Price Wars and Food Politics in Mid-Twentieth-Century Canada

Radical Housewives is a history of Canada's Housewives Consumers Association. This association was a community-based women's organization with ties to the communist and social democratic left that, from 1937 until the early 1950s, led a broadly based popular movement for state control of prices and made other far-reaching demands on the state. As radical consumer activists, the Housewives engaged in gender-transgressive political activism that challenged the government to protect consumers' interests rather than just those of business while popularizing socialist solutions to the economic crises of the Great Depression and the immediate postwar years.

Julie Guard's exhaustive research, including archival analysis and interviews with twelve former Housewives, recovers a history of women's social justice activism in an era often considered politically dormant and adds a Canadian dimension to the history of politicized consumerism and of politicized materialism. *Radical Housewives* reinterprets the view of postwar Canada as economically prosperous and reveals the left's role in the origins of the food security movement.

(Studies in Gender and History)

JULIE GUARD is an associate professor of labour studies at the University of Manitoba.

STUDIES IN GENDER AND HISTORY

General Editors: Franca Iacovetta and Karen Dubinsky

Radical Housewives

Price Wars and Food Politics in Mid-Twentieth-Century Canada

JULIE GUARD

UNIVERSITY OF TORONTO PRESS
Toronto Buffalo London

© University of Toronto Press 2019
Toronto Buffalo London
utorontopress.com
Printed in Canada

ISBN 978-1-4875-0215-7 (cloth)
ISBN 978-1-4875-2181-3 (paper)

♾ Printed on acid-free, 100% post-consumer recycled
paper with vegetable-based inks.

Studies in Gender and History

___

Library and Archives Canada Cataloguing in Publication

Title: Radical housewives : price wars and food politics in
mid-twentieth-century Canada / Julie Guard.
Names: Guard, Julie, 1952–, author.
Series: Studies in gender and history ; 47.
Description: Series statement: Studies in gender and history ; 47 |
Includes bibliographical references and index.
Identifiers: Canadiana 20190045647 | ISBN 9781487502157 (cloth) |
ISBN 9781487521813 (paper)
Subjects: LCSH: Housewives Consumers Association – History –
20th century. | LCSH: Consumer movements – Canada – History –
20th century. | LCSH: Housewives – Political activity – Canada – History –
20th century. | LCSH: Women – Political activity – Canada – History –
20th century. | LCSH: Food – Political aspects – Canada – History –
20th century. | LCSH: Cost and standard of living – Canada – History –
20th century. | LCSH: Price regulation – Canada – History – 20th century. |
LCSH: Social justice – Canada – History – 20th century.
Classification: LCC HC120.C63 G83 2019 | DDC 381.3/2097109045 – dc23

___

This book has been published with the help of a grant from the Federation
for the Humanities and Social Sciences, through the Awards to Scholarly
Publications Program, using funds provided by the Social Sciences and Humanities
Research Council of Canada.

University of Toronto Press acknowledges the financial assistance to its publishing
program of the Canada Council for the Arts and the Ontario Arts Council, an agency of
the Government of Ontario.

 Canada Council for the Arts   Conseil des Arts du Canada

ONTARIO ARTS COUNCIL
CONSEIL DES ARTS DE L'ONTARIO
an Ontario government agency
un organisme du gouvernement de l'Ontario

Funded by the Government of Canada   Financé par le gouvernement du Canada    Canadä

MIX
Paper from responsible sources
FSC® C016245

Contents

List of Illustrations vii

Acknowledgments ix

Introduction 3

1 Price War: Housewives Organize in the Great Depression 17

2 Housewife-Patriots and Wartime Price Controls 50

3 Fighting for the Working Class: The Struggle for Postwar Price Controls 81

4 Mothers, Breadwinners, and Citizens 116

5 Citizen Consumers or Kitchen Communists? 163

6 "Reds," Housewives, and the Cold War 198

Notes 217

Index 285

Illustrations

1.1 "Threatened for Her Fight against High Prices" 20
1.2 "Fighting the High Cost of Living" 27
2.1 "Milk – Facts behind the Rise in Price" 57
2.2 "Public Ownership of Milk" 58
3.1 "To Ensure Enough Milk for Our Children" 90
3.2 "Buy No Meat for One Week" 93
3.3 "Milk Prices to Rise Again, 1946" 95
3.4 "The Case of the Dwindling Dollar" 106
3.5 "Milk: What You Must Make Drew Do!" 111
3.6 "16 Cent Milk" 112
4.1 "The Case of the Shrinking Steak" 126–7
4.2 "Candy Bar Boycott, Montreal, May 1947" 129
4.3 "Here, You Can Finish Him Up" 134
4.4 "What Goes Up Had Better Come Down!" 142
4.5 "Call and Invitation to the March of Million Names Delegation" 156
4.6 "If This Is Your Letter" 157
4.7 "Meat Racket" 158
4.8 "Mrs Housewife, the Price of Milk Must Not Go Up" 159
4.9 "My Mommy and Daddy Were Talking Last Night" 160
4.10 "Roll Back Prices, Tax Excess Profits, Say Housewives" 161
4.11 "The Dwindling Staff of Life" 162
5.1 "Toronto Housewives Delegation to Ottawa" 170
5.2 "Roll Back Prices" 171
5.3 "Nation Is Aroused" 173
5.4 "Somebody Is Lying" 180

Acknowledgments

Writing this book has been a remarkably long journey, but I remain as excited about the bold and committed women whose history it recovers as I was at the outset. I am grateful to those who have made the process of discovery possible. Miguel Figueroa, former leader of the Communist Party of Canada, endorsed my project and helped me contact former members of the Housewives Consumers Association – Mona Morgan, Audrey (Modzir) Staples, Peggy Chunn, Helen Weir, Janet McMurray, and Mary Prokop – all of whom agreed to be interviewed. Mercedes Steedman connected me with former Housewife Pat Chytyk. These women generously shared their time with me, and their recollections provide an invaluable inside view of the movement they initiated and led. Ester Reiter introduced me to Lil Ilomaki and Alice Maigis, both of whom are remarkable women, and shared an interview with Becky Lapedes. John Marshall of the People's Coop and a Housewives ally talked to me about his role in this history, and Ann Ross's daughter, Dee Dee Rizzo, shared her memories of her mother's experiences. Archivists at Library and Archives Canada, the Manitoba Archives, York University Archives, the Archives of Ontario, the BC Archives, and the Fisher Rare Book Room at the University of Toronto, and the library staff at the Toronto Public Library, the University of New Brunswick's libraries, the University of Toronto's Robarts Library, and the University of Manitoba's Dafoe Library provided generous help. Darrell Rankin, head of the Communist Party in Manitoba, gave me unfettered access to party records. I am deeply grateful to all of them.

The research was supported by funding from the Social Sciences and Humanities Research Council of Canada and by the History department and the Faculty of Arts at the University of Manitoba, for which

I give thanks. Thanks also to the wonderful team at the University of Toronto Press, particularly Len Husband, Frances Mundy, and Marilyn McCormack, as well as to Jonathan Adjemian, Krishna Lalbiharie, and the anonymous readers. Barbara Cameron and the other members of the Cecil-Ross Society, Wendy Terry and Andrew Oliver from the Workers' Educational Association of Canada, and David Fairey of the Trade Union Research Bureau generously allowed me to publish the many images that add visual interest and help locate the events within the dynamic context of their time.

During the years that this work was in progress, many colleagues have provided helpful comments as well as support and encouragement. Special thanks to Franca Iacovetta, Ester Reiter, and Mercedes Steedman, whose friendship and encouragement supported me throughout the project. Thanks also to Kate McPherson, Bettina Bradbury, Ian Radforth, Craig Heron, and the other members of the Toronto Labour Studies group, and to Tina Chen, Brenda Austin-Smith, and David Churchill at the University of Manitoba. Karen Naylor helped me through some of the difficult times. My biggest debt is to my family, who have seen the project through from the start. Seth Wigderson read many drafts, gave valuable suggestions, and shared his acute insights about the Cold War era and the left, while providing warm comradeship and enthusiastic support. Bronwyn Guard, always my biggest fan and most loyal supporter, cheered me on while providing comfort, food, friendship, and love. Special thanks for all you've done.

RADICAL HOUSEWIVES

Price Wars and Food Politics in
Mid-Twentieth-Century Canada

Introduction

From 1937 to the early 1950s, the Housewives Consumers Association (HCA), a loosely federated organization of activist consumers, led hundreds of thousands of women and men in a rights-based movement for fair prices and more responsive government.[1] Led by women of the political left, the HCA's affiliated housewives' associations and consumers' leagues mobilized women across the country in protest against the high cost of living, named the firms that they claimed extorted consumers, and demanded government intervention to control prices and punish profiteers and price-fixers. For over a decade, the Housewives captured media attention: prices, the price campaign, and the Housewives' brand of performance activism preoccupied the mainstream, labour, and left press. The most popular grassroots movement of the era, the Housewives-led price campaign was ostensibly a women's issue, but health advocates, social welfare activists, progressive clergy, and municipal and other politicians endorsed and supported it; indeed, the social democratic Cooperative Commonwealth Federation (CCF), the Communist Party of Canada (CPC), and the Congress of Canadian Labour (CCL) not only supported it but claimed to lead it. Inspired by, and part of, the international wave of activist consumer movements that erupted in the early to mid-twentieth century,[2] the Housewives tapped the urgent concerns of working- and middle-class people buffeted by a decade of economic depression and another six years of war. Supported by a majority of Canadians, they campaigned for state control of prices and public policy to ensure adequate access for all to affordable, nutritious food, demands that were broadly shared by the party and popular left.

The prices movement the Housewives initiated and led, and the support they mobilized across the country for an interventionist state, reveal a dynamic – but under-studied – period of Canadian history, one in which an exuberantly activist left played a meaningful role in wide-ranging public debates about the rights of citizens and the responsibilities of the state. Through the 1930s and 1940s, thousands of women and men were inspired by the left's vision of a better world; by joining or supporting left-led movements, parties, unions, and ethnic organizations, many found a political voice. Collectively, this comprised the popular left, a formation distinct from the much better-known party left in its freedom from institutional ties and party discipline, the prominent role within it of women, as well as its relative omission from most left history. The recovery of this history complicates the standard characterization of the postwar years as an era of rigidifying gender divisions and political quiescence. A focus on the years before, during, and immediately following the Second World War reveals a social and political climate that was very different from the insularity and retrenchment that has come to define the 1950s that followed.[3] Canadians, educated by the experiences of the Great Depression followed immediately by a "total war" effort that demanded full mobilization on the home front, were confident in their rights as social citizens and outraged that their wartime sacrifices were not compensated by the "peace dividend" they had been repeatedly promised.[4] This heightened political awareness, along with the economic and social crises that fueled it, provided fertile ground for these militant Housewives.

The spirit of civic engagement that empowered and supported the Housewives was reflected in a leftward shift in the political consensus. The social democratic CCF, precursor to today's NDP, was established in 1932 and, as James Naylor argues compellingly in his recent history, struggled to chart a course between divergent visions of a socialist future through its first decade.[5] Membership fluctuated during those tumultuous years, peaking in 1948 at over 38,000.[6] Its popularity shifted, sometimes dramatically, but the debates over vision and strategy were earnest and its appeal broad, so that, even in the midst of turmoil, it eclipsed the Communist and Trotskyist alternatives to become the pre-eminent party of the left. By the mid-1940s the CCF was the predominant left force in the labour movement and community-based social justice organizations, and remarkably, by September 1943, a Gallop poll reported that the CCF's popularity had surpassed that of the Liberals.[7] The CCF and its successor, the NDP, were and continue to be the most important progressive force in Canadian social, political, and intellectual life. The popularity of the Communist left also peaked in this period, although under less favourable conditions.[8] Established in 1921 at a secret meeting in Guelph, Ontario, the Communist Party of Canada (CPC) was inspired by a more radical vision of a better world, although in practice most party activities were directed towards more readily achievable reforms of the existing system, often the same ones advocated by the CCF. Its members and supporters were overwhelmingly non-Anglo-Celtic Canadians and immigrants, mostly Ukrainian, Finnish, and Jewish. Officially banned as an illegal organization in 1940 and reconfigured in 1943 as the legal Labor-Progressive Party (LPP), it reported peak membership of 20,000 during this period.[9] Far less successful in electoral politics than the CCF, which formed the official opposition in three provinces – British Columbia in 1933, Saskatchewan in 1934, and Ontario in 1943 – and formed the Saskatchewan government in 1944, the LPP enjoyed sufficient popular support for its candidates to win a number of elected positions, mostly at the local level, and to make a strong showing in other campaigns.

The political and social contexts of this brief period provided an unusually receptive climate for the Housewives. Only a minority of Canadians belonged to a left party, but opinion polls indicate that a majority agreed with the left's economic vision. Buffeted by chronic shortages and extortionate prices while the state intervened to protect the profitability of retailers, manufacturers, and agricultural industries, a majority of Canadians believed that the state had an obligation to intervene in the economy and should use its power to ensure fair prices and more equitable distribution of goods.[10] Not only was organized labour exceptionally militant during this period[11] but, as Lara Campbell reminds us, a wide diversity of Canadians – consumers, farmers, butchers, and even school children – were ready to take direct action to challenge authority and express disagreement with their elected representatives' political decisions.[12]

The Housewives' call for state management of the economy, one of the urgent political debates of the era, resonated with many Canadians. Between the beginning of the 1930s and the end of the 1940s, Canadians experienced the sharpest possible contrasts between an uncontrolled economy and centralized economic management. A decade-long Depression in the 1930s, during which the Canadian government refused to intervene, was followed by the economic stability of the Second World War, when Canada adopted the most invasive and far-reaching program of market intervention of any combatant country. The wartime experience of sweeping state control of the economy provided ample evidence that the state was fully capable of ensuring the general well-being of its citizenry by managing markets, production, and prices. Support for such economic management was reinforced when the Liberal government, led by Prime Minister Mackenzie King, began to retreat from the market in the late 1940s, resulting in rising prices, stagnant wages, and spiralling inflation and prompting widespread demands for a return to some measure of state control. Indeed, an overwhelming majority of Canadians endorsed the Housewives' demands that the state manage the economy, or at very least control prices, as it had during the war.[13]

Canadians who had lived through the Depression and the war were preoccupied by food's price, distribution, and accessibility.[14] Food not only absorbed a third of the average household budget, but shortages and high prices often put even basic necessities out of reach for the many who lived on low or irregular incomes. Many fixed at least some of their frustration on governments, aware that the state's prominent and expanding role in the regulation of agricultural industries such as dairy was inconsistent, poorly executed, and designed to support industry, often at the expense of consumers.[15] The national economic reconversion program, adopted at war's end, encouraged economic expansion with measures that raised the price and reduced the supply of domestic goods, including food. The imposition of the wartime command economy demonstrated clearly that government had the capacity to make food affordable but, as Joy Parr argues, its program for economic reconversion prioritized export trade over the needs of ordinary households. Federal policy makers, in other words, designed a program for achieving economic stability that, for pragmatic reasons, advanced the interests of business while it deferred or denied the needs of Canadian households.[16]

Alert to the impact of these policies, Canadians widely rejected official claims that this reconversion program actually protected working people's interests. The country was therefore ripe for the kind of grassroots movement initiated by the Housewives, who politicized food by redefining the everyday problems of feeding a family as not an individual problem but the result of systemic inequities built into the political economy. Consumer activism was further encouraged, albeit unintentionally, by the politicization of food by the state. Ian Mosby observes that Canadians were bombarded by wartime propaganda that stressed their collective responsibility to maintain proper nutrition, their patriotic duty to comply with rationing and price controls, and the proper role of citizen-shoppers. Inspired in part by their experience as volunteer price-checkers during the war, he argues, women's "expansive vision of social citizenship" and newly acquired confidence in their political rights inspired a collective demand for state intervention in the "affairs of the kitchen."[17]

Maintained by strong popular support, the HCA spanned some thirteen or fourteen years, surviving a remarkably long time for a grassroots movement and furnishing a rare example of a successful popular front organization. Inaugurated in the midst of the Communist party's Popular Front period (1935–1939), the Housewives embodied precisely the kind of "mass organization" envisioned but rarely achieved by the LPP: a grassroots movement of ordinary people with little or no political experience or affiliation, led by communists – although in the case of the Housewives, also by a few left-leaning CCFers. In contrast to the party's own women's organizations, the Women's Progressive Associations and the Congress of Canadian Women,[18] which were clearly party-run and thus not widely popular, the Housewives were enthusiastically supported by the CPC but, my evidence indicates, never under its control.

Led by members of the communist ethnic and labour left, and advocating much the same program as the rest of the party, labour, and ethnic left, including state control of prices and the retention of food subsidies, the HCA was an integral part of Canada's popular left. Its absence from most accounts of left history reminds us that much historiography still overlooks women, even after decades of feminist scholarship intended to address this gendered myopia. It is also a remnant of the Cold War anticommunism that continues to shape twenty-first century consciousness. Scholars of left feminism have correctly identified the Housewives as an organization close to, although not of, the Communist party, although there is a tendency among some to accept the designation of the conservatives of their time, who dismissed them as a "Communist front" or, more derisively, as "Communists in women's clothes," a construction that reveals how anticommunists could strip gender, and thus motherhood, from women simply by referring to their radical politics.[19] I interrogate that relationship, paying particular attention to the complex relationship between the Housewives, a community organization in which communists (not all of them party members) were active, and the Communist party. This more nuanced perspective on the relationship between the Communist party and the broad communist left is consistent with the current trend in left history, reflected in the work of Ian McKay and John Manley, among others, who argue that not every Communist, and certainly not every activist in the broad communist left, was subject to, or obeyed, Moscow's rules.[20]

Challenging those assumptions and recovering new evidence that suggests a more complicated relationship between the Housewives and the Communist party than has been generally acknowledged deepens our understanding of left history, particularly with regard to women. Canadian communists, particularly those who were active in social movements such as the Housewives, played a crucial role in advancing the socialist ideas of the 1930s and 1940s, ideas that underpinned the formation of the Canadian welfare state and that are still reflected in institutions such as universal medicare, publicly funded education, and a publicly provided income retirement system, among others, that define the character of Canadian society and inform Canadians' sense of our distinct identity. Indeed, radical women were so vital to those movements that the history of women's popular activism is largely the history of the female ethnic left.[21] Housewives Associations across the country were organized and led by women of the ethnic left such those identified by Varpu Lindström, Frances Swyripa, Rhonda Hinther, and Franca Iacovetta, among others, and are among those Ester Reiter celebrates in her recent study of the secular Jewish left, *A Future without Hate or Need: The Jewish Left in Canada*.[22]

The Housewives, the most popular social movement of the period, offer us a unique and critical perspective on the political history of the period before, during, and immediately after the Second World War. They were part of the broad-based wave of activist consumers who used their moral authority as mothers and their economic leverage as consumers to demand radical, even revolutionary change. Like the activist consumers in the United States identified by Dana Frank, Meg Jacobs, and Lawrence Glickman, among others,[23] Canadian consumers were politicized by changes in the political economy that exposed the hidden political dimensions of prices and products and revealed the taken-for-granted quality of unequal class relations. They made similar claims as economic citizens and inserted state responsibility to contain inflationary prices into the public debate.

Despite their many similarities, there are important differences between the U.S. and Canadian consumer movements. U.S. consumers were supported by liberal and leftist economists and other professionals who staffed the New Deal administration of the 1930s and initiated socially progressive policies. But, as Landon Storrs explains, the advantage of such progressive bureaucrats was temporary, aborted by the Cold War-era purges that drove most progressives out of office and overturned virtually all pro-consumer policies.[24] Unlike their U.S. sisters, Canada's Housewives faced a hostile federal government. Yet, as Joseph Tohill argues, "Canadian consumer activists" achieved "a more auspicious outcome." He attributes their success to "Canada's centralized parliamentary system," which "facilitated more decisive, co-ordinated action" than was possible within the U.S. administration. The relative independence of senior bureaucrats within Canada's parliamentary system, he explains, shielded policy-makers from the anti-consumerist lobby that derailed the progressive policies of the U.S. Office of Price Administration (OPA).[25]

Canada's federal bureaucracy included few progressives, aside from a small number of Keynesians in the Department of Finance.[26] But the Housewives' delegations, petitions, and letter campaigns were sufficiently popular to inspire concern, and perhaps fear, within the federal Cabinet and among officials in the Department of Finance, the Wartime Prices and Trade Board (WPTB), and the Prime Minister's office. Prime Minister Mackenzie King and Donald Gordon, head of the WPTB and a powerful member of the corporate elite, hoped to contain popular outrage about rising prices, shrinking paycheques, and spiralling inflation with official statements meant to reassure Canadians that the government could be trusted to resolve the economic crisis. News of a forthcoming Housewives' delegation or a deluge of letters demanding that the Cabinet explain its policy decisions could therefore send bureaucrats scurrying to contain the predictable political damage. The CCF, at the forefront of the popular shift to the left, allied itself with the HCA. Countless references in the records of the Prime Minister's Office, the Department of Finance, the House of Commons debates, and the Royal Canadian Mounted Police (RCMP) to the Housewives' letters, delegations, and campaigns indicate the extent to which CCF members of Parliament (MPs), and sometimes members of other parties, used the Housewives to advance their parties' agendas on price control and other aspects of postwar reconstruction. In this and other ways, this grassroots movement influenced political decision-making by strengthening the arguments of opposition parties and, on occasion, of opponents of government policy within the Liberal party.

The evidence for this study draws on a diverse array of sources, including previously unexcavated documentary evidence. It includes some of the thousands of petitions and postcards with which Housewives and their supporters lobbied for the reinstatement of price control, taken from the files of the federal Department of Finance, which was responsible for Canada's wartime price control program, including the WPTB and its Consumer Branch, in which the Housewives were active as volunteer price-checkers and administrators.[27] The sheer volume of these petitions and postcards is tangible evidence of the strength and geographical reach of their popular support. Correspondence between the Housewives Associations and the prime minister, finance ministers, and various members of Parliament, reveal much about the reaction within the government to the Housewives' campaigns and the influence the Housewives wielded on Parliament. The RCMP, preoccupied as they were through these decades with identifying and exposing suspected leftists and other so-called subversives,[28] maintained close surveillance on the Housewives from their first appearance in the late 1930s and continued to watch them into the 1960s, long after the organization's decline. Surveillance records of RCMP divisions in British Columbia, Alberta, Saskatchewan, Manitoba, Ontario, Quebec, and Nova Scotia that watched the Housewives yielded many thousands of pages of detailed information on Housewives organizations in those provinces, including the Housewives' activities, the multi-ethnic composition of their membership, and the influence they had within their communities. They also shed light on the state's response to this extraordinarily popular social movement. RCMP agents and their superiors, up to and including the commissioner, defined the Housewives' criticism of the government as subversive. They also treated women's traditional organizing strategies as chaotic and ineffective – despite their evident success – and assumed, without evidence, that they were secretly controlled by the male-dominated Communist party.

RCMP agents and informers watched Housewives members and secretly attended their meetings as well as their public conferences, social gatherings, and protest demonstrations. They also gathered hundreds of articles on the Housewives from the mainstream, left, labour, and ethnic press. Even so, the RCMP's clippings files, while numerous, represent only a fraction of the media coverage. The Housewives were excellent organizers who cultivated the media with innovative performance strategies that emphasized their maternalism and respectability and provided ready-made, eye-catching headlines for an eager press. Their campaigns for affordable milk, meat, fuel, and other necessities that families living on wage-earners' salaries could barely afford, promoted by parades of women pushing baby prams or carrying picket signs urging others to boycott over-priced meat, milk, or butter, shamed government and business elites and garnered extensive coverage in both the national and regional press.[29] The Housewives also got vigorous support from the Communist newspapers of the time, which were widely enough read to include, until 1940, a national daily.[30] They were covered as well by Canada's major magazines: *Saturday Night*, *Time* (Canada), and *Chatelaine*.

The Housewives' campaigns tapped pervasive concerns about what we would now call food security: through the 1930s and into the post-war years, the communist and, to a lesser extent, the social democratic left's campaigns for affordable food, of which the Housewives were an important part, established the historical roots of the contemporary food security movement. At the forefront of this movement, the Housewives played a prominent role in the contentious debates in the media, the legislature, and the streets about purchasing power, free markets, and the proper economic role of the state. These debates reveal ideological divides, exacerbated by emergent Cold War anxieties, that shaped news coverage of the Housewives. Media coverage was initially widely supportive, even if some treated the spectacle of women organizing politically as farcical, but became increasingly polarized as evidence of Housewives' connections to the Communist left mounted. Some continued to support the Housewives, often while lamenting their leftist political taint. Others seized every opportunity to denounce them as devious agents of a malevolent foreign power. No such ambiguity afflicted the RCMP, whose surveillance was predicated on the firmly held but weakly supported conviction that they were a "subversive organization" operating under direct Communist party control. These records, like most historical documents, were produced by people with a variety of perspectives. In combination, they provide a rich and diverse array of sources on the Housewives.

Non-elite subjects tend to leave few historical records, and the mostly working-class women who were politically active consumers in the 1930s and 1940s are no exception, but a number of interviews with Housewives activists, their family members, and allies provide rare glimpses from the front lines of the struggle. Winnipeg Housewife Anne Ross's personal papers, and those of Marjorie Mann, a long-time CCF member, activist in the CCF Women's Committee, and fierce

Housewives' opponent, add intimate detail from opposing perspectives. The archived records of Communist party member Robert Kenny and the Communist Party of Canada, and the published biographies of a few prominent Communist party activists who played a role in the Housewives, provide additional depth. But personal records and memoirs of working-class women, especially those on the left, are rare, and we cannot know how much material has been lost or deliberately destroyed. In her book on women who organized politically during the Cold War, Tarah Brookfield tells of a Women's International League for Peace and Freedom (WILPF) executive who destroyed membership lists to protect members from being vilified as suspected Communists.[31] Such record destruction was common among organizations targeted by anticommunists and therefore susceptible to raids by the RCMP and demonization in the press, and helps explain why there are no extant sources aside from those identified above from which to reconstruct the history of the Housewives Consumers Association and its members.

Maternalism as Political Strategy

The Housewives' use of their identities as wives and mothers to claim political space and justify behaviour that would otherwise be regarded as transgressive earns them a place in the long continuum of citizen-mothers who used maternalism strategically to overcome the limitations imposed on them because of their gender.[32] But maternalism, as feminist historians have long argued, is a complicated historiographical category, which makes it an unpredictable strategy. Women's claims to an empowered motherhood have long legitimated and supported female activism.[33] Like the Housewives, women have invoked motherhood as political "cover" to defy traditional notions of acceptable womanhood by engaging in public protest.[34] But motherhood inevitably also invokes traditionalist assumptions about women's common nature and values that limit women to narrowly defined roles and reinforce women's subordination.[35] Denyse Baillargeon illustrates both the power and limitations of motherhood as a strategy in her study of twentieth-century Quebec women who deployed it to wrest medical and social services from a reluctant state. She shows how female activists, often strategically allying themselves with medical and other experts, drew on powerful discourses that linked motherhood to nationhood to legitimate their demands for publicly funded milk and medical care for themselves, their babies, and children. Through collective action, women eventually won systemic support for the health and well-being of mothers and babies, but at a cost. Maternalism, she argues, reinforced medical and social discourses that assumed maternal ineptitude and subordinated women's needs to those of the state, discourses women were obliged to negotiate, resist, or accept.[36] Nationalist claims, moreover, are intrinsically regressive and such discourses subsume female agency while encouraging the extremist views that we see today among the radical, racist right.

Despite these complications, generations of women have used motherhood to justify their occupation of political and social space defined as exclusively male. Annelise Orleck, for instance, argues that, whatever its ambiguities and despite its limitations, women have long used the language of motherhood as a "powerful political identity around which they have galvanized broad-based and influential grassroots movements for social change."[37] Although not acting directly in the interests of children, they nonetheless perceived their motives as grounded in some innate female quality related to their capacity for motherhood and therefore as different from, and indeed more virtuous than, men's.

Maternalism thus deployed is an abstraction; it applies even when there is no direct relationship to actual children.[38] And, perhaps ironically, women who invoked motherhood to justify their political activism have all too often faced daunting obstacles to combining that commitment with motherhood. One particularly poignant depiction is found in Faith Johnston's biography of Communist MP Dorise Nielsen. The party's gendered expectations of female self-sacrifice alongside its failure to provide parental support wreaked havoc in her family, leaving her permanently estranged from her daughters.[39] Nielsen's case is sadly not unique. Motherhood was notoriously difficult for politically active women, who were expected to demonstrate a political commitment that equalled or exceeded that of their male counterparts. The rare references in the literature suggest that the few women who played major roles in the CPC, such as Becky Buhay, Annie Buller, Bella Gauld, Florence Theodore, and Louise Watson, faced daunting challenges attempting to balance family commitments and political life.[40]

Not just Communists, but many women have justified their political activism with reference to an abstract maternalism. Tarah Brookfield, for instance, has recently shown how both right- and left-wing women in postwar Canada used maternalism to explain their deviation from prescriptively gendered behaviour and justify political demands that ranged from anticommunism to disarmament.[41] In a similar vein, Brian

Thorn has recently highlighted the maternalism in which women activists in post-World War Two Canada across the political spectrum grounded their political convictions. He argues that Communist, CCF, and Social Credit women relied on a "common maternalist ethic" to justify their struggles for radically divergent visions of a better world and their incursion into normatively masculine political terrain. Although few of these women would have called themselves feminists, Thorn identifies them as maternalist feminists who laid the foundation for the women's movement that emerged in the decade after their own decline.[42] In this regard, they remind us of the maternalist movements in many countries, now recognized as also being feminist, that made significant political gains, perhaps most significantly by forcing governments to enact progressive policies that codified twentieth-century welfare state programs.[43] Many of these were contemporaneous with the Housewives.

These radical Housewives nuance our perspective on female agency and political activism and illuminate how not only historians of the left, but also the left itself, have been largely blind to women's political activism, especially when they acted, or claimed to act, in ways deemed socially appropriate to their gender.[44] It reminds us of the many women activists who defined themselves, as did most women, in relation to their familial responsibilities, even when they took to the streets in angry protest or devoted themselves to building socialism as members of the various organizations of the left. Acknowledging the political activism of such women not only expands the historical record of popular protest but, by acknowledging women's distinctly gendered forms of activism, provides a more inclusive view of that history.

Women such as these Housewives, who claimed to speak as mothers, invoke the ongoing discussion about left and working-class feminisms. Brookfield traces the maternalism that inspired other left activists from the Women's International League for Peace and Freedom (WILPF) and the Voice of Women (VOW) to the suffrage and social gospel movements of the late nineteenth century.[45] Some Housewives, especially those who were members of the CCF, may have drawn inspiration from the social gospel. Others were inspired less by primarily middle-class movements like suffrage and more by the traditions of female activism within their own ethnic and labour left histories that we now recognize as feminist. The excavation of left and working-class feminism in Canada and elsewhere has successfully challenged the assumptions that, in the past, defined feminism as an exclusively middle-class phenomenon.[46] Evidence of left and working-class women's sustained struggles for rights and status, often within labour unions, also complicates the traditional assumptions that divided feminism into two distinct waves.[47] The Housewives, like most women at the time, particularly among the working class, would not have called themselves feminists. Yet they are undeniably part of feminist history. They made demands of the state as citizen-mothers and called repeatedly for a larger role for women in the public sphere. They put their vision of female emancipation into action. Without waiting for enabling legislative or social endorsement, they engaged in direct political action and inserted themselves into public space. They mobilized thousands of women and men in a broad-based popular movement for state control of prices and fostered a public debate about the responsibilities of the state. Women such as these, whose class and political identities precluded their self-identification as feminists, nonetheless defied and upended the very restrictions they appear to have embraced as they expanded the boundaries of acceptable female behaviour, claimed the right to a public voice and public space and, confident in their rights as citizens, made bold demands of the state.

Maternalism gave the Housewives licence to deploy the kinds of strategies of resistance available to those with little power that the sociologist James C. Scott so compellingly terms the "weapons of the weak."[48] They led national boycotts of overpriced milk, meat, jam, and butter, advertising their campaigns with flamboyant street parades and demonstrations, and held countless public meetings to educate other women about the political economy of prices and to debate the proper relationship between citizens and the state. They organized intensive lobbying campaigns, persuading dozens of unions, women's auxiliaries, city councils, religious and community groups, and individuals to send letters to members of Parliament. They stood on busy street corners with petitions and handed out protest postcards for women to send to their elected representatives. Along with their allies in the community and the labour movement, they mounted five delegations to Ottawa, two of them several hundred strong, where they confronted members of Cabinet and demanded a change in policy. They attacked industry directly, publicly accusing dairies, meat processors, sugar refiners, and bakeries of profiteering and forming illegal trusts, and called for government investigation of high food prices and prosecution of price-fixers under anti-trust legislation. They demanded a voice in developing food policy and lobbied for permanent state control of prices, insisting that an adequate supply of staple foods was a natural right of all citizens and that ensuring a secure source of affordable food was an inherent obligation of the state.

1
Price War: Housewives Organize in the Great Depression

On 4 November 1937, a delegation of eleven women, one accompanied by her child, converged on Toronto's Board of Control, the city's most powerful elected body, to protest a one-cent increase in the price of a quart of milk. Led by Mrs Bertha Lamb, a twenty-three-year-old housewife from the lower-middle-class East End of the city, and claiming to represent all women's organizations in the East End, the women urged the city government to support their demands that the province override the price hike authorized by its Milk Control Board, the government agency that regulated the industry, and investigate the high profits earned by the dairies. Speaking with the moral authority of concerned mothers, they blamed the prevailing high rates of childhood malnutrition and illness on the rising price of milk. Oranges and cod liver oil (widely recognized as protective foods, essential to health),[1] were already "beyond the reach of the average family." Now, Lamb averred, "they are putting milk beyond reach as well."[2] Charging big companies with "making millions at the expense of our children," they demanded that "something be done" to end this "outrage." Unlike the previous delegations of women that had expressed similar concerns to the Board, they planned to put teeth into their demands by forming a city-wide housewives' union that would "go on strike against every dairy in the city" if necessary. They also proposed a remedy, advising the city to cut the costs of milk delivery by providing it as a public service, "as it does water." The women cheered "lustily," the press reported, when the entire council agreed that higher milk prices were "just another profit grab by the big companies" and promised to petition the province to reduce milk price to "its former level and even lower if possible." Despite the small size of the delegation, by that evening, news of the housewives' "high prices boycott" had spread through the city under a banner headline on the front page of the *Toronto Daily Star*, the country's most widely read paper.[3] The rival *Telegram* noted that telephone calls from women wanting to join the boycott "had started to come in by the time Mrs Lamb reached home." By the time the next day's papers went to press, Lamb and her committee, with the help of the Toronto District Trades and Labor Council, had organized a mass meeting the coming week to establish a Housewives' League.[4] Both city papers, the national *Globe and Mail*, and the Communist *Daily Clarion* reported that many housewives had immediately begun boycotting milk and some had stopped milk delivery entirely.[5]

At least a thousand women flocked to the Housewives' founding meeting on the evening of 8 November. Over eight hundred of them, including representatives of women's organizations from each of Toronto's nine wards and adjacent municipalities, filled Toronto's Labour Temple to capacity and constituted themselves as the Toronto Housewives Association. A hundred more, unable to get in, gathered outside, in addition to an estimated two hundred who had given up and returned home. Asserting the maternalism that would define the organization, Lamb barred men from the meeting, although word circulated among the throng that at least one "gentleman housewife" was present. Following elections for ward captains in all areas of the city, the affiliation of the left-led East York Housewives, who had organized in advance of the Toronto women, and a noisy debate about strategy, meeting organizer and founding president Bertha Lamb fired the first salvo in the Housewives' "war on prices," announcing a city-wide milk boycott. Unanimously endorsing plans to "defeat the milk trusts" and "enable the mothers of Toronto to keep within their family budgets," the women pledged to reduce their household milk consumption to a bare minimum until the price dropped from 13 cents to 10 cents a quart. Banner newspaper headlines announced a "price war" as the Housewives began organizing a "city-wide union" of consumers, vowing to strike against every dairy in the city if their demands were not met.[6]

Even before it was established, the Toronto Housewives Association had, for the second time in two days, made front-page news, taking second place only to rumblings of war on the horizon. A banner headline in the *Globe and Mail* announced that, hours before the meeting, Lamb had received an anonymous letter, mysteriously signed M.A.O.T., advising her to "mind her own business." If she went ahead with the milk boycott, it warned ("and you won't be warned again, either"), she would be "very sorry." "You have a very nice child," it concluded menacingly; "don't jeopardize its future." The milk boycott leader, "not afraid of anyone," spurned a police guard and dismissed the threat as "ridiculous." Demonstrating the feisty maternalism that would become the organization's hallmark, and to the evident approval of an admiring press, she arranged for the "safety of her baby" and arrived at the meeting as scheduled.[7]

Two days later, the Housewives Association, now formally organized, was again in the news, as two hundred women, standing three deep, made a formal presentation to the Board of Control. Accompanied by the newly elected ward captains, Mrs Lamb demanded a "public investigation into the milk business" and a serious consideration of the "merits of incorporating milk as a public utility, therefore cutting distribution costs to a minimum."[8] Reiterating their demands at Housewives' meetings, Mrs E.A. Havelock explained that the Housewives' goal was not to reduce families' milk consumption, but to increase it. To do that, "we must repeat our demands until the price comes down." If the Milk Board refused to reduce the price, she warned, it might be necessary to ask the city to take over its distribution.[9] By December, their weekly delegations to municipal councils around the province prompted Alderman R.H. (Robert Hood) Saunders, a popular politician who would subsequently be dubbed "Grassroots Bob," to point out the failings of the other councillors in relation to the Housewives. The first of their many male supporters who would do so, Saunders congratulated the Housewives while simultaneously patronizing them as mere women. City council, he chided, "should take an interest in the welfare of the citizens" and not "wait until a committee of women is organized to protest increases in commodity prices." Echoing the Housewives, he called for an investigation into the prices of milk, bread, coal, and gas.[10]

Although no clear evidence emerges about its impact, a day into the boycott, milk delivery drivers on some routes reported that receipts were down three or four dollars.[11] In less than a week, the *Clarion* announced that milk consumption had dropped "appreciably," and the *Star* reported that one of the city's largest dairies acknowledged a "slight falling off" in sales, although at least one refused to speak to the press and others insisted it was "too early to determine."[12] By the end of the second week, the Housewives claimed that 5,000 Toronto and area women were participating in the boycott and others reported that they had been offered free butter by dairies in return for maintaining

1.1 "Threatened for Her Fight against High Prices," *Daily Clarion*, 9 November 1937, 1

their regular milk delivery.[13] By the end of November, determined to continue but unwilling to deprive their families of an essential food, they resolved to extend the boycott by buying no milk one day a week.[14] Seven months later the price dropped to 12 cents per quart and the Housewives' claimed victory, although the *Telegram* suggested it was merely a seasonal adjustment. Seasonal or not, it remained at 12 cents for the next two years. When the Milk Board proposed a one-cent increase in January 1941, the resulting outrage spilled over into another round of demands for "municipalization," a consumer vote on the Milk Board, and a public investigation of the industry. Led by the Housewives and supported by municipal councils and many others, the public debate about fair milk prices thus continued into the next decade.[15]

Whatever the effect on milk sales, the Housewives' campaign focused intense scrutiny on the industry by the public and the press, and their aggressive reaction to the Housewives indicates that the big dairies, the Milk Board, and the Producers' Association considered the women a significant threat. Advertisements in local papers challenged the Housewives' allegations and insisted that farmers and dairy employees would reap most of the benefits of a price hike. Dairy spokesmen claimed they could not afford to sell milk for less than 13 cents a quart and, meeting two days after the Housewives, the executive of the Toronto Milk Producers' Association publicly thanked the Ontario Milk Board for approving the price rise.[16] Taking the offensive against the Housewives, Dr J.B. Reynolds, president of the Producers' Association, retorted that the price rise was necessary, warned that a boycott could result in dairies going bankrupt, and described the Housewives' demand for consumer representation on the Milk Board as not only unnecessary, but "obnoxious."[17] A few dairy industry representatives, reported by the press, admitted publicly that Toronto milk prices were too high and confirmed the Housewives' claims that the controversy had, in fact, stopped further price increases, a prediction that proved accurate.[18] Meeting privately, the dairies began planning ways to make up their losses by forcing lower prices on producers and initiating new efforts to increase milk consumption.[19] Publicly, dairy industry representatives dismissed the Housewives' boycott as a "flash in the pan" that, three weeks into the boycott, had already "blown over." But the press reported that sales of tinned milk had increased "tremendously" while those of the fresh product were down by 7 per cent, despite offers of free butter and cream to milk customers who placed regular orders.[20]

Small dairies began threatening to defy the Milk Board and cut their prices, and several municipalities began looking for legal ways to circumvent the Milk Board.[21] The Housewives, for their part, refuted the dairies' claim that the boycott would only hurt milk drivers and farmers. Lamb acknowledged that they "might have to suffer for a while," but threatened to reduce milk consumption even more drastically "if any of the dairies attempt to take it out on the farmers or drivers."[22] Rather than bribing their customers with free butter, Lamb suggested, dairies should cooperate with the Housewives. Any dairy "endorsed by organized labor" and willing to sell milk at the Housewives' price of 10 cents per quart would have their support.[23]

Workers, Farmers, and Consumers

Like the Housewives, organized labour blamed the milk price increase on the big dairy companies that controlled most of the Toronto market and, many claimed, dominated the Milk Control Board. The Toronto District Trades and Labour Council supported the boycott and pointed to record high profits, observing that the four big Toronto dairies reported earnings in excess of $8 million. Although the Milk Distributors Association disputed that figure as "entirely false," the claim was a red flag to the milk delivery drivers, some of whom were in the midst of a long and sometimes violent strike for union recognition and minimum earnings of $25 a week.[24] Key figures in the labour movement supported the Housewives, including J. Kellythorne, secretary of the Milk Drivers' Union local 647, Toronto District Labour Council President John Noble, and Labour Council secretary and long-time socialist John W. Buckley, who was probably the husband of Housewife Mrs Dorothy Buckley. But not all drivers did. Based on evidence from a handwriting expert, the police identified the writer of the anonymous threat as a "disgruntled" milk delivery driver, and reports circulated that milk drivers whose milk orders had declined were being penalized by the dairies. Drivers, who worked seven-day weeks delivering milk to customers' doors on horse-drawn wagons and earned commission on sales, also reported lost earnings as a result of the boycott.[25]

The Housewives also sought alliances with farmers, arguing, as did Mrs Ewart Humphreys, that "it would be all right" if the farmer got the milk price increase, "but he doesn't. There is far too much profit going to the distributors."[26] But dairy farmers, like some of the drivers, were ambivalent. Investigations into milk price in a number of cities after World War One, including Toronto and Winnipeg, had confirmed that the dairies engaged in sharp practices and led to the conviction of executives in one dairy for illegal profiteering. Two others were prohibited from reducing what they paid milk producers. But when Ontario (along with other provinces) created a Milk Control Board in 1934 to stabilize the industry, it did little to improve the circumstances of the farmers who produced fluid milk for the retail market. Lacking a strong political voice, they were largely ignored by government policies, which prioritized production of butter and cheese for export.[27] The Housewives' milk price protests shone a light on the economics of the dairy industry, revealing that farmers earned about 4 cents per quart for their milk, which many claimed was insufficient to make a living. Rising costs combined with low prices paid by the dairies, they claimed, left them earning as little as 15 cents per hour.[28] Some blamed consumers, as did the farmer who suggested that "dumping all the milk for a few days" would "bring the housewives to their senses." A letter from a farmer to the *Globe* illuminated the divide between the concerns of farm women and those of the Housewives. "It almost broke my heart," she wrote, to see the "foolish (but no doubt well-meaning)" Housewives parading with placards demanding "Buy no butter until it is 30 cents per pound" as she prepared to milk seven cows. Farmers such as herself work "very, very hard for the ordinary comforts of life," she explained, and "perhaps in the golden-age-to-be we may even persuade our city sisters to campaign for higher prices for our products when they fail to bring us a margin of profit."[29] Others opined that, although producers were not getting paid enough for their milk, "at the same time the consumer is paying too much." Most agreed that the price spread between the 4 cents paid to farmers and the 13 cents paid by consumers was "too much." Profits, some suggested, should be "divided between farmers and consumers."[30] Small dairies, likewise, believed that "small operators" like themselves had no voice at the Milk Board. Unable to absorb a decline in sales, ten suburban dairies attempted to circumvent the Ontario Milk Control Act, which forbade the selling of milk below the price approved by the Ontario Milk Control Board, by establishing an Independent Milk Distributors Association and offering milk to consumers at 12 cents per quart.[31]

Politicized, in part, by the Housewives, milk price became a synecdoche of the political crises of the decade, as prices rose while earnings declined. Through the last two years of the Great Depression, Housewives Associations became a lightning rod for popular outrage about governments' failure to address the daily crises of unemployment, poverty, and hunger. They tapped the widespread frustration of working people who had struggled through eight years of hard times only to see prices rise with no increase in wages. They ignited a public debate about the industry and the political economy of milk price and inspired others in surrounding communities to organize local Housewives Associations.[32] Housewives' leagues and associations, some but not all of them affiliated to the Toronto group, sprang up in communities across Ontario. They were endorsed by organizations across the political spectrum, including Home and School associations, ratepayers' groups, and Liberal women's organizations, which were far from radical, and some, such as the Women's Christian Temperance Union, the Canadian Daughters League, and Local Councils of Women, that were socially and politically conservative. The Reverend R.J. Irwin of Donlands United Church, one of many religious leaders who agreed publicly with the Housewives, supported the municipalization of milk and advised housewives to establish dairy cooperatives to circumvent the over-priced dairies.[33] The Toronto District Labour Council called on the city to reduce the cost of milk distribution while increasing returns to the farmer by "municipalizing" milk, and to do the same with bread, coal, and gas, commodities that they claimed had "become a monopoly by trustification."[34] The Toronto *Telegram* ran a special Saturday feature on the economics of the dairy industry.[35] Industry supporters, including the right-populist *Telegram* and the pro-business *Globe*, disputed the solution proposed by the Housewives, labour, and the left, pointing out that the Milk Board had increased security in Ontario's important dairy industry. But the Housewives' campaign had made equally clear that the Milk Control Board, a provincial regulatory body, had failed to justify an increase in milk price, a decision with far-reaching community impact that caused particular hardship during an economic downturn in the eighth year of the Depression.

Milk, widely regarded as an essential food, had been a national problem since the start of the Depression, which a 1933 federal inquiry and the creation of provincial milk boards did little to quell.[36] Chronic instability in the dairy industry, as Andrew Ebejer has argued, reached crisis proportions in 1932, when a "price war" drove down retail milk prices from 11 cents to as little as 5 cents a quart. The low price was a boon to consumers, many of them struggling to buy milk and other necessities while family breadwinners were unemployed or earning starvation wages. Distributors, however, passed the losses on to producers, whose wholesale price dropped from $2.12 to $1.30 per hundredweight, a disproportionate 39 per cent decline. The industry, having petitioned for years for government regulation, seized the opportunity to pressure the province for legislation. Enacted in April 1934, the Ontario Milk Control Act used licencing rules to restrict the number of dairies and producers, effectively barring new entrants, and created the Milk Control Board to negotiate and approve consumer and producer milk prices. One consequence, unforeseen by many, was concentration within the industry. Small dairies were effectively "squeezed out," leaving the four largest dairies – Borden, Silverwood, Eastern, and Dairy Corp. – with over 50 per cent of the city's milk business. The Milk Board thus secured the industry but at the expense of producers and consumers, and was widely condemned as wielding too much power – according to some, "almost as great as Mussolini."[37]

By December 1937, a month after its founding, the Toronto Housewives Association had hit on a new remedy for high milk prices. Excited by the possibility of emulating successful dairy cooperatives in Winnipeg, Nova Scotia, Illinois, and New Zealand, Toronto Housewives began pressuring the Ontario legislature to amend the Milk Control Act, which restricted purchases to shareholders and prohibited rebates to consumers, a provision that was interpreted by the Milk Board to disallow profit-sharing between cooperative dairies and their members.[38] They lobbied the Premier and petitioned the legislature for an amendment to the legislation to permit dairy coops and presented their case at a four-hour meeting with the Milk Board, all to no avail.[39] Unable to form dairy cooperatives, they moved on to other commodities. By June they had established a consumer-producer coop with six Peel county farmers, who began trucking in fruit, vegetables, eggs, and butter twice weekly to their members.[40] Pleased with their initial success, they announced their commitment to "raise the general standard of living by a greater cooperation between producers and consumers."[41] This strategy was reflected in the first issue of the *Housewives Report*, published in April 1938, which featured an article on cooperatives by H.H. Hannan, secretary of the United Farmers of Ontario, signalling both the Housewives' continued enthusiasm for cooperatives and their hope of forging alliances with farmers.[42] Both projects, however, resulted in failure.

Milk, Butter, Bread, and Fuel

Milk's special significance as an essential food, believed indispensable for the health of children, as I have argued elsewhere, made it an ideal target for the Housewives' campaigns, but Housewives' groups also demanded lower prices for other necessities.[43] A month after its founding, the flagship group of Toronto Housewives, alarmed that food prices had increased 40 per cent since the previous year whereas wages had gone up only 10 per cent, and "some not at all," formed a committee to study food prices. "We are working for lower priced milk now," ward captain Mrs M. Garrison explained. "Later we will go on to other foods."[44] Other Housewives groups refused to wait. Less than two weeks after the Toronto group organized, a hundred members of the Lakeshore Housewives Association voted to petition the premier for lower public transit fares and telephone rates in addition to the milk price. Declining to affiliate with the Toronto association, they criticized Bertha Lamb, whose campaign, they charged, had achieved nothing. By contrast, their own organization, President Mrs Edith Harrison declared, would address the "problems that affect the working class," and would not stop "until we have received a satisfactory solution to these problems."[45] York Township Housewives agreed, vowing, "We are not going to stop when we have the milk problem solved. Bread and other essential foodstuffs will be next."[46] That kind of optimism is evident, as well, in their letters to the papers. One such writer predicted that "Just one week and no sales would make them all sit up and take notice." As evidence, she offered an optimistic assessment of the results of consumer activism in the United States: "Housewives in the States started a meat war, and in two weeks won out."[47]

In February 1938, Toronto Housewives launched a new campaign, in a meeting at which hundreds of Housewives members rose to their feet and pledged to buy no butter until the price dropped. They called on all city housewives to join them in "Butter Boycott Week" and predicted that as many as 8,000 women would do so.[48] Already skilled organizers, they engaged in an energetic round of activities that foreshadowed the performance activism that would keep them in public view throughout the coming decade. In the days before the boycott, they generated headlines with revelations that a local radio station considered them too "controversial" to allow their broadcast; that a majority of Toronto women, surveyed by telephone, supported them; and that hundreds of Housewives had sent letters to every member of the Ontario legislature.[49] The broadcast went ahead on 22 March, marking

Fighting the High Cost of Living

On Tuesday afternoon more than 200 members of the Toronto Housewives' Association paid a call on the Ontario legislature and left a resolution asking for an investigation into the high cost of living. Pictured above are Mrs. Phyllis Poland, publicity director of the association and Mrs. Anne Usprich and her daughter Cecile as they left the parliament buildings. Yesterday a delegation from the association visited the board of control and asked for support in the housewives' battle against rising food costs.

1.2 "Fighting the High Cost of Living," *Daily Clarion*, 24 March 1938, 1

the first day of the boycott and again making news in Canadian papers as well as in New York State, where the radical Dairy Farmers' Union – a model for the Housewives – had been using direct action tactics to challenge the pricing policies of the dairies through the 1930s.[50]

The next day, fifty Housewives secured tickets to the Ontario legislature to see Premier Mitchell Hepburn receive their petition urging a commission to investigate high food prices. One hundred more, led by Toronto Housewives Ward Two President Mrs Elizabeth Brown and Campaign Director Mrs Phyllis Poland, converged in an open-air meeting at the Ontario legislature with placards calling for a food price investigation and reminding legislators that the butter boycott continued. They were joined at Queen's Park by members of the Communist party, there to register their opposition to British Prime Minister Neville Chamberlain's policy of appeasement with Germany and call on Prime Minister Mackenzie King to take a stand against fascism in Europe.[51]

A second delegation, this one five hundred strong, reiterated their demands the next day in a meeting with Toronto city council. In addition to lobbying, they picketed stores and posted homemade signs on cars and in home and store windows urging women to join the boycott. They canvassed door-to-door to gather signatures on petitions and, each Housewife taking a page of the telephone book to call, drummed up support on the telephone. At week's end, they ramped up the campaign with a "postcard parade," singing as they marched down city streets, wearing sandwich boards demanding "we want milk for 10 cents or less," and urging women to use "peanut butter, honey butter, and jam" as substitutes for butter. Demonstrating their developing skills in street theatre, the protestors lined up at the busy Adelaide Street post office where, one by one, they bought cards, wrote messages asking for an investigation of the dairy industry, and mailed them to Ontario Premier Mitchell Hepburn. The capstone event was a mass meeting in the Labour Temple, to which all housewives, as well as "gentlemen," were invited. Two hundred men and women gathered to celebrate a successful week of boycotting butter. Speakers included George Watson, president of the Trades and Labor Council, Dr Edmund T. Guest, Chairman of the Board of Education, Russell Pawley, a Brampton farmer, and Dr Rose Bronstein, national secretary of the pro-Communist Association for Jewish Colonization in the Soviet Union (ICOR), all of whom offered their support.[52]

Two months later, the Toronto Housewives resumed their delegations to city council and began petitioning the Ontario legislature in a new campaign. The Consumers' Gas Company, they complained, not only levied higher rates on households than on businesses, but charged an exorbitant 50 cents per month for the meters that calculated customers' usage. A commercial client with a $100 monthly gas bill could easily absorb the extra 50 cents, they explained, but the same charge added 25 per cent to the average housewife's bill of $2 and would double the costs for poor families, who might use as little as 50 cents worth of fuel.[53] Mrs Ena Albon, secretary of the Toronto Housewives' Association, outlined the issues in an article published in the *Clarion*. Housewives, she posited, knew that the rates for natural gas were too high. Shareholders, by contrast, who received dividends, "in good times, in bad times, without any competition," were guaranteed annual returns of 10 per cent, making Gas Company shares "the only profitable investment left." To solve the problem, she suggested, "I wish that we could use that very effective method – boycotting the company." But the poor, who could least afford high rates, were unable to switch fuel because they "generally can't afford the $35 or $40 for an electric stove." The gas company, she accused, "has them at its mercy." "Talk about dictators," she concluded, making a clear reference to the fascist threat looming in Europe, "we have them right here – for that's what the Consumers' Gas company is."[54]

Not only did the Housewives frame their demands in the same language as (and sometimes more vehemently than) the party and labour left, but consumer activism added traction to the left's efforts to advance the price struggle. While the Housewives lobbied city councils and provincial legislatures, protested through the streets, and engaged in other direct action tactics, Joe Salsberg, one of Toronto's two Communist aldermen, managed to wrest a small, albeit symbolic, concession from city council on the gas meter charge. His initial motion that the city petition the provincial government to eliminate the meter charge and reduce the statutory dividend to shareholders from 10 to 5 per cent failed, but passed when amended to omit the call to halve dividends, a sticking point due to the large number of shares held by the city.[55] The campaign got additional support from the Toronto District Labour Council and the *Clarion*, which published evidence from the company's year-end report. Debunking the Gas Company's claim that its financial stability depended on the meter charge, the *Clarion* revealed that, with $2.5 million in profits, it had actually done better during these Depression years than other Toronto corporations and had even been able to increase dividends.[56]

The gas meter campaign was prominent, as well, on the agenda of the Housewives' first annual convention. On 30 November, over a hundred delegates resolved to redouble their efforts to abolish the gas meter charge with tactics that included a boycott, a city-wide petition, and a survey of the positions of candidates for the forthcoming municipal election. In addition to electing a new executive led by Mrs Elizabeth Brown as incoming president, the women declared themselves "determined to build a strong association that will be a mighty power against the cost of living." Margaret Gould, the left-leaning *Toronto Star* reporter who, as Ian Mosby notes, produced many editorials exposing the misery of the poor during the Depression, and who spoke at the Housewives' convention, assured them that "there is nothing that a group of determined women cannot get." They also resolved to continue the fight for lower milk price, abolish the Milk Board, and amend the Milk Control Act to permit dairy cooperatives.[57]

An unsuccessful meeting with the Gas Company's general manager in December convinced the Housewives that determination and lobbying were insufficient to effect change, and they bolstered their efforts at persuasion with direct action. On the morning of 8 February 1939, two hundred Housewives, led by President Elizabeth Brown and Mrs Isobel Johnson, the campaign manager, presented their petition to the board of control. They were watched by four members of the police Red Squad and an unspecified number of newspaper reporters. Press coverage of the event, while sympathetic to the Housewives, emphasized the spectacle of gender inversion, in which feisty and determined women appeared to impose their political agenda on powerful men, and depicted the struggle between the Housewives and their male adversaries as somewhat ridiculous. Bearing a huge banner demanding "Abolish the 50 cents Monthly Gas Meter Service Charge," and brandishing dozens of petitions, the Housewives paused for press photos on the city hall steps. Inside, the four controllers and the mayor, who, the press noted, "blushed slightly" in response to the women's cajoling, signed their petition, accompanied by the "cheers and laughter" of the women. The women then marched to the offices of the Consumers' Gas Company and mounted four flights of stairs to the general manager's office. Told the manager was at lunch, the *Star* reported, the women "chattered excitedly" while Mrs Johnson scoffed that he was "afraid to meet us." Fifty women returned the following day and, after their five leaders were admitted, the others "started for the stairs." A fracas ensued when five company guards barred them from proceeding. The Housewives, who evidently perceived no contradiction between their social entitlements as women and their rights as citizens to a voice in public policy, chided the men, who they said "ought to be ashamed" of themselves for "pushing helpless women."[58] Yet they made no headway with the Gas Company. A private members' bill proposing their amendments to the Milk Control Act introduced by Eric Cross, the minister for municipal affairs, who had been successfully lobbied by the Housewives, also failed.[59] A conference held in May at the upscale Royal York Hotel and heavily covered by the *Clarion*, but ignored by the other papers, similarly failed to sway legislators or the Gas Company.[60]

A National Organization

Optimism and their collective confidence in their ability to force the government to make progressive change propelled the Housewives onward, confident that, "with persistence and determination," they could "compel the government to act."[61] After all, less than three months after organizing, the Housewives had mounted dozens of delegations and sent hundreds of letters to city councils, the Ontario Milk Control Board, and the Ontario legislature; they had organized a mass meeting in Toronto's Mutual Street Arena, capable of seating at least 5,000. They had paraded through Toronto's business section bearing picketed signs announcing, "Down With Butter," "Dairy Combines are unfair to housewives," and "Do not buy any more butter until it is 30 cents a pound or less." City councillors and members of the provincial legislature had attended their meetings and pledged their support. They had held huge meetings at which hundreds of women had stood and vowed to boycott butter until the price dropped.[62]

Confident that they were on the brink of becoming a national force, sometime in late 1937 or early 1938 they formed the Canadian Housewives Association, engaged legal counsel, and began corresponding on letterhead stationery emblazoned with its own coat of arms, with its thirteen-member executive listed on the masthead. Membership dues were set at 10 cents per month or one dollar per year. In January 1938, publicity director Mrs Phyllis Poland reported in the *Clarion* that the Association had a membership of nearly 10,000 and members in every ward in the city.[63] In May, a report on the organization in their paper, the *Housewives' Report*, no longer extant but described by Housewife Alice Cooke in the *Daily Clarion*, affirmed that the Association was "non-political and non-sectarian" and set out its ambitious objectives: "To reduce the high cost of living," "facilitate and advance the interests of all housewives," "collect all available information regarding prices of food products, fuel, rent, articles of clothing," "devise ways and means to reduce those prices to a minimum," and "distribute information relating to every aspect of household economy."[64] Over the following months, new organizations formed in Oshawa, Orillia, Whitby, Ottawa, Kingston, North Bay, London, Hamilton, and Windsor. By fall 1938, membership in the Canadian Housewives Association, with groups in Vancouver, Winnipeg, and Montreal, had increased to an estimated 15,000.[65]

Montreal women had organized a branch of the Canadian Housewives League in February 1938, encouraged by Bella Hall Gauld, a Communist party member and at that time chairman of the Central Labour Forum – the gender-inappropriateness of her title unnoticed, even within the Communist Party.[66] Hall became a socialist in her early 30s and was active first in Brandon, Manitoba, in J.S. Woodsworth's All People's Mission, before taking a position as the first director of the University Settlement of Montreal. At the age of forty-two, she attended the American Socialist Society's Rand School in New York, where she encountered Marxism. Inspired, she returned to Montreal, joined the Communist party and, along with other socialists, including her life-long friend and comrade Annie Buller, organized the Montreal Labor College. The College survived only four years, but party activists agreed that it laid the foundation of the Montreal Communist party. Hall remained active in the party the rest of her life, as an organizer for the Canadian Labor Defence League, the Young Pioneers, and Friends of the Soviet Union. Her relationship with the Housewives is typical of leading comrades like herself, Annie Buller, and Becky Buhay, who endorsed the Housewives and described themselves as participants, but whose absence from media accounts and RCMP records suggests played no consistent role in the organization. Hall's party-authorized biography, significantly, includes no mention of her involvement in the Housewives.[67]

Instead, President Mrs Newey led the League's 250 members in protests against high rents and pre-wartime profiteering. An RCMP report on a symposium on profiteering in January 1939, at which President Newey spoke on behalf of the Housewives League, summarizes her statements on the rising cost of living, the sugar shortage, and the need for everyone to send protest postcards to Ottawa. But it offers no opinion on Newey's possible political affiliation, an omission that suggests the Mounties had no reason to believe she was a communist, given their preoccupation with identifying those who were.[68] In addition to participating in public protests like the symposium, the Housewives collected signatures on petitions to protest the rising price of sugar, and sent resolutions to all provincial members of Parliament. Initially, at least, whatever the political views of its president, the group maintained its ties to the Communist party. CPC general secretary Tim Buck, Canada's best-known Communist, spoke to the women about the gas meter struggle in Toronto and Mrs Newey addressed a meeting of the Young Communist League, at which she urged the comrades to sign their petitions and invited "all ladies present" to join. By February 1940, the Montreal Housewives had attracted the attention of the mainstream press, when Mrs Sylvia Ledoux, described by the *Globe* as a "comely French-Canadian housewife," made headlines as she fired "the first shot" in their renewed fight against rent increases by nailing a placard to the door of her home.[69]

Women in Vancouver were also organizing around prices, although as Effie Jones recalls, the BC Housewives League "was started by some women and a man of the Liberal party," who, she recalled, "did nothing, but they met socially. Well, the times called for something more than social meetings." The solution, she decided, was "to get into this Housewives League and make it work. That's what I did, and quite a lot of my friends."[70] Jones was an effective and energetic organizer. By March 1938, at least one Housewives League had formed and by November, the *Globe and Mail* reported, the BC Housewives League had fifteen branches and six more starting to organize.[71] Over the following months, with inflation and, they charged, profiteering driving up food prices, the Housewives called a week-long "meat strike," threatening that, unless the price came down, they would call one every month "until we can convince retailers that we mean business." They picketed stores that sold over-priced meat and called on the government to regulate meat prices, complaining that suppliers were sending only top-quality grade A beef to market, which many, living on low wages, could not afford.[72] They held public meetings and conferences on rising food prices and wartime profiteering, with speakers that included Vancouver's CCF mayor, Lyle Telford, and Mrs Stuart Jamieson, a regular patron of progressive causes, who articulated the demand for a planned economy, a proposal that would preoccupy social planners over the coming decade.[73] Together with women's and community groups and labour unions, they established the Consumers' Research Council, probably modelled on Consumers' Research, known for its product testing and consumer education in the U.S.[74]

Conditions during the Depression were dire, Jones recalled, and the League members were unwilling to restrict themselves to fighting prices. They also had to fight evictions. "They were putting people out in the snow. We had to work on all kinds of things. There was no other organization working, none at all."[75] Jones recounted one eviction in which the sheriff and his "goons" were taking people's furniture out the front door and the Housewives League members and others were bringing them in at the back. She also recalled an attempted eviction of two old people in which the crowd of about two hundred resisters lit a woodstove the sheriff's men had put outside, thus blocking any further removals. League members were also active in the unemployed workers movement, organized as the communist-led Relief Project Workers Union, for whom they prepared meals during their month-long sit-down strike at the Vancouver post office. Interviewed four decades after the event, Jones recalled clearly the day the strike ended, on 19 June 1938, in one of the most dramatic expressions of police violence against the unemployed, an event memorialized as Bloody Sunday.[76]

As yet not organized into Housewives groups, Winnipeg women made news in January 1938 with the strong language they used to express their opinions about the milk price hike.[77] By the end of April, members of the Communist-led Women's Progressive Club joined others from the right-wing Social Credit Party to create Homemakers' Clubs. They established a temporary committee to campaign against high prices and, by September, had joined Toronto Housewives in the milk boycott. Like Housewives elsewhere, they organized public meetings which they advertised in radio broadcasts. Winnipeg's tradition of electing socialists and communists to city council, together with its activist left ethnic culture, prominent among which were the Ukrainian Labour Farmer Temple Association (ULFTA) and the United Jewish People's Order (UJPO), was reflected in the diversity of their speakers, who displayed a more visibly ethnic and more socialist composition than their counterparts in Ontario. But like other Housewives groups, they were perceived as very respectable, as evidenced by the prominence of their speakers. These included the city's socialist mayor, John Queen, Alderman Jack Blumberg, a member of the CCF, and the well-known Ukrainian activist Andrew Bilecki, manager of the ULFTA-run People's Cooperative Dairy and a Communist.[78]

Canada's declaration of war in September 1939 helped to shift media attention and thus the public conversation away from the Housewives. Anticommunist allegations against the organization in fall 1938 and the temporary silencing of the Communist press in 1940, following its banning by Justice Minister Ernest Lapointe in October 1939, combined to thin out the available evidence of Housewives' activities. Still, media coverage confirms that the Housewives continued to respond to the concerns of ordinary people, denouncing profiteering and urging the federal government to immediately begin controlling prices. They also called for fair tax policies, including a tax on excess profits, especially on food. With branches now reaching from BC to Montreal and allies elsewhere, they kicked off a coordinated campaign with delegations, public conferences, and protests in cities across the country. Hundreds of BC Housewives, in collaboration with the Victoria Council of Women and Vancouver Mayor Lyle Telford, met in convention to demand state control of prices and consumer representatives on the Wartime Price Control Board. These were the same demands made by more than two hundred who attended a meeting called by the left-led Workers' Cooperative in Timmins, Ontario, which also established a committee to investigate profiteering. Winnipeg Homemakers joined with the Winnipeg Trades and Labour Council to protest wartime profiteering and propose that a woman be appointed to the Wartime Prices and Trade Board. London's Trades and Labour Council, London's and Regina's city councils, and Toronto Alderman Stuart Smith joined the protest. Similar actions by Housewives and labour unions were reported in Port Arthur, Windsor, and Hamilton, although the *Clarion* declared the "people's movement against profiteering" to be most powerful in BC.[79]

Who Were These Housewives?

The Housewives' broad appeal owed much to the apparently unthreatening maternalism that distinguished them from the overtly political and male-dominated organizations of the left. Their founder, Bertha Lamb, identified herself as "just an average Toronto housewife," motivated to act by seeing "children suffering while the profits of the large milk distributors go sky high." "Realizing that her feelings were the same as thousands of others," she told the press, she "decided to do something about it."[80] Even as a political neophyte, she took pains to ensure that the Housewives would be seen as apolitical and, even more important, as non-Communist, establishing a rule at the outset that "office-holders in other women's organizations" were not eligible to hold office in hers. The new organization, she insisted, "must have no strings attached to it, political or otherwise." Members were to be "ordinary housewives who, under other circumstances, take no part in organizational activities."[81] Her unilateral ruling provoked an inconclusive debate that did little to deter the members of the CCF and the Communist party, labour women, members of ethnic organizations, and other members of the broad communist left, who, within the year, formed the organization's activist core. The influence of such women is apparent in the emergence of Housewives groups in cities such as Vancouver, Winnipeg, and Montreal, all of which had a significant Communist presence.

Among those at the founding meeting were a number of Communist party women and others with ties to the non-party communist left, including representatives of the left-led East York Housewives and United Women's Association, which met with their town council to urge support for a milk-price protest days before the Toronto women's delegation.[82] At least two East York Housewives, Mrs Elizabeth Morton, a frequent Communist party candidate for East York Town Council and a member of the Communist-led Canadian League for Peace and Democracy, and Mrs Ewart Humphreys, were probably Communist party members.[83] Neither the press nor the historical literature provide much information about Mrs Humphreys, whose name before marriage was probably Ethel May Watts, but Ewart had been a staff member of the Communist Worker's Unity League before his election as East York's reeve.[84] All three were active in the radical East York Workers' Association and involved in the unemployed workers movement and resisting evictions.[85] Likewise, at least a few members of the Communist-affiliated Progressive Women's Associations attended the Housewives' founding meeting, as did Mrs Alice Cooke, who wrote a "weekly letter" for the women's section of the *Daily Clarion*, and Mrs Alice Buck, wife of CPC general secretary Tim Buck. Also present was Mrs Rae Luckock, a charter member of the Ontario CCF who had been organizing for the party since 1933.[86]

Effie Jones joined the BC Housewives League in 1938, the same year she joined the Communist party. Jones was active during the Depression in the Mothers' Council as well as the Housewives League, where she played a leading role for a decade. She was involved in a wide range of progressive causes, but, unusual at the time, she preferred to work with women. Convinced that women were "more effective" politically than men, she espoused an inversion of the widespread belief on the left that men were inherently more class conscious and should therefore educate their wives. Instead, she believed that radical women would influence their husbands. Jones spent many years organizing grassroots movements with other women and also became prominent in civic politics, where she ran for election on platforms that called for more affordable transit fares and utilities. Of her many achievements, she is remembered primarily for her strong showing in the 1947 mayoralty race, winning 19,218 votes to her opponent's 24,135 and twenty-seven of fifty-one polls.[87]

While this is an impressive achievement, the emphasis on the male-dominated sphere of electoral politics offers a clue about why so little has been written about Jones and other women on the left, and why we know so little about the women who were active in the Housewives, the most popular left movement of their decade. Her comrade Maurice Rush, in his memoir of a life in the Communist left, credits her as having played an important role in shaping history, but outlines her contribution in three brief paragraphs and one footnote.[88] As Irene Howard observes in her valuable article on the Mothers' Council of Vancouver, "the task of writing left-wing women into the history of Canada will not be an easy one," because so few records exist. Archival materials on large, mainstream organizations such as the National Council of Women are recognized as important and have been preserved. But "women in less permanent regional and local organizations, no matter what their politics, have not had sufficient sense of their own importance to preserve their records." "When storage space was a problem," she notes, "a woman might find room for her husband's 'more important' papers and destroy her own." Omitted from history and eclipsed by the records of men, often within the same organizations, "it is little wonder that when it came time to deal with their accumulated papers, they destroyed them." Such, sadly, was the case with Effie Jones, who destroyed her papers in the 1970s, believing that they were "of no interest to anyone."[89]

A few women can be traced because they or their husbands were involved in progressive causes that attracted the attention of police red squads or other coercive arms of the state and have thus left public records. Mrs Nora Rodd helped organize the Windsor Housewives League in March 1938, served as its first vice-president, and remained a consumer activist into the 1940s. She was a member of a number of other progressive causes in which Communists were active, including the Canadian-Soviet Friendship Society and the Women's International Democratic Federation (WIDF), an influential international women's organization of the post-1945 era but largely forgotten today.[90] In 1951, she chaired a delegation of twenty-one women to North Korea, then at war with the U.S., to investigate evidence of allied war crimes, an action that brought her to the attention of the federal External Affairs Committee. External Affairs Minister Lester Pearson termed her behaviour "vicious" beyond exaggeration and suggested she might be prosecuted for treason when she returned, although (other) Canadian Communists, he admitted (along with other anti-war activists) "who had stayed home, remote from North Korea, were saying publicly what Mrs Rodd was saying over Moscow radio."[91]

Married women are hard to identify, as they almost always took husbands' names. Exceptional circumstances helped to identify Mrs Phyllis Poland, publicity director of the Toronto Housewives Association through the 1930s and 1940s and almost certainly the wife of Fred Poland, who was charged and later acquitted in the 1946 espionage trials that followed the defection of Soviet cypher clerk Igor Gouzenko. Mrs Poland, who was Phyllis Lane before her marriage, attracted media scrutiny when she petitioned the court to release her husband on the grounds that he was illegally detained without charge and denied access to legal counsel. Her valiant attempt to persuade the court to release her husband, who was later found innocent, made front-page news. Fred and Phyllis Poland subsequently disappear from the public record, but the notoriety of such a public trial during the Cold War era would have tarnished their reputations and they would almost certainly have remained under police surveillance.[92]

Women who did not attract such damaging media attention or were not prominent members of a left party are harder to trace. One exception is Mrs E.A. Havelock, a frequent spokesperson for the Housewives, whose name, before she married Eric A. (Arthur) Havelock in 1927, was Ellen Parkinson. Aside from a few references to her in the press that identify her as a professor's wife as well as a Housewife, little has been recorded about Ellen, but Eric was a professor of classics at Victoria College of the University of Toronto and a socialist. He was one member of the small group of left-wing academics who established the League for Social Reconstruction (LSR), the intellectual organization of the CCF, in fall and winter 1931–2, and was known to support left causes, including the 1937 United Autoworkers strike in Windsor. Havelock played a major role in the *Canadian Forum*, the LSR's scholarly journal. Like many others on the left, he was regarded with suspicion by the authorities, including the administrators of his university, where his political activism was regarded as an "indiscretion." He was ordered to resign from his position in the CCF provincial executive and acquired a reputation as a dissident.[93] Mrs Havelock's work in the Housewives suggests that she and her spouse were both progressives. These women and others brought their organizing skills and political acumen to the Housewives, forming the activist core that kept the organization alive for over a decade, but their presence was used by the red-baiters who attacked and would eventually discredit their movement.

Left Politics and Food Security

Through the Depression years and after, the two prominent parties of the left, the CCF and the Communist party, campaigned actively for what we would now call food security. As candidates and elected members of municipal councils and provincial legislatures, Communists and CCFers called for state action to reduce high prices and, by relentless effort, occasionally wrung concessions from government. Both parties had urged state intervention in the dairy industry and proposed nationalization – or "municipalization" – of dairies to reduce milk price through the 1930s. Indeed, until the Cold War drove a final wedge between them in the late 1940s, the two parties were virtually unanimous on the prices issue, as they were on many other matters. CCF election platforms frequently included nationalization of milk, and municipal control of milk was supported by Toronto Mayor James (Jimmy) Simpson, Vancouver Mayor Lyle Telford, and Winnipeg Mayor John Queen, as well as Toronto Alderman William Dennison, all of whom had connections to the CCF. Dennison also joined the Housewives in advocating reducing milk delivery drivers' work week to forty hours.[94] Articles in the Communist press, which until 1940 included a daily and some weekly papers, research papers from Communist-led unions, and booklets and pamphlets produced by the Communist party were intended to educate consumers and provide research for activists. *Milk for Millions*, a forty-five-page booklet published in 1938 by the New York State Communist party and circulated widely, outlined the party's proposal for solving the milk problem: genuine consumer and farmer participation on milk boards, municipal distribution, and support for cooperative dairies.[95] *Milk for Millions* articulates the same demands as the CCF, the Communist party, the Housewives, and the other organizations of the broad social democratic and communist left.

Communist and CCF women had certainly protested high prices, especially those of essential foods, well before the emergence of the Housewives. Communist-led Women's Progressive Clubs and United Women's Councils, including the very active East York United Women, had protested through the 1930s against high prices and advocated for families on relief, demanding government intervention to bring down the price of milk, bread, and meat. In the months before the Housewives organized, delegations of these women's organizations, along with unionists and rate-payers' groups, had confronted Toronto's city council when the milk price increase was first announced to register their objections. The left-wing York council, which included a number of future Housewives, held public meetings to protest the increase in milk price and launched a house-to-house signature drive on a petition to the premier.[96]

The CCF continued to protest high prices, although most party women were forced out of the Housewives during the purge within the CCF in the late 1940s and, because they failed to create an alternative consumer group, little of their activity took place at the grassroots. In the 1930s and through the war years, however, a number of left-leaning CCF women were active in or supported the Housewives. Rose Henderson exemplifies the activist maternalist stream within the CCF that led women to support the Housewives. Although Henderson died on 30 January 1937, eight months before the Toronto Housewives Association was formed, she worked with Communist women in the Women's Progressive Associations who organized around political issues that they perceived as having most relevance for women – poverty, child welfare, inadequate relief, pacifism, and prices – and who brought these concerns to their activism in the Housewives.[97] Henderson, whose politics were informed by her maternalist feminism and was willing to work with Communists, would no doubt have been active with the Housewives, as were other CCF women with a similar outlook, most prominently Rae Luckock. Indeed, as Peter Campbell argues in his illuminating biography, Henderson perceived no contradiction between feminism and socialism; on the contrary, he contends, her "anti-capitalist politics flowed directly out of maternal feminism."[98] That political philosophy seems likely to have motivated others who have left no record of their thoughts.

Red-Baited!

Anticommunism, of course, long predated the Cold War, and the prominent role of communist women and the active support of the Communist party in the struggle for lower prices dictated caution among the Housewives. Many Canadians endorsed socialist ideas during the Depression years and a significant minority supported left parties. Indeed, as John Manley argues, the party's successful mobilization of the unemployed had so enhanced its popularity that it prompted a repressive response by the state. In 1932, eight prominent party members, including general secretary Tim Buck, were jailed on convictions of seditious conspiracy and membership in an illegal revolutionary organization. Hundreds of immigrants who were active in the unemployed workers' movement were deported and violent police action was used to halt the movement's On-To-Ottawa trek in Regina in 1935 and end the sit-in at the Vancouver post office in 1938. These events were clearly designed to demonstrate the coercive power of the state and its determination to repress socialism, and that repression did undermine the party's popular support. But as the thousands who flocked to hear Buck on his country-wide tour after his release from Kingston penitentiary attest, it simultaneously enhanced the party's status among some as a voice for the powerless.[99]

Anticommunism was thus a very real concern for the Housewives, while at the same time communists' participation in the organization was acceptable to many non-communist consumer activists. From the outset, Lamb had taken pains to ensure that the organization was regarded as respectable, and had insisted that members cultivate an appealingly maternal public image. Proper decorum, she insisted, was especially important. "We are housewives, not fishwives," she reminded the noisy crowd at the organization's founding meeting, pointing out that reporters were present. But she was equally concerned about the threat of anticommunism, noting that the press tended to describe organizations like theirs as "reds." The Housewives, she insisted, were neither political nor sectarian, but merely "a group of indignant housewives tired to death of trying to make both ends meet."[100] Yet like many organizations at the time, the Housewives depended on the energy and organizing skills of communists. Their commitment, skill, and visionary leadership, in the Housewives and elsewhere, was legendary. As one participant in the U.S. unemployed movement of the 1930s recalled, the communists did much of the organizing, helping transform individual distress into collective action by bringing "misery out of hiding" and parading it "with angry demands." Communists, he said, "channelled their formidable self-discipline and energy" into these movements and initiated direct action, helping to "raise the pitch of anger to defiance."[101] Likewise, the Housewives' tolerance of open Communists such as Alice Buck, Alice Cooke, Elizabeth Morton, and

Hilda Murray, all of them very active Toronto Housewives, suggests that the potential stigma of being red-baited was more worrisome than the presence of actual communists.

The issue erupted in September 1938, when accusations of Communist domination in the Toronto Housewives flashed across the front pages. The drama that unfolded on the pages of local and national papers exposed the conflict that rocked the membership and split its executive, and led the press to pronounce, inaccurately, the organization's demise. Following a secret meeting of just over half of the Housewives' executive, Lamb announced to the press that she was dissolving the organization. Supported by Mrs Malcolm Malloy, president of the Hamilton Housewives Association, who had coincidentally discovered communists in her own organization at precisely the same time, she informed the press that the Housewives Association was being "systematically throttled by the forces of communism." The "the worst of it," she confided, was that only eight members of the thirteen-member national executive members were alert to the danger. The other members, she explained, had been "won over" by "the convincing arguments and smooth diplomacy of the Communist bloc." Two of the eight, Mrs Claude Hill and Mrs B. Kemppfer, affirmed their agreement in statements to the press.[102] The news, which was carried in papers across the county, sparked similar denunciations of communist members in Housewives groups in Port Arthur and Vancouver, discoveries that are more likely to have been motivated by fears of red-baiting that would delegitimize the organization than by genuine ignorance that community activists with strong records of activism on the left might have been communists.[103]

Although Lamb had long been attentive to the risks that accusations of communist domination posed to the organization, her conversion to anticommunism was sudden and not easily explained. Only recently, she and her mother, Housewives' secretary Mrs Ena Albon, had not only spoken freely to their allies in the Communist press, but had organized signature drives and spoken at rallies to protest Quebec's anticommunist Padlock Law. She assured the *Clarion* that, were Ontario to pass similar legislation, it would be used to target the Housewives, because "the Housewives' Association is a threat to the big monopolies and such laws are aimed at protecting them."[104] Yet barely four months later, she and her mother pronounced themselves amazed to discover communists in their midst. "We were either blinded by our own zeal or more gullible than we thought," they confessed. The communist faction came to light, they protested, only when it had grown strong enough to oppose "everything constructive." "When I presented a constructive idea," Lamb complained, "they wouldn't let me carry it out." The communists, she contended, "did not want conditions to be improved through our efforts, because they believe the more people suffer, the larger their ranks will swell." Lamb lodged a formal complaint with the Ontario government, and Attorney General Gordon Conant, a zealous anticommunist, promised a full investigation, although there is no evidence that one was initiated.[105]

Those on the other side explained things very differently. Following an emergency meeting of the remaining members of the executive, Mrs Hilda Murray (herself an open Communist), informed the press that the organization was not dissolved but "is functioning efficiently." Labelling Lamb's statement "ridiculous" and her behaviour "unconstitutional," the other members of the executive described the matter as a simple power struggle. Lamb, they explained, had attempted to open food stores "under the guise of a cooperative." The majority of the executive opposed the plan, whereupon "Mrs. Lamb arbitrarily suspended the organization for failing to 'cooperate.'" Lamb, they charged, was "unwilling to abide by majority decision" and "refused to attend executive meetings." Refuting her accusations of Communist control, they insisted that the organization's principled commitment to be "non-political and non-sectarian" had been "rigidly upheld," pointing to the diversity of their members as evidence. Their claims, they pointed out, were supported by the Housewives' legal advisor, Mr J.R. Cadwell, who agreed that Mrs Lamb's attempt to dissolve the organization was "entirely unconstitutional." "Surely intelligent people," Murray concluded, "will not be fooled by the old Communist bogey." She was seconded by Mrs Rae Luckock, a member of the CCF, who affirmed that "only the membership can dissolve the organization." She acknowledged that there were communists in the Housewives, "but they certainly are not in the majority." Mrs Archibald (probably Elizabeth) Brown dismissed the entire episode as "plain silliness," insisting that "we have been getting along splendidly."[106]

Yet a third version was circulated among the Royal Canadian Mounted Police (RCMP) security service, which was engaged primarily in watching communists and had been conducting surveillance on the Housewives. In a memorandum to the commissioner, based on information that in all likelihood came from an informer, Superintendent W. Munday reported that the rift within the organization erupted in a disagreement about tactics during a Housewives' support picket for striking workers at Child's Restaurant. Sixteen members of the Communist-affiliated Women's Progressive Association, who were also Housewives, the Mountie reported, decided to increase the effect of their protest by staging a sit-down strike, "occupying" the restaurant by sitting over a single cup of coffee during the entire lunch hour. The episode revealed, he concluded, that "most of the members of WPA were also Housewives."[107]

Following a brief skirmish over ownership of the constitution, which their lawyer confirmed the anticommunist group had forfeited, Lamb announced that the Housewives had been "reorganized" as the Housewives' National Association and that she was its new president. Claiming an obviously exaggerated membership of 2,000, she said the organization would publish a twenty- to thirty-page newspaper distributed free to members, and would "strive for the maintenance and preservation of Christian family life and protection and security of Canadian homes." British ethnic origins, ancestry in Canada, and Canadian birth, as Lara Campbell has observed, was understood by many to confer special status, and Lamb made ready use of the social capital enjoyed by those with long tenure in the country.[108] Citing her credentials in nativist terms, she proclaimed, "I am a Canadian and my great grandparents were Canadian." But those of the other group, she suggested, were dubious. "If these people don't like Canada," she stated, "I do." Invoking the xenophobia that her audience would understand equated Communism with an inherently untrustworthy foreignness, she pledged the new organization to work for "Canadian womanhood" and oppose those who would "disrupt the fundamental principles of Canadian unity."[109]

The Toronto Housewives Association resumed their milk and gas meter campaigns and began new campaigns to force down the price of bread, which remained at 10 cents per loaf even as the price of wheat had declined drastically. Hoping to make allies of farmers and rural women, they framed their demands in terms of reducing the price spread between producers and consumers. They also proposed to host conferences with farmers' and, especially, farm women's groups so as to foster closer ties and pursue joint action against monopolies. These efforts, as subsequent chapters will show, were unsuccessful. As war drew nearer, they opposed compulsory military training in schools and approved in principle a boycott of fascist-associated Japanese, German, and Italian goods.[110] Like Housewives organizations in BC and Winnipeg, Toronto women took up the cause of unemployed men denied relief, organizing to provide food aid and cash to some three hundred unemployed and homeless Toronto youth. They joined with other organizations on the left, including the communist-led Canadian Youth Congress, to resist the eviction of twenty-six members of the communist-led Toronto Single Unemployed Men's Association who were living together in a house at 53 Duke Street and operating a cooperative business selling cord wood for fuel. The address was also the headquarters of the Single Men's Unemployed Association.[111]

Red-baiting and their close association with Communist organizations led inevitably to some negative repercussions. Unsympathetic school trustees began charging them for the use of school auditoriums and they were watched closely by the RCMP and local police red squads, who sometimes generated damning headlines by dispersing their protests and rallies.[112] But these setbacks were temporary and had little influence on the Housewives' growing legitimacy as an organization of respectable consumer activists with a commitment to social justice. Their meetings and protests continued to be covered by the mainstream press. The city confirmed their legitimacy by sending official greetings to their second annual convention in November 1939, delivered in person by Alderman Adelaide Plumptre, active in the conservative Canadian Council of Women, and Mrs H.E. McCullagh from the Board of Education. Their speakers, eminently respectable and prominent community figures such as Mrs Anderson Wingham, president of the women's section of the United Farmers of Ontario (UFO), Mrs Margaret Spaulding, vice-president of the Toronto Welfare Council, and Mr Drummond Wren, general secretary of the Workers' Educational Association, were further testimony to the Housewives' good standing in the community.[113] Membership, moreover, had grown to two thousand in nineteen branches across Ontario.[114]

Meanwhile, Bertha Lamb and her mother, Ena Albon, had joined the anticommunist crusade. At the only meeting of the new National Housewives Association covered by the press, in January 1939, the members pledged to "maintain Christian doctrines," to "prevent the distribution and circulation of godless literature in the city of Toronto," and to advocate against the "teaching of anti-Christian and godless doctrines" in Toronto schools. Their speakers, the professional anticommunist Catholic priest, Father Charles Lanphier, Alderman David Balfour, and Councillor George Treadway, also stressed the importance of the struggle against Communism.[115] Anticommunism had percolated through the Depression in response to the rising popularity of the left, as the federal government's refusal to assume responsibility for relief and municipal governments that prioritized balanced budgets over ameliorating the suffering of the low-waged and unemployed fuelled popular outrage. Communist-led neighbourhood associations, unemployed workers' associations, and women's groups took to the streets in noisy street protests through the 1930s.[116] Toronto, although by no means the only municipality in which protest erupted, was the headquarters of the Communist party, whose members and supporters mobilized and led radical groups across the city. As Lara Campbell observes, conditions were enough to provoke people who considered themselves "respectable citizens" of all political persuasions to join in lobbies and direct action to demand more generous relief and affordable food and other necessities.[117] Progressives also ran for election, and by 1936, two Communists, Stuart Smith and Joseph Salsberg, had been elected to city council. The state, predictably, responded with repression, and Toronto's police Red Squad was infamous for the brutality with which it broke up meetings and demonstrations. The city's repressive apparatus also included the Protestant Orange Order and, as Paula Maurutto has demonstrated, the Roman Catholic Church. The election of David Balfour to city council in January 1939 gave the Catholic anticommunists a strong voice in city hall. In alliance with Balfour and the Toronto police Red Squad, the National Housewives Association became participants in one of the most bizarre episodes in Toronto's history.[118]

Brandishing the National Housewives Association's resolution, Balfour launched his attack with the startling announcement that Toronto was secretly home to forty Communist schools. A motion to council from the National Housewives, developed in in collaboration with Father Lanphier, urging the city to prevent the circulation of anti-Christian and godless literature in Toronto schools, set the process in motion. These schools, Balfour elaborated, were "stealing the souls of little children" who were taught to "spit on the Cross" and "everything holy." The National Housewives Association therefore called on the city to take "immediate action to abolish the teaching of anti-Christian and godless doctrines in the Toronto Communist schools." Attorney General Conant was urged to do likewise.

The Civic Legislation Committee complied with the National Housewives' request by launching an immediate investigation that included testimony from members of the police Red Squad but, inexplicably, none from the school board. Attempting to refute the allegations, Communist Alderman Stuart Smith called the accusations "damnable, despicable lies" and demanded that the accusers produce evidence. Testifying on behalf of the Red Squad, Detective William Nursey claimed that schools on Ontario, Bathurst, and Cecil streets and on Manning Avenue were among those teaching "atheism and Communism." Nursey provided no actual evidence, but bolstered his allegations by accusing Smith of teaching a course on public speaking. Also entered into evidence were Smith's responses to questions about whether Communists were "loyal to King George" and whether "Communists ever teach your children about God."[119]

Such was the persuasive power of anticommunism that the National Housewives' accusation, although far-fetched and without evidence, was widely accepted, not only by inveterate anticommunists in the church, the police force, and the city council, but also by the mainstream media. The rather stuffy *Globe and Mail*, apparently swayed by the "shocking disclosures" of Detective Nursey before the city's legislative committee, pressed for amendments to strengthen Section 98 of the Criminal Code, which had been used at the beginning of the decade to jail Communists and other dissidents on suspicion of planning subversion. Although teaching atheism was not, in most cases, illegal, the paper warned: "If Ontario children are being taught to hate Christianity, to plan sedition and to plot the overthrow of Canadian institutions, people should be prepared for the worst."[120] A follow-up editorial by H. Ivers Kelly linked the Communist school problem to ethnic groups – mostly Ukrainian, but also Finnish, Macedonian, Jewish, Bulgarian, and Russian – and Communist summer camps, which, he claimed, invested "millions of dollars" into teaching "Communist doctrines to young children."[121]

The existence of a second Housewives' organization led briefly to some confusion. Mrs Dorothy Vickery, for instance, complained that a resolution presented by East York Councillor George Treadway, a member of the anticommunist faction, asking the council to "abolish the teaching of anti-Christian and godless doctrines in the communistic schools of East York" was not from the radical East York Housewives Association, of which she was a member, but from the anticommunist National Housewives Association. Explaining that the East York Housewives were not the source of the resolution, she insisted, "We are not concerned with such matters, our sole aim being to better conditions in the home."[122] No further record of the National Housewives

Association or Bertha Lamb appears after this date, and it seems likely that she pursued her new career in relative obscurity.[123]

Housewives on the Home Front

The Housewives marched onto the war's domestic front battle-scarred but with valuable tactical experience. They had emerged relatively unscathed from their first encounter with red-baiting, with branches in four provinces and allies and supporters from among a cross-section of society and across the political spectrum. Members of provincial legislatures and city councillors, religious and medical authorities, and prominent social reformers attended their meetings and endorsed their proposals for progressive policy change. As Housewife Phyllis Poland wrote in her article to mark International Women's Day in the *Clarion*, the "success of this movement" could "not be estimated." In just a few months, women in Montreal and Winnipeg and cities across Ontario and British Columbia had "learned more about the way things are run under the present system than they did all the rest of their lives." In addition to a new understanding of the workings of "the monopoly trusts," which were "their enemies," they had also learned about "the trade union movement and the need to stand by organized labor." Putting this new awareness into action, most of the members, she affirmed, "are now buying their milk from the five dairies recognized by the Milk Drivers' Union."[124]

Despite, or perhaps because of, their new understanding of how the price of milk and other commodities was integral to the class struggle, the Housewives Consumers Association was widely perceived as a highly respectable association of concerned, civic-minded women who had responded as mothers and homemakers to the crisis in their homes by creating Canada's first and only consumer organization. Some of them, as everyone now knew, were communists. But anticommunist attacks had failed to dislodge their legitimacy or their popularity. Even within government circles, the Housewives had become a synecdoche of Canadians' dissatisfaction with their legislators. "The strikes of housewives on milk and other prices," announced Ontario MPP Leopold Macaulay, leader of the Opposition, in March 1938, were clear evidence that federal transfers to the province for relief benefits were inadequate.[125] The failure of anticommunism to seriously harm the Housewives during this period affirms the contention of Cold War scholars such as Franca Iacovetta and others that the Cold War was necessary, not to protect Canada, but to demonize communists.[126] It also reveals the potential of such demonization to assault even the most popular of movements and raise doubts about the legitimacy of its participants. Although anticommunists in politics, religious institutions, workplaces, unions, schools, the media, and elsewhere made significant advances in their efforts to vilify the Communist Party and the rest of the broad communist left in the 1920s and 1930s, not until anticommunism solidified in the late 1940s did they succeed in discouraging progressives of all stripes from working alongside communists. That, however, remained in the future. Canada's engagement in total war created new opportunities for the Housewives, who adopted a new role as highly respectable citizen-housewives.

2
Housewife-Patriots and Wartime Price Controls

In March 1943, Mrs Elizabeth Brown, president of the Toronto Housewives Consumers Association, outlined consumers' concerns to the listeners of National Farm Radio Forum, a popular civic education program designed to promote informed, active citizenship among Canadians, with a particular focus on farm families.[1] In wartime, she asserted, housewives looked to government to control food supply and prices. Consumers therefore endorsed the federal government's program of price ceilings and subsidies, which held inflation in check in part by freezing retail prices. But, she suggested, they had been promised that the required sacrifices would be shared equally. In an implicit reference to the widespread scepticism Canadians expressed in response to the official propaganda campaign that promised wartime measures were predicated on a commitment to "equality of sacrifice," she affirmed that women were even prepared to do without for the war effort, as long as their sacrifices were necessary and shared equally through a fair and equitable system of rationing. Brown had no need to refer directly to the all-too-familiar experience of shortages, black markets, and profiteering that revealed the program's flaws. But she did explain that women expected the government to ensure that adequate supplies were available at fair prices. They therefore could not understand why, in a country that produced enough agricultural products to support an expanding export market, anyone should be short of food.[2] "Most of us don't mind substituting or going without if beef, bacon, milk, eggs or anything else is actually going overseas off to the boys and girls in the services," she stated. "But if it's not, there's something wrong somewhere and I'd like to find out what it is. Why," she queried, "should there be food shortages in Canada?"[3]

In a scripted dialogue, Brown and three male agricultural experts sought common ground between the consumers' and the producers' perspectives on the government program of rationing, price control, and subsidies, outlining the problems that retail price ceilings, imposed by the state and favoured by consumers, created for farmers concerned about rising production costs and declining incomes. Introducing her as "a housewife from Toronto with her own family to feed," and thus authentically maternal, host Neil Morrison described her quest for reliable information, a testament, he implied, to her civic consciousness and propensity for collective action. "Mrs Brown wasn't content with asking questions at the butcher shop or grocery store," he explained. "She's worked through the Toronto Housewives Consumer Association, of which she's president. She's discussed these problems in conference with government officials and food processors. And now," he concluded, "she's here in our Toronto studio tonight to get the farmers' point of view."

Farm Radio Forum's identification of Brown as the country's leading authority on consumers' concerns would most certainly have resonated with Canadians, as would her criticisms of the federal price control program. As the Housewives' leader, Brown personified responsible civic activism in an unthreatening domestic form, her maternalism successfully cloaking her implied challenge to the policies of the Liberal government of Mackenzie King. A more explicit critique of the rationing and price control program might well have been called subversive, particularly in the midst of wartime, when even "Grandma" thoughtlessly buying too much scarce fabric was considered hoarding and could tag her as a "saboteur."[4] Canadians would also have understood and agreed with her allusion to shared sacrifice. Official pronouncements by Prime Minister King and other federal officials, informed by the Wartime Information Board, the propaganda office created in September 1942, extolled participatory citizenship and called on all Canadians to do their part for the war effort in the language of shared sacrifice and fairness.[5] And indeed, many people were far better off than ever before, due to vastly increased public spending, high levels of employment at government-pegged wage rates, and state-managed price ceilings. But shortages were common, even of commodities such as meat and butter that were produced domestically, and the Wartime Prices and Trade Board (WPTB), the body responsible for controlling prices, was admittedly reluctant to prosecute businesses for infractions. As a number of others have observed, people were generally willing, even eager, to support the war effort, but were outraged by profiteering and unfairness.[6] Interviews by the *Toronto Star* with retail merchants, women's organizations, dairies, and municipal officials suggest that even those who would not normally agree were unanimous in applauding the introduction of butter rationing in December 1942 precisely because they believed it would eliminate butter shortages and ensure that henceforth "everyone will be treated equally." Housewives President Brown described herself as "awfully pleased," as were the many other women who had telephoned her. Most had already been "playing fair and using as little butter as possible." But, voicing the scepticism that she shared with others, she remarked that "it seems odd that there isn't enough butter in Canada for all our requirements."[7]

During the war years, the Housewives Consumers Association, while remaining a community-based network of women's organizations, cemented its reputation as a prominent and highly respectable civic institution that was recognized as the authoritative voice of consumers. As married women and therefore housewives, they knew what worried ordinary people because they faced the same problems, and were able to identify and politicize the most urgent concerns people faced every day. As they frequently reminded the reporters who wrote many articles about them, they were homemakers first and, they insisted, consumer activists second. Yet as an organization of the left and the only organization that spoke for Canadian consumers, they had a dual role. As prominent leaders of a well-respected women's organization and part of the army of women home front volunteers, the Housewives were an integral part of the government's price control program. At the same time, as consumer-activists, they were at the forefront of consumer protest and among the government's most vocal critics.

Hoarding, Profiteering, and Prices

Food was front of mind for many during the war years, just as it had been during the Depression. Although more people had jobs and average incomes had risen, poverty did not disappear completely and was still a significant problem at war's start. As of March 1940, some 600,000 workers were still on direct relief and 160,000 more were on partial relief, probably working but at lower-than-subsistence wages.[8] War, moreover, added profiteering, shortages, and inflation to existing problems. Food might not literally have "won the war," although, as Ian Mosby points out in his recent history of food in wartime Canada, that claim was made repeatedly in the country's wartime propaganda. But it was nonetheless integral to Canadians' wartime experience and a daily reminder of state intervention in the economy. The history of the Housewives confirms Mosby's claim that the everyday experience of food rationing and price control politicized consumers, transforming "popular notions of social and economic citizenship by mobilizing consumers around the responsibilities of both citizens and the state." But Mosby's claim that it contributed to "Canadians' growing faith in the state's ability to intervene in and manage" the economy in wartime and after fails to account for the widespread dissatisfaction expressed very forcefully by the many Canadians who took to the streets in protest.[9] This study presents a very different perspective. Far from evincing greater faith in the state, politicized consumers joined the Housewives' broadly based movement in huge numbers to protest its failure to control inflation or restrain prices in order to ensure that wage-dependant families could afford adequate food, fuel, and shelter. The eruption of periodic protests over unexplained shortages, high prices, and a rising cost of living suggests that, although the state's capacity to intervene in the economy may have been evident, confidence in its willingness to do so was far from universal. The progressive potential of the state's economic control, combined with its reluctance to use its extensive powers to restrain rising prices until two years into the war, strengthened the popular appeal of the Housewives' persistent demands that the state use its power to protect the well-being of wage-dependent families by controlling prices.

Food price and supply became central planks of the country's war economy, as the Liberal government, which had refused to consider intervening to mitigate the widespread hardships of ordinary people in the 1930s, prepared to assume total control of the economy. Anxious to avert the inflationary spiral that had wreaked havoc with federal finances during the First World War, the federal government had acted even before the Second World War was declared to establish a powerful arm of the state to manage the economy. Yet the Wartime Prices and Trade Board (WPTB), established on 3 September 1939, initially fell far short of meeting its broad mandate to prevent "undue" price increases and ensure an "adequate supply and equitable distribution" of all essential commodities. While Housewives-led consumers' groups and others in the labour, party, and ethnic left called for swift government intervention to control prices and contain inflation, for its first two years the WPTB attempted to control inflation by regulating suppliers and urging voluntary restraint on consumers and retailers.[10] Those measures failed. Widespread shortages from 1940 through spring 1941, accompanied by rising prices, especially food costs, drove up the cost of living, which rose nearly 18 per cent during the first two years of war and a precipitous 6.7 per cent between March and August 1941.[11]

The Housewives, along with other organizations of the left, blamed big companies which, they said, took advantage of the wartime situation to increase their profits. Government spokesmen initially denied any incidence of profiteering and blamed shortages on hoarding, but the Housewives retorted that firms, not individuals, created shortages by withholding goods from the domestic market until prices rose.[12] Less apparent to the Housewives, perhaps, but also contributing to domestic shortages, were the large exports of pork, eggs, and cheese to Britain. Still, their economic analyses were generally consistent with those of the experts. The Housewives, along with the rest of the left, claimed that, even as war was declared, prices were already being "boosted by big monopolies" and "big food wholesalers."[13] Contemporary accounts from leading economists agree, confirming that the sharp increase in the cost-of-living index in April 1941 was due mostly to rising food prices, primarily for meat. By October, the index had advanced a further 6.9 per cent and was 14.6 per cent above its 1939 level.[14]

As Graham Broad points out in his history of wartime consumer culture, even though food production more than doubled during the war and supplies of butter and meat were more than sufficient to meet both domestic requirements and export commitments, shortages were common. Consumer frustration erupted in confrontations between shoppers and storekeepers; opinion polls, initiated to assess the public response to wartime policies, found consistently that Canadians wanted a more interventionist state that increased fairness through rationing and price controls.[15] That collective sentiment found expression in consumer protest.

At war's start, the Housewives were well-placed to mobilize consumers. Their national organization, established in 1938, published a monthly newspaper, the *Housewives' News*. Housewives organizations were well-established in British Columbia, with groups in Victoria, Vancouver, New Westminster, and Nanaimo; groups also existed in Winnipeg, Montreal, Toronto, and Windsor, and in small and medium-sized cities across Ontario, with a total membership of about 15,000 women who had experience mobilizing against rising prices, high rents, and low relief rates. The drop-off in news coverage of the Winnipeg and

Montreal groups suggests that they lapsed during the war, whereas the Toronto and BC Housewives appear to have been the most active and certainly generated the most police surveillance reports. The RCMP reported that the BC Housewives League had branches in Vancouver, Victoria, and "other outside points," and representatives in "the majority of community organizations," including taxpayers' organizations and "on various auxiliaries of unions." The Mounties estimated the BC League's actual membership at about 150 but, like similar community-based organizations today, all Housewives groups had a small group of activists who did most of the work as well as a much larger number who came out for demonstrations and other events. The BC Housewives League, for instance, regularly mobilized hundreds at protests and meeting attendance was sometimes three hundred or more. They also published their own newspaper, the *B.C. Consumer*.[16]

In addition to organizations in four provinces and sufficient notoriety to attract police surveillance, they had allies on the left. Their calls against rising prices, profiteering, and public ownership of essential goods were also on the CCF's municipal, provincial, and federal agendas; CCF women, city councillors, and members of provincial and federal parliament supported Housewives' campaigns. The *WEA Labour News*, a left paper aimed at working-class readers of all political stripes, published research explaining the "facts behind the rise in [milk] price" and extolling the benefits of "public ownership of milk."[17] They could count, as well, on strong support from the Communist left, not just the national and provincial party organizations and the Communist press, including ethnic newspapers such as the *Kanadia Magyar Munkas* (Hungarian Worker), but more importantly, the women of the pro-communist ethnic left. Like other social movements, their social networks were critical to their success, enabling them to mobilize large groups on short notice and to achieve maximum impact by coordinating campaigns in many places across the country. Their most important networks in this regard were among women on the left. Although the sources do not yield information about how many such women were involved in the Housewives, RCMP surveillance reports often note Housewives' activity among women of the Ukrainian Labour-Farmer Temple Association (ULFTA) (reorganized as the Association of United Ukrainian Canadians [AUUC] after it was banned in 1940), the Finnish Organization of Canada, the United Jewish People's Order (UJPO), the Federation of Russian Canadians, the Canadian Federation of Democratic Hungarians, and the Croatian Organization. Mary Prokop, a life-long Communist and an activist in the Ukrainian left, recalled that women such as herself in the ethnic organizations played a significant role in the Housewives. "Each province, really each city, had a [ULFTA] committee going," she explained, and the women's auxiliaries of the left-led unions also did "a lot of the work."[18] As soon as war was declared, Housewives everywhere began organizing protests against rising prices, events that were rarely reported in the mainstream media but were covered by the *Clarion* and the left ethnic press and watched by the RCMP.

Barely three weeks into the war, three hundred women in attendance at the Housewives' conference at the Toronto Labour Temple on profiteering and prices heard presentations by Herbert Hannam, General Secretary of the United Farmers of Ontario; George H. Hougham, Secretary of the Canadian Retail Merchants Association; and Marjorie Bell, a prominent dietitian and public health advocate. Housewives President Elizabeth Brown assured the gathering that, "As one small group of women we cannot do much, but if all women in Toronto band together to wipe out wartime profiteering we can accomplish a great deal."[19] The delegates urged the government to stabilize prices and crack down on profiteering and advised the WPTB to research living costs and appoint a woman, preferably "a trained dietitian," to the Board as a consumers' representative.

Two weeks later, Winnipeg Homemakers' Clubs held a conference at which they scorned the WPTB's attempt to blame hoarding on consumers, pointing out that, in Winnipeg, 13 per cent of people lived in one room, 27 per cent in two rooms, and 50 per cent in two or three rooms, making food storage of any significance virtually impossible. Like their Toronto sisters, the delegates advocated that the WPTB appoint a woman and urged the union movement to take an active role in the struggle against profiteering.[20] At month's end, four hundred members of the Housewives League in Vancouver joined with others in Victoria to demand that the government fix food prices at the level they were on 20 August and appoint a consumer representative to the price control board. By mid-November, BC Housewives had established a fifteen-member Consumers' Research Council to combat profiteering, consisting of six Housewives and representatives of the women's auxiliaries of the Canadian Legion, Cooperative Society, Electricians' Union, Brotherhood of Railway Carmen, Old Age Pensioners' Benevolent Association, Bricklayers' Union, and Stockmen's Association. The Council's research included a survey of housewives with questions

LABOUR NEWS

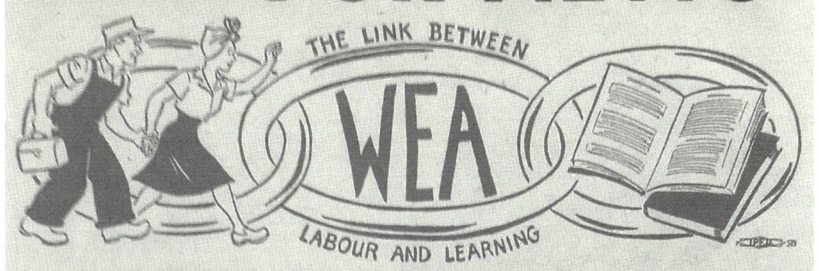

THE LINK BETWEEN **WEA** LABOUR AND LEARNING

AN INFORMATION SERVICE FOR THE LABOUR MOVEMENT

Vol. VI, No. 13   Sept. 16, 1946 $1.00 Per Year

MILK — FACTS BEHIND THE RISE IN PRICE

The living standard of Canadian workers will be seriously threatend by a further rise in the price of milk beginning September 30th. The following facts, taken from reports issued by the Dominion government, reveal the importance of milk and other dairy products in food standards.

FAMILY PURCHASES

In its survey of "Family Income and Expenditures in Canada, 1937-1938", the D.B.S. found that the average weekly outlay for dairy products comprised more than one-fourth of all food purchases, the highest cost shown for any single group (other groups being meat, eggs, cereals, fruits, vegetables, etc.). According to the survey, "dairy products were an exceedingly rich source of calcium, supplying over 70 per cent of the total quantity purchased". **Almost nine-tenths of this amount was obtained from milk**, and most of the remainder from cheese. Dairy products also contain one-third of all phosphorous, one-fourth of calories, and almost one-fifth of the protein supply (Survey, page 138).

NUTRITIONAL VALUE OF DAIRY PRODUCTS

In estimating food purchases in relation to the "Canadian Dietary Standard", the survey found that "the most pronounced deficiency in food values was in the calcium available to survey families". Only among families at relatively high income levels was the supply of calcium found to be adequate. For the average family the calcium content of foods purchased was 87 per cent of the "Canadian Dietary Standard" (Survey, page 141).

The "Canadian Dietary Standard", moreover, is based on the requirement of 2,800 calories per day for an adult male employed in "light manual work". For the great majority of workers, therefore, the calcium deficiency is probably 40 to 50 per cent. This is confirmed in comparing the "weighting" for milk in the D.B.S. cost-of-living index (based on the results of the survey) with the minimum allowance in the Toronto Welfare Council. The D.B.S. index uses a "weighting" of 10.5 quarts of milk per week for an average of 4.3 persons in a family; the Toronto Welfare Council allows a minimum of 25 quarts of milk for a family of two adults and three children (Toronto Welfare Council Study, 1944, page 7).

Applying the Dietary Standard of milk consumption requirements to the age and sex distribution of survey families it was found that 0.35 grams of calcium per man value should be supplied from this source daily. The amount shown as being provided was considerably lower, averaging 0.24 grams per man value, or about 70 per cent of the Standard (for "light manual labour") (Survey, page 141).

MILK PURCHASES VARY WITH DIFFERENT INCOME

The serious deficiency in milk purchases occurred in families with an average income in 1938 of $1,500 a year. Workers getting less

2.1 "Milk – Facts behind the Rise in Price," *WEA Labour News*, 16 September 1946, 1

LABOUR NEWS

THE LINK BETWEEN WEA — LABOUR AND LEARNING

AN INFORMATION SERVICE FOR THE LABOUR MOVEMENT

| Vol. VI, No. 15 | Oct. 14, 1946 | $1.00 Per Year |

PUBLIC OWNERSHIP OF MILK

We confront a food crisis which affects the health and living standards of every Canadian family. Within recent months the price of adequate supplies of food has been placed beyond the reach of a large section of the Canadian people. Unless concerted action is taken to check the growing food crisis, more lives will be lost or permanently disabled in the postwar fight against hunger and disease than during the war itself.

No valid excuse can be given for the failure of our government to control the price of food and other basic necessities. No valid excuse can be given for the food crisis created here at home by removing controls and letting the food trusts amass enormous profits.

The most serious and immediate threat to the health of Canadian families is the sharp rise in the price of milk. Adequate supplies of milk have been placd beyond the reach of 85% of our urban families—the families who earn less than $1800 yearly.

"Milk is the most complete single food." That is the opinion of the experts of 44 nations at the United Naitons Conference on Food and Agriculture which met in June, 1943, when the representatives of the United Nations declared that "Freedom from want of food can be achieved." "We have the tools", the Conference said, but "we have to find the strength and the common sense and good will to use them efficiently and rightly."

FOOD PRICES DURING WAR

During the war the federal government cut through red tape to build the health and strength of the nation by keeping food prices within the reach of the Canadian working people. In recognizing milk as "the most complete single food", the government reduced the price of milk to 10 cents a quart. Milk consumption jumped 50%. By 1945 we were well on the way to making possible an adequate consumption of milk by Canadian families. We still had a long way to go — but the trend was upward and steady. The government was taking seriously the advice of such experts as Dr. Frederick F. Tisdall who told the National Dairy Council of Canada to "put your efforts on increasing the use of milk by the coming generation of Canada."

When the war ended we were reassured by the federal government that the wartime policies which benefited the people would continue into the peace. We were assured that the government's successful policy of price control to keep down the cost of living would continue.

THE RISE IN MILK PRICES

Under the pressure of Big Business price controls began to slip with the removal of price ceilings on over 300 items last February. This vicious policy continued despite the protests of the Canadian people, and is still going on today.

Accordingly — and again, despite the protests of the Canadian people — the consumer

2.2 "Public Ownership of Milk," *WEA Labour News*, 14 October 1946, 1

about household size, organization and church activity, budget and income, their views on labour unions, the Defence of Canada regulations, extension of the civic franchise to age 21, low-rent housing policy, school textbook rental, and whether there should be a housewives' organization. In Montreal, the Canadian Housewives League urged the government to impose a 100 per cent tax on excess profits and ration "any item that threatens a shortage," and make those items available to everyone "at equal prices."[21]

Others on the left also responded. Two hundred people in Timmins at a meeting sponsored by the left-led Workers' Cooperative urged government to immediately initiate price control and establish a broadly representative committee to investigate profiteering; the London Trades and Labour Congress and the Winnipeg Trades and Labour Council approved similar actions. Regina's left-dominated city council undertook to prepare a brief on the problem and Vancouver's CCF Mayor Lyle Telford, credited with taking "an active part in the fight against profiteering," suggested that "not all our enemies are on the Rhine" and opined that if people "in the lower income brackets" were "good enough to be called upon to fight, then the government should show a little concern for them," presumably by controlling prices.[22]

Elizabeth Brown's appeal on National Farm Radio articulated consumers' growing dissatisfaction with the King government's demonstrably inadequate efforts to restrain inflation, control prices, and prevent shortages of food and other necessities. Shortages of sugar and other imports, as well as butter, which was produced domestically, began early in 1940, despite the fact that prices had risen only slightly and supplies of butter and sugar were more than adequate. Sensational headlines cited WPTB spokesman David Sim, who blamed panic buying and spectacular hoarding by consumers, such as the school teacher with 8,000 pounds of butter and the "insurance man" with 30,000 pounds.[23] To be sure, some Canadians did buy on the black market, and a minority of Canadians – 18 per cent according to a November 1941 poll – admitted to stockpiling food to prepare for shortages, perhaps partly in response to newspaper advertisements urging consumers to stock up on hard-to-find items.[24] Despite a well-publicized meat shortage in 1942, which some ascribed to the low price ceiling that encouraged some retailers to withhold meat from the market, historian Jeffrey Keshen points out that Canadians consumed more meat per capita than they could obtain as legal rations.[25] But while newspapers ran sensational stories about hoarders, most people were fiercely patriotic and staunchly supported both the war effort and rationing. In any case, most would have been hard-pressed to find space for much hoarding, as the housing shortage that had been a problem during the 1930s became acute during the war.[26]

Prompted by continual shortages and in response to consumer anger and a vibrant black market, the WPTB initiated coupon rationing in 1942, starting with sugar in July, followed by tea and coffee in August, butter in December, and meat in March 1943.[27] Although both Broad and Mosby concur with WPTB head Donald Gordon's insistence that the agency was coping effectively with the crisis, the evidence suggests otherwise, revealing persistent problems that appear to contradict their argument. Despite rationing and the most comprehensive and rigid price controls of any country,[28] shortages were endemic. Rarely a week went by, Broad acknowledges, "without at least one important item being in short supply in any given town or city."[29]

Milk Wars and Butter Battles

Butter shortages and rising prices frustrated consumers across the county. A year-long attempt by the WPTB to negotiate prices with the provincial milk control boards was unsuccessful, and when prices rose, protests ensued. Butter mattered to consumers; the ban on margarine, in place to appease the country's powerful dairy lobby, was not lifted until December 1948, and although lard, shortening, and meat drippings were also used, butter was the most common fat used in Canadian households. With few acceptable alternatives, Canadians were among the world's largest consumers of butter.[30] Accordingly, butter price and wartime profiteering dominated the agenda of the BC Housewives League's annual convention in November 1940. Delegates linked the rising price of butter to inflation, hardship, and profiteering. Nor, they contended, were consumers' sacrifices being matched by those of business. Rather, "Terrific profits are being made out of the war at the expense of the Canadian people." At the same time, Housewives League organizer Effie Jones proclaimed, "poorer people are facing malnutrition." Since the war began, the meeting was told, the wholesale price index had increased 16 per cent. But by controlling prices, they advised, the government could "eliminate further wartime profiteering." A strategy committee was struck to organize a butter strike in collaboration with other organizations "if prices were not adjusted immediately." "Our husbands will kick at such a strike," one

Housewife admitted, "but they'll have to keep kicking." After lengthy discussion, the delegates sent a telegram to federal Minister of Trade and Commerce James MacKinnon, urging immediate action to reduce butter prices.[31]

Consumers' frustrations sometimes erupted at the shop door, as they did in Toronto on 28 November 1942, when, as Broad recounts, WPTB official Christine White, investigating reports of hostile encounters between shoppers and grocers, encountered a "mob" of three hundred women. Unable to buy butter, he writes, they instigated a "near riot" and "had to be turned away" by police. WPTB food administrator J.G. Taggart denied there was any shortage. Yet, apparently seeing no contradiction, he insisted that consumer hoarding accounted for 8 or 9 million pounds of missing butter.[32] Within days, Elizabeth Brown and a delegation of more than thirty "indignant Housewives" converged on Toronto's Board of Control to protest the butter shortage. Terming the butter situation "shocking," she dismissed Taggart's accusation and instead blamed dairies for profiteering. Women would accept a genuine shortage, but were "outraged at having to do without" while dairies withheld 50 million pounds of butter in anticipation of "the higher prices in the spring." If housewives could not buy butter and other foods with less difficulty, she warned, they would have to take absences from their jobs at war factories to search for groceries, and would even "take to storming the packing houses" if the shortages continued. The city's solicitor disputed the Housewives' calculations, asserting that only 42, not 50 million pounds of butter were in storage in Canada, some 10 million of it in the Toronto area, data that appear to support, not contradict, the Housewives' claims. The Housewives also articulated consumers' scepticism and challenged official finger-pointing, rebutting Toronto WPTB Women's Advisory Committee chairman Mrs W.P.M. Kennedy's claim that "some unpatriotic people" were hoarding butter and making rationing necessary. On the contrary, the Housewives insisted, people were not hoarding butter "to any appreciable extent"; rather, the current crisis was caused by speculators and wholesalers, who were "ganging-up" on consumers by profiteering.[33]

Toronto's Board of Control, led by Mayor Frederick Conboy, a progressive liberal, agreed that the Housewives' proposal for butter rationing would help solve the problem and sent a telegram to Ottawa urging immediate action. In a response that may help explain consumers' dissatisfaction with the Prices Board, Taggart accused both the media and Mayor Conboy of fear-mongering, predicting that "the more the people in Toronto yell and the more the press carries these stories, the more frightened will people become." Evidently not a "people person," he not only suggested that the press ought to suppress information about shortages, but dismissed consumers' complaints, retorting evasively that Toronto was already consuming "more butter than previously."[34] By contrast, following a meeting with the Price Board, Mayor Conboy predicted that rationing was imminent, and indeed, by the end of the month, the WPTB had finally acceded to calls by the Housewives and others. Butter rationing began on 20 December 1942.[35] Butter protests were no longer reported by the press, suggesting that rationing stabilized its price at about 40 cents per pound, but as Mosby reports, following its rationing, butter consumption declined to 83 per cent of its pre-war levels.[36]

Milk was at least as important to Canadians' diets as butter, and as the Housewives had so frequently pointed out, consumption decreased in direct relation to price increases. Milk price's disproportionate economic influence reflected its primacy in the daily diet. The Dominion Bureau of Statistics attributed a 1.7 point reduction in the cost-of-living index in December 1943, from 118.8 to 117.1, entirely to lower food prices, of which fully 48 per cent was the result of a 2 cent-per-quart drop in milk price.[37] As these data suggest, milk prices did eventually drop, but the battle over milk price continued through the war years. Milk price stabilized at 12 cents per quart in May 1938, following the Housewives' protests. But the battle erupted again in January 1941, once again making headlines, when the Ontario Milk Board called a public meeting at Queen's Park to announce a planned increase to 13 cents. The Housewives, present at the event, challenged the Board's assertion that "every cent of the increase would go to the producer and none to the distributor." While they agreed that the farmer "did not get enough for his product," they argued that the real problem was the cost of distribution. Any increase in the price, they contended, would cause hardship for poor families, "already hard hit by the rising cost of living." Toronto Controller R.H. Saunders, the Milk Board's consumer representative and Housewives' ally, protested that the increase, which would cost Toronto residents an estimated $900,000 annually, was being "railroaded through" without consultation, underscoring his point by walking out of the meeting. The debate resumed the next day in Toronto city council, where Saunders raised the stakes by questioning the Milk Board's legal right to set prices which, he contended, contravened the Combines Investigation Act by "stifling competition to the detriment" of Toronto citizens. Elizabeth Brown, leading a deputation of Housewives, protested the Milk Board's treatment of the mayor and the controllers, observing that it more closely resembled a distributors' board "than one set up to protect the consumers," and recommended that it be abolished.[38] On 23 January, Ontario Premier Mitchell Hepburn, who styled himself a left-wing populist but who had close ties to the province's agricultural sector, settled the matter, at least temporarily, by permitting the 1-cent-per-quart increase.[39]

In May, Toronto city council re-engaged the battle by creating a milk committee to address the milk question. The committee was chaired by William Dennison, the sole CCF member of council; its other members, Controller Saunders and Aldermen Ernest Bogart, John Innes, Hiram McCallum, and John Quinn, reflected a diversity of political positions. The committee allied itself with the Housewives and included them in its public meetings and in at least some of its deliberations. In a deliberate challenge to the Milk Board, it solicited tenders from dairies to supply milk below the set price, a clear provocation to which the Board responded by revoking the successful dairy's licence. The city council retaliated by asking the combines commissioner to investigate the Milk Board, contending that it was operating as an illegal combine "against the interests of the public" by setting prices, which, as Saunders pointed out, were higher in Toronto than in the surrounding area. Dennison added that high milk prices had made it "impossible for low-income families to purchase the amount of milk recommended by welfare and health agencies," and that it was mainly the children that suffered.[40]

The combines commissioner dismissed city council's request, but at the end of August the milk price warriors got a new weapon when the WPTB acquired additional powers that allowed it to override prices set by any provincial body, a measure clearly intended to address the simmering conflict between Ontario's most powerful city and its milk board. In the wake of the ruling, the milk committee, meeting with several members of the Ontario legislature and the Housewives, agreed that an increase in milk price was "unwarranted" and turned to the federal Price Board to hold the line on milk price. Saunders, echoing the sentiments of the Housewives, blamed the dairies, proclaiming that "No man ever became a millionaire by farming, but we do know that many men have become millionaires by distributing milk."[41] Within the week, six other municipalities had joined Toronto in the struggle against the Milk Board. Saunders, now representing seven municipalities, met with Hector McKinnon, head of the Prices Board until he was replaced by Donald Gordon in November 1941, who advised him that no price increase was imminent. Suggestive of the rising tension between the Milk Board and the city was McKinnon's revelation that he had already met with the Board without the milk committee's knowledge.[42] By early December, with no change in the milk price, the Ontario Holstein breeders' representative was threatening that farmers, already struggling to compete with the wages being offered by industry, would "sell their cattle at a good price and get a job where they can earn some money," thus creating a milk shortage.[43]

The Housewives and the Toronto milk committee were only part of the Price Board's problem. It was under pressure from organized labour, health experts, and municipal governments on one side to reduce milk price. On the other, milk producers, big dairies, the agricultural community, and their allies in the Ontario legislature and the federal Cabinet demanded an increase in prices paid to producers and distributors. The Board was also anxious to avoid paying wage-controlled workers the cost-of-living bonus that was tied, by wartime legislation, to a rise in the cost-of-living index. Its solution was to underwrite the cost to consumers and ensure the sustainability of the industry by instituting subsidies that the federal government paid to milk producers and manufacturers of concentrated milk products.[44]

When the milk subsidy was introduced, the Housewives and their supporters claimed victory. Implemented on 16 December 1942, it reduced the retail milk price by 2 cents per quart without reducing the price paid to producers, a savings to Toronto households, the *Globe and Mail* estimated, of $1.5 million annually. The prices of three other commodities, tea, coffee, and oranges, were likewise reduced by means of a subsidy. Together with reduced prices in other food items, these measures made a major contribution to reducing the cost-of-living index, which dropped by 1.7 points by January 1943 to 116.2, only 0.8 points above the base level (set at 100 in 1939).[45] The 2-cent drop in milk price accounted for 48 per cent of the drop in the food index. Summing up the year's activities at their April 1943 annual meeting, Housewives outgoing president Brown pointed with pride to their achievement of "more concrete results" than ever before, "the result," she concluded, "of all the spade work done." One of the most important of these was the milk subsidy.[46] Her sentiments were reflected, as well, in letters to the editor, such as the one in the *Globe and Mail* from Mrs Mary Aveline of Toronto, whose wording suggests she was probably a Housewives member, and who credited them with impressive achievements. "We are pleased to note that the long-sustained effort of the Housewives' Association has at last been crowned with success: the price of milk has been reduced to the consumer."[47] Indeed, even H.J. Clark, president of the Ontario Milk Producers Association, acknowledged that fear of another Housewives-led protest placed a brake on milk price. Predicting a 4-cent-per-quart increase when government subsidies were removed, he admitted that the Milk Producers knew "from past experience" with "the Housewives League, the Federation of Women and other municipal bodies – not forgetting our friends the politicians, who are always ready to ride into office on the milk wagon – that we would be classed as the biggest rogues in history if the increase were passed on to the consumer."[48]

The index itself was a matter of dispute in which the Housewives joined their allies in the labour movement. As Ian Mosby points out, "organized labour often complained that the official cost-of-living index was being manipulated" by the government to avoid payment of bonuses tied to the index, a trade-off designed to encourage compliance with wage control. Food costs, he observes, represented 31 per cent of the index, but forty-seven items, including fresh fruit and vegetables, were excluded. These were precisely the items most likely to rise in price.[49] At the Toronto Housewives' 1943 annual meeting, Mrs Christine Chappel, convenor of research, proposed changes to make the cost-of-living index more accurately "reflect reality." Pointing to the Board's failure to arrest price increases, the Housewives proposed to "wage an educational campaign to instruct homemakers" about what to buy and vowed to use "all legal means within our power to have these prices righted and the price ceiling maintained."[50]

Housewives on the Home Front

Through the war years, media coverage of their activities indicates that the Housewives were regarded by the press and within their communities as authorities on a wide range of matters. At war's start, Toronto Housewives called for elimination of the gas meter rental charge and criticized the excessive profits earned by the gas companies; with others on the left and liberal social reformers, they condemned the government's continued refusal to provide relief benefits to single unemployed men and opposed compulsory military training in public schools. During the war years, they joined city councils and labour unions advocating that, to increase safety for drivers and save precious fuel, home milk delivery be limited to daylight hours and that milk also be available in stores. With city aldermen and wartime fuel committees, they organized protests and lobbies to demand federal control of coal in order to eliminate shortages and guarantee fair prices. They joined with labour and the left in calls for changes to the calculation of the cost-of-living index, which excluded many essential foods. With the Canadian Red Cross Society, Women Electors, Ontario Federation of Home and School Associations, Local Council of Women, and the Toronto Welfare Council – as well as communist women – they called on the government to reform and expand its publicly funded day nursery program. Along with these groups, they advised the government to expand eligibility to children "of all mothers," not just those who worked in war industries, "regardless of where they were employed." They urged the city council to provide public housing and enforce laws restricting minors' access to movies, supported calls for public health insurance and old age pensions, and advocated for full state support for education. Similarly, BC Housewives advocated requisitioning of capital for the war efforts, including mines, lumbering, and sawmills, creating local fuel rationing boards, and employing prisoners of war and enemy aliens on fuel projects. BC did not extend the franchise to Asians until 1949, but during the war years the Housewives League, along with organized labour, petitioned the city to include all citizens of Vancouver in the city franchise.[51] Housewives in a number of cities were also active in electoral politics, continuing to lobby politicians and send delegations to municipal councils. Some of them ran for political office. Housewives Elizabeth Morton and Alice Buck ran in a number of Toronto civic elections, as did Gertrude Partridge in Montreal and Effie Jones, Elizabeth Wilson, and Jean Mason in Vancouver. Although not elected, these women used their political platforms as candidates to insert the Housewives' demands into the public debate.[52] In these and other ways, the Housewives, together with their allies among social welfare advocates and public health authorities, in the labour movement, and in the party left, responded to changes in the political economy and struggled to reshape it in the interests of working people.

Their popular appeal was enhanced by their prominent role as volunteer price-checkers for the Consumer Branch of the Wartime Prices and Trade Board. This work affirmed their legitimacy as citizen-consumers and gave concrete expression to their principled insistence that consumers had a natural right to participate in developing state policy, principles they had espoused in the 1930s. It also added a gloss of domestic patriotism to the good reputation they had established as civic-minded women. Wartime reinterpretations of women's proper place, together with universal acceptance of a larger role for the state, rendered the Housewives' more clearly political stance entirely consistent with mainstream political sentiments and popular notions of female propriety.

The Housewives' prominent role in the Consumer Branch, the federal agency that mobilized volunteer price checkers, made them integral to Canada's war effort. Price control was the linchpin of the government's anti-inflation program but the WPTB lacked the resources to enforce its extensive legal authority. Public compliance and volunteerism were therefore crucial to its implementation. Acknowledging the importance of compliance in his 1945 report to the Cabinet, WPTB head Donald Gordon observed that "success or failure of wartime economic controls depends in large measure on the extent to which they are accepted by the public."[53] To compensate for its lack of staff, the Board relied on a vast volunteer army of price-checkers whose vigilance made the program work. In contrast to wage controls, which historian Jeffrey Keshen argues were widely flouted, prices, policed rigorously by thousands of consumers, were largely kept in check. Well-known public health authority Dr F.F. Tisdale predicted that mobilizing housewives would "do as much toward winning the war" as mobilizing soldiers.[54] Even economists set aside their tendency to aggregate households and acknowledged the important role of housewives, concurring that enforcement depended on women's unpaid price-monitoring and noting that most prosecutions of price-control violators relied on evidence gathered by volunteer price-checkers.[55] As the popular *Saturday Night* magazine affirmed, "Price Control Depends Largely on the Women."[56]

The Housewives' ongoing efforts to inform themselves and others "about the way things are run under the present system" and to develop their own and others' ability to be active citizens were advanced by their involvement as Consumer Branch volunteers, where Housewives and other women took an unprecedented role, as ordinary citizens, administering public policy.[57] In Canada and elsewhere, historians have noted, women who monitored prices not only acquired organizational skills but became more confident in their entitlement as citizens. Mosby argues that a nationalist vision reinforced women's identification with the domestic, contending that, by "fulfilling their obligations to the nation and empire as wives and mothers," women redefined notions of "gender, citizenship, and the value of women's unpaid labour."[58]

While no doubt true for some, such an identity would have been anathema to left-wing Housewives, who turned their already impressive organizing skills to monitoring prices in the interest of ordinary families rather than an imperialist state. The many apolitical women who checked prices for the Consumer Branch and subsequently joined and supported the Housewives' campaigns may have more closely resembled those described by Meg Jacobs, who checked prices for the Office of Price Administration (OPA), the U.S. equivalent to the WPTB. Such women, she argues, acquired economic expertise through their direct engagement with policy and began to think of themselves as economic citizens, an experience that supported a new sense of political entitlement and an identity as citizen consumers.[59]

War work also augmented the celebrity of Housewives President Margaret Rae Morrison (Rae) Luckock, elected in April 1943, and a future president, Lily Phelps. Both were celebrated by the media as "outstanding women" who demonstrated "citizenship in action." Both were involved in many civic activities in addition to their work in the Housewives, perhaps most prominently as members of the Emergency Committee of Canadian Women, which advocated better care for wounded servicemen. There, they worked alongside other well-known community leaders such as surgeon and community health activist Dr Minerva Reid, one of the original directors of the board of Women's College Hospital, philanthropist Lady Flora McCrea Eaton, and the human rights advocate, peace activist and feminist lawyer Margaret Hyndman.[60]

Rae Luckock, who was present at the Toronto Housewives Association's founding meeting, made feminist history when she was elected to the Provincial legislature as the CCF member for Toronto-Bracondale in August 1943. The Ontario election was an important landmark for the CCF and the country: Luckock and her better-known counterpart, Agnes Macphail, were the first two women elected to the Ontario legislature. Yet only Macphail has been widely celebrated in the historiography as a feminist and identified as the first woman elected to the Ontario legislature.[61] Luckock, like Macphail, had been a member of the United Farmers party. She helped launch the Ontario CCF in 1933 and worked on socialist feminist Rose Henderson's election campaign in 1934. She was a strong advocate for women in electoral and grassroots politics. But, as her biographer Michael Dawber demonstrates, she has been virtually forgotten by feminists and deliberately written out of CCF history because of her work in the Housewives.[62] Macphail disagreed with consumer activism in general, believing, as Joy Parr observes, that consumers' interests would be advanced only by electing CCF governments.[63] This was a view shared by other prominent CCFers, including Ontario CCF Women's Committee head Marjorie Mann.[64] As a strong advocate for farmers, Macphail also disagreed with the Housewives – and her own party – about lower milk prices, the Housewives' signature campaign.[65]

Like her friend Rose Henderson, Luckock was a progressive, a socialist feminist who was on the left in the CCF, and a principled, caring person who was both a maternalist and a feminist.[66] Her 1943 election platform included expanded day care for children of working mothers, including "hot, nourishing meals" and "an attractive 4-6 pm program to keep children off the streets and prevent juvenile delinquency." Interviewed by the *Globe and Mail* before the 1945 Ontario election about the "question" of women candidates, she set about challenging prevailing gender ascriptions, asserting that Canada could "not afford to do without the practical minds of women" in elected positions.[67] Before her election to the legislature, as a Board of Education trustee she was among the minority of CCF members who fought for an increase in the city's scholarship allocation for students in vocational and commercial programs, who were overwhelmingly working-class, from $1000 to $3000 per year. As an MPP, she weighed in on a contentious city council meeting to support a proposal that the city collaborate with the federal government to build three hundred temporary houses on the edges of city parks and harbour lands to help mitigate the acute housing shortage. In response to the right-wing members of council who opposed the plan, Luckock responded that "Human beings are much more important than money. This means a lot to the working man."[68]

Lily Phelps, also a member of the CCF, was active in a wide range of the community causes, including the Women's Section of the League of Nations, an organization for the advancement of human rights, world peace, and universal collective security through education and disarmament. Led by Phelps, Toronto Housewives played a prominent role in a clothing drive for the millions of Russian people, Canada's allies, displaced during the battle of Stalingrad, part of the Canadian Aid to Russia campaign. The U.S.S.R., which jeopardized its relations with the Allies with the Molotov-Ribbentrop pact in 1939, regained favour when it joined the Allied war effort in June 1941. By winter 1942, Canadians were anxious to support Aid to Russia, a national campaign supported by many prominent organizations and individuals, including the wealthy Bronfman family.[69] The initial group of fifty or sixty Housewives who began volunteering in December 1942 soon swelled to over four hundred participants, half of them employees of Simpson's department store seconded to the campaign to help out three evenings per week. In addition to the Ukrainian-Canadian Association, a government-sponsored umbrella organization representing the non-communist and anticommunist Ukrainian community,[70] and the Ukrainian Labour League, the drive was supported by the media, the Home and School Associations, the Women's Voluntary Service Corps, and a number of church groups. Creeds, an upscale department store, provided storage space and its owner served as chairman. With strong popular support and extensive media coverage generated in part by the Housewives, donations of clothing, household items, and cash to the Toronto appeal and others like it across the country poured in at the rate of 12,000 articles per day.[71] Like Luckock, Phelps was also a feminist who advocated for more opportunities for women. Speaking at the Women's School for Citizenship, she spoke on the topic, "This New Era – A Moment for Women." An op-ed in the *Globe and Mail* challenging the prevailing assumption that women were "disinclined to train their minds" cited, as evidence to refute that view, Mrs Lily Phelps, who "points to the increasing number of study groups for women."[72]

Not just the HCA's leaders, but also the organization's extensive membership was active in volunteer war work. Thousands of Housewives who had spent the last years of the Depression lobbying city, provincial, and federal governments and organizing conferences, letter-writing and postcard campaigns, fund-raising picnics, card parties, and social evenings, turned their formidable organizing talents to war work. At the outbreak of war, months before the Consumer Branch began recruiting women as volunteers, Housewives seized the new opportunities for active citizenship presented by the war effort. Along with other women's organizations, they raised funds and organized classes and public meetings for the Health League of Canada's "Nutrition in Wartime" campaign. They volunteered on local ration boards, where they did essential war work administering the ration system. They harvested crops, sold war savings stamps, knitted socks for soldiers overseas, and collected used clothing for war-devastated Europe.[73]

As home front volunteers led by respected community leaders, the Housewives acquired new legitimacy, their stature enhanced by the unprecedented social value attached to women's domestic work during wartime. Government propaganda exhorted women to engage in collective action for the good of the nation and celebrated female domesticity in the service of home-front defence as the highest form of womanly patriotism. In her classic study of women's voluntary work in the Second World War, *They're Still Women After All*, Ruth Roach Pierson argues that women's patriotic domesticity was perceived to shore up shaky social relations, acting as an antidote to what many saw as the impending social breakdown caused by so many women out of their proper place, replacing men in industry, agriculture, and service jobs, and even joining the military. Government rhetoric celebrated women's "everyday labour as housewives and mothers" in support of the war effort as the highest form of "practical patriotism."[74] As this suggests, the strategic value of Housewife activists' domestic and maternal identities worked overtime during the war; their work on the home front confirmed that they were patriots as well as mothers and affirmed the legitimacy of their aggressive style of consumer activism.

The Housewives' identification with price controls – a program that resembled closely their pre-war demands for government intervention to bring down unfair and extortionate prices – cemented their position as the authentic voice of Canadians and appeared to confirm their ability to influence public policy. Yet official accounts confirm the Housewives' scepticism that government policy was genuinely intended to address the concerns of ordinary people. Political economist and influential Wartime Prices and Trade Board Secretary K.W. Taylor acknowledged, in his May 1945 presidential address to the Canadian Political Science Association, that price control was "sold" to Canadians as a measure to protect their purchasing power. But its primary purpose, as Robert B. Bryce, a Finance department economist, later explained, was actually to avoid the financial disaster that had followed the First World War, when the interest on wartime debt escalated along with inflation, leaving the government with crippling payments of $164 million per year.[75] The government's deliberate promotion of what Taylor described as an "illusion" was completely justified, in his view, by the need for mass compliance to make price control work. Indeed, persuading Canadians that the price ceiling was "an end in itself" was, he explained, "a remarkable achievement by a small group of persons who organized and developed the Information and Consumer Branches of the Wartime Prices and Trade Board."[76]

WPTB head Donald Gordon publicly identified price control as a "direct attack upon a threatened rise in the overall cost of living" that, if not stopped, would "lead to national disaster," and inflation as the "arch-enemy of the common man." To be sure, state-negotiated wages pegged (albeit inadequately) to inflation, rationing of hard-to-find goods, and state management of prices and production ensured a far more equitable distribution of goods than Canadians had ever before experienced. But the social and economic levelling effects of the price and wage control programs were incidental and never intended to extend past the war emergency. In the back rooms of the Finance department, everyone agreed that inflation-controlling price ceilings were not intended primarily to improve the lot of "the common man," but to reduce governments' postwar financial burden.[77] The consensus among bureaucrats, politicians, and economists was that eliding the real policy goals of price control was a necessary expedient to assure popular compliance, even if that involved telling half-truths to the public.[78]

Economists and Finance bureaucrats applauded the price control program, but for different reasons than did consumers. Even dyed-in-the-wool free-marketers, including prestigious economists, admired Canada's price control program because it was simple to administer, comprehensive, and effective. Economists praised its simple elegance and approved the assignment of sweeping administrative power to the WPTB. Robert B. Bryce affirmed that Canada's price controls were "the most severe" of any nation's, even more "rigid" than the "German 'price stop' of 1936."[79] Economist Jules Backman, who wrote extensively on price control (and later taught Alan Greenspan), wrote approvingly of Canada's price control program's extensive regulatory scope, comparing it favourably with price control programs elsewhere. In the U.S., the Office of Price Administration (OPA) had less power and was more inclined to adjust prices to accommodate powerful business and political interests; Britain's price control program, while equally comprehensive, was complex, cumbersome, and, unlike Canada's simple across-the-board price ceilings, difficult to administer.[80]

Whatever its real objective, price control was enormously popular with ordinary people, not only during the war, but well into the postwar period, because it stabilized the economy and protected the purchasing power of working people's wages. From 1941 until 1946, the WPTB controlled not only prices, but also the supply and distribution of most commodities, business and residential rents, and the prices of most services, including public utilities. It determined what items were essential, forbade the production of those that were not, and restricted the use of scarce materials. Price ceilings, together with subsidies on essential items, stopped war-induced inflation in its tracks. During the first two years of war, rising prices, especially food costs, drove up the cost of living nearly 18 per cent. But price ceilings, introduced on 1 December 1941, effectively ended inflation by fixing the retail price of virtually all goods at a level no higher than they had been during the four-week "base period" in the previous September and October. Between October 1941 and April 1945, prices rose a negligible 2.8 per cent.[81]

Housewives and Wartime Anticommunism

The Housewives' criticisms of government policies that failed to address the interests of working people, together with their campaigns for more aggressive prosecution of profiteers and more stringent control of prices, were virtually identical to the reforms advanced by the CCF, the Communist party, and the labour and ethnic left. Left ideas such as these, which had gained currency during the Depression, remained popular with Canadians during the war, particularly, as John Riddell and Ian Angus point out, among the workers in Communist- and CCF-led unions, but also among voters.[82] But left-led labour militancy and the spectre of a CCF electoral victory alarmed the political establishment, who construed criticism by the left, particularly during wartime, as evidence of subversion. Indeed, official anticommunism, as Chris Frazer points out, was "ultimately based on ideological considerations" rather than evidence of any actual security threat.[83]

On 6 June 1940, the *Globe and Mail* proclaimed a "vigorous blow" had been struck "at enemies within [Canada's] gates," with Justice Minister Ernest Lapointe's announcement that sixteen organizations, including the Communist Party of Canada and the (fascist) National Unity Party, had been ruled illegal under the Defence of Canada Regulations (DOCR). As a number of Cold War scholars have noted, the list was skewed towards communist, and thus anti-fascist, organizations, even though Canada's enemies were fascists, not communists.[84] Official anticommunism was at work again on 13 June 1940, when Conservative MP Herbert Bruce rose in Parliament and announced the identity of nineteen organizations and ten publications "known to have been actively associated with the spreading of subversion." He urged Justice Minister Lapointe to "take action against them" by a "broadening of the present measures to provide a better safeguard against subversive activities." One of those organizations was the Housewives, whose trenchant criticisms of the state's inadequate response to the needs of its citizens together with their many ties to the communist left made them easy targets for anticommunist attacks.[85]

Lapointe justified the repression of communists with reference to events abroad, particularly the 23 August 1939 Molotov-Ribbentrop non-aggression pact between the U.S.S.R. and Germany, and the CPC's non-support for the war effort. But official repression of left-wing radicals was already an established state practice when the Liberals used the DOCR to ban the Communist party and intern real and suspected Communists, labour organizers, ethnic leftists, leftist city councillors and a number of people with little or no connection to the left. As Reg Whitaker points out, Lapointe considered communism to be as bad as fascism, "regardless of what military pacts were signed."[86] He notes that RCMP Inspector Rivett-Carnac, chief of its intelligence section and one of the drafters of the DOCR, stated publicly that communism was a greater threat than fascism, opining that fascism was the "reaction of the middle classes to the Communist danger," and that it actually incorporated a modified form of capitalism. Even during a war against fascism, he regarded Communists as "the main threat to Canadian security." His views were reiterated by RCMP Commissioner S.T. Wood, who confirmed that, "it is not the Nazi nor the Fascist but the radical who constitutes our most troublesome problem."[87]

By spring 1940, the war in Europe had begun in earnest and there was considerable public support for such harsh measures in the interest of state security. Under the DOCR, any organization's or individual's refusal to support the war effort had become cause for suspicion. As Frazer observes, the regulations were used not just to restrain those who authorities believed might "subvert the war effort," but also to "suppress those who opposed the war," including people who did not actually sympathize with the enemy. In addition to the organizations of the pro-communist left, the round-up included the Jehovah's Witnesses, union leaders, and even "well-known public figures like the mayor of Montreal, Camillien Houde, who opposed conscription." Within days, the RCMP began arresting Communists and suspected Communists on the vaguely defined grounds that "representations had been made" that they were Communists and thus likely to act "in a manner prejudicial to public safety or the safety of the state." One hundred and thirty-three communists, mostly men, were interned, most of them labour unionists, members of pro-communist Ukrainian, Finnish, and other ethnic organizations, and a few high-ranking Communist party officials who had not gone underground.[88]

The Toronto Housewives responded within hours of Bruce's announcement with a telegram to Justice Minister Lapointe strongly protesting Bruce's statements. They also affirmed their loyalty to Canada and their support for the war effort. Their letter, mailed the next day, declared their political independence (presumably from affiliation to the Communist party) and described their patriotic activities in more detail. The Association's aims, they explained, were to "promote the welfare of housewives and their families ... We interest ourselves particularly in food; the manufacture, distribution, conservation, business practices in relation to the manufacture and sale of food," as well as in "workers' conditions." On September 10, the day after Canada entered the war, they stated, they had "expressed their loyalty" in a letter to the Prime Minister and commenced war work. They helped "pick, truck, and distribute apples that would have been wasted to families with children, in the very low income group"; "assisted the Health League of Canada in its 'Nutrition in Wartime' campaign" by participating in its first and subsequent tag days; and sold War Savings certificates. "Members of our city-wide groups," they added, "are doing the usual knitting, etc." They also wrote to Dr Bruce "to inform him of his erroneous information" and ask that he retract his accusation "on the floor of the House where he made it."[89] No such retraction was forthcoming.

The Housewives were never banned, but RCMP files and correspondence between the Mounties and the Department of Justice reveal that Housewives associations, leagues, and clubs across the country were targeted for closer surveillance and reports were generated on these groups' activities and the political views and affiliations, real and suspected, of their members, summaries of which were forwarded to the Justice department. Nor were any Housewives interned; but at least four of the internees were husbands of Housewives or future Housewives. Winnipeg (future) Housewife Mary Prokop's husband Peter and Toronto Housewife Helen Weir's husband John, both active in the ULFTA, and Vancouver Housewife Nellie McKean's husband Fergus, secretary of the Communist party in BC, were interned at Kananaskis. Port Arthur Housewife Kay Magnuson's husband Bruce, president of Local 2786 of the Lumber and Sawmill Workers union and secretary of the Port Arthur Trades and Labor Council, was interned at Petawawa and later moved to Hull.[90]

These Housewives, the other wives, and their supporters began a campaign to lift the ban on anti-fascist organizations and secure the release of the anti-fascist internees. Kate Magnuson, as Ian Radforth recounts, "fought relentlessly for the release of her husband and his comrades," writing many letters to newspapers and members of the government and travelling to Ottawa in a failed attempt to speak directly to the Justice Minister.[91] Mary Prokop's recollections in William and Kathleen Repka's collection of first-person accounts of internment, *Dangerous Patriots*, details how she and the other women began meeting weekly to share survival strategies and organize for their husbands' release. Over the next two years, organizing demonstrations and mass meetings, circulating petitions, and writing letters, telegrams, and protest cards became an "everyday way of life." "Our regular meetings and mutual support and the support of our friends was what kept us going," she recalled. Collectively, these women and their many supporters wrote hundreds of letters and telegrams to the Minister of Justice and the Prime Minister urging the release of the anti-fascist internees and the restoration of democratic rights such as access to legal counsel, proper trials, and the right to appeal. Prokop wrote more than anyone else, because she composed most of the hundreds of telegrams of protest drafted at the weekly house gatherings and, in addition to her own many letters, she wrote "on behalf of a number of wives who could not write in English."[92]

These women of the left, many of them activists in the ULFTA, drew on their extensive social networks and experience organizing fundraisers, rallies, meetings, and delegations to form a new organization, the National Council on Democratic Rights (NCDR). They held large conferences in Winnipeg, Montreal, and Port Arthur to publicize the injustice of internment without trial and indefinite detention and to raise money for delegations to Ottawa. Their campaign attracted broad popular support, particularly after June 1941 when Germany invaded the U.S.S.R. and the Communist party and the internees pledged full support for the war effort.[93] On 30 March 1941, a delegation of fifteen women, including Kate Magnuson and Mary Prokop, several children, and some labour unionists, arrived in Ottawa bearing a brief they hoped to present to Justice Minister Lapointe and the Parliamentary committee to review the Defence of Canada Regulations. They urged the Minister to release their husbands, and until their release, to reclassify them not as prisoners of war and thus state enemies but as political prisoners, and to improve their living conditions by allowing family visits, uncensored mail, "frequent letter writing and receiving, and the right to receive newspapers and other printed matter."[94] Prokop was there again as part of a second delegation in February 1942 making much the same demands, shortly before the internees were finally released. Peter Prokop was released in Toronto, where Mary had work at a war plant and would subsequently become active in the Housewives' campaigns for postwar price control.[95]

Prokop, interviewed decades after the event, had a clear memory of the morning the RCMP came before dawn to their Winnipeg apartment and took her husband Peter away. She believed that her husband and the sixteen other members of the ULFTA were interned, not because they were Communists, but "because they had supported the trade union movement." When the NCDR was organized in 1940, Mary Prokop, at age 26, was already a seasoned activist. The daughter of illiterate immigrants from Ukraine, who were not radical, she had joined the Communist party in her teens and the Canadian Labor Defence League (CLDL) as a young woman and was active in the ULFTA. "Any strike that the workers had," she recalled, "we were right there with them." In 1932, she had been part of the CLDL's delegation to Ottawa to protest the arrest of the eight party leaders and call for the repeal of Section 98.[96] When the CLDL, banned in 1940, was replaced by the NCDR, Prokop became acting secretary. Not only was she a hardworking and skilled organizer for the rights of the anti-fascist internees and their families, she was a clever writer who raised the spirits of the internees by embedding news in her letters to Peter by means of a code that allowed it to pass uncensored.[97] Prokop, who had delayed having children until after the Depression, was not yet involved in the Housewives, but she joined the Toronto Housewives Consumers Association in the late 1940s. As an activist in the CDR, she worked with at least one other future Housewife, Winnipegger Peggy Chunn, who, like Prokop, would join the campaigns for peacetime price control in the late 1940s.[98]

Other Housewives spoke out against the DOCR. When Parliament struck a committee to review the DOCR, the New Westminster, West End Vancouver, and Finnish branches of the BC Housewives League sent telegrams urging it to remove the ban on anti-fascist organizations, which, they contended, hurt the war effort.[99] Members of the Vancouver branch submitted articles to the editor of its newspaper, the *B.C. Consumer*, rebutting Dr Bruce's accusations and urging the government to release their member Nellie McKean's interned husband and, until his release, allow her to visit. These activities became news when the paper's editor, Mrs Mable Norton, refused to publish their articles, perceiving that her sister activists' "real purpose" was to "co-operate with other progressive bodies," including the Communist party, "in protesting section 21 of the Defence of Canada Regulations." Her principles, she proclaimed, would not "allow the *B.C. Consumer* to be made an organ of left-wing support." Following an executive meeting from which Norton was excluded but at which her resignation was read, she took her complaint to the press.

The episode, which sparked a brief flurry of articles in the press and close scrutiny by the RCMP, offers a glimpse of the destructive power of anticommunist attacks. Mable Norton, a non-communist, had been the victim of red-baiting only months prior to the event, when the *Financial News* incorrectly identified her as a member of the Women's International League for Peace and Freedom (WILPF), an organization they red-baited as a Communist front. Housewives Secretary Grace Greenwood defended Norton in print. But subsequent events suggest that the attack had hit its mark, making Norton wary of giving cause for further attacks – no doubt suspecting, quite accurately, that she could be demonized without having any direct connection to communism. Indeed, as Greenwood pointed out, the *Financial News* revealed its true motives when it acknowledged that "as long as it believed that the Housewives' League was a harmless collection of home bodies just out the kitchen it was not interested." But when the League began "investigating business and prices," it became "very interested indeed – and looked around for the handiest cudgel." Red-baiting provided just such a weapon.[100] To be sure, Mabel Norton and other League members would almost certainly have known what the Mounties knew: that some of the members were communists. RCMP reports at the time identified eleven such women out of the League's one hundred and fifty members, although their sources were unreliable and they often used suspected left-wing political views, non-British ancestry, or family connections to the left as evidence, and thus were often wrong.[101]

Conclusion: Housewife-Citizens and the Responsible State

The Housewives' evolution into a mainstream organization of the left was compatible with the zeitgeist of the war years. Like other successful social movements, they adapted in their tactics to accommodate changing political and economic circumstances without deviating from their core demands and while continuing to articulate the everyday concerns of ordinary people. Popular opinion, which had been increasingly critical of big capital and a non-interventionist state during the

1930s, continued to shift leftward. Responding to the popular will, even conservatives endorsed a bigger role for the state in providing for citizens and increased government spending. As the CCF, which had been advocating central economic control and increased public spending for a decade, increased its share of the popular vote, not only the Liberals but even the Conservative party adopted progressive programs as defensive measures.[102] Within this context, the Housewives' critiques of businesses that profited from human suffering and government policies that failed to ensure a minimum standard of living for all expressed the real concerns of ordinary people and seemed neither extreme nor radical.

Leonard Marsh, commenting on his 1943 *Report on Social Security for Canada*, observes that, by the 1940s, social security had become "an international idea" animated by world-changing events.[103] The experience of the Great Depression had changed the way people across the world thought about their governments and forced governments to take more responsibility for social welfare. Informed by a series of widely read reports extolling the social and economic benefits of public spending to enhance human well-being, Canadians began to expect more from the state and wanted opportunities to be more active as citizens. Through the war years, Britain's Beveridge Report (1942) and Canada's Marsh Report shifted public and official positions in favour of state planning and increased public spending on social security and public welfare. It is noteworthy that a similar study in the U.S., the *Report of the Committee on Long-Range Work and Relief Policies to the National Resources Planning Board* (1942), produced by economist Eveline Burns, had far less impact. In the purge of liberals and leftists from the U.S. federal administration, which Landon Storrs argues led, in large part, to the demise of the New Deal, Burns herself was demonized as a probable communist and her report, thus tainted, was largely ignored.[104] Yet despite the growing influence of anticommunism in the U.S. and elsewhere, public statements by political elites in virtually all of the Allied nations, including Canada's own Prime Minister King, confidently projected a postwar "era of freedom."[105] Public opinion was also shaped by the Atlantic Charter's promises of expanded rights and freedoms for the world's citizens, including freedom from want.

Encouraged by politicians and community leaders to expect that wartime sacrifices would be shared equally, Canadians expected increased fairness and were ready to hold politicians to account. Mainstream newspapers and magazines seemed to have taken a page from the left-leaning (but anticommunist) *Canadian Forum*, with discussions about whether, after the war, the state should continue to manage the economy to ensure greater fairness and whether socialism should replace the "free market" system.[106] Emerging notions of fairness among progressives also included increased equality for women, demands articulated by the Housewives along with other prominent women. Whatever the final distribution of resources, people generally expected a peace dividend of more rights and social justice.[107]

The Housewives occupied a pivotal place in this shifting political landscape. Maternalist Housewives who welcomed all women "with responsibility for a home" straddled the political mainstream while advancing the policies of the left.[108] Aside from the women's organizations of the Communist and CCF parties, which had little appeal to apolitical women, no other women's organization protested official accusations that consumers were hoarding scarce goods, argued that shortages were actually created by producers, or called on government to prosecute profiteers. Similarly, none attempted to tackle the urgent problems of high prices, unresponsive political leaders, and inaccessible corporations that defied the law with impunity.

As the political landscape shifted towards the left, the Housewives' demands, positions they shared with the party, labour, and ethnic left, remained consistent with the political mainstream and continued to resonate with a majority of Canadians. Women who held no strong political views and would have avoided joining any overtly political organization were therefore comfortable joining the Housewives. During the war, they added a reputation for civic responsibility to their maternalism. Housewives leaders rose to prominence as respected community leaders who were accepted as the authoritative voice of Canadian consumers, and the organization's identification with the extremely popular price control program reinforced their legitimacy as civic-minded women. Canadians had experienced directly the benefits of state economic management, food subsidies, and controlled prices, confirming the reasonableness of the Housewives' pre-war demands. Many therefore supported the Housewives' campaign to resist the Liberals' plan to terminate price controls at war's end.

3
Fighting for the Working Class: The Struggle for Postwar Price Controls

On 2 April 1946, the Wartime Prices and Trade Board (WPTB) announced the news that many Canadians had been dreading: price controls were ending. With the war now over for some eight months, regulatory price ceilings on many everyday items would be eliminated as government relaxed its hold on the economy. The Liberals were well aware that the majority favoured continued government economic management, at least during the transition to peacetime or, as some proposed, permanently.[1] Indeed, from the end of the war until the end of the decade, well over 70 per cent of Canadians consistently told pollsters they supported government control of prices, most of them until the economy had stabilized. But a significant minority – 18 per cent in 1944 – wanted prices controlled indefinitely.[2] The Liberals staunchly opposed the idea, however moderate, of a planned economy. The government signalled its commitment to that view in January 1946, with the announcement that it would begin eliminating price ceilings and subsidies "at the earliest possible moment," beginning with the least essential, reminding Canadians that they were "never intended to be a permanent feature of the economy."[3] Finance Minister J.L. Ilsley insisted that a swift return to a market economy would "enable Canadians to preserve the economic advantages gained from nearly five years of self-discipline on the economic front."[4] As price de-control continued, WPTB Chair Donald Gordon reiterated assurances that the return to a market economy would be gradual and orderly, so as to avoid rapid price increases that everyone, including the Price Board, feared would lead to "a serious [economic] collapse."[5] But official predictions of a smooth and painless transition from state control to competition were belied by precisely what everyone feared: steeply rising prices and shortages. As consumers squared off against industry across the nation, producers' strikes, consumer boycotts, panic buying, and black markets were again front-page news.[6]

The Housewives, so recently at the forefront of patriotic efforts to control prices, voiced the sentiments of most Canadians by calling on government to continue the wartime policies that, since December 1941, had halted inflation and kept prices within wage-earners' reach.[7] Toronto Housewives were among the first to react to the WPTB's dreaded announcement. A letter from Toronto Housewives' executive secretary Lillian Colgate to Finance Minister Ilsley on 19 March 1946 declared the Housewives Consumers Association to be "absolutely opposed to the lifting of any price controls for at least a year," asserting that "the high cost of living must be curtailed."[8] Two weeks after the WPTB's announcement, Colgate sent a second letter to Ilsley and to Prime Minister King, informing them that the delegates at the Housewives Consumers Association's eighth annual convention had expressed their grave concern that if inflation were allowed, it would "menace the health and well-being of Canadian families" whose "sons and fathers fought and died to preserve the Atlantic Charter," which, as they well knew, guaranteed freedom from want. They therefore resolved unanimously to "reaffirm" and, indeed, reinforce their demand that "no further controls," neither price ceilings nor subsidies, be eliminated "for at least two years."[9] A week later, with the papers reporting a "beef strike" by retailers intended to pressure the government to raise the price ceiling, an "out of control" black market in meat, and widespread "panic buying," they sent a third letter. In it, they informed King and Ilsley that an emergency meeting of the Housewives' Central Executive had passed additional resolutions approving the WPTB's statement that the price ceiling on beef would be maintained, affirming the benefit of the anti-inflation program that had "worked to the benefit of the Canadian public during the war," and trusting that the government would take immediate action to "stop rising prices."[10] Senior bureaucrats in the Prime Minister's Office, the Finance department and the WPTB dealt carefully with the Housewives, acutely aware of their ability to mobilize a large number of supporters quickly in response to a price increase or a government announcement. Letters such as these, along with their many telegrams and postcards, circulated through the executive branch like so many hot potatoes. Charged with responding to their letters and, presumably, with containing their implied threat of more direct action, the administrator in charge of the Prime Minister's office declared himself "at a loss" about how to deal with the Housewives.[11]

There was probably little the government could do to forestall the onset of Housewives' direct action. Toronto Housewives lost no time in mounting a delegation and presenting a brief to their allies at city hall, urging the board of control to support their request that the King government retain the subsidy that had reduced milk price to 11 cents per quart and kept it there since December 1942. Housewife Elizabeth Morton, the press reported, referred the councillors to the government's "nutrition in wartime" campaign, reminding them that to maintain good health, "we need milk," but that "higher prices would affect getting it." Housewife Ann Arland disputed the dairies' contention that consumption would not drop in response to a price increase. "Milk is one of the most essential foods," she reminded the councillors, and "the health and growth of our children" depends on getting enough of it. Controller Stuart Smith, a Housewives' ally and a well-known member of the Communist Labor-Progressive Party (LPP), which had replaced the banned Communist party (CPC) in 1943, assured the Housewives that city council would do "everything in our power" to retain the subsidy. Some days later, at their annual meeting, reported by the press, the Housewives re-affirmed their commitment to push for price ceilings "until wartime shortages have vanished."[12]

On 16 May, Agriculture Minister James Gardiner rose in the House of Commons to deal another blow to Canadian consumers. The milk subsidy would be terminated on 1 June and pricing authority would revert from the WPTB to provincial milk boards. Without the subsidy, milk price would immediately rise to the "legal price" of 13 cents per quart.[13] The next day, Toronto Housewives and two Toronto members of provincial Parliament, Harry Jackman (PC) and David Croll (Liberal), participated in a highly unusual joint meeting with city council, including Housewives' long-term ally, former Controller and now Mayor R.H. Saunders, to plan strategy. Alderman May Birchard suggested that the politicians "should be ashamed" to increase milk price after "making speeches about our future citizens and telling mothers to give their children more milk." Controller Smith predicted the new milk price would lead to a "full point jump" in the cost-of-living index. Saunders, the meeting decided, should travel to Ottawa to make the city's case to Parliament.[14]

Restore Price Control!

Anger erupted across the nation as prices rose on de-controlled essentials through spring and summer 1946 while supplies of items still under price ceilings dwindled. Price Board head Donald Gordon insisted that shortages were "temporary, seasonal and local," or, in a few cases, the result of "selfish panic buying," but many blamed companies for shifting goods from legal sale to the black market or creating shortages deliberately to force the government to lift price ceilings.[15] Consumer Branch head Byrne Hope Sanders defended the government's position, arguing that, in the transition to a peacetime economy, "it is natural that some prices will give a bit" but that the government would, "as far as possible ... make the stabilization program a success." She called on women to make the struggle against postwar inflation their "biggest wartime job yet," invoking their wartime work as price-checkers by insisting that stabilization "cannot succeed without the consumer." Suggesting that women could stop profiteers and black marketers by simply monitoring prices, just as, she implied, they had during wartime, she enjoined them to "stick to the end."[16] But the Housewives, who had played a major role in the Consumer Branch during the war, ridiculed their former leader's suggestion that housewives alone could stop profiteering and rejected her assurances that the government was managing the economy effectively. Taking up Sanders's challenge parodically, they surveyed Toronto grocery stores to highlight the "uncertainty and confusion" that surrounded price ceilings. "When we have completed this week's survey," Toronto Housewives President Anne Arland announced to the press with obvious irony, "we will then ask the wartime prices and control board if there is still a ceiling on these foods and what it is."[17]

Despite repeated government assurances that price de-control would be orderly, internal Finance department documents reveal that the King government had resolved to ignore "demands for the maintenance of price control," although senior bureaucrats warned them that rising prices would generate "serious public resentment."[18] Their decision, although not publicly acknowledged, was pragmatic. As Joy Parr explains, the Canadian government, forced to choose between rebuilding industry and meeting wage-earners' and households' demands for jobs and domestic goods, opted to postpone action to address consumer demands. As early as November 1944, federal economic planners had prioritized mechanisms to encourage private investment, particularly in the export industries that had historically been the country's most dynamic sector. "In Canada," she notes, "the economy was to be rebuilt by private investment rather than, as in Britain, by the nationalization of key industries." Consumers' interests were thus quite deliberately subordinated to those of capital.[19]

The predictable consequences of this policy decision included rapidly rising prices and shortages of domestic goods, and these were front-page news through much of the immediate postwar period. In spring 1946, meat-packing companies, determined to force the government to rescind price ceilings, created widespread shortages by refusing to send livestock to slaughter. By April, with only 8 per cent of the meat in retail stores available at legal prices, customers were competing for legally priced meat or paying well above the government-controlled price on the black market, which by all accounts had reached "enormous proportions." As the stand-off between meat packers and the state continued, papers reported that the "flow of cattle into the [stock] yards dried up to a trickle" and meat supplies in the city dwindled. Although half of the butchers in attendance at an "uproarious meeting" in Toronto rejected the Mayor's plea that they pledge not to sell meat on the black market, there was so little meat available at any price that, by early May, most butcher shops simply closed.[20] Meanwhile, the bakeries announced plans to brazenly circumvent price ceilings by replacing the standard 24-ounce bread loaf with a 20-ounce version to sell at the price of the larger loaf, and dairy farmers threatened to create "serious" milk shortages if they did not get higher returns, punctuating their demands with a "milk strike" and mass rally at Toronto's Queen's Park and a delegation to Ottawa.[21]

The government's intention to eliminate the milk subsidies that had held milk prices steady through the war, despite a two-point increase in the cost-of-living index, prompted general outage. Across the country, "civic groups, consumer and producer associations" took to the streets in mass protests. In an emergency session of Toronto's Board of Control with local members of Parliament, Mayor Saunders extolled the benefits of the retail milk subsidy because it "went directly into the home of the small wage-earner" and had increased consumption in his city alone from "93 million quarts per year to 133 million." The popular LPP city controller Stewart Smith dubbed the milk subsidy the "linch-pin that is holding down prices," without which, he warned, costs would "balloon." To underscore the city's displeasure with the milk policy,

Saunders vowed to speak directly to the federal Finance Minister to urge retention of the milk subsidy.[22]

Housewives' groups everywhere began mobilizing their communities in resistance to high prices, citing the termination of the extremely popular milk subsidies as indicative of a larger problem. Leading the movement and speaking as the authoritative voice of consumers, Toronto Housewives blamed industry and the government in equal measure for the crisis and called on the Liberals to solve the problem by re-imposing price control. They accused business of creating meat shortages, raising milk prices, and shrinking loaves of bread, and pointed to "the responsibility of the Dominion government" to protect "the Canadian public" by implementing anti-inflation measures such as the price controls and subsidies that had worked so well during the war. They urged Prime Minister King to "stop rising prices" by imposing price controls "for at least two years of the post-war period." They also proposed that the state "take over the [meat] packing plants in this crisis," "just as they did," they pointed out, during the recent strike of packinghouse workers, and forbid "any increase in bread [price] whatsoever," including by the subterfuge of producing a smaller loaf.[23]

Making Millionaires out of Manufacturers

Like their milk price campaign of the 1930s and their anti-profiteering activities during the war, the Housewives' campaign for postwar price control tapped popular outrage about government policies that advanced business interests at the expense of ordinary people. While manufacturers, producers, retailers, and chambers of commerce pressed for immediate elimination of price ceilings, most wage-dependent families were struggling to cope with rising prices and stagnant incomes. This was a far cry from the postwar prosperity people had been promised, and in the difficult first years after war's end, the Housewives' call for postwar price controls resonated with working people, whose food costs had declined by an average of $18 to $36 per month under wartime price controls but who saw inflation eroding their newly acquired food security as controls ended.[24] Hourly wages declined along with hours of work in the months following war's end, and by the end of 1946 the average household was spending over two-thirds of its total income on food, clothing, and shelter, of which food alone constituted almost one-third.[25] As Alvin Finkel observes, corporate profits and the gross national product rose rapidly during this period, but popular images of postwar prosperity ignore the 27 per cent of non-farm Canadians who could afford only bare necessities, and the 14 per cent more who lived barely above that level.[26]

Popular demands for state control of prices in peacetime began to appear even as the Housewives launched their campaign. Finance department files reveal dozens of letters from wage-earners, homemakers, pensioners, clergy, farmers, and small business owners urging the Prime Minister, the Finance Minister, the Price Board, and members of Parliament to retain wartime controls, as well as many from businesses demanding their termination. One of the many who wrote was Ann Emard, a former wartime electrical worker and possibly a member of the militant United Electrical, Radio and Machine Workers union (UE), which led the Ontario labour campaign for peacetime price control. In her letter to Finance Minister J.L. Ilsley, Emard, now living in Vancouver, noted that the impact of rising prices on household budgets varied by social class – a reality, she suggested, that eluded the wealthy. She took particular exception to the Minister's description of anticipated price increases as "modest," observing that "a person with your income wouldn't mind paying a few cents more for everything." But price increases were harder on wage-earning people like herself, "members of the poor working class," struggling to get by on $16 a week, "from which $6.50 goes for room, $6 for board, $1 for tax and $2.50 for spending money." From wartime wages of a dollar per hour, and "with 5 years and 10 months experience in electrical work," in addition to "5 years school teaching in Ontario," she stated, "I've been offered jobs ranging from 35¢ to 45¢ per hour with cost of living still climbing." Yet, she continued, "I suppose you would also approve of this 'modest decrease' in salary." Accusing the government of making "millionaires out of manufacturers," she hoped for "someone who would fight for the working class."[27]

Dozens of others wrote to express similar sentiments. Mrs E.A. Lightfoot of Regina, a self-described housewife who was nonetheless "the wage earner of the home," advised the Minister that removing wartime price controls was "a very poor idea." It was already "impossible to make ends meet," and if prices rose further there would be "many homes with not enough food." Mrs Cecilia L. Hill, of Pacific Junction, Manitoba, wrote to tell Ilsley that she was "appalled" at the removal of price ceilings and blamed him personally. Was the problem, she asked, that "you have budgeted badly? ... If I buy anything I expect to pay for it and budget accordingly consequently I feel if you don't do the same you are a mighty bad example to little folks like me. I honestly never expected such a let down from you," she concluded. Seventy-three-year old A.F. Smith of Toronto, living on an annual pension of $2,380, thought it unfair that those, like himself, living on fixed incomes faced rising prices for milk, cheese, and especially butter, which had risen from 43 cents to 64 cents per pound. Hinting at clothing price increases, he explained that he was "afraid to buy clothes, fearing the taxes will be increased. Bought a suit in 1937, cost $85 and am compelled to still keep it for best wear, afraid to buy another." Smith cautioned the Finance Minister to avoid lifting price controls too early, reminding him of the spiralling inflation in the U.S., which had removed most of its own price controls by fall 1946. "Don't follow that United States crowd," he advised. "We love them and are sorry for them."[28] Members of the Labor-Progressive Party, labour councils, and unions across the country sent in hundreds of postcards and dozens of petitions, each of which bore hundreds and even thousands of signatures. Ordinary citizens organized among their neighbours, circulating petitions among the immediate community. Mrs Ethel Clare of Cudworth, Saskatchewan, for instance, gathered seventy-one signatures; Mrs Lorna Elliott of Owen Sound gathered ninety-seven; and the Reverend Anthony Friebert, a United Church minister in Hartney, Manitoba, gathered fifty.[29]

A National Movement of Housewives

With the enthusiastic support of people like Emard, Lightfoot, Hill, and Smith across the county, Housewives mounted a nationwide lobby against rising prices. Community organizations, women's groups, and producers' associations everywhere joined their call for government action.[30] At public meetings across the country, many of them organized by the Housewives, and some so "stormy" that "speakers could not be heard," people accused "packing barons" of a conspiracy to raise prices while forcing farmers to accept lower prices for their livestock, and predicted that "rising prices would pose problems for the average family."[31] Ratepayers, unionists, and consumers at one Toronto meeting resolved to "flood" the Prime Minister's office "with postcards in the shape of milk bottles" to protest the price rise.[32] Toronto's Board of Control met with Housewives to coordinate a joint strategy to fight increased prices.[33] Canadian unionists, inspired by the massive rallies of unionists and consumers in the U.S., who demanded the state reinstate price controls there, cited the U.S. Congress of Industrial Organizations (CIO) President Philip Murray, who raged that "No amount of phoney phrasing about 'modest increases' can explain away or bolster the government's position of permitting further jack-ups in the prices of goods, food-stuffs and services," and insisted that "it was the business of the organized workers to carry on a militant and vigorous fight to retain reasonable price control."[34] Labour unions, councils, and federations from BC to Nova Scotia endorsed the retention of price ceilings to protect "the best interests of the majority."[35] Urging Christians to support calls for fair prices, Reverend J.R. Mutchmore, of the United Church Evangelism and Social Services Board, observed that "Jesus had much to say about wages, prices, workmen, fair dealing and related matters," and, in an innovative interpretation of scripture, attributed "Christ's early death" in part to "his attacks on privilege."[36]

On 21 May, Housewives' ally Mayor Saunders, heading up a delegation of mayors and dairy farmers, travelled to Ottawa where, speaking "on behalf of the consumers of the Toronto area," he urged Ilsley to retain the milk subsidy. But despite reminding the Minister that Price Board head Donald Gordon had "only the day before" urged the "housewives of Toronto" and elsewhere to "assist the government in holding down the cost of living," his pleas were not successful. Declaring himself "amazed" by this intransigence, Saunders predicted that the government's decision would result in "an increase of 20 percent in the price of a basic commodity." Days later, on 25 May, Toronto Housewives, their union allies, and community supporters held a mass meeting at Queen's Park where they signed milk-bottle-shaped postcards to the Prime Minister. Fifty Ontario mayors and reeves held an emergency conference on the milk question. Unionized milk delivery drivers voted unanimously to put notices protesting the milk price increase in every bottle they delivered and warned that "thousands of children in low-income families will go without milk as a result of the increase in price."[37]

Meanwhile, one hundred and fifty-five Winnipeg women, organized by the Labor-Progressive Party women's council – some of whom may have been active in the pre-war Homemakers' Clubs – constituted themselves as the Winnipeg Housewives Consumers Association. They joined with the People's Cooperative Dairy – a business of the pro-communist Association of United Ukrainian Canadians (AUUC) – the Manitoba Federation of Agriculture and Cooperation, the left-led United Packinghouse Workers, the Labor-Progressive Party and the

A FREE glass of MILK for EVERY School Child Every Day!

3.1 "To Ensure Enough Milk for Our Children," milk-bottle-shaped protest card, Archives of Manitoba, Anne Ross fonds, MHCA Releases, Reports, Activities, [1946–8], P5941/5

city's family bureau to "speak with a single voice on the issues facing the woman consumer." Within two weeks, their membership had almost tripled to four hundred and fifty and they had representation from women's groups across the city. While Toronto Housewives and their supporters protested in Queen's Park, a delegation of seventy-five Winnipeg Housewives, led by Mrs Anne Ross and Mrs K. Bolton, appealed to members of the provincial legislature to support their appeal to reinstitute milk subsidies and rent controls. Cancelling the milk subsidy, Ross announced, was "a blow below the belt" because "the burden thus placed upon the shoulders of 60 percent of the

Canadian people," those with fixed incomes, "was far too great."[38] Taking their cue from Winnipeg, women in Saskatoon also organized, and by July the Saskatoon Housewives Consumers Association had forwarded to the Prime Minister a petition urging continuation of price control and the reduction of prices on items on which ceilings had been lifted, signed by more 6,000 citizens and a variety of organizations, including old age pensioners, commercial travellers, veterans' organizations, benevolent societies, and church groups, in addition to labour unions, the AUUC, and the LPP.[39]

Through the crisis, the Liberals repeated their promise that reconversion policies would "protect the real value of the workman's wage and the purchasing power of the housewife's dollar," and assured Canadians that the government had "no intention of dismantling the system of price control so long as the emergency exists." Rejecting such assurances out of hand, Manitoba Housewife Anne Ross observed that government was supposed to "represent the interests of the majority," but was instead "completely disregarding the welfare of those same people."[40] Because milk subsidies benefited not only urban voters but also milk producers, who represented a significant segment of the important agricultural vote, King and his cabinet faced determined opposition to their program of de-control, not just among consumers, in local governments, and the press, but within Parliament and even within their own party. Yet, in the midst of a fractious debate in Parliament about price controls and under intense pressure from powerful agriculture and dairy interests and their political supporters, the government raised price ceilings.[41] Even Price Board head Gordon, who advocated voluntary compliance with price controls during the reconversion period and contended repeatedly that "self-restraint" by business, rather than regulation, would suffice to assure "a planned and orderly re-adjustment," acknowledged that business was eager to supply pent-up demand and aware that "money could be made in an uncontrolled market." In a series of public broadcasts, he distanced himself from both sides of the debate, the CCF's call for state management of the economy and the Liberals' program of rapid de-control, contending that, although permanent price control was not "realistic," it would nonetheless be "safer" for the government to discontinue controls "in a more gradual and orderly fashion over a longer period."[42] The U.S. Congress's abrupt elimination of price controls in July, amidst a highly charged debate between liberals and conservatives, put further pressure on Ottawa to relax price ceilings.[43]

Official statements that the "runaway spiral" of prices "will create big problems" in the U.S. but "will not be permitted to wreck orderly ... removal of price ceilings in this country," where controls had kept the cost of living 10 to 12 per cent lower, proved misleading. The government instead moved to restore normal trading relations with the U.S., eager to encourage commerce with its major trading partner by allowing prices to rise.[44]

In July, with better cuts of meat up 6 cents per pound, utility-grade meat up a cent, and prices on fruits and vegetables, fats, and sugars soon to follow, Housewives in Winnipeg and Toronto called a "beef strike." Emulating radical consumers in the U.S., who were taking to the streets to protest rising meat prices, Housewives, together with labour unionists, veterans, and faith and community groups, held rallies and parades and picketed stores to demand lower meat prices.[45] In a coordinated action, Housewives in both cities distributed tens of thousands of circulars, issued press releases, and telephoned their neighbours to urge that they "eat lamb, chicken and liver, fruit, vegetables and eggs and drink lots of milk," but "buy no beef" from July 20 to 26.[46] Some Toronto butchers acknowledged that sales were "slower than usual" and even the conservative and business-friendly *Globe and Mail* acknowledged the campaign to hold down meat prices in an editorial cartoon suggesting the one who was "getting hooked" was the "consumer," although it expressed its antipathy to the Housewives by locating them among those, including beef producers, meat packers, and retailers, who were "hooking" the consumer.[47]

Housewives everywhere kept up the pressure, and by autumn, women in towns and cities across the West, many of them members of the Ukrainian, Finnish, Hungarian, Polish, and Jewish left, had organized Housewives Associations in Moose Jaw, Regina, Edmonton, Calgary, and Vancouver, as well as the northern Ontario mining towns of Sudbury and Porcupine, notable for their high numbers of Eastern European immigrants and their strong, left-led unions.[48] In July, Saskatoon Housewives joined with the Old Age Pensioners Organization, United Commercial Travellers, Navy League, Army and Navy veterans, Sons of England, Saskatoon Musicians Association, women's church groups, the AUUC, the LPP, and unions in a street-by-street signature drive, gathering more than six thousand signatures on their petition to restore price control.[49] In Windsor, members of the Democratic Hungarian Society's women's group joined with those of the women's auxiliaries of United Auto Workers Locals 195 and 200

3.2 "Buy No Meat for One Week," poster, Archives of Manitoba, Anne Ross fonds, MHCA Releases, Reports, Activities, [1946–8], P5941/8

to revitalize the Housewives Association they had organized in the 1930s, and immediately set about collecting fifty thousand signatures and raising funds to send a delegation to the Ontario government demanding that the price of milk be lowered to 12 cents a quart.[50] By October, the Montreal North End Housewives Association and Central Consumers League had launched milk price protests. In December, the Housewives from the tiny but radical mining town of Coleman, Alberta, sent the Minister of Finance a petition bearing two hundred and twelve signatures urging the government to halt the removal of price ceilings and reinstate both price controls and milk and flour subsidies. As was the case in Vancouver, Edmonton, Regina, Saskatoon, Winnipeg, Sudbury, Toronto, Windsor, and Montreal, the Housewives' strength in Coleman was no doubt due to its heavy concentration of left ethnic organizations and labour unions. Although only big enough for one secondary school, Coleman had both a Ukrainian Labour Temple and a Polish Hall, reflecting the ethnic concentration of its residents, as well as its well-established history of left labour militancy.[51]

Housewives Associations almost everywhere relied heavily on the social networks, political, organizing, and fund-raising skills of the women of the ethnic and labour left. Housewife Mary Prokop, a member of the Ukrainian left, recalled that the important role of left ethnic women was often overlooked, partly because Housewives leaders were usually women without ethnic-sounding names.[52] This may have been a strategic decision by the Housewives, although many left-ethnic women Anglicized their names or took their husbands' Anglicized names, in part because, as Franca Iacovetta has demonstrated, during the 1940s and beyond, "foreign-ness" was regarded by many, including the police and government officials, as cause for suspicion.[53] Winnipeg Housewives, for instance, were led by Anne Ross, whose Anglo-sounding name disguised her identity as part of Winnipeg's significant Jewish left. Ross was born Hannah Glaz in Eastern Europe, now part of Ukraine, in 1911 and emigrated to Winnipeg in 1922. Her husband, Bill Cecil Ross, also from Ukraine, was born Cecil Zuken and was also an activist, part of the Jewish labour left, and leader of the Manitoba LPP from December 1948 to 1981. She was a community activist who is best remembered today for her dedication to the Mount Carmel Clinic. Mount Carmel was the first community health centre in Canada, created by the social-justice-oriented Jewish community to provide services to mostly Jewish immigrants. In 1948, during the period when she was active in the Winnipeg Housewives, Anne was the Clinic's

3.3 "Milk Prices to Rise Again, 1946," Archives of Manitoba, Anne Ross fonds, MHCA Releases, Reports, Activities, [1946–8], P5941/5

only full-time employee, working as a nurse, X-ray technician, and lab technician. She became its Director in 1964. Under her directorship, the Clinic grew into a major community health centre that, even today, specializes in community outreach. She also worked to provide services to teen parents and seniors. One of Winnipeg's most prominent Housewives, Ross was known at one time as "Anne of the Milk Subsidies," and honoured for her community health activism by being appointed a Member of the Order of Canada (1985) and the Manitoba Order of the Buffalo Hunt (1987). The Anne Ross Day Nursery, which she established in 1976, is dedicated to her legacy.[54]

Winnipeg Housewives had ties to both the Jewish and Ukrainian left, and worked closely with the People's Cooperative Dairy, a not-for-profit business affiliated with the left-led Association of United Ukrainian Canadians (AUUC) and the LPP to form the Citizens Committee on Milk. Linking the demands of consumers with those of producers, the Dairy's education director, John Marshall, wrote on behalf of this coalition to Finance Minister Abbott complaining that the elimination of the producer milk subsidy and subsequent increase in milk price resulted in a 7 per cent decline in milk consumption in Winnipeg, during a time when it would be expected to rise at least 3 per cent. The Citizens Committee, perhaps provocatively, invited the Milk Producers Association to a public meeting to "present their case for a milk price increase before a body of Winnipeg consumers."[55] Weeks later, Saskatchewan Housewives president and provincial LPP leader Florence Theodore led a delegation of Housewives with similar demands to the Saskatchewan legislature. In response, the CCF government announced that it was considering a provincial milk subsidy to replace those terminated by the federal Liberal government. Both the Manitoba and Saskatchewan governments rejected the Housewives' proposal that they assume responsibility for milk distribution by making it a public utility, although the more progressive CCF Saskatchewan government agreed to support the Housewives' delegation to Ottawa and to send a member of the provincial Cabinet as a delegate.[56]

With consumers battling the meat packers and butchers, the Liberals assured the Housewives that the government was doing "everything possible to maintain stable prices" and "prevent inflation," even as they eliminated price ceilings, terminated subsidies, and gave provincial milk boards the power to negotiate higher milk prices with producers' associations.[57] Articulating the scepticism of the wider community, the Housewives pronounced themselves unconvinced. Chiding federal Agriculture Minister James Gardiner, who had announced his intention to allow pork prices to rise, Manitoba HCA President Anne Ross warned that housewives who, like herself, were "at our wit's end trying to make ends meet," were "getting progressively more disillusioned with the Government's attitude."[58] Mrs E. Molinski, president of the Mothers' Club of the politically progressive All People's Church (established by CCF founder J.S. Woodsworth) and an ally of the Housewives, expressed her "alarm and disapproval" at the Liberals' "lifting [of] both the subsidy on milk and the ration on alcoholic beverages." Dropping the subsidies on milk, a staple in most families' diets and a substitute for higher-priced protein foods, raised its price from 10 or 11 to as much as 17 cents per quart, an increase of more than 50 per cent, between June and September.[59] Pointing to this increase, Molinski accused the government of hypocrisy, noting that politicians "express concern over the nutrition and health of the citizens," but then "jeopardize the health of children by making it so difficult to obtain such an indispensable food." Such policies were "not sensible," she insisted, "not to mention [not] being Christian."[60] Even the *Globe and Mail*, like its populist counterparts, ran milk price as front-page news and featured hardship stories like that of the Houston family, with "twelve children to feed," and "hard hit" by an increase in milk price. Mrs Houston, it reported, had been "buying seven quarts daily" at 13 cents, but with the price rise, "the mother fears she will have to cut down to six quarts a day or less."[61]

Milk in Politics

The Housewives, supported by the labour, party, and ethnic left, initiated and led the popular demand for the re-imposition of price ceilings and subsidies, but as the battle between consumers, producers, and corporations progressed, it was clear they had a tiger by the tail. By fall, Kenneth Craig, the *Globe and Mail*'s parliamentary reporter, observed that "the milk subsidy question" had become "much larger" than a matter between producers and consumers, and indeed, embodied "the entire issue of [postwar] stabilization."[62] This was precisely the argument made by the U.S. consumer activists who so inspired the Housewives, and who linked their own desire for material goods to the progressive economic theories of the time. Those politicized consumers urged their federal government to continue fighting inflation by controlling prices while supporting organized labour's demands for higher wages, a strategy that, they insisted, would support adequate purchasing power to form a secure foundation for economic stability and general prosperity.[63]

The Housewives were encouraged by the apparent achievements of their U.S. sisters, who mounted a massive grassroots campaign that linked calls for controlled prices in peacetime to those for higher wages, referencing their demands to the influential Keynesian conviction that insufficient purchasing power was a threat to economic recovery. Powerfully supported by organized labour, the U.S. consumer movement, described by Lawrence Glickman, among others, was both more numerous and more diverse than in Canada, with a number of organizations as opposed to Canada's one.[64] As Landon R.Y. Storrs has shown, it also had important allies in the federal bureaucracy, including several New Deal Democrats in the Office of Price Administration (OPA), the U.S. counterpart to Canada's Wartime Prices and Trade Board.[65] Although, as Meg Jacobs shows, U.S. consumers failed to persuade the government to retain price control into the postwar, they mobilized in unprecedented numbers around that demand.[66] Their meat boycotts and buyers' strikes, many of them led by the Communist-affiliated League of Women Shoppers, inspired Canadian Housewives, who followed their activities in the left and mainstream papers and adapted their tactics to their own campaigns. The Housewives shared their enlarged sense of entitlement as citizen-housewives and perceived themselves as part of an emergent and, they imagined, unstoppable international movement that included citizen consumers who demanded expanded rights and a more responsive state, not just in the U.S., but also in Europe.[67]

In both countries, consumer activists' confidence in the capacity of the state to control inflation and ensure economic stability through the economic levers of price ceilings and subsidies lay at the root of their demands. Canada's Housewives, like their U.S. sisters, argued for greater purchasing power. But the Canadians, perhaps reflecting their different view of the state, articulated their demands in terms of government's responsibility to ensure the well-being of citizens and the natural justice of income redistribution through taxation and subsidies. These consumer activists tapped the collective wartime experience of sufficiency under tight government controls and rationing, which contrasted favourably with the laissez-faire conditions of the 1930s. Moreover, no less an authority than WPTB head Donald

Gordon credited the federal wage and price control program as having "brought the country through the great strains and stresses of war in better order than that of any other country" precisely because it was an "anti-inflation program" that had "succeeded beyond the most optimistic hopes expressed at its inception."[68] But King, along with Ministers C.D. Howe, J.L. Ilsley, and Douglas Abbott, the most powerful members of Cabinet, was eager to terminate controls and shed the onerous obligation to finance subsidies. The latter, they observed, accounted for over $130 million in public expenditures in the last year of war, continued to absorb $90 million annually, and showed every sign of increasing further as milk consumption rose in response to the subsidy.[69]

The Liberals' termination of price ceilings and subsidies didn't just exacerbate inflation; it created real hardships for the many families living on stagnant and inadequate wages. During the immediate postwar period, many wage-dependent families were considerably worse off than they had been during the war, and rising food costs played havoc with household budgets. A study by the Toronto Welfare Council found that a family of five needed $40.11 per week, or an annual income of $2,085.72, for food and other basic needs, but that 1.75 million earners had income of under $2,000 in 1946.[70] The Edmonton Housewives League reported similarly that, in their city, a family of five needed $14.40 per week for food alone, equivalent to $748.80 per year, a cost that would leave a low-income family with too little for other necessities.[71] Their data may have been drawn from the nutrition study conducted by the Canadian Council on Nutrition (CCN), the expert panel created by the federal government that produced research reports on low-income families in several cities in 1941.[72] The Housewives and their allies pointed to the importance of the milk subsidy in low-income household budgets and its contribution to the "health and welfare of families of millions of wage earners." As the Housewives also noted, milk was the "largest single expenditure on a minimum diet," and its consumption increased when its price was frozen, rising from 95 to 100 million quarts when the subsidy was introduced and to 133 million quarts in its final year in Toronto alone. Correspondingly, consumption declined as milk price rose.[73] So essential were milk and other dairy products in the average household's budget that they accounted for over a third of food costs, and some predicted that a price increase would result in a full point rise in the cost-of-living index.[74]

According to the Housewives, subsidies were not only a sound investment; they also socialized the cost of milk and thereby increased fairness. The public cost of price control was "under $200 million per year," they explained, whereas the "direct savings to consumers were $1,500 million." Indeed, Dominion Bureau of Statistics data showed that price control had reduced the household costs of the average Canadian family substantially.[75] Milk subsidies, moreover, increased economic equality by redistributing wealth progressively. Subsidies were financed from taxation which, during this era, became even more steeply progressive. The costs, the Housewives observed, were thus distributed according to income. Their termination shifted those costs back to "the people with large families" and "the low income group." "Removal of the subsidy," they concluded, "took milk away from children."[76] Others on the left, such as the Workers' Cooperative of New Ontario, saw things similarly, noting that for "every $1 spent on price control the people saved $12.50." Linking the termination of price controls directly to rising inflation, they urged the Liberals to "reimpose price controls and subsidy payments with utmost dispatch" to "hold the line on present price levels," warning that the "rampant inflationary potential of the present economic condition can conceivably lead to the most terrible economic crisis of all time."[77]

Control Prices, Not Wages

The battle over milk subsidies strengthened and significantly broadened the Housewives' long-standing connection with organized labour. Since their founding meeting in Toronto's Labour Temple in 1937, the Housewives had collaborated with unions, and those ties had strengthened, in part through the overlapping memberships of prominent Housewives such as Mona Morgan and Kay Magnusson, who were active in women's auxiliaries of left-led unions, and through their joint efforts with the Milk Drivers Union, the Packinghouse Workers, and others whose jobs were directly affected by price controls and subsidies. Many, although importantly not all, of these allies were part of the labour left.

Workers and their unions had good reason to support the Housewives. In contrast to the war years, when rationing had democratized access to commodities, especially food, improving the diets of those on low incomes while reducing the luxuries available to the better-off, the termination of price control had increased the prices of meat and bread and the withdrawal of the milk subsidy had raised retail milk price by as much as 50 per cent.[78] Yet wage controls continued to cap pay hikes at 20 cents per hour.[79] Unions struggled to achieve the "high and rising standard of living" Canadians had been promised during the war years while inflation eroded the value of workers' wages, still constrained by government-imposed wartime wage ceilings even as price controls were relaxed. Increased milk costs had a noticeable impact on the cost-of-living index and thus the real value of wages. Always an important part of the average family's diet, milk had been more affordable under subsidies, which not only lowered its price to consumers but encouraged producers to allocate more fluid milk to the retail market. Thrifty homemakers could substitute milk-based dishes for scarce and expensive meat, which, unlike milk, was rationed.[80] Milk production, moreover, had increased during the war, as had household consumption, which peaked in 1946 at a remarkable annual average of five hundred quarts per person, or one and a half quarts daily, an increase of 50 per cent since the inception of subsidies and an amount even larger than the one pint per adult and one quart per child per day recommended by Canada's Food Rules.[81] So significant was milk to household economies that, as one commentator observed, an "increase in milk price affects the consumer faster than an increase on almost any other food product." "Every price increase has the same effect as a reduction in wages," the Canadian Congress of Labour noted. Workers, still unable to negotiate wage increases, would see their wages undermined by a dramatic increase in the price of an essential food that, as the Edmonton Housewives League explained, constituted "the largest single expenditure on a minimum diet" and a major expense even for workers earning higher than minimum wages.[82]

Postwar unions enjoyed unprecedented strength that, despite their tendency to regard direct action on prices as a domestic matter that was best left to women, made them useful, if often disappointing, allies for the Housewives. Unionization drives, led by the left-led CIO, had grown the organized labour movement from 16.3 per cent of the labour force in 1940 to 27.9 per cent in 1946, spurred by full employment and wartime labour legislation that, for the first time, provided some measure of union security.[83] As the government announced plans to terminate the milk subsidy, unions from BC to Nova Scotia were poised to begin one of the longest and most successful struggles of the twentieth century in a strike wave that secured union rights and laid the foundation for the working-class prosperity that prevailed for the next four decades.[84]

The surge in organization was more than a happy consequence of job security during wartime. Wendy Cuthbertson credits the popularity and power of unions in this period to the CIO's careful construction of a "union public sphere" that advanced a narrative of workers' rights and entitlements to more than just bigger paycheques, but also to more democracy and a "stronger voice in the country's affairs."[85] The social justice work of the left-led CIO unions, in other words, complemented that of the Housewives; both movements informed an enlarged notion of the rights of citizens and the duties of the state.

The endorsement of the male-dominated labour movement, particularly that of the CCF-affiliated and conservative unions, added to the Housewives' stature and legitimacy, even if labour's most powerful organizations gave the Housewives little more than token support. The Housewives had official standing in the anticommunist Toronto District Labour Council, the official support of at least thirteen other labour councils and at least four federations of labour, and their milk price campaign was endorsed by both labour centrals, the CCF-led Canadian Congress of Labour (CCL) and the more conservative Trades and Labour Congress (TLC).[86] The CCL, representing more than a third of unionized workers, took up the call for postwar price control and dubbed itself the "chief supporter of price-control," despite the largely rhetorical nature of its efforts. Research Director Eugene Forsey introduced the CCL's nationwide lobbying campaign in the September 1946 issue of *The Canadian Unionist*, pronouncing labour's belief "that price-control, at least for the necessities of life, is an essential and permanent part of a full economy."[87]

The Congress soon dropped its demand for permanent price control, but continued to petition the government to restore price controls until the end of the decade. In 1949, however, it signalled its support for the Liberal-sponsored Canadian Association of Consumers (CAC) and, by implication, its opposition to radical movements like the Housewives, with the unprecedented inclusion of a two-page report on the CAC's annual meeting in its monthly magazine, *The Canadian Unionist*. An initiative of the socially conservative National Council of Women of Canada (NCWC), the CAC was created in April 1947 with a $15,000 grant from the Liberal government. Joy Parr, who compares the two groups in her study of postwar consumption, notes that the CAC owed this generous start-up grant in part to "its willingness to adopt many government priorities as its own" and thus become a politically unthreatening alternative to the radical Housewives. In the vortex of community protest led by the Housewives, the Liberals "needed a national women's voice to urge domestic consumers to patience," Parr writes, as they "embarked on economic policies which, in the short and medium term, gave priority to export and capital goods." The CAC, which allied itself with economic liberals who believed "well-functioning markets" would meet consumers' needs better than an interventionist state, acted as an advisory, rather than activist, group that expressly rejected the use of boycotts. It distinguished itself from the better-established and more populist Housewives by invoking the Cold War polarity of patriotic nationalists and traitorous Communists, repeatedly calling itself the only genuinely "Canadian" consumer group.[88]

Congress leaders disputed King's repeated assertion that prices could not be controlled unless wages were also managed, but suggested that, if wage control became necessary, the government could count on "the good sense and public spirit of the trade unions" which, as "partners," would help find a solution.[89] As this suggests, the CCL's position on price control was consistent with its postwar strategy of labour statesmanship and its categorical renunciation of militancy as "irresponsible." It hoped such a stance would distinguish it from the left-led unions that refused to ban communists but, as a number of labour historians have observed, it achieved little more than weakening its bargaining power.[90] The Congress thus took no visible action on its resolutions to "organize public opinion" around demands for the re-imposition of price controls and subsidies, but "advised and petitioned the Government to maintain an effective price control over all price levels." It admitted, however, that its "warnings" had been given "little heed."[91]

The endorsement of the anticommunist unions was important to the Housewives because it demonstrated the breadth and diversity of their support, but only the left-led unions, which were also more militant on the labour front, organized their members behind the price campaign. Those unions, particularly the United Electrical, Radio and Machine Workers (UE), the International Woodworkers of America (IWA), and the Mine, Mill and Smelter Workers (Mine-Mill), worked closely with the Housewives and mobilized support from among their members by circulating Housewives' petitions to their locals, soliciting members' contributions, and recruiting members to attend Housewives' rallies and conferences. The UE's national office, headquartered in Toronto, led the labour wing of the Ontario prices movement. In a joint prices campaign with Toronto Housewives, the union assigned staff, sent telegrams, co-hosted public conferences, and held press conferences. It was the UE's Director of Organization, Ross Russell, who initiated the idea of postcards in the shape of milk bottles, a tactic that became a Housewives' signature. Urged on by their national executive, UE leaders in virtually every local pressured their members to take an active role in petition-signing and other activities, and kept the campaign front of mind within the union through circulars and newsletters to its membership in which they explained that, through such determined effort, workers could "play a decisive role in forcing the Government" to reduce prices and reinstate milk subsidies.[92]

Yet despite the obvious enthusiasm of their support and their efforts to make the price campaign a union issue, unions frequently treated the prices campaign as the preserve of its women's auxiliaries. Strong language notwithstanding, they effectively framed demands for lower prices as supporting unions' more important, and implicitly more manly, struggles for higher wages. In her letter to LPP organizational secretary Stanley Ryerson, the party's BC education director Minerva Miller praised the BC women for "doing a very good job in the prices campaign" despite the attacks of "red-baiters," but complained that the LPP-led trade unionists had the "'unbalanced' attitude" that only the women's organizations should be "worrying their heads about" the price campaign.[93] To be sure, as homemakers with direct experience keeping house on shrinking incomes, and sometimes as wage-earners too, Housewives in unions and auxiliaries understood and expressed the concerns and desires of ordinary women in ways that their union brothers could not. But union support for the movement was undermined by its uncritical identification of prices as a distinctly feminine and, by implication, less important concern. Oblivious to Miller's criticism of the unions, the party's paper similarly urged readers to support the Housewives with sex-specific direct action: "If you are a woman, join a Consumers' group; men can take up the question through their trade unions."[94] Similarly, male-dominated labour organizations tended to link their support for lower prices to their implicitly masculine demand for higher wages. The Toronto District Labour Council, the Housewives' long-standing ally, expressed its support in the language of labour militancy, threatening a general strike for higher wages to offset rising cost of living as "the only way we can keep our purchasing power in line with present prices."[95]

Not surprisingly, perhaps, the Housewives' most reliable labour allies were women's auxiliaries of the left-led International Woodworkers of America (IWA), United Mine, Mill, and Smelter workers (Mine-Mill), and United Auto Workers (UAW), and of these, the IWA and Mine-Mill auxiliaries formed the core of labour women's membership in the Housewives.[96] Mona Morgan, IWA auxiliary president and leader of the BC Housewives, regarded women's activities as Housewives as continuous with her work in the labour movement and saw prices as just as critical as the demand for higher wages. In spring 1946, when the IWA auxiliary got a letter inviting them to join the Housewives' first delegation to Ottawa, Morgan recalled, they had been "protesting the milk subsidy removal" and high prices "for over a year." Along with some "twenty-five women's organizations," she recalled, the auxiliary took up the proposal on International Women's Day by creating a group. Marge Croy and Morgan, both Communists, were elected leaders, "because we were both officers of the District Council of the IWA that had been carrying on these prices [protests]." "All the auxiliaries participated in raising money," together with "the AUUC and the other ethnic organizations," including "the Scandinavian," she recalled, and collectively raised enough to send a delegation to Ottawa. In most cases, women's auxiliaries did the work on the price campaign. According to Manitoba Housewife Peggy Chunn, union men took no active role in the price campaign. There wasn't "anybody from the labour council," she recalled, "other than the women's committees."[97] Union auxiliary women in the IWA, Mine-Mill, and the Port Arthur Trades and Labor Council were among those who organized their labour sisters to write protest letters to the Finance minister "and urge other organizations to do the same."[98]

With only token support from the male rank-and-file, Canada's price campaign lacked the collective muscle U.S. unions were flexing to emphasize their demands for postwar price control. Still, the endorsement of the labour press, the vocal support of many union leaders and other labour officials, and the hard work of labour women added heft to the Housewives' demands. A deluge of letters from labour unions, women's auxiliaries, local labour councils, union councils, and labour federations urged the Liberals to reinstate price control and subsidies. Incomplete records in Finance department files provide a snapshot view, including dozens of telegrams, letters, and resolutions from more than twenty-two local unions, four union district councils, ten union women's auxiliaries, two provincial labour

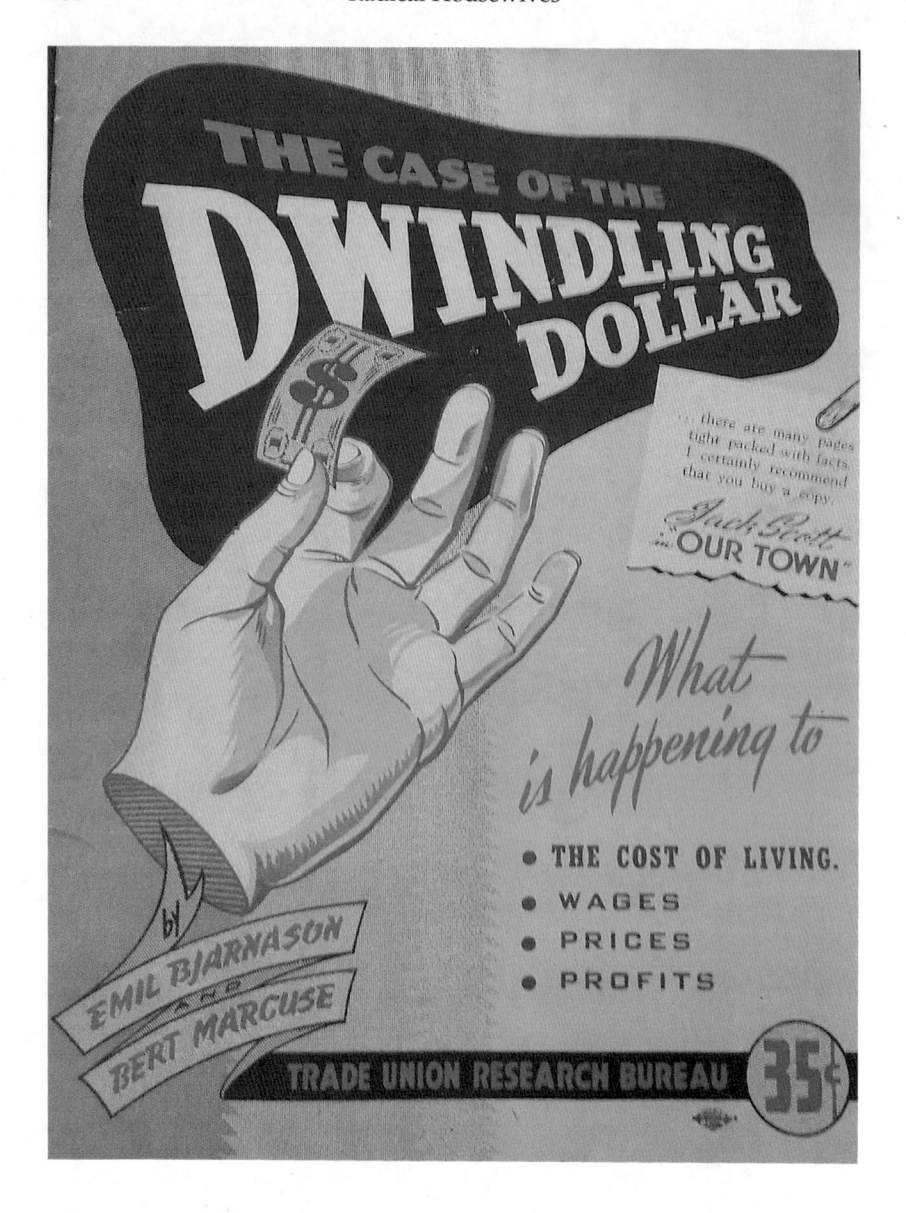

3.4 "The Case of the Dwindling Dollar," Archives of Manitoba, Anne Ross fonds, MHCA Releases, Reports, Activities, [1946–8], P5941/9

federations, twenty-eight district labour councils, and a worker cooperative.[99] Local labour councils in cities and towns across the country, particularly in regions of left-labour strength such as Liverpool, Nova Scotia and Vancouver, British Columbia, passed resolutions in favour of the continuation of price control. Most unions did so as well, not just the left-led CIO affiliates such as Auto, Mine-Mill, Packinghouse, Steel, Rubber, Boilermakers, Woodworkers, and Lumber and Sawmill workers, but also more conservative AFL affiliates such as Teamsters, Machinists, and Carpenters. Several small independent unions, including the Railway, Locomotive, and Sodium Sulphate workers, and unions of fire fighters, musicians, commercial travellers, and university workers, did so as well. Research provided by labour organizations also played a role. Labour provided much of the data for the Housewives' many petitions and briefs to the government, including educational pamphlets, booklets, and broadsheets with titles like "High Profits = High Prices," "Removal of Price Control and Subsidies Leading Canada to Economic Recession," and *The Case of the Dwindling Dollar*. The UE and Mine-Mill's jointly published book, *How High Are Living Costs?* presented labour's perspective on the postwar economy not only to their members, but aimed at the general public as well.[100]

Price Control and the Left

Although they called for revisions to federal policies, like many other women activists, the Housewives achieved their best results at the local level, where their alliances were strongest. Their local allies included not just the CCF and the LPP, whose positions on lower prices, public ownership of milk, and a managed economy coincided with their own, but progressives of all stripes. In Winnipeg, LPPers Joseph Zuken, Mary Kardash, and Peggy Chunn (the latter of whom was a Housewife) promoted the price campaign as members of city council.[101] Most of the Toronto city council, including not only the LPP aldermen Stewart Smith and Dewar Ferguson, but also Mayor Robert Saunders, a lawyer with corporate connections who was strongly endorsed by the business press, and Alderman May Birchard, a Liberal anti-poverty activist, supported them, as did Alderman William Dennison, the CCF's most vocal advocate of accessible milk through the war years. In 1941, as chairman of the city's milk committee, Dennison took an aggressive stance against the dairies and argued consistently in favour of the Housewives' proposal to make milk a public utility, suggesting that milk delivery could be "taken over by the people" and operated as a publicly funded service like the municipal transit system. Under his leadership, the committee attempted unsuccessfully to persuade the provincial government to take away the Milk Board's price-setting power, demands that were also made by the Housewives and the LPP. Dennison was supported by the Toronto CCF Council, which argued that publicly owned milk distribution would generate sufficient profits to justify the public cost. Like the Housewives, the Council pointed to the hardships suffered by low-income families, although unlike the Housewives, they expressed special concern for the working poor, who were "less able to afford milk than those on relief."[102]

The CCF, whose continued popularity with voters had forced both the Liberals and the Conservatives to add social welfare provisions to their own electoral platforms, and which, in June 1945, had won third-party status in the federal Parliament, became a vocal advocate of milk subsides and the extension of price control. The party condemned the Liberals' termination of milk subsidies, which they charged not only "sabotaged" its own anti-inflation program but struck a "blow against the living standards of our people" and discriminated "against children," especially those in "families with low incomes." Reminding the government that milk price was "a serious matter for the people of Canada," highly regarded party leaders such as MP Stanley Knowles and CCF Women's Council head Lucy (Mrs J.S.) Woodsworth urged them repeatedly to restore the subsidy, pointing out that, without the subsidy, milk would cost the average family with three children an "extra 42 cents per week," which was "equal to the loss of a week's pay per year for a man earning $25 per week."[103]

Riding a wave of popularity based in large part on the appeal of their call for a planned economy, the CCF argued fiercely in Parliament and in public for peacetime price control. As William Bryce, CCF Member of Parliament for Selkirk, Manitoba and a milk producer, argued, the expenditure of $20 million in milk subsidies was "the finest investment in health this country ever made."[104] The CCF's twenty-eight MPs had considerable, if qualified, support from both opposition and government members. Several Conservatives, along with Solon Low and other members of the right-wing Social Credit Party, overcoming their distaste for state intervention, argued that price ceilings be extended temporarily to slow inflation, as did Liberals representing agricultural ridings, the most powerful of whom was J.G. (James) Gardiner,

Minister of Agriculture, who fought vigorously for the continuation of farm but not consumer subsidies. Gardiner, however, was not popular with consumers because he fought equally hard for increased retail food prices.

The milk question was behind one of the year's most dramatic moments in the House, coming within a hair of bringing down the Liberal government. The CCF had consistently pushed the milk question in Parliament, bolstered by a steady stream of letters from their constituents, no doubt prompted by the Housewives. In August, the party almost made history when it marshalled enough support from its temporary allies to defeat a government motion to terminate producer milk subsidies by a vote of 69 to 41. Because this was a budget matter, according to the rules of Parliament, such a vote should have brought down the government. Only quick action by Reconstruction Minister C.D. Howe, aided by a generous interpretation of the rules of Parliament by the deputy speaker, retroactively ruled the decision a "free vote" and not a vote of non-confidence.[105] In the end, King managed to have his way through a subterfuge, returning control over milk price to provincial milk boards, which immediately terminated the subsidy. Across the country, retail milk price, which had increased in June, rose again, from 10 or 11 cents to between 15 and 17 cents per quart.[106]

In October, a federal by-election to replace anticommunist MP Herbert Bruce, who had resigned from his seat in Toronto's Parkdale riding, created yet another opportunity for the Housewives. Even the anticommunist *Globe and Mail* observed that the "milk issue" was "the chief Communist bid for election." Bruce's seat was contested by five candidates, one of them LPP member and Housewife Elizabeth Morton. Attempting to harness state power in pursuit of the Housewives' demands, or at least rattle their opponents, Morton filed for an injunction against the Ontario Milk Control Board, the Whole Milk Producers' League, and the Ontario Milk Distributors' Association, charging that the milk price agreements negotiated among these bodies was "illegal, invalid, against public policy and restraint of trade." By filing a legal application and contending that "the consumer has the right to be represented when and if any further agreement on the price of milk" is negotiated, Morton hoped the court would rule illegal the agreement that raised Ontario milk price by 3 cents per quart without any public consultation and would stop any further such trilateral agreements on milk price. Even if the court ruled against her, of course, it was an excellent way to keep the unfairness of the milk price increase in the newspapers. The court eventually conceded that the Milk Board had exceeded its mandate after first ruling against Morton on a technicality.[107]

Royal Commission on Milk

Housewives believed they had achieved an important victory on the first of October 1945, when Ontario Premier George Drew announced a Royal Commission to investigate the milk question. Through the fall and winter of 1946 and into the new year, confident that the government had acceded to their calls for a public investigation of milk price in the interest of consumers, communities across the province responded by organizing citizens' committees that called conferences to solicit public opinion on the milk question and prepare for the Commission's public hearings. The most active of these ad hoc groups was the Toronto-based Consumers' Federated Council, effectively a popular front organization of which a number of the executive committee members, including Aldermen Stewart Smith and Dewar Ferguson, Housewives Louise Watson and Elizabeth Morton, and unionist Sam Lapedes – husband of Housewife Becky Lapedes – were LPPers. The committee also included a number of other social reformers, the most prominent of whom was Alderman May Birchard, who were not only willing to work with Communists, but who endorsed their proposals for resolving the milk crisis. A public meeting attended by over two hundred delegates from Toronto churches, unions and consumer organizations similarly approved the Council's submission to the Royal Commission, which urged the restoration of subsidies, called for an investigation of dairy industry profits, and advocated for consumer participation in developing milk policy and monitoring the Milk Board. It also advised the Commission that, as the court hearing on Morton's application had eventually conceded, the Milk Board had acted without legal authority to set milk price. Because the price increase was "illegal," it contended, the proper price for milk was still 13 cents per quart. All of these positions were held jointly by the Housewives, the LPP, and the Ontario CCF.[108] The Housewives and the LPP continued to campaign for 13-cent milk, circulating pamphlets informing consumers that "16 cent milk" was "illegal" and urged "Mr. and Mrs. Consumer" to protest "the illegal price of milk" to the Ontario government.

3.5 "Milk: What You Must Make Drew Do!," Archives of Manitoba, Anne Ross fonds, MHCA Releases, Reports, Activities, [1946–8], P5941/10

16 CENT MILK?

- City Council says..................................No!
- Housewives Consumers Ass'n says........No!
- Milk Distributors say............................No!
- Citizens' Committee says ....No!
- Organized Labor says............................No!
- W.B.A. and Ukrainian Canadians say....No!
- People's Co-operative says....................No!
- The Consumer Says................................No!

•

Here is the story of the Milk Control Board Conference held on Monday, January 6th, in the Normandy Hall. The purpose of this Conference was to consider the application of the Winnipeg District Milk Producers' Co-operative Association for an increase in the price to the producer which, if granted, would have raised the price to the consumer from 14 to 16 cents a quart.

> The decision of the Board, as announced on Jan. 14, was NOT to raise the price above 14 cents. This is a great victory for the organized consumers of Greater Winnipeg, and a tribute to the fight which consumers have been waging on milk prices and subsidies.

MILK SUBSIDIES? YES!

3.6 "16 Cent Milk," poster, Archives of Manitoba, Anne Ross fonds, MHCA Releases, Reports, Activities, [1946–8], P5941/6

The calling of a Royal Commission appeared to be a clear victory for the Housewives, who had long demanded a public inquiry into milk price. But Drew, a "visceral" anticommunist who considered the Housewives subversive and, unlike most other politicians, refused to meet with them, used the Royal Commission, as have many other politicians, to forestall criticism and sidetrack dissent while appearing responsive to citizens' concerns.[109] Facing not only irate citizens but a potentially explosive legal finding if the court ruled that the Milk Board lacked the authority to set prices, Drew tasked the Commission to advise the government how to rectify the situation and forbade discussion of the matter in the legislature pending its report, thus sidelining the problem for a year.[110] Although forced to admit that the price hike had no legal basis, he nonetheless allowed it to stand, pending the inquiry's outcome, and ignored the resultant outrage.[111] When the Commissioner, Ontario Supreme Court Justice Dalton C. Wells, reported on his findings a year later, many were surprised and disappointed.[112] Dozens of community groups, organizations, and individuals had testified before the inquiry and submitted briefs outlining the importance of affordable milk to families and communities; many had appeared before the Commission to argue for state control of prices and distribution. These Canadians had accepted the Premier's assurances that the inquiry would investigate milk "production, processing, distribution, transporting and marketing," as well as "the prices at which it should be sold." It was therefore widely expected that, in addition to milk price, the inquiry would consider the charges of excessive industry profits, the potential benefits of public distribution, and the right of consumers to participate in policy. These were the questions that had animated the public debate and galvanized consumers, unionists, farmers, the left parties, producers' and distributors' organizations, and a host of political commentators. But following a full year of testimony, the Commission rejected evidence from community groups and workers' organizations that explained the importance of milk to families, particularly those on low incomes, who did without other necessities to buy milk for children. It also ignored the many who urged legislation that would eliminate exploitative pricing and inefficient distribution, ideally by making milk a public utility. Taking the part of the dairy industry, the final report, released in October 1947, far from curtailing the Milk Board's power, recommended expanding it, including the right to set prices, and rejected outright proposals for consumer representation.[113]

On to Ottawa

At war's end, the Housewives turned their attention from checking prices for the Consumer Branch of the Wartime Prices and Trade Board and exposing the businesses that were profiting from war at the expense of ordinary people to another patriotic activity, that of re-shaping the postwar economy. Indeed, as Leonard Kuffert, among others, has observed, mass media and educational organizations, along with the state, encouraged citizens to participate in planning the postwar, depicting it as the duty of an engaged and active citizenry to ensure that the West "won the peace."[114] The Housewives epitomized activist citizenship, although not, of course, in the ways that the elites who advocated it actually hoped. Their demands for continued state control of prices reflected collective expectations of a larger role for citizens and a more compassionate and responsive state, their movement drawing strength from the general shift to the political left. Housewives' demands for state economic management were consistent with those of the LPP and the CCF, and the labour and ethnic left, all of which supported their campaigns.

Confident in their rights as economic citizens, the Housewives reflected the hopefulness of the postwar era. They sparked a national discussion about the rights of citizen-consumers and the proper obligations of the state to ensure collective access to affordable food and other necessities, a debate that, although wide-ranging and newsworthy at the time, has since been forgotten.[115] As policy-makers and economists across the Western democracies, including Canada, debated the economic theories of Friedrich Hayek and John Maynard Keynes, newly empowered citizen-consumers considered the potential benefits of a managed economy over the old orthodoxy of laissez-faire.[116] At war's end, and despite the government's determination to withdraw as quickly as possible from direct control of the economy, the Housewives helped keep the question of peacetime price controls on the political agenda in Parliament, in the media, and on the streets. Housewives-led price protests sparked countless similar protests, for example the East York high school students, probably inspired by the Housewives, who launched their own buyers' strike when their school cafeteria raised the price of half-pints of milk from 5 to 6 cents. Politicians, business people, and economists debated whether peacetime price controls were "a suitable weapon to fight the present war against inflation" or part of "a socialist form of planning" incompatible with "a free society in which men have an opportunity to develop and expand." Even school children researched projects on "whether price control should be re-instated."[117]

The transitional character of the immediate postwar period and the rise of the popular left propelled the Housewives to the forefront of a dynamic popular debate about the future of the postwar world. As rising prices and shortages eroded the security they had enjoyed through the war years, Canadians switched their votes to the parties of the left and joined the Housewives-led campaigns for postwar price control. Energized by their success, the Housewives raised the stakes in their struggle with the government. They forged new organizations across the country and began mounting delegations to Ottawa, two of them several hundred strong, who confronted Members of Parliament directly, criticized the Finance Minister's management of the economy, and demanded a change in public policy. Through 1947 and into 1948, their delegations to Ottawa kept the Housewives on the front pages of the country's papers and bolstered their conviction that, with sufficient popular support, they could alter the course of national politics.

4
Mothers, Breadwinners, and Citizens

Through 1947, as inflationary prices continued to drive up the cost of living, the Housewives-led movement for peacetime price control grew stronger. By mid-summer, they had mounted two delegations to Ottawa and were preparing for more and bigger spectacles. Housewives in a number of cities held signature drives and organized parades, mass meetings, and conferences, activities that mobilized the support of thousands of Canadians. By year's end, fully three-quarters of Canadians, sceptical of official assurances that the Liberal reconversion program was the best and only route to a stable economy, favoured state control of prices.[1] Indeed, so popular were the Housewives that Canadians remained receptive to their socialist economic strategies even as the anticommunist attacks escalated. Red-baiting in the business press by professional Cold Warriors claimed to "expose" their already publicly acknowledged alliances with pro-communist unions and ethnic organizations, published the names of their communist members, and used that information as evidence to denounce them as being nothing more than a "front" for the Communist party. Their detractors' accusations that the Housewives were neither authentic consumers nor truly interested in price control were wrong, but they correctly identified the Housewives as an exceptionally popular organization of the left and thus a potential threat to powerful business people (all of them men) and their friends in government. The association refused to tie themselves formally to either the CCF or the LPP, although they allied with the organizations of the labour, party, and ethnic left. Their program, while centrally concerned with prices, also included other reforms demanded by the left. Like the rest of the left, the HCA advanced proposals that, they insisted, would give substance to the Liberals' wartime promises of a safe, secure, and prosperous postwar world. In concert with labour, they demanded higher wages and more progressive taxation, including more generous income tax exemptions for wage-earners, not just business owners. With their allies in the left-leaning Farmers Union, they called for lower freight rates and parity pricing, a program that would raise farm incomes by pegging agricultural product prices to the price index for other products.[2] Along with municipal reformers, anti-poverty activists, faith groups, and public health authorities, they proposed better social services, including subsidized housing and continued rent controls. With their friends in the CCF and the LPP, they urged lower sales taxes, higher taxes on luxury goods, and legal curbs on profits.

Their anticapitalist and pro-welfare-state demands and their program of boycotts and mass protest achieved their widest popularity during this period by tapping the widespread outrage that, two years after war's end, wartime sacrifices were not reaping the promised benefits of general prosperity and increased democracy. Thousands of women and men across the county joined the Housewives' campaigns, frustrated and angry that the federal government that had managed the economy so effectively through the last half of the war now claimed it was unable to control escalating prices, spiralling inflation, and profiteering. As the cost of living rose to unprecedented levels, consumers organized new Housewives-affiliated groups across the country.

In less than thirteen months, the HCA mounted five delegations to Ottawa to confront Cabinet members and other members of Parliament and demand state control of prices. The first, a delegation of twelve women from the three Western provinces who arrived in Ottawa on 31 March 1947, was praised as a group of "determined women" by a sympathetic press.[3] They were also attacked by their opponents, who contended that as many as eight of the twelve were communists, although the actual number was probably six.[4] The first delegation was quickly followed by a series of larger groups, culminating with a delegation of some five hundred Housewives and their supporters on 14 April 1948. Each trek to Ottawa received extensive media coverage, much of it positive, but also enraged their opponents, who accused the Housewives of "Communist domination." To be sure, some Housewives were members of the LPP and the pro-communist ethnic and labour left. These women – particularly the members of the ethnic groups – had the fund-raising skills and female networks that supported many grassroots organizations at the time and that were crucial to the Housewives. They were also seasoned activists who were familiar with direct action and, embedded as they were in working-class immigrant and ethnically identified communities, not encumbered by middle-class, Anglo-Celtic notions of respectable womanhood. But many other Housewives were women who had no previous experience as political activists but for whom the HCA, a respectable organization with a maternalist orientation that was "doing something" about rising prices, provided an acceptable way to communicate their distress and dissatisfaction to the politicians in Ottawa.

The Housewives' maternalism continued to shield them from anticommunist attacks well into the early Cold War. Women who would not have joined a party of the left were enthusiastic participants in the Housewives, who advocated many of the same proposals for social and economic reform as the LPP but were not yet effectively demonized and delegitimized by anticommunists. The resilience of this grassroots consumer movement, which advanced the same proposals for economic and social reform as the social democratic and communist left, suggests that there was more popular resistance to the state-led anticommunist program of threat, coercion, and re-education that shifted popular opinion to the right than most Cold War histories acknowledge.[5] Until 1948, and thus a full year into Canada's Cold War, the hopefulness and sense of entitlement of the immediate postwar period still played a larger role in the collective consciousness than the fear-mongering that, already underway in the 1940s, would define the 1950s.

More dynamic and more democratic in practice than either left party, the Housewives embodied the exuberant spirit of the immediate postwar years. They were also more resilient in the face of growing anticommunism. Even as the CCF-led CCL purged the Communist-tolerant and left-led unions from the house of labour, and communists, real and presumed, were ejected from liberal social justice organizations and social democrats who were willing to work with communists were expelled from the CCF, the Housewives' protests were supported by pro- and anticommunist labour groups, the CCF, and the liberal populist press. They inspired ever larger numbers of women to take to the streets in political street theatre that promoted their serial boycotts and captured the attention of the press. Their creative protests informed consumers about high living costs while underscoring their maternalism by reframing street demonstrations as unthreatening baby parades, to which mothers were urged to bring infants, events that often featured twins, and bread-and-butter marches to protest rising bread and dairy prices and promote their bread and butter conferences.[6]

As advocates of a more socialist postwar Canada, the Housewives embodied the fierce contradictions of their era. Their ability to mobilize large numbers of people from all sections of their communities around the ideas of the left, together with the obvious presence of LPP, labour, and left-ethnic women, antagonized the mainstream political parties, professional Cold Warriors, the RCMP, and the anticommunist and business-friendly press. These powerful adversaries fought back. Their public vilification by prominent anticommunist journalists and business leaders and the disruption of their parades by local police red squads jeopardized the maternalism and respectability that were their most important political assets. Outraged Housewives, communist and non-communist alike, denied charges that their organization was dominated by its communist members and that they themselves were either devious and dangerous subversives or naive dupes who, although innocent, were, their accusers implied, weak-minded women who were easily misled. Despite these attacks, the Housewives remained popular – indeed, far more popular than the male-dominated left, which could only aspire to engage such a broad swathe of Canadians. Appeals to their maternalist credentials and the continued support of the CCF, "respectable" non-communist and anticommunist labour leaders, and the majority of ordinary Canadians provided temporary protection as, fuelled by anger at the government and confidence in the Housewives' vision, consumers and their allies struggled together to make a better world.

Hundreds of thousands of Canadians, outraged by rising food prices and shortages while profits rose, demonstrated their support for the HCA by joining or supporting the five delegations that took their demands for peacetime price controls to Liberal Cabinet ministers, party leaders, and members of Parliament. Between delegations, hundreds of women across the country from Victoria, British Columbia to Halifax, Nova Scotia led local parades, boycotts, and protests and organized national postcard and petition campaigns that generated hundreds of thousands of signatures. Housewives-led boycotts of high-priced food, household essentials, and everyday luxuries like jam and chocolate bars provoked denials and justifications from meatpacking, dairy, bread, and candy manufacturers, forced merchants to reduce stocks and drop prices, and stimulated a broad public debate about the state's obligations to citizens and the viability of state economic management. By the end of the year, this remarkable record of achievements encouraged the Housewives to believe that "with persistence and determination," women such as themselves, organizing as citizen activists, could reform the state, influence state polices, and "compel the government to act."[7]

Complete Disregard for the Welfare of the People

In January 1947, the Liberals began dismantling the programs that had stabilized the economy through the war years, prompting immediate and drastic price increases in basic items such as meat, butter, and bread and shortages of many items, as suppliers held back products in anticipation of yet higher prices.[8] Housewives in Toronto, Winnipeg, and Vancouver, who had been mounting regular delegations to their municipal governments, and occasionally to provincial legislatures and official bodies such as Milk Boards, since the 1930s, began turning their sights on Ottawa. New branches formed in cities and towns across the country and Housewives-led boycotts and protests erupted everywhere, sparked by regular Housewives' reminders that the reality of rising living costs and declining real wages contradicted Prime Minister Mackenzie King's repeated assurances that the transition would be well-planned, competently administered, and painless. Housewives in Saskatoon urged their neighbours and supporters to "do what we can in every way" to stop the "run-away inflation that threatens to overwhelm us unless the government policy is changed." Men and women, they advised, should "sit down at once and write to your member of parliament" and "get a group of people together and send a wire" to the prime minister.[9]

Such letters deluged the Prime Minister's Office, many of them agreeing with the Housewives that the government was deliberately sacrificing the well-being of ordinary people to aid business recovery. Working people's everyday experience contradicted the Liberals' repeated insistence that its record on price control confirmed its "wise" and "courageous" decisions, that its orderly readjustment plan had "avoided violent fluctuations," and that the outcome of these policies would be "continuing prosperity."[10] In reality, Liberal assurances were intended to obscure the fact that the primary objective of federal economic policy was to reduce government's role in the economy, and that the federal reconstruction program prioritized the expansion of industrial capacity and encouraged export-led business development while it suppressed domestic consumer spending. The postwar recovery program therefore made little use of the economic stabilization measures that would raise household standards of living. Profits, encouraged by these policies, soared, while the consumer price index was allowed to rise rapidly in 1947 and 1948 in response to the termination of price controls.[11]

The HCA's vocal disbelief in official assurances that the transition to peacetime would be carefully and skillfully planned resonated with wage-earners and their families just as they provoked the animosity of business. The federal bureaucracies, as historian Peter McInnis notes, lacked the skills and knowledge to ensure the smooth transition to peacetime that Prime Minister Mackenzie King repeatedly promised.[12] This ineptitude was painfully obvious to the Housewives, who openly mocked Finance Minister Douglas Abbott's argument that "the only way to bring prices down" was to "boost production and let the law of supply and demand operate." On the contrary, they insisted, "if the government could introduce controls in wartime, they could do it now."[13] Its refusal to do so, Housewife Edith Beveridge suggested, revealed that "the federal government no longer is interested in legislating in behalf of the majority of the people." Labelling Abbott's manner "evasive" and his responses "equivocal," Toronto Housewives President Lily Phelps averred, "we can only assume that Mr. Abbott has lost all contact with the realities of the price situation and is not concerned with the welfare of the Canadian housewives and their families."[14]

The Housewives were correct in disputing Abbott's confident assertion, as he announced the first of three reductions in income taxes and the elimination of excess profits taxes in spring 1947, that Canadians were "enjoying their most prosperous time in memory." In fact, only business owners and shareholders experienced much prosperity. Inflation, which by the end of 1947 had increased by almost 15 per cent over the previous year, and especially food costs, which had increased over 22 per cent, eroded the value of wages. Profits, on the other hand, increased over the decade by an extraordinary 153 per cent.[15] These economic disparities fuelled the nearly unanimous perception that legislators were not making policy in the interest of ordinary people and helped to light the spark of mass protest.[16] In spring 1947, Housewives in the Western provinces, outraged by what Manitoba Housewives President Anne Ross, writing to federal Agriculture Minister James Gardiner, called the government's persistent and complete disregard for the "welfare of the Canadian people" and, supported by their allies on the labour, ethnic, and party left, organized the first of five delegations to Ottawa.[17]

The Western Delegation

On 31 March 1947, newspapers across the country reported that "twelve attractive but determined and articulate women," representing Housewives Associations from British Columbia, Alberta, Saskatchewan, and Manitoba, the women's sections of the Alberta and Saskatchewan United Farmers Union, and the Alberta branch of the Association of United Ukrainian Canadians (AUUC), had converged on Ottawa.[18] In the weeks before their trek, Housewives had taken to the air waves and issued press releases to inform Canadians that they were going to Parliament to urge the Liberals to stop the "alarming trend towards run-away inflation that threatens to overwhelm us" with a change in policy. "Since before the war ended," they advised the press, the federal government had assured Canadians that "the post-war objective of our domestic policy is social security and human welfare" and promised that price controls and subsidies "will remain in effect in order to prevent undue increases in prices." But, they pointed out, the government "has said one thing and done another." High prices and rampant inflation had left an astonishing 82 per cent of families with insufficient income to maintain "health and self-respect," of which 44 per cent had "less than half" enough to do so. "Bigger profits for wealthy monopolies," they advised, meant "less milk for babies." They had prepared a brief, which they presented to Finance Minister Abbott, advocating measures similar to those used in wartime to mitigate the postwar emergency. In addition to price controls, they advised the government to re-institute milk subsidies and reduce milk price, establish a low-rent housing program and maintain rent controls, and re-impose restrictions on new food products, clothes, and luxury goods. To oversee this program, the women called for a peacetime prices and trade board with broad citizen representation from labour, farmers, and women.[19]

In Ottawa, the delegation was warmly received by CCF leader M.J. Coldwell, who, the press reported, "recognized a couple of the women from Saskatchewan as strong CCFers," and, according to one delegate, promised "to bring the subject up in the House."[20] The delegates vowed to stay "right here in Ottawa until we get results," counting on Abbott's assurance that he would give their proposals "careful consideration." But the delegation, the press reported, felt betrayed and discouraged when, the following day, as they watched from the visitors' gallery of the House, Abbott announced additional decontrol measures. They were also "exposed" by the anticommunist *Montreal Standard*, which revealed that eight of the twelve delegates were, "rightly or wrongly," identified as communists. Housewife Mrs Ann Latham of Moose Jaw, Saskatchewan, rejected the accusation as irrelevant.

"We come here as housewives and representatives of thousands of other housewives," she protested, "not as politicians or political agitators." The press confirmed that they were, as she claimed, "getting the run-around" from the Cabinet ministers. "But we can't be pushed off," she insisted. "This is too serious."[21]

The Housewives' first delegation to Ottawa, although small, hit a raw nerve among the public and generated extensive media coverage that embarrassed the government by exposing the real beneficiaries of its reconversion program. In the rubric of the Cold War, embarrassing governments and revealing disunity were evidence of subversion, and fortunately for their opponents, these Housewives had not anticipated the possible consequences of including a number of communists and women with other left connections among the delegation. Neither they nor other Housewives would make that mistake again. Indeed, a RCMP file memorandum related to their second delegation in June includes a (redacted) list of LPP members present, and notes that "Party members have instructions to remain in the background."[22] The presence of such women, who constituted half of the first delegation, fuelled a series of articles in the anticommunist *Winnipeg Free Press* that were reprinted in similarly anticommunist papers across the country. Hoping to discredit the Housewives in advance of the second delegation's arrival in Ottawa in June, their critics claimed to expose them as a covert Communist "front" with its "central headquarters" in Winnipeg, where Housewives President Anne Ross and delegate Peggy Chunn were well-known left activists. Anticommunist journalists accused the Housewives of misrepresenting themselves as "apolitical" when, in fact, some of them were (real or suspected) communists, and of duping "hundreds of unwary housewives" into supporting their movement. These "Communist leaders," they insisted, had "seized control and sowed Communist propaganda among members with all the dexterity they could command." Not only were communists among the delegation, they charged, but the association itself was dominated by communists. The presence in various Housewives associations of women such as Beatrice Levis, Anne Ross, and Ann Swanky, who were married to prominent members of the LPP, Mrs Norman Brudy, whose son was reported to be a member, as well as openly LPP members such as Mona Morgan, Josephine Gehl, Audrey Staples, Florence Theodore, and Margaret (Peggy) Chunn, although a tiny fraction of the Housewives' membership, was proof, they alleged, that the organization was "under the direct control of Communists." Further incriminating evidence was their association with suspected communists such as John Marshall, educational director of the People's Cooperative Dairy, an important ally of the Manitoba Housewives, and guest appearances at Housewives' meetings by several local LPP celebrities, including the popular Member of the Manitoba Legislative Assembly (MLA) William Kardash, well-known political activists Mitch Sago and Abe Zailing, and Winnipeg city aldermen Joseph Zuken and Jacob Penner. Housewives, who distinguished between their activities as party members and their consumer activism, protested that they went to Ottawa as housewives, not as Labor Progressives. But anticommunists dismissed those objections as false "cries of innocence," proving only that "Communists" were "angry at the truth."[23]

Children, Chocolate Bars, and Butter Boycotts

Refusing to be deterred by the attacks on their organization, Housewives from British Columbia to Nova Scotia, no longer formally affiliated but functioning as a network of consumer groups, began organizing a larger delegation to Ottawa in June. Housewives from BC to New Brunswick coordinated a busy cross-country schedule of parades, boycotts, signature drives, and postcard campaigns, canvassing their neighbours door to door and through telephone trees, and setting up tables outside stores on shopping days to promote their boycotts and galvanize support for their June delegation to Ottawa. On 1 May, Toronto Housewives President Lily Phelps, a CCF member of long standing and thus clearly not a communist, announced the first of a nationwide series of boycotts to promote the planned delegation. Housewives associations across the province urged women to "refrain from buying butter for one week" to protest "the heavy increase in the price of such an important food," which had risen, depending on region, from about 36 cents to between 42 cents and 46 cents per pound. The following day, a hundred and fifty Housewives paraded through downtown Vancouver to signal the beginning of a week-long boycott of butter, shortening, and lard, a second week-long boycott of jam, marmalade, peanut butter, and canned fruit, followed by a two-week clothing boycott, co-sponsored by the Vancouver Labour Council. By week's end, the Regina Housewives' League had announced its own month-long buyers' strike and was picketing stores and restaurants to protest high prices, including the 10-cent butter increase and an increase in the price of restaurant coffee. The League's two hundred members had commissioned and decorated two trucks, equipped with loudspeakers, to "build public support" and were planning a "baby parade" of Housewife-mothers and their infants, complete with twins, to promote the "butter question." By the following week, Winnipeg Housewives, supported by the local labour council, were conducting a "house-to-house canvass" distributing "The Case of the Shrinking Steak" leaflets, and asking women to boycott meat. The Vancouver Labour Council called a "city-wide buyers' strike" for 2 May to demand the restoration of price ceilings, subsidies, and rent controls. Left activist Mona Morgan, one of the five hundred delegates at the Labour Council meeting, invited "all women" to join the newly reconstituted consumers' league. Left-led Montreal unions began re-organizing Housewives organizations in Notre Dame de Grace and other areas of left support. Vancouver and Port Arthur Housewives established telephone chains to spread their boycott message; Saskatchewan Housewives called their own "baby parade"; and Edmonton Housewives distributed pamphlets and prepared to picket "large stores" bearing "cards listing numerous boycotted items."[24] Others wrote letters to the editors of their local papers. Helen Noble of Toronto, for instance, asked women to consider whether their patriotic war work checking prices and fighting inflation should be used to let "big corporations to fatten up" now that war was over. Clearly, she fumed, the "government is not working for the benefit of the common man, but is catering to the capitalists." "Come on, ladies," she urged, "organize a buyers' strike in your community."[25]

In tandem with the Housewives' boycotts, and with the Housewives' support, the Communist-affiliated National Federation of Labor Youth (NFLY) called a month-long candy bar boycott to protest an increase from 5 to 8 cents per bar, kicking off the campaign on the symbolic first of May, when workers and socialists around the world celebrate May Day. News media across the country reported that thousands of eager teenagers across the country were taking direct action.[26] An excited press reported hundreds of Montreal youths parading through the streets bearing "down with chocolate bars" signs. Three thousand Toronto students, the press announced, signed "anti-eight-cent candy-bar pledge cards" and several hundred more, according to NFLY secretary Norman Penner (who remained a life-long Communist) joined a "chocolate bar parade" at the end of classes. Newspapers reported "bedlam" in Vancouver as "200 school children" stormed the BC legislature, chanting, "We want five cent chocolate bars," accompanied by loud "catcalls and whistles." Another eight hundred marched in Regina. Three hundred Ottawa

The Case of the Shrinking Steak

- Trying to give your family enough meat these days is an uphill task. Meat prices have swelled like a balloon. And the amount of meat your dollar buys has shrivelled like an autumn leaf.

- It's like this:

	1939	1948
1 lb. sirloin steak	23c	68-75c
1 lb. round steak	17c	67-73c
1 lb. shoulder roast beef	15c	49c
1 lb. prime rib roast beef	22c	70c

- **WHO GAINS?** You certainly don't. But someone does. Between 1939 and 1947, profits of four big meat companies rose 430%.

- **YOUR WAGES**—Since pre-war years, most meat prices have trebled. Your wages have not trebled to meet these prices. With all other necessary foods equally high-priced, your family's health suffers. The black word "malnutrition" becomes more than just a word.

- **LID OFF BEEF EXPORTS**—Recently the Dominion Government lifted the embargo on beef shipments to the U.S. This means you are competing with the American consumer, who can afford to pay more. Our Government took no steps to protect Canadian families. So meat prices have jumped clear out of sight, and quality of meat sold to us has become poorer.

- **OBVIOUSLY** a bad situation. But can we do anything to correct it?

YOU BET WE CAN!

Let's Get Together!

- By ourselves, each of us can only sigh over shrinking steaks. But together we can DO something about it!
- Griping won't put more meat on your table. But buyers' resistance and organized consumer protest will!
- Heres' what we mean:

The Manitoba Housewives' Consumers' Ass'n.

announces

A MEATLESS DAY CAMPAIGN

When? October 15th to December 15th.

How? Refuse to buy meat on Tuesdays and Fridays. Tell your butcher why. Get your group or club to exchange meatless recipes.

Why? Strong buyer resistance can bring pressure to bear on meat companies; can make meat stocks pile up; can force prices down.

But That's Not All:

- Forcing prices down by buyer resistance is necessary in this crisis. But it is not enough.
- The permanent solution rests with the Government.
- Only price ceilings and subsidies on meat can ultimately solve the whole problem.
- How can we make the Government take this step?

By Organized Consumer Protest!

- Write your local M.P., Prime Minister McKenzie King, and Mr. Abbott.
- Join in the work of the M.H.C.A., a non-subsidized, independent organization which has campaigned against high prices for over two years. Phone 46 835 or 53 920.

25

4.1 (a and b) "The Case of the Shrinking Steak," 2 pages, Archives of Manitoba, Anne Ross fonds, MHCA Releases, Reports, Activities, [1946–8], P5941/4

high school students marched to Parliament Hill at lunchtime bearing placards threatening, "We'll eat worms before the eight-cent [chocolate] bar." High school students in Halifax "toured retailers' shops" to check candy bar prices, and "when told, registered disgust and marched to the next." Fredericton teenagers were reported to be saving their sugar rations "to make fudge at home." Despite some anticommunist attacks in the right-wing press that "definitely identified" the teenagers who appeared to be "innocently parading" as a "Communist front," by the end of the week, Vancouver retailers reported "a definite drop in sales of chocolate bars." Some Moose Jaw stores had lowered their price to 6 cents, at least one Montreal merchant reported he hadn't sold a case of candy bars "this week," and Ottawa merchants were refusing to take their normal shipments "because they can't sell them."[27]

Housewives and teenagers parading down the streets of Vancouver, Victoria, Regina, Moose Jaw, Toronto, Montreal, Ottawa, Fredericton, and other cities made front-page news, bringing into clear view the hardships suffered by working-class families, for whom rising prices, high inflation, and declining real wages entailed the loss of small, everyday luxuries such as candy bars. The Housewives' support for and participation in the country-wide May Day children's chocolate bar boycott, the year's most spectacular act of street theatre, together with their pram and baby parades and other kinds of performance activism, also highlighted their public persona as mothers and homemakers acting politically only out of concern for families. In this regard, they presaged the similar claims made more than a decade later by the Voice of Women (VOW), an organization started in 1960 that, as Frances Early argues, spoke similarly as "militant mothers" and organized actions with and in the name of children to advocate the cause of peace. Like the Housewives, the VOW organized large delegations to Ottawa to confront politicians and demand progressive reforms to safeguard children and their families, similarly attracting hundreds of supporters among apolitical women who just wanted to "do something" about a grievous social ill. Like the Housewives, by presenting itself as an organization of "serious-minded and responsible mother-citizens," the VOW acquired legitimacy and a "public hearing for its views." And like the Housewives, they were excellent political strategists who embraced and expanded traditional understandings of motherhood in pursuit of their vision of a better world.[28]

On 9 May, following a meeting of nine hundred Housewives, the BC Housewives Consumers Association kicked off a week-long boycott of

4.2 "Candy Bar Boycott, Montreal, May 1947," Library and Archives Canada, accession number 1974-264 NPC, box 03453, *Canadian Tribune*, Price Campaign, Montreal, QC, PA-093691

butter, lard, and shortening with a placard parade through downtown Vancouver. They followed this with a second week-long boycott of jam, marmalade, peanut butter, and canned fruit and a two-week boycott of clothing. Deploying the street theatre for which they were becoming famous, the BC Housewives and their labour allies, all dressed in "overalls, slack suits, and old clothes," engaged in "mass picketing," the press reported, "led by two marchers in barrel-like costumes" bearing the slogan, "Roll Back Prices." Although the police did not interfere, the RCMP watched them closely and maintained detailed records of their events, and Board of Trade President Thomas Braidwood's accusations that the BC Housewives were dominated by Communists briefly drew unfavourable media attention. Braidwood urged business and labour leaders to "cooperate to bring prices down" and thus subvert the "Communist-inspired buyers' strikes and boycotts" of the Vancouver Housewives Consumers Association (although he did not explain how the outcome would be different). In a statement to the press, Braidwood denounced the Housewives as "adjuncts" of the Labor-Progressive Party who disguised their true nature in that their placards "are never trade-marked with the Communist hammer and sickle," as would, he thought, be proper.[29]

In addition to participating in the children's chocolate bar boycott, Montreal Housewives prepared for their trek to Ottawa by uniting their twelve Housewives Leagues, with a combined membership of over five hundred women, in the Montreal Consumers' Federation. They also affiliated thirty-three provincial organizations, "French, English, and other nationalities," home and school associations, women's union auxiliaries, and the Canadian Congress of Labour (CCL). Their announcement in May of a buyers' strike and an "interview drive" in which members would ask local merchants to reduce their prices voluntarily by 10 per cent prompted a quick response from the anticommunist unions. Representatives of Montreal unions affiliated to the American Federation of Labor (AFL) and the Catholic Syndicates issued a press statement denouncing the Montreal Housewives Consumers Leagues, who they accused of attempting to "infiltrate" and take command of labour-led protest against "the rising cost of living." A month later, the press reported, the Housewives applied for a permit to set up a table and hand out protest postcards on downtown streets just as other Housewives were doing, but they were refused. Between thirty-five and fifty of them, according to varying reports in the press and RCMP surveillance reports, along with some twenty-five children, a decorated truck, and three cars, went ahead and protested without the permit, marching through downtown from the corner of Jeanne-Mance and Sherbrooke streets bearing banners and placards calling for the reimposition of price controls and protesting the price of candy bars. Six members of the Montreal police Red Squad and six more uniformed officers who were standing by broke up the parade and confiscated the placards, whereupon the women reformed on St. Catherine Street re-equipped with new placards. The women were eventually dispersed, although two of the drivers, the press reported, were charged with driving without a licence.[30]

Regina police took a similar tack against the Regina Housewives Consumers League. The Housewives, who had received a permit to parade with some 1,000 school children in the May Day protest against the 8-cent candy bar, applied for another to promote their month-long buyers' strike to support their demands for a 10-cent drop in the price of butter, reduced prices of a host of other items, and a drop in the price of restaurant coffee to 5 cents per cup. They planned a "baby parade," featuring twenty sets of twins, at which women would march with perambulators down city streets on a Friday afternoon. But, as Mrs C.A. Farrow, the organization's secretary, informed the press, when she applied for a parade permit, Police Chief Duncan MacDougall refused it, informing her that "any attempt to hold the parade would be halted by police officers." The event spawned a flurry of articles in the press, in which Chief MacDougall blamed the Housewives for giving insufficient advance notice of their request, and Housewives' spokesman Mrs Mable Hanway accused Chief MacDougall of attempting to justify his refusal on the grounds that "Regina babies were not starving like German children" and labelled him a "fascist." Popular sentiment seemed to be with the Housewives, however. Months later, CCF Premier T.C. (Tommy) Douglas, LPP head Nelson Clarke, the provincial leaders of the Social Credit and Progressive Conservative parties, and representatives of the AFL and CIO labour councils spoke in support of the Housewives at a protest rally at Regina City Hall, where the Housewives announced a forthcoming conference on prices and promoted their campaign to gather 75,000 signatures on their roll-back-prices petitions.[31]

Housewives everywhere announced small victories, such as Winnipeg Housewife Anne Ross, who reported that nylon stockings were "piling up," the price of fruit and meat was down in some stores, and butter had dropped 5 or 6 cents per pound. In Regina, Housewife Evelyn Farrow reported that "chocolate bars and butter" were "not being sold" and sales of "perishable foodstuffs" were "slow," and one Regina store offered meat at an 11-cent reduction as a "Housewives' strike" special. In support of the Housewives, Beland Honderich, financial editor of the left-liberal *Toronto Star*, argued that their first delegation to Ottawa, followed by a month-long rotating boycott in several provinces, had significant "indirect benefits." The Housewives' campaign, he asserted, sent a "danger signal that prices and wages" were "out of line," drew national "attention to high prices," deterred additional price increases, prompted retaliatory sales by beleaguered retailers, and resulted in the organization of "about fifteen" new HCA branches "almost overnight."[32]

The anticommunist press, by contrast, described their demands as "fantastic and unreasonable," pronounced the boycott a "dismal failure," and attributed evidence of "a falling off in business" to "selective buying rather than the [buyers'] strike," without bothering to explain how those were different. The head of the Vancouver Board of Trade dismissed the boycott as merely "an attempt by Communists to gain leadership over many non-Communists." In June, an article provocatively titled, "Will Fellow-Travellers Control Housewives' Cavalcade to Ottawa?" by anticommunist journalist Ronald Williams denounced the "housewives' crusade against rising prices," like "so many other popular agitations," as the work of "the communists and their sympathizers." He also provided a province-by-province summary of Housewives associations and, deploying the Cold War method of assigning guilt by association, named known or suspected communists, socialists, and sympathizers as well as their incriminatingly left-wing allies.[33] Like many other red-baiters, he named names, providing a long list of Housewives with both influential positions in their own organization and incriminating ties to the LPP, including Housewives Vice-President Louise Watson and corresponding secretary Edna Hahn, noting as well that "at least one" of the Housewives' ward presidents was a Communist and two more were "sympathizers." Other Housewives' husbands provided the incriminating links to the Communist party. These included Margery Ferguson, "wife of Dewar Ferguson, LPP alderman and business agent" of the Communist-led Canadian Seamen's Union, the "wife of Reg Wright, officer in the Communist-led Chemical Workers Union," and Helen Weir, Housewives Campaign Director and "wife of John Weir, former managing editor of the Communist newspaper."[34]

Shaken but undeterred by the red-baiting, the Western Housewives promised to return "with a larger delegation," determined to "tell the government that the people of Canada have finished playing the role of passive victims while their pockets are picked by the profiteers."[35] Canadians seemed to agree, as Housewives Consumers Associations and Housewives Leagues grew in numbers and popularity, spurred by the country's frustration with the slow pace of the recovery and the disproportionate benefits to business of the federal government's postwar recovery policies. Tapping the collective anxiety that rising prices would erode the gains many had made during the war years and the widespread support for postwar price control, they quickly recruited new members among their friends and neighbours, assisted in the formation of many new Housewives groups, and persuaded a variety of other organizations to join them in coalitions. By the end of the year, some forty Housewives organizations, representing as many as 100,000 members in cities and towns in every province, formed a network from Nova Scotia to British Columbia.[36]

Prices continued to rise through the coming months, giving credence to the Housewives' detractors, who claimed that neither the children's chocolate bar boycott nor the Housewives' rotating buyers' strikes had more than a temporary impact on prices. While this was no doubt true, the boycotts caused a "strategic disruption" that engaged thousands of ordinary people in acts of politicized consumption and sparked a heated public debate about the political economy of prices in a market economy and the right of citizens to criticize the state.[37] Whether or not their boycotts actually brought down prices, they transformed high prices from a personal problem into a political issue, foreshadowing the central insight of the late twentieth-century women's movement that the personal is political.

Whatever the impact on prices, the Housewives' month-long rotating boycott generated an upsurge of grassroots activity across the country, culminating in the Toronto Housewives' "bread and butter conference" at the end of May. Two hundred delegates from several provinces approved a seven-point program to "increase consumer purchasing power" and curb corporate "greed." The Housewives' economic plan to restrict excess profits, boost consumers' purchasing power, and create a peacetime prices and trade board that included housewives, workers, and farmers was consistent with reforms advanced by the communist and social democratic left. The same demands were advanced by the LPP in its paper, the *Tribune*. Prepared by the Housewives' economics expert Edith Beveridge, with the assistance of the research departments of three large labour unions, the Toronto Welfare Council, and the Visiting Homemakers, it was disseminated widely through the labour movement and at public meetings and press conferences. Using powerful facts and figures, they showed that price control saved consumers $1,500 million annually at a cost of under $200 million, thus effectively transferring wealth from the rich to the poor. Between 1945 and 1946, as the Liberals terminated the excess profits tax, Canadian food companies increased their profits by 62 per cent while 1.75 million taxpayers reported income of less than $2,000, insufficient for the average family to meet basic needs.[38] Armed with strong arguments supported by data, delegates confidently approved the proposal and resolved to mount a second delegation to take it to Ottawa.[39]

4.3 "Here, You Can Finish Him Up," cartoon, *Canadian Tribune*, 10 June 1947

Over the following weeks, Housewives and their allies took to the streets to build momentum for the forthcoming delegation. Hundreds of Toronto Housewives set up tables at busy street corners and, in two weeks, collected 35,000 signatures on price protest cards from enthusiastic shoppers to send to the Prime Minister. "It was almost impossible to cope with all the people who stopped and asked for a card," one Housewife reported. "In some places," women were "standing six deep" to sign cards.[40] Montreal Housewives, as noted earlier, requested a city permit to set up tables and collect signatures, but their request was denied by the police, who justified their refusal on the grounds that the women might disrupt traffic.[41] Housewife Rae Luckock took to the airwaves to remind Canadians that the Liberals were ignoring their needs, reneging on their promises, and failing to account to the electorate for the policies that were causing them so much distress. Parodying a well-known advertisement for a women's remedy, she asked rhetorically, "Does your budget feel tired toward the end of the week? Do you get that saggy feeling when you see the grocery bill? Do you get dizzy spells when you pay the rent out of your husband's pay?" If so, she prescribed, "You need help," although not what "the political medicine men like Finance Minister Abbott wants to give you." But instead of Lydia Pinkham's patent medicine, she recommended a "good scientific dose of price control and subsidies." The remedy was direct action. "If you feel a towering rage coming over you when you look at today's prices, if you go all hot and cold when you think how much it will cost to buy Johnny a new summer outfit – don't see a psychiatrist – there's nothing the matter with your nerves – just get in touch with the Housewives' Consumer Association. Our Association is the best tonic you can find after weeks of struggling with the Dwindling Dollar."[42]

Calling another round of boycotts, dubbed "buyers' resistance week," Housewives in Ottawa, Winnipeg, and Toronto asked consumers to "buy only a minimum" of essential foods such as "bacon, butter, fresh vegetables and fruit, shortening, sugar, pastries and cake," and refrain entirely from buying canned goods, candy, clothing, and furniture.[43] "Resistance" of this sort made significant demands on homemakers, who were still constrained by rationing and shopped carefully from a limited selection in the stores to stretch too-small budgets, but it gave women everywhere the chance to participate in direct action. Although there is no evidence that they did so strategically, the Housewives tapped the moral outrage of supporters and combined personal sacrifice and direct action, two qualities that are essential to boycotts' success. Like latter-day boycotts, including the twentieth century's best-known and most widely supported boycotts, the United Farm Workers' campaign against California grapes and the Montgomery Bus Boycott, as well as many other less famous boycott campaigns, the Housewives combined direct action with shared moral principles, providing opportunities for their supporters to demonstrate their commitment to the cause through modest personal sacrifices, such as doing without meat.[44] Whether or not she did so consciously, Lily Phelps justified the association's audacious demands by pointing to the morality of shared sacrifice, a strategy that campaigns like the grape pickers', the civil rights activists', and other contemporary campaigns have shown strengthens supporters' commitment to the cause. Observing that "people can live without those articles for a week," she enjoined consumers to "prove" that "public opinion is behind us." Not only was the sacrifice manageable, she suggested, but people in Europe were "living on a great deal less."[45]

The "Roll Back Prices" Delegation

On 24 June 1947, the Housewives' second delegation of more than two hundred Housewives from six of Canada's nine provinces, a few men representing labour councils and left-led unions, and seventeen-year-old Shirley Endicott, chosen as the youth delegate for her work collecting "hundreds of signatures in high schools protesting the price of chocolate bars," captured headlines across the country. Lily Phelps, who led the delegation, explained that their proposals for alternative economic policies were based not on "politics" but on "human need." The Housewives, it appears, had learned from the mistakes of the failed Western delegation, and were careful to emphasize the maternalism that they hoped would distinguish them from communists. Some delegates were, in fact, communists, including Endicott, who was head of the National Federation of Labor Youth. But, in anticipation of anticommunist attacks, the delegation was led by eminently respectable CCF women: Lily Phelps, well-known for her war work in the Consumer Branch and the Emergency Committee of Canadian Women, and her second-in-command, Rae Luckock, a former CCF MLA. With such women at the helm, the Housewives no doubt hoped to avert the red-baiting that had tarnished the maternalist credentials and undermined the credibility of the first delegation.

Demonstrating the public relations skills that had kept their campaigns in the news, and maintaining the maternalist cover that deflected demonizing attacks, the Housewives took care to distinguish this delegation from the previous one. Phelps acknowledged that their brief was "roughly" the same as the previous delegation's, but insisted (accurately, in the sense that Housewives groups were linked only as members of an informal network) that the two groups were unrelated. "Our association has a broader basis than the Western group," she explained. She also stressed the unthreatening gender composition of the Housewives, as well as the anti-discrimination policy that it shared with the communist left, pointing out that "It is open to any woman in charge of a home, irrespective of age, race, or political belief." To emphasize their difference from the previous delegation, which was tagged by hostile papers as "openly Socialistic," the Toronto-led delegation reiterated that they were "non-political" and had been "in the business of watching consumer interests since 1937." Although only unionists from the pro-communist labour left participated as delegates, the HCA could point to broad labour support, noting that their brief had been endorsed by the leaders of the CCF-dominated and anti-communist Canadian Congress of Labour (CCL) and Toronto Labour Council.[46]

Emphasizing the feminine domesticity that they hoped would imply the antithesis of socially deviant and dangerous communists, however, increased their risk of being defined as irrelevant. This dichotomy has plagued generations of socialist feminists, such as CCF activist Rose Henderson (1869/71–1937), whose political ideas clearly influenced her former campaign worker Rae Luckock.[47] Identifying them as the "ladies of the rolling pin" and the "rolling pin brigade," papers across the country applauded the Housewives' efforts even as they snickered at the spectacle of upstart women out of place in the halls of (male) power. The Housewives, they reported, arrived "armed with miniature rolling pin" lapel pins, which, Phelps emphasized, "we made ourselves." Papers' sniggering suggestion that the "rolling-pin ladies" had proven that "the female of the species is deadlier than the male" was clearly meant to underline the incongruity of women challenging legislators in the overwhelmingly male domain of Parliament. Emphasizing the inherent ridiculousness of the confrontation, reporters labelled their rolling pins a "kitchen weapon" and described the Housewives as bearing down "on the mere male legislators" and demanding that they "roll back prices," or, they threatened, they would "roll out the rolling pin." Pundits described Phelps as the "motherly type" and, with heavy irony, compared her "dainty" rolling pin, "decorated in the delegation's colours of blue and white," to the parliamentary mace, a stylized male weapon used to symbolize authority in the House of Commons. But hers was a distinctly maternal authority, and even though the "housewives brigade" hadn't left "a single stone unturned" in its attempt to "get prices down," some members of the press questioned whether a mere "rolling-pin" could "make a government change its mind."[48]

Their maternalism, which differentiated these Housewives from the male-dominated party, ethnic, and labour left, all of which were being red-baited, demonized, persecuted, and purged, thus embodied its own risks. Although it shielded them, at least temporarily, from the anticommunism that was decimating the mostly male left, like other women elsewhere who use maternalist strategies as cover, the Housewives' invocation of domesticity left them vulnerable to attacks on their credibility as genuine political actors. As the press coverage of the delegation suggests, some papers seized the opportunity to portray women lobbyists as inherently ridiculous. Relishing the spectacle of "motherly" Housewives delivering "the housewifely economic-facts-of-life" to "statesmanlike" Cabinet ministers, several right-wing papers embellished the apparent absurdity of the event, describing "irate Housewives" in "picture hats" and "chic print dresses" who "stormed" at high-ranking government officials. Anxious to escape the women, two of the ministers "made their leaps for life" while Abbott "elbowed his way to freedom" by squeezing by the "ample figure" of Mrs Florence Flowerdale. He then ran down the hall of the East Block to the sound of "100-odd soprano Lou Costellos calling, 'Mr. Abbott! Mr. Abbott!'"[49]

The Housewives' performance of domestic and unthreatening femininity, although caricatured by the press, was both a genuine expression of their identities as wives and mothers and integral to their political activism. Indeed, historian Brian Thorn has recently argued that politically active Western Canadian women in the 1930s and 1940s on both the right and left were motivated by a common belief that, as actual or potential mothers, women had a collective responsibility to protect the world's children. Their quest for a better world was animated by the same belief in women's innate capacity to nurture, even if the future worlds for which they struggled were diametrically different.[50] Similarly, we can look to anarchist women, many of them immigrants, whose commitment to "anarchist motherhood" often made them more militant their male comrades, a reality that, as José Moya tells us, shocked the police, who counted them as more dangerous than the men.⁵¹ Although anarchist women's political principles often led them to reject normative notions of femininity, as Caroline Merithew explains, they perceived no contradiction in framing their revolutionary politics in maternalist terms. In contrast to their male comrades, early twentieth-century American anarchist women defined their politics in relation to their emotional connections to family and community. Like others elsewhere, they perceived their primary contribution to the revolution in terms of "anarchist motherhood," which entailed a commitment to sustaining the revolution by mothering anarchist children.⁵²

Maternalism, as many feminist historians of the left and of social movements have shown, can be both an effective strategy used by disruptive women and a genuine expression of their familial ties and commitments. Protesting women have, moreover, on various occasions used the symbols of domesticity as real weapons, such as the Italian-American mother who, as Jennifer Guglielmo informs us, not only encouraged her garment-worker daughters to organize for the union, but accompanied them on their organizing rounds with a rolling pin tucked under her arm "in case of trouble."⁵³ Temma Kaplan, who has written extensively about women protesters, describes how left-wing Chilean and Spanish women protested the dictatorships in their respective countries by beating pots and pans in demonstrations, emphasizing their femininity and creating "feminine cover" that excused and, indeed, justified their taking to the streets in what would otherwise be condemned as "unwomanly" and possibly dangerous political actions.⁵⁴ They also remind us of the same tactic used by residents in Montreal neighbourhoods during the student protests of Quebec's 2012 "Maple Spring," thus demonstrating the ongoing power of such tactics to audibly affirm community support. Likewise, anarchist women's leadership in rent strikes in early twentieth-century Buenos Aires was sufficiently prominent to inspire the epithet, "the strike of the broom."⁵⁵

At the same time, maternalism can be an unreliable strategy in that women's radical political views can be invoked by their enemies as evidence that invalidates their claims as mothers. Historian Kathleen Kennedy's insightful investigation into the prosecution of U.S. women anti-war activists during World War One illustrates the phenomenon, rarely acknowledged in the historiography but common in practice, of accusations against radical women that elide their political activism and their deviance from accepted gender norms, whereby one becomes de facto evidence of the other. The case of anti-war activist Kate Richards O'Hare is particularly relevant here in that, unlike most of her contemporaries on the left, she adopted a maternalist position and advocated socialist motherhood as an alternative to the patriotic motherhood demanded by the pro-war U.S. state. Her position enraged the judge at her subversion trial, who sentenced her severely, ranking her socialism as more serious than that of her male comrades in that it not only attacked capitalism, but promoted an unnatural subversion of genuine motherhood. Her actions threatened the state itself, he contended, by corrupting citizenship and promoting moral decay.[56] Other women have of course also been vilified as "radicals of the worst sort" by enemies who defined their deviance from, or rejection of, middle-class notions of feminine propriety and motherhood as corroborating evidence of a dangerous and socially deviant radicalism.[57]

Activists who invoke traditional gender dichotomies hope to justify their apparently gender-inappropriate behaviour as an expression of responsible motherhood, but they risk confirming the very gender ascriptions that delegitimize their capacity as political actors. Tarah Brookfield argues, in her study of Canadian women's political activism during the Cold War, that women in Canada's Voice of Women (VOW) justified their campaigns for peace and disarmament in the 1960s in the name of children. Ursula Franklin, VOW's charismatic leader, appealed to women as mothers who, "above everyone else," could understand the need to protect future generations from nuclear warfare, and thus motivated "thousands of women to join the movement." The movement's appeal to maternal responsibility for all the world's children proved effective, Brookfield argues, becoming the enduring face of the Canadian peace movement. But like other activists who used maternalist arguments, VOW's strategically useful appeals to women on emotional grounds invoked traditional gender assumptions that provided fuel to their opponents, who used gendered arguments about women's inherent emotional nature to challenge the plausibility of the movement's scientific evidence.[58]

Yet, despite these hazards, the Housewives' maternalism and appeals to normative domesticity, augmented by careful selection of delegates, were an effective, if temporary, antidote to anticommunist attacks. In many cases, the presence of well-known LPP members and other communists among Housewives delegations went unremarked by the press. As late as June 1947, despite the escalating Cold War, no one complained about the presence of Toronto Housewives' secretary and long-time LPP member Louise Watson among the delegates, or exposed Edith Beveridge as a member of the University of Toronto's

Communist Club and the communist-affiliated Finnish Organization of Canada, or Sinefta Kizema as a member of the pro-communist AUUC, although these facts were known to the RCMP.[59]

The CCF, despite the growing anticommunism among its executive and the particular antagonism towards the Housewives by its Ontario Women's Committee, remained sympathetic to the Housewives and endorsed the delegation, which included several of its own members.[60] That endorsement, and the ongoing participation of CCFers such as Lily Phelps and Rae Luckock, and even briefly of Eileen Tallman, offers a bellwether of the continued protective cover provided by the Housewives' maternalism and their strong and genuine links to their communities. In a June 1947 meeting between CCF MPs and the Housewives, party leader M.J. Coldwell assured them that they had the party's "sympathy and support." MP Stanley Knowles pronounced Abbott's treatment of them "a crying shame," and no doubt referring to their reckless inclusion of communists in their first delegation, urged them to avoid "what had happened" to it. Offered literature on the CCF's price control program, Phelps offered to "give you our literature too," remarking, to a chorus of laughter, that the Housewives had been calling for price control "for a longer time than had the CCF."[61] Others, such as the editorial cartoon captioned "What goes up had better come down!" that depicted a determined Housewife striding purposefully towards Parliament beside piles of "statistics on prices" with the "family budget" in hand, applauded their "business-like" manner and obvious competence, evident in the "50,000 protest postcards" they had mailed to the Prime Minister.[62] Noting that the Housewives enjoyed "a good deal of popular sympathy" and had the "good wishes" of "thousands of ordinary men and women," who believed the Housewives were "on the right side of the issue," others observed that they were "seriously intent on advancing their purpose," and that their "gift for debate" and "unshakeable belief in the justice of their demands" were "potent" weapons.[63]

From their own perspective, the Housewives declared their delegation a resounding success. Ukrainian-Canadian Mrs Paska felt that "something important had happened," and Finnish-Canadian Mary Latva thought that, although the delegation had "no direct results," the Housewives had aroused "great interest." School trustee, city councillor, anti-poverty activist, and self-described left liberal May Birchard, who was also a highly regarded humanitarian and "a fourth-generation Canadian" of "United Empire Loyalist stock," reported that she

4.4 "What Goes Up Had Better Come Down!," *Toronto Daily Star*, 24 June 1947, 6

had "never been on a delegation" that "had made such an impression." "If we got a brush-off," she said, "I don't know what a brush-off means," adding that federal Labour Minister (and former Ontario Premier) Humphrey Mitchell, enlisted to "do the blustering," had been silenced by the excellence of their arguments.[64] "As far as we are concerned," Phelps agreed, "we came out on top in our interview with Mr. Abbott." The delegation, she determined, was a "victory," because it "exposed the complete failure of the government's postwar program to protect the health and welfare of Canadian families" and demonstrated conclusively that the Housewives' "actions and public statements" were "entirely correct." "Acting as "mothers, breadwinners, and citizens" out of concern for "the health and welfare" of their families, she asserted, they had advocated alternatives to the Liberals' reconversion policy that they were sure reflected "the feelings and needs of a great share of the Canadian people," and demanded "bold and decisive action" to halt "rising and unprecedented prices." Refusing to be discouraged by the government's "brush-off," they set about establishing a national organization, the Housewives and Consumers Federation of Canada, electing Phelps as its provisional head.[65]

"Eat Less Abbott"

The Housewives Consumers Association was far from alone in pointing out the government's mishandling of the postwar reconstruction. But their appeals to the well-being of families, especially children, who, they insisted, suffered most from the governments' poor policy choices – arguments that were endorsed by their huge number of supporters – made them particularly troublesome critics. Their criticism of the government was inflamed by the government's business-friendly strategies to deal with the economic crisis. Canadians watched in dismay as prices rose ever upward through the summer and fall of 1947, threatening to surpass those in the U.S., where "frightened" consumers were demanding the restoration of price controls, and veterans had threatened to "throw rocks," rather than sell apples, if inflation led to another depression.[66] By mid-summer, inflation had risen almost ten points in eight months, and prices of essentials such as butter, tea and coffee, meat, eggs, and bread were rising daily.[67] United Church social services secretary Dr J.R. Mutchmore warned that wages were too low for working-class families to "meet the cost of essential food," and a Toronto social worker complained that people on low incomes who had once survived by living "with no frills," including coffee and tea, now regarded "bread, butter and milk" as unaffordable luxuries.[68]

The resulting rising prices, food shortages, and rampant profiteering fuelled what the press described as a "rising tide" of public protest, led by the Housewives, which kept the troublesome question of price control on the order paper in the House of Commons through the winter session.[69] To the embarrassment of the Liberals, the Housewives used Dominion Bureau of Statistics data to show that the average wage-earner was unable to "provide adequately for family needs," and pointed out that welfare agencies were becoming "seriously alarmed" about rising rates of malnutrition. Despite average wage increases of some 10.7 per cent, unchecked inflation pushed up the cost of living, which rose 16.8 per cent, cutting real wages by 6.1 per cent.[70] The CCF, still supporting the Housewives, decried the "lack of planning" by government and the federal policies that gave concessions to the "rich and powerful" while "old age pensioners were eking out a miserable existence" in "slow starvation" and "those in the lower [income] brackets were not earning sufficient to provide themselves with the bare necessities of life." Canadian people, CCF head M.J. Coldwell charged, were "being sacrificed to the discredited ideology of so-called free enterprise."[71]

Support for the Housewives' campaign rose in tandem with inflation, as the 55 per cent of Canadians polled in July who blamed "big profits" for high prices and wanted government to control prices rose to 76 per cent by December.[72] The United Farmers party hinted at a possible farm strike. The CCL's four-point program paralleled the Housewives' demands for price controls, the re-imposition of an excess profits tax, and the removal of new excise taxes on Canadian goods. All of the communist-led unions, as well as the anticommunist Trades and Labour Congress and CCF-led United Steelworkers (USW), warned the Liberals that "allowing prices to spiral" was "asking for trouble." Economics experts, quoted in the press, advised the government that it would be "politically wise" to "find some means of fighting prices."[73] Articulating the moral outrage that animated the unions, the communist-led United Electrical, Radio and Machine Workers (UE) reminded the Prime Minister that prices were rising "at a rate never before matched in Canadian history," and proclaimed that the removal of price controls and subsidies were accelerating the rise of "unprecedented corporation profits." It urged Parliament to "protect the living standards of the Canadian people," pointing out that, as profits rose, average per capita food consumption had "declined 3.5 percent" in one year, and milk consumption fell 4.5 per cent.[74] The Canadian Council of Churches called "record or near-record" high prices of 142 per cent of pre-war levels, a "threat to world peace," and urged the Prime Minister to convene a special session of Parliament to resolve this "urgent matter."[75] In Parliament, CCF leader M.J. Coldwell warned of another Depression and Conservative MPs, who stood firmly in support of "free enterprise," nonetheless voted to extend "rent controls and other wartime measures through the crisis."[76] Rae Luckock, who had succeeded Lily Phelps as HCA president, predicted that, unless controls were restored, "families everywhere will suffer."[77]

Tightening the Canadian Belt

With winter approaching and rising prices of butter, milk, and other basics still front-page news, wage-dependent families had another shock when, in mid-November, the Liberals announced a largely domestic solution to the country's foreign trade crisis. Closely identified with the Finance Minister, Abbott's "austerity program" was the government's response to a critical shortage of U.S dollars, a crippling loan to Britain, and a growing federal deficit created, in part, by an unequal balance of trade with the U.S.[78] Averse to devaluing the Canadian dollar, and committed to a program of economic reconstruction through business expansion, the government opted to reduce its dependence on American dollars by severely restricting U.S. imports, including a long list of fresh fruits and vegetables. At the same time, they imposed 25 per cent taxes on domestic products to create an "exportable surplus" intended to generate U.S. dollars and improve Canada's faltering balance of trade, a strategy that would create hardship for households but would not slow the growth of export-dependent business profits.[79]

Prime Minister King, determined to "tighten the Canadian belt," announced "emergency steps" to contain the crisis, including "sweeping" restrictions that banned imports of food and other goods deemed "not entirely essential" and lower tariffs on exports of Canadian meat, butter, milk, cheese, poultry, eggs, tree fruits, and vegetables to the U.S. Declaring that Canadians had been "living beyond" their means, and assuring them they would not miss "luxury" vegetables such as lettuce if they ate "turnips and beets this winter," Finance Minister Abbott placed temporary price ceilings on canned goods meant to replace the fresh fruits and vegetables that many could no longer obtain or afford. Prices on meat, milk, butter, and other essentials rose precipitously, increasing as much as 150 per cent. Even root vegetables, which Abbott advised consumers to substitute for U.S. imports, were in short supply, with the sole exception of turnips, for which demand was reported to remain "singularly low."[80]

The federal embargo on imports, at the heart of Abbott's "austerity plan," blocked supplies of lower-priced fruit and vegetables from the U.S., causing high food prices and shortages of even domestically produced staples such as butter, meat, carrots, and cabbage.[81] Federal Health Department head Dr L.B. Pett denied that food costs had become onerous, insisting that, as an experiment, he had fed his own family of five (although there were actually only four) for a week on $16.36 and they had "survived." The Housewives derided his figures as "highly improbable."[82] By eliminating "luxuries" such as tea and coffee, the Toronto Welfare Council calculated that a family of four could subsist on $45 a week, although the many who depended on the average weekly wage of $41.25 would have struggled on considerably less. The Housewives disputed even that figure, arguing, along with organized labour, that the official cost-of-living index, developed during the war, significantly underestimated real costs. Complaining that the government had so far failed to establish "an adequate or even desirable Canadian standard of living," the Housewives described the *Toronto Star*'s financial editor, Berland Honderich's proposed minimum budget of $54 as more "realistic."[83]

Housewives branches and HCA-affiliated consumers' councils everywhere organized protests, delegations, and petitions. Two more groups of Housewives, a delegation of twelve in November followed by one of seventy-five in December, joined the many other "austerity delegates" in Ottawa to protest the "Abbott Austerity Plan."[84] Like the rest, including many business people, they left disappointed.[85] In Montreal, watched by members of the RCMP's Red Squad, delegates from fifty-seven organizations to the Housewives' "Roll Back Prices" conference, representing the Montreal Trades and Labour council, the Catholic Syndicate, labour unions, home and school associations, Canadian legions, church and community organizations of teachers, students, social workers, nursery schools, health care workers, and mothers, as well as the pro-communist United Jewish People's Order (UJPO), the Federation of Russian Canadians, and left-wing Ukrainians, agreed that it was hypocritical for the Liberals to oppose price controls to protect consumers while imposing import controls to protect industry. As the Ottawa Consumers Association explained, Canadians "find it difficult to understand" why subsidies for business are good "when subsidies on bread and milk are intolerable."[86] Surely, insisted Montreal Housewives President Ethel Leigh, the government could pass legislation "to protect the health and welfare of Canadian families" in peacetime as it could during the war.[87] Confident that their own expertise rivalled that of government economists, the Housewives cited official government data, including wage and profit rates and the cost-of-living index, to contradict the Liberals' assurances that Canadians were relatively well-off and real prosperity was imminent. They deluged their communities with an impressive array of literature, including press releases, leaflets, and briefs to Royal Commissions, the Cabinet, and other government bodies. On countless occasions, they mobilized dozens, hundreds, and even thousands of members and supporters, often on short notice, in response to a sudden price increase, a change in policy, or a speech by a cabinet minister or other public figure.

Price Control and the CCF

The CCF's endorsement conferred legitimacy on the Housewives, who never hesitated to remind the press and the public of the party's ongoing support. But it also rankled the Liberals, who, like the Conservatives, had been forced to shift their own election platforms to the left as the CCF's popularity with the voters – bolstered by their endorsement of peacetime price control – transformed it from a fringe party into a serious political rival. The CCF, determined to increase its share of the popular vote and desperate to recover from its disastrous loss in the 1945 Ontario election, was running on a platform that included peacetime price controls. Reminding voters that they had advocated price controls since war's end, the CCF's 1948 campaign called for the "re-imposition of price controls on all the basic necessities of life – food, clothing and fuel," renewal of subsidies, and a new tax on excess profits, demands that echoed those of the Housewives.[88] Their support for price control and for the Housewives was entirely consistent with the party's position during these years. Indeed, as historian Ian McKay points out, there was, at this time, little difference between the CCF program for social reform and that of the rest of the left, including the LPP.[89] The party also allied itself publicly with the Housewives, congratulating them on their March of a Million Names campaign and assuring them that, together, the Housewives and the CCF could influence the government on the price issue.[90]

The apparent alliance, even on only one issue, between the CCF and the Housewives exacerbated Liberal anxieties about the CCF as a political threat. The CCF's demands that government take action to control rising prices, tied as they were to those of the very popular Housewives, were a constant reminder that the Liberals had failed to meet popular expectations, fuelled by the government's own wartime promises of a postwar world of general prosperity, full employment, and social and economic security.[91] Mobilized by the Housewives, women and men in communities across the country had expressed their dissatisfaction with the government by sending hundreds of letters and postcards to the Prime Minister demanding government accountability and state control of prices. In these and other ways, they not only reminded people of the Liberals' failures, but they helped to normalize the previously unthinkable possibility of a CCF government. As "non-political" mothers and homemakers who were above politics, moreover, their widely supported campaigns for state control of at least some aspects of the economy and direct democratic participation in policy-making rendered these and other proposals they shared with the CCF, ideas that were often demonized in the popular press, a domesticized and unthreatening socialist alternative.

Labour Allies, Left, Right, and Centre

Labour's support, like that of the CCF, bolstered the Housewives' campaigns, enhanced their credibility, and antagonized the government. Organized labour, as historian Peter McInnis reminds us, figured prominently in the collective struggle over postwar reconstruction and the shaping of the postwar world. It was this struggle that laid the foundation for the labour relations regime that secured the living wages, decent working conditions, and collective bargaining rights that industrial workers and others enjoyed through much of the last half of the twentieth century.[92] But the labour militancy of this period was as much about the relationship between wages and prices as the better-documented struggle for "jobs and justice."[93] Unions of all political stripes joined the Housewives' campaign for peacetime price control, linking rising prices to declining real wages and threatening to use their strike power against the state to punctuate their demands. Hundreds of local and national unions, as well as newly established labour councils and labour centrals, whose members watched their real wages fall while profits soared, collaborated with the Housewives in public meetings, parades, demonstrations, and letter-writing campaigns demanding higher wages, a 10 per cent drop in prices, and higher corporate taxes. Newly powerful unions, constrained by wage ceilings and no-strike pledges during the war, had flexed their muscle in an unprecedented number of strikes and bargained impressive wage gains at war's end, but unionized workers were angered and dismayed by the high prices and rising inflation that all but erased union wins. Fewer than 30 per cent of Canadian workers, moreover, were unionized.[94] And, as the CCL pointed out, only 20 per cent of workers actually got wage increases, and "thousands of girls and men," according to the United Office and Professional Workers union, were earning only 18 dollars a week, at a time when, according to the Toronto United Welfare Council, the minimum needed to support a family of five was $40.[95]

Unionists, newly empowered by the unprecedented achievements of their nationwide strike wave, linked wage demands to high prices and demanded an end to the inflation that eroded their standard of living. Pro- and anticommunist unions across the country, along with their federations and councils, resolved to support the Housewives' buyers' strikes and petitions, organized joint conferences with them on prices, and threatened labour strife if prices were not reduced. In "fighting speeches," they accused labour leaders of being "too law-abiding" and "docile," urged their union brothers and sisters to demand price controls as well as higher wages to offset rising prices, and called repeatedly for, but did not initiate, a nationwide general strike to "fight back" against inflation.[96] Left-led and communist-tolerant unions such as the United Electrical, Radio and Machine Workers (UE), the Shoe and Leather Workers, the United Rubber Workers, the United Packinghouse Workers, the Textile Workers Union of America (TWUA), the United Garment Workers, the International Woodworkers of America (IWA), and the United Auto Workers (UAW) threatened "widespread wage troubles" if prices continued to rise, and centrist labour leaders concurred, warning that if price ceilings were lifted, it would be "difficult to maintain labour peace" despite their well-established "desire to do so."[97] Even the CCF-led, mostly anticommunist unions who were in the process of distancing themselves from the more militant, and thus less "responsible," pro-communist unions by rejecting the strike weapon in favour of a more statesmanlike commitment to negotiating labour peace, vowed militant action on prices. Anticommunist Trades and Labour Congress (TLC) President Murray Cotterell warned that the removal of the government price ceiling on bread and its anticipated increase to 14 cents a loaf would "seriously endanger peaceful industrial labour relations."[98] Similarly, the anticommunist Toronto District Labour Council debated the question of a general strike for higher wages to offset the rising cost of living as "the only way we can keep our purchasing power in line with present prices."[99] In reality, however, unlike their union brothers in the U.S., where the UAW led the campaign against high prices and tied price control and wage demands to the public interest under the slogan "Purchasing Power for Prosperity," Canadian unions took no strike action against the government.[100] More in keeping with the Congress of Canadian Labour's postwar strategy of "statesmanlike" conciliation was its strongly worded argument for state control of prices, which appeared in its annual memoranda to the federal government until 1949.[101] In Canada, it was the Housewives, not the unions, who led women and men across the nation in direct action. Their rotating boycotts, parades, rallies, mass meetings, store pickets, and postcard and petition campaigns kept homemakers and their husbands engaged in active struggle, kept wage-dependent households' struggle with high prices in the news, and kept the political economy of prices in the public debate.

Communists and the Ethnic Left

Just as important to the Housewives were the women of the pro-communist ethnic left, but unlike their labour and CCF allies, who provided a bulwark against anticommunism, the presence of ethnic women, particularly those who were LPPers and members of pro-communist organizations, increased the risk of anticommunist attack. As Franca Iacovetta has so clearly demonstrated, immigrant and ethnically identified communities, and especially immigrant women, were particular targets of the anticommunist institutions and policies of the Canadian state, which endeavoured to "reshape" immigrant lives and consciousness by instilling "Canadian values," the foremost of which was anticommunism.[102] Yet these experienced activists, with their extensive networks and well-honed fund-raising skills, were critical assets to the Housewives. Unlike their Anglo-Celtic sisters, who were careful to emphasize their feminine propriety, women in the Ukrainian, Jewish, Finnish, Russian, Hungarian, Polish, and other groups of the ethnic left drew on traditions of socialist maternalism that expressly rejected bourgeois womanhood and provided alternative models of female identity that justified and encouraged political activism. Left culture, particularly left ethnic culture, valued feminine courage and strength, and women who were part of that milieu were less constrained than others by the postwar era's restrictive constructions of gender normativity.[103] British-born Alice Maigis, a proudly working-class woman of Lithuanian descent who was active in the prices campaign in Toronto, recalled being ridiculed and even spat upon by newer immigrants for picketing her struck workplace and for selling the Communist party newspaper. In an interview many years later, Maigis explained that "working-class women" had "different ideas about respectability than middle-class women. We weren't worried about polishing up and diamond rings." Her friend and comrade Lil Ilomaki, of Finnish and Polish background, echoed her sentiments, recalling that "from the time I was sixteen or seventeen I used to speak on street corners." During the 1930s, Ilomaki and another comrade and Housewife, Becky Lapedes, were arrested and charged with sedition for distributing strike leaflets.[104]

Yet despite their rejection of middle-class constructions of proper womanly decorum, most women on the left accepted gender differences without criticism and perceived their work on the price campaigns, which reflected their concerns as women, as profoundly different from activism that they saw as political. Ilomaki, for instance, explained that she wasn't as interested in "feminine" issues as in "class issues." Similarly, Sudbury Housewife Pat Chytyk distinguished between her activities in the communist-led Mine, Mill and Smelter Workers union, the Mine-Mill women's auxiliary, and the Association of United Ukrainian Canadians (AUUC), and her work in the Housewives, which she saw as "not political," because organizing against high prices was just a natural concern of women.[105] BC Housewives President Mona Morgan, who worked as a union secretary and was active in the women's auxiliary of the communist-led International Woodworkers union (IWA), recalled that most of the Housewives members "weren't political," but "just interested in the prices campaign." Left women like herself, she explained, did their political work outside of the Housewives, which in her own case included the LPP's city and provincial committees, the peace movement, the Spanish Civil War movement, and the Communist party clubs.[106]

Housewife Mary Prokop recalled that the women's branches of her organization, the AUUC, played a critical role in the Housewives. "We sent letters, circulars, asking the [other] women to collect these signatures," which they did "everyplace that we went to. We carried petitions in our purses all along and any time we had a chance to collect a signature. For other things, but for the Housewives, too." They also raised money, "because we had to have money for publicity and for going from one city to another." Ukrainian activists were skilled fundraisers, who, she explained, "always came out for raising one-third of the finances." The AUUC was especially important because of its size and scope, with "over one hundred branches. We had contact with Vancouver, Lethbridge, Calgary, Edmonton, all over Saskatchewan; Manitoba was more around Winnipeg, the suburbs, Ontario, Thunder Bay, Windsor, Hamilton, any number of places." Similarly, in Manitoba, Peggy Chunn recalled that "a number of the women would be from the ethnic groups, the Ukrainian, the Russian, the Polish, they would all be there." In Winnipeg, the two most prominent were the AUUC and the United Jewish People's Order (UJPO). Chunn recalled "a woman from Wellington Crescent, from the UJPO, a tony kind of lady," who she thought, because of her social class, was more likely to be in the B'nai Brith, but who had a Housewives meeting "in her home, a beautiful big home."[107]

Ethnicity carried its own stigma, however. The pervasive xenophobia and nativism of mid-twentieth-century Canada was embedded in state policies and social conventions and, indeed, often went unrecognized until it was challenged by the left. This unconscious, everyday racism translated Eastern European and Jewish identify as a predilection for disunity, totalitarianism, and subversion. Even the Communist party, the majority of whose members were from the so-called "language groups," was wary of acknowledging the role of these ethnic, mostly Eastern European, members, who were regarded by others with suspicion and were thought to undermine the party's appeal to the Anglo-Celtic mainstream. This sidelining occurred within the Housewives as well. Even the Mounties, within whose own organization an identifiable "ethnic" – that is, non-British – identity was regarded as inherently suspicious, noticed that women of the ethnic left, who performed extraordinary service for the Housewives, were rarely part of its public face.

Their certainty of purpose, their political savvy, their organizing skills, and their extensive networks among ethnic organizations and union auxiliaries across the country were integral to the Housewives' success, and most of the non-communist members recognized and appreciated their vital contribution. The non-communist majority of HCA members, fully aware of the political affiliations of their communist sisters, voted them regularly into leadership and, with a few notable exceptions, defended them vigorously when they were attacked. One instance that illustrates this is a statement issued to the press in response to the attack in the *Winnipeg Free Press*, in which Mrs A.E. Martin and Mrs Donna Hunt, non-communist executive members of the Winnipeg Housewives, firmly denied that their association was dominated by the Communist party. "We are fully aware that our president (Mrs Anne Ross) and delegate to Ottawa (Mrs Margaret Chunn) belong to the Labor-Progressive party," they stated. But both were "elected in open meetings and have conducted themselves to the entire satisfaction of us all."[108]

But at the same time, like others on the left, both communists and those who were willing to work with communists, the Housewives also strove to dodge politically lethal accusations that they were a Communist front by minimizing the role of the ethnic organizations. The accusations that the first delegation was "Communist dominated" were based on the presence of known or suspected LPP members such as Peggy (Margaret) Chunn, Sinefta Kizema (whose name also appears in RCMP records as Cynest and Cynefta), Anne Swankey, Audrey Staples, Florence Theodore, Margaret Croy, and Mona Morgan. Henceforth, Housewives chose CCF women who appeared to be Anglo-Celtic as the organization's public face.[109] This practice, which was common among organizations that remained open to communists, obscured both the political affiliations of some of its leading activists and the organization's ethnic diversity. Its diversity, and the extent to which the HCA depended on the largely unrecognized work of women in the ethnic left, was further minimized by the many Housewives who bore Canadianized or Anglicized names. Many Canadians, anxious to avoid the stigma of foreign-ness in a nativist and xenophobic society, altered their non-Anglo-Celtic names, a practice that was perhaps even more common among those who were active on the left. Mary Prokop's husband John was a left-wing labour organizer who had changed his name from Prokopchuk because of state harassment and the strongly anti-immigrant mood of the wider public. Anne Ross, formerly Hannah Glaz, wife of Winnipeg Communist party leader Bill Ross, was a Jewish Russian-Ukrainian immigrant whose husband belonged to the politically active Zuken family. Toronto-based HCA campaign manager Helen Weir, born Kucherian, was a Ukrainian Canadian and an active member of the Association of United Ukrainian Canadians (AUUC). Her husband, John Weir, who came from the Viviurski family of Communists, wrote for several Communist newspapers, and was one of the mostly

Ukrainian-Canadian communists interned during the war. Yet some Housewives, such as Audrey (Staples) Modzir, recovered their ethnic names when their marriages ended, and others, such as Mary Kardash, Pat Chytyk, and Becky Lapedes, were embedded within ethnic communities that, to a large extent, shielded them from stigma.[110]

The presence of such obviously "ethnic" women was an opportunity for their opponents, most specifically the federal government, who traded on the xenophobia of the Anglo-Celtic mainstream, further inflamed by the Cold War, to vilify the Housewives as an un-Canadian, "foreign" organization. That appellation included native-born Canadians of immigrant parents, as well as Jews of any national origin. The Liberal government's provision of start-up funds for the creation, in September 1947, of the Canadian Association of Consumers (CAC), a rival consumer organization that emphasized its "Canadian-ness," was part of the state's attempt to discredit and delegitimize the Housewives. Referencing Cold War anxieties about dangerous and untrustworthy foreigners, the CAC advised consumers who might be "confused by the existence of other groups of housewives or consumers" that theirs was the only organization that had "Canadian" in its name.[111] Trading, as well, on emerging Cold War notions of domestic containment and closer adherence, especially by women, to prescriptively gender-appropriate behaviour, it also presented itself as ladylike and middle-class.[112] In this regard the CAC reflected the coming Cold War consensus that rejected collective struggle in favour of polite negotiation and declined to acknowledge the existence of power relations. Its public persona was also a sharp contrast to the Housewives, who appealed to a great diversity of women, both middle and working class, but whose leaders were mostly working-class women and whose egalitarian proposals had particular relevance for the wives of wage-earners and those living on low incomes. The CAC, by contrast, was led by elite women, the wives of senior government bureaucrats, prominent businessmen and academics, "society ladies" who were active in church and charity work and conservative women's organizations such as the National Council of Women of Canada and the Women's Canadian Club.[113] Its leaders expressed concern about the high price of commodities, but adopted the more refined strategy of politely "asking the government to do all in its power to hold off an increase in essential foods until other prices stabilized," and proposed to "enlighten and train consumers" to become more skillful shoppers.[114] When the *Globe and Mail* announced that the Housewives were "on the warpath" against high prices, CAC President Mrs R.J. Marshall, who also served as president of the National Council of Women of Canada, advised them that a buyers' strike "would be a poor way of going at the problem."[115]

Duped by Reds?

The struggle over the Housewives' campaign for peacetime price control resonated with all the fury and vitriol of the Cold War. Indeed, the attacks on the Housewives embodied the fundamental conflict between the competing postwar visions of the pro-business right and the populist left. The better world for which the Housewives struggled was incompatible with the loyalty, patriotism, and unity that framed their opponents' vision of a domestically contained nation defined by its commitment to a "free market" and national security. Domestic anticommunism was central to that vision.[116] Businessmen representing both large and small enterprises, ranchers, lumber barons, and other commodity producers lobbied government with considerable vigour to accelerate the termination of controls. As their many letters to the Finance Minister, the Prime Minister, and their own MPs reveal, they addressed a business-friendly federal Cabinet, with whom many were on familiar terms and thus able to trade on personal acquaintanceships and invoke patronage in their appeals. Yet despite these considerable advantages, they were profoundly threatened by the Housewives. The all-out attack on the Housewives and their delegations suggests just how much was at stake.

As the anxiety and fear of the Cold War seeped into the collective consciousness, anticommunist accusations became normalized even as they grew more hysterical. This transition from postwar to Cold War redefined the social conditions that had, for more than a decade and to varying degrees, provided fertile ground for the Housewives' campaigns. Unaware that the ground was shifting under them, increasingly outraged by patently false reassurances from the Liberals as inflation rose ever upward, and confident of their wide popular support, the Housewives launched into a new round of activities in winter 1947 as they prepared for their most ambitious campaign, planned for April 1948, the March of a Million Names.

COMITE POUR LA BAISSE DES PRIX
1906, RUE STE-CATHERINE OUEST — WI. 3807 — MONTREAL

APPEL et INVITATION
pour
L'ENVOI D'UNE REQUETE D'UN MILLION DE SIGNATURES ET
D'UNE DELEGATION A OTTAWA
le 16, 17 avril 1948, Little Elgin Theatre

le 25 mars, 1948

Cher ami:

La campagne qui se poursuit à travers tout le pays pour un million de signatures demandant des contrôles sur les prix et leur baisse, et qui a été conduite par les organisations de ménagères et de consommateurs, les unions ouvrières, et leurs auxiliaires, des associations religieuses, de professionnels et de parents, des groupes professionnels, des succursales de la Légion canadienne, et par plusieurs autres organisations, a aussi pour but d'envoyer une délégation à Ottawa le 16 avril prochain.

Avant de rencontrer les représentants du Gouvernement, les délégués se réuniront au Little Elgin Theatre, à Ottawa, pour régler l'organisation de la délégation et la présentation de la pétition. Après l'entrevue avec les représentants du Gouvernement, il y aura une autre réunion dans le but de préparer des projets pour l'avenir.

Nous croyons que l'augmentation exhorbitants des prix, et du coût de la vie en général, a créé une situation intenable pour tous les Canadiens. Nous demandons votre coopération et votre appui pour cette importante délégation. Nous lançons un appel urgent à tous les consommateurs pour qu'ils viennent à Ottawa. Nous demandons encore à toutes les organisations d'élire des délégués et qu'elles paient leurs dépenses.

La Ligue des Consommateurs et des Ménagères propose de tenir un congrès national dans le but d'établir une organisation nationale permanente. Tous les délégués à Ottawa sont invités à prendre par à ce congrès. Un projet d'agenda vous sera envoyé bientôt.

Vos tout dévoués,
LE COMITE EXECUTIF POUR L'ABAISSEMENT DES PRIX

PARRAINS
MAIRE EDWARD WILSON, *Verdun*
MAIRE J. A. LEROUX, *Ville Lasalle*
M. P. VAILLANCOURT, *Dir. régional du C.C.T.*
M. H. LAVERDURE, *Prés. du Con. Central des Synd. Cath.*
M. J. THOMPSON, *Rep. int. des Ouvriers Unis de l'acier de l'A.*
REV. WILLIAM ORR MULLIGAN, *l'Eglise Presby. Melville*
REV. R. G. KATSUNOFF, *de l'Eglise de toutes les Nations*
DR M. F. McCUTCHEON, *First Baptist Church*
M. DAVE ROCHON, *Conseiller de la ville*
M. RENE MICHAUD, *Prés., Conseil Fédéré de Québec et Lévis*
MME S. McALLUM, *Prés. l'Union Int. des Mach., aux. fém.*

LE COMITE EXECUTIF
M. T. PAYNE, *Syndicats nationaux de Montréal*
M. T. GARRETT, *Conseil du travail de Montréal, CCT*
REV. J. WAGLAND, *St. Saviour Mission, N.-D. de G.*
MME H. ORME, *Auxiliaires féminines Côte-St-Paul, Lég. Can.*
M. S. PRESSMAN, *Fairmount Home and School Association*
M. T. HARDIE, *Assoc. prov. des professeurs protestants*
MME M. RICHARDSON, *Ligue des consommateurs de Verdun*
MME ROSE PETCH, *Fédération des consommateurs de Mtl.*
MME ETHEL LEIGH, *Fédération des consommateurs de Mtl. et Comité Pour l'abaissement des prix*
MLLE ALICE BOOMHOUR, *Student Christian Movement*

Appuyé officiellement par:

Des conseils de ville à travers le Canada; le Board of Control de Toronto; la Fédération du Travail de la Colombie Canadienne (FAT et CCT); la Fédération du Travail d'Ontario; les conseils des métiers et du travail d'Edmonton et de Calgary (FAT et CCT) et du Cap Breton (FAT); le Comité conjo'nt des contrôles sur les prix de Winnipeg; le conseil des consommateurs d'Edmonton; le Congrès National de l'Association des Canadiens Ukrainiens; l'union des fermiers d'Alberta; l'Ordre des Juifs Unis,

4.5 "Call and Invitation to the March of Million Names Delegation," Archives of Manitoba, Anne Ross fonds, MHCA Releases, Reports, Activities, [1946–8], P5941/7

4.6 "If This Is Your Letter," *Canadian Tribune*, 24 July 1948, 7

4.7 "Meat Racket," *Canadian Tribune*, 10 June 1948, 1

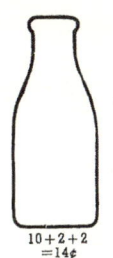

Mrs. HOUSEWIFE
the Price of Milk Must NOT Go *Up!*

10 + 2 + 2 = 14¢

Yesterday we were paying 10 cents a quart.
Today we are paying 12 cents.
Tomorrow we'll be paying 14 cents.....

If You, the Housewife, Do Not Act... *Now!*

- SIGN THE CARD AND MAIL IT TO THE PRIME MINISTER TODAY!
- GET YOUR ORGANIZATION TO SEND A RESOLUTION OF PROTEST.
- JOIN THE HOUSEWIVES' ASSOCIATION—the organization which fights to protect our family living standards.
  Its membership meets every 1st and 3rd Wednesday at 2.30 p.m. in the Y.W.C.A. Membership fee 25 cents a year. For information, call Mrs. H. J. Benson, 1203 Monroe Avenue. Phone 91041.
- ATTEND THE HOUSEWIVES' RALLY at the TECHNICAL SCHOOL on SEPT. 12th.

PUBLIC PROTEST MEETING
TECHNICAL SCHOOL
THURSDAY, SEPTEMBER 12th, at 8 P.M.

Speakers:
Representative of PROVINCIAL GOVERNMENT
Acting Mayor S. A. EARLY
and representatives of local organizations.

"WHEN THE PRICE OF MILK GOES UP THE HEALTH OF OUR CHILDREN GOES DOWN!"

Issued by Saskatoon Housewives' Consumer Association

4.8 "Mrs Housewife, the Price of Milk Must Not Go Up," Archives of Manitoba, Anne Ross fonds, MHCA Releases, Reports, Activities, [1946–8], P5941/6

MY MOMMY AND DADDY WERE TALKING LAST NIGHT

They said I wasn't getting enough vegetables and milk because prices were too high. Daddy was real worried... said I needed lots of good food or I wouldn't be strong and husky.

Mommy was mad and said maybe there were too many bachelors in the government who didn't know what kids needed. She said if a *million people* spoke up the government would *have* to lower prices, then I'd get more to eat and wear. She was pretty mad all right. So am I!

I want to be strong and healthy. I need good food that daddy can afford to buy. I want to grow up to be a big fellow so I can do big jobs and be a good, useful citizen.

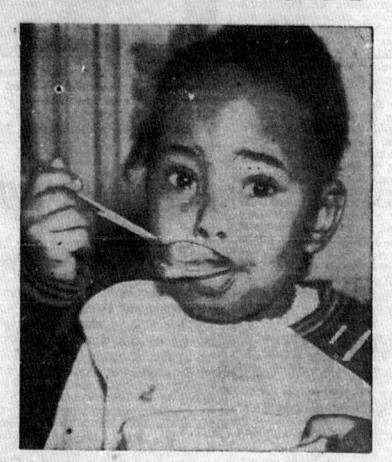

Maybe you've got kids, too, and feel the same way as Mommy and Daddy. They said they were going to sign a petition demanding that the Government "roll back prices."

Maybe you, too, will sign it for me *and your own little guy.*

- - - - - - - (CUT HERE) - (CUT HERE) - - - - - - -

THE "MARCH OF A MILLION NAMES" PETITION

RT. HON. W. L. MACKENZIE KING, Prime Minister of Canada, and Members of the Government of Canada, Ottawa

We, respectfully, petition you to restore price ceilings on essential foods, at the level of January, 1946, and to introduce subsidies where necessary.

NAME	ADDRESS
....	....
....	....
....	....
....	....
....	....

Please get your neighbors to sign and return to the address below for presentation to the Government on April 16th next: HOUSEWIVES' CONSUMER ASSOCIATION, Mrs. Rae Luckock, President, 1 O'Hara Ave., Toronto 3

4.9 "My Mommy and Daddy Were Talking Last Night," *Canadian Tribune*, 10 April 48, 14

Roll back prices, tax excess profits say housewives

Led by the Toronto Housewives Consumer Association and organizations in Montreal, Windsor and other cities, protest petitions are being circulated with the objective of reaching a million names. Toronto housewives at their meeting (ABOVE) undertook to sign up 200,000.

4.10 "Roll Back Prices, Tax Excess Profits, Say Housewives," *Canadian Tribune*, 24 January 1948

THE *Dwindling* STAFF OF LIFE

HOW MUCH BREAD DOES A DOLLAR BUY?

ONE POUND LOAVES
Vancouver

1939 — 13 LOAVES
1947 DEC. — 9⅓ LOAVES

HOW MUCH MILK DOES A DOLLAR BUY?

QUARTS *Vancouver*

1939 — 10 QUARTS
1947 — 6⅔ QUARTS

4.11 "The Dwindling Staff of Life," *The Case of the Dwindling Dollar*, 23, Archives of Manitoba, Anne Ross fonds, MHCA Releases, Reports, Activities, [1946–8], P5941/9

5
Citizen Consumers or Kitchen Communists?

Inflation continued to rise through the winter of 1947–8, despite the Liberals' claims to be managing the crisis. With prices up and wages declining or remaining stagnant, support for the Housewives' demands for peacetime price control and effective government economic management remained strong. Hundreds of thousands of people across the country demonstrated their supported for price control by taking direct action, joining Housewives-led boycotts, attending Housewives-sponsored conferences on the high cost of living and rising prices, and signing the Housewives' postcards and petitions demanding peacetime price control. But the social and economic upheavals of the Depression and wartime and the exuberance of the immediate postwar period, all of which had favoured the Housewives, were giving way to a new social transformation. By 1947, the exaggerated fears evoked by the Cold War were beginning to displace the climate of hope and expectation that had emerged at war's end, foreclosing the public debate that had fostered progressive visions of a more just and egalitarian postwar society.

The Liberals, cognizant of the country's collective shift to the left, were strategically maintaining the appearance of liberal tolerance while authorizing intrusive surveillance by the RCMP and quietly supporting the exposure and purging of communists by non-state actors from workplaces, labour unions, and community organizations, among others. As Reg Whitaker and Gary Marcuse point out in their study of Canada's Cold War, Canada was regarded as a moderate in the international debate between those who argued for extreme measures to combat what they saw as Communism's grave threat to "the security of Western nations," and those who urged restraint, worried about the chilling effect the repression of political ideas would have on political freedoms in liberal democracies. The Liberals were no doubt genuinely concerned to preserve such liberal values, but during the early Cold War years, Whitaker and Marcuse suggest, it was primarily Prime Minister Mackenzie King's "healthy instinct for self-preservation" that underwrote his refusal to revive the illiberal anticommunist laws that had been used to incarcerate communists in the 1930s.[1] Indeed, the slow uptake of popular anticommunism and the emergence of what Dominique Clément identifies as a "revolution" in human rights suggest that the political climate in Canada was not yet tempered by the politics of fear as it was in the U.S. in this era.[2] But tolerance faded with the rise of anticommunism through the latter half of the decade, encouraged by the hardening of the Cold War and expressed in the more openly anticommunist position of the King government. For the Housewives, the shift in government policy played out in spectacular fashion on 15 April 1948, when five hundred Housewives were publicly humiliated, turned away with short notice from a meeting with one of the most powerful members of the federal Cabinet and a long-time Housewives foe, Finance Minister Douglas Abbott.[3]

Anticommunist Attacks

Anticommunism had plagued the Housewives since 1938, contributing to a number of internal ruptures that led to unflattering coverage in the press and intensified police surveillance. In spring 1938, the Port Arthur Housewives Association imploded over the "discovery" that its president, Kate Magnuson, was the wife of Bruce Magnuson, one of the best-known Communist labour organizers in the region and, in an area that depended on the logging industry, a key figure in the struggle to found the left-wing Lumber and Saw Mill Workers union.[4] In September, as we saw in chapter 1, the Toronto Housewives Association – the movement's flagship organization – was riven by the defection of its founder, Mrs Bertha Lamb, who informed the press that Communists were "systematically throttling" the organization's "high principles" by "opposing everything constructive" and "fomenting" discontent. She announced that she was dissolving the organization in order to "prevent communism from taking full charge."[5] Following a brief skirmish between Lamb's faction, which included most of the original executive, and the rest of the members, including several communists, Housewives Vice-President (and LPP member) Hilda Murray advised the press that, contrary to Lamb's accusations, the Housewives was a "non-political and non-sectarian" organization in which there was never "any suggestion whatever of Communistic control." It was still "functioning efficiently" with the majority of its membership intact.[6] A similar scandal erupted in 1940 within the BC Housewives League, when Mrs Mable Norton, the editor of its publication, the *B.C. Consumer*, resigned on the grounds that the organization's executive was "influenced by or friendly to the Communist party." Acting President Mrs H. Ross dismissed the accusation as "too absurd to merit a reply," and urged the public to "judge our organization by its future activities, now that our internal troubles have been solved."[7] Similarly "absurd" claims purporting to "discover" that some of the most prominent Housewives were communists, appeared from time to time in the press, and escalated in tandem with the Cold War.

A Turning Point in the Cold War

Spring 1948 was a turning point for the Housewives, whose ambitious March of a Million Names campaign coincided with some of the pivotal events that escalated the Cold War. The Prague coup, the Marshall Plan, and the Berlin Blockade signalled the hardening of East–West antagonism in Europe. In the U.S., the McCarthy-era "HUAC" trials of the Special House Committee on Un-American Activities – better known as the House Un-American Activities Committee – were well underway.[8] In Canada, the right-wing Union Nationale government of Quebec reactivated its anticommunist Padlock law, which criminalized gatherings and publishing related to the Communist left. The red-baiting articles continued, fuelled by escalating Cold War hyperbole. Typical of these was a January 1948 article in the Hamilton *Spectator* that scoffed at Toronto Housewives President (and long-time CCF member) Rae Luckock's insistence that the association was "non-sectarian and non-partisan." It cited the presence among the delegation of "Comrade Helen Anderson, ex-controller, and Miss Mary Jennison, among others of reddish hue," such as Toronto City Controller Stewart Smith, as clear evidence that the association had a "Red taint." Yet, in a surprising acknowledgment of those same people's skill in organizing popular community protests, it concluded that "the presence of such activists ensured that "the campaign here will be carried out with enthusiasm and determination."[9]

In February, the anticommunist Vancouver *Daily Province* announced that the Housewives were being secretly and, perhaps worse, "skillfully," managed by communist Effie Jones. "Never," the paper intoned, "was the public given a hint" that Jones was a Communist "of long standing." In reality, Vancouverites with even the most passing interest in local politics would have needed no hints, since Jones was a well-known political activist who, among other activities, had more than once run for election, as either a CCF or an LPP candidate. In December 1947, just two months previously, in one of the most publicized elections in years, she had nearly won an upset victory in her run as a candidate for mayor on a platform of lower transit fares. Jones had gathered wide public support for her opposition to the business-dominated Non Partisan Association that controlled city hall in a hotly contested election in which, to distinguish her from her pro-business opponent with the same last name, she was pegged as "Low-Fare Jones." Despite being grossly out-spent by her opponent, Jones garnered 42 per cent of the popular vote.[10] In a similar vein, the *Ottawa Journal* informed readers that the Housewives Consumers Association, like other organizations "with high-sounding names," was in fact a "Communist front." Trapping the "unwary" with "protests against fascism" and false calls for "democracy," the paper warned, was a "famous Communist technique" of the "Hammer and Sickle crowds," such as the Housewives, that were "doing the work of Moscow."[11]

As the Cold War took hold, official and popular tolerance of dissent underwent a profound transformation. In the U.S., McCarthyism was underwriting a new climate of fear and demonizing dissidents – not just Communists but, as Landon R.Y. Storrs demonstrates, also New Deal liberals.[12] As the emerging Cold War consensus among the Western powers legitimated the persecution of dissidents and redefined the suspension of rights as not only fully compatible with democracy, but as essential to preserving it, even King, the most cautious of politicians, adopted a more aggressive stance. By late 1947, the Prime Minister was signalling his government's more explicitly anticommunist policy in speeches that identified Communism as the world's "greatest menace" and boasting of his government's exposure of Communists and other "subversives" in the public service.[13] In March, while denouncing Canada's own Communists as "not loyal Canadians" because their true allegiance was to Moscow, Justice Minister J.L. Ilsley warned the CCF that its left wing, which had consistently supported the Housewives, was suspiciously friendly with communists.[14] Indeed, tracking

Communists had for some time been part of the regular business of Cabinet, with information on the activities of "subversive organizations," including the Housewives, provided through regular briefings to Ilsley by the avowed Cold Warriors in the RCMP's Special Branch. Within the RCMP, red-hunting had become at least as important as pursuing criminals, a priority that reflected the state's heightened emphasis on identifying and extinguishing domestic Communism.[15] Anticommunist hyperbole was increasingly normalized in the press, further exacerbating the collective anxieties that would delegitimize dissent and enable the state to impose repressive "domestic containment" through the coming decade.[16]

The Housewives' ability to deploy legitimizing maternalism to neutralize anticommunist attacks was compromised by their close identification with the LPP and exacerbated by the twists and turns of the Communist International (Comintern) during this period. The temporary non-aggression pact between the U.S.S.R. and Germany from August 1939 until June 1941 and the Comintern's instructions to national Communist leaders to oppose the war effort had cost the LPP considerable popular support, undoing much of the progress it had made among mostly working-class Canadians during the party's Popular Front period (1935–9). The Popular Front had encouraged communists to set aside sectarian and other political differences and work collaboratively with other progressives in the labour, human rights, and social justice movements. As a result of this policy, the party experienced unprecedented popularity.[17] But just as communists were being purged from those movements,[18] the Canadian leadership, on orders from the party's Moscow-based international headquarters, adopted a new "United Front" program intended to reassert Moscow's dominance.[19] The comrades were issued new instructions to align themselves publicly with the U.S.S.R. in matters of foreign policy, a position that was becoming increasingly unpopular in the wake of the February 1948 Czech coup and the general hardening of antagonisms between the West and the East.[20] Although the Housewives, like most others in the broad communist left, ignored those instructions and took no public position on such matters, the national leadership's defence of Stalin's brutal transformation of Europe further alienated potential allies and reinforced the perception that all communists marched alongside Stalin.

The shifting political climate manifested in an increase in red-baiting by the press and other anticommunists who were determined to derail the Housewives' campaigns. In April 1948, just as Housewives and Consumers Associations across the country went into high gear, organizing prices conferences, pickets, parades, and signature drives to promote their forthcoming delegation to Ottawa, the papers reported that police raids on at least two Montreal homes turned up Toronto Housewives' pamphlets and petitions, and a series of articles appeared in the press claiming to expose the Housewives as a Communist front.[21] No doubt timed strategically to appear in the weeks before their well-publicized delegation, these anticommunist attacks helped to shift the political discourse to the right and legitimize attempts to redefine the Housewives as subversives and thus not entitled to rights as citizens. As their nationwide campaign to gather a million signatures on their "Roll Back Prices" petition gained momentum, an article by reporter Don Cameron of the *Windsor Star* claimed to expose the association as a "Communist front." These articles and the many others that followed depicted the Housewives as not merely one of many organizations in which communists were active, but as the very embodiment of the Communist threat to Canada. Described by the paper's editor as the "most complete account ever written of Communists in Canada," Cameron's articles vilified the Housewives as a "red fifth column," a "unit of the invisible army which has enlisted countless women who have no use for Communism but are quite understandably worried about the increasing cost of feeding a family and running a home." Their hundreds of thousands of supporters, he charged, had been "duped" into becoming "unwitting collaborators" in "the violent seizure of Canada's material and human resources to enrich the world's most tyrannical dictatorship." It was their gender, it seemed, that made the Housewives so dangerous. As communists, he suggested, they could not be real housewives; the Housewives' appropriation of terminology that evoked gender-normative femininity was therefore a fraud. Along with their male comrades, he inveighed, such women were "remorseless" in their determination to "devour" the "freedom of everyone who does not obey Communist dogmas." These fraudulent "Housewives," he claimed, had deliberately deceived the Canadian public. Dismissing their decade-long campaign against high prices as a deceptive trick designed to "to stir up trouble" and "spread discontent," he proclaimed that the Housewives "do not care a straw about price control." On the contrary, they were merely exploiting a "genuine public grievance for their own selfish and dangerous ends."[22] Another inflammatory article, provocatively titled "Reds and Housewives," in the June issue of the

Financial Post, by well-known red-baiting journalist Ronald Williams, similarly described them as a "Red Fifth Column" secretly controlled by the Communist party. The Housewives Consumers Association, Williams charged, was not only a Communist group masquerading as consumers, but it embodied a particularly dangerous brand of communism. Like Cameron, he invoked gender as a weapon, pronouncing the Housewives Association the "most effective" such organization "the Reds have had for a long time," precisely because, he implied, as a group of women concerned about high prices and their effect on families it was as familiar and unthreatening as the lady next door.[23]

Cold Warriors Cameron, Williams, and the others whose red-baiting articles followed demonized communists and denigrated as "dupes" anyone else who joined them in expressing legitimate criticism of the state. For such anticommunists, dissenting political views were not just misguided, but dangerous. As they reiterated frequently, the actual number of communists in the Housewives was irrelevant. Indeed, even the prolific red-baiting journalist Ronald Williams, whose evidence of Communist party membership relied heavily on women's husbands' affiliations, described the Housewives groups in Regina, Saskatoon, and Calgary as being dominated by the CCF, and noted that the "Red-led" Edmonton group's delegation included Mrs J. Geddes, "reputedly a [right-wing] Social Crediter."[24] Regardless of how many were actually communists, however, it was their deceptively maternal appearance and their ability to mobilize innocent others in support of dissent that made them such a dangerous security threat. These Cold Warriors did not hesitate to use the Housewives' maternalism, the very quality that had protected them, as a weapon. On the contrary, they implied, the Housewives' gender rendered them a far more devious and dangerous threat to the nation than their male comrades or, indeed, even the Communist party itself. The Housewives' dissenting views, they insisted, not only made their maternalist claims unbelievable, but revealed them as transgressive women who had breached the normative gender boundaries disrupted by the war. Part of their mission, therefore, and, as Elaine Tyler May has argued, that of the Cold War itself, was to shore up those boundaries.[25]

March of a Million Names

The devastating impact these changes would have on the Housewives was not yet apparent on 15 April 1948, when some five hundred

Lead Toronto Housewives delegation to Ottawa —Photo by Helene Wasse

More than 150 delegates will go from Toronto to Ottawa next week to carry the price protest campaign right to Mackenzie King's doorstep. Along with delegates from every part of Canada representing hundreds of organizations of housewives, trade unions, veterans, churches, social workers, students, etc., the national delegation will present the government with a million protests demanding price controls and a rollback of prices to January 1946 levels. Leading the Toronto delegation are: BACK ROW left to right: Mrs. M. Ferguson; Mrs. E. Hahn; Mrs. Rae Luckock, president of the Housewives Consumer Association; and Mrs. S. Hart. FRONT ROW: Mrs. L. Watson and Mrs. A. Binley.

5.1 "Toronto Housewives Delegation to Ottawa," *Canadian Tribune*, 10 April 1948

5.2 "Roll Back Prices," cartoon, *Canadian Tribune*, 17 April 1948, 6

Housewives and their supporters converged on Parliament Hill in a powerful demonstration of Canadians' widespread support for state control of prices.[26] Unaware that the anticommunism they had successfully dodged for over a decade was about to destroy their movement, the Housewives were convinced that the impressive growth of their organization and the strength and diversity of their support had transformed the price movement from "just another campaign" into "a crusade."[27] And indeed, their rally in Ottawa was front-page news across the country. The Housewives brought with them hundreds of petitions demanding the government "roll back" prices.

With 709,573 notarized signatures, which the Housewives and the Communist *Tribune* claimed was the largest petition ever presented to the Prime Minister of Canada,[28] the Million Names campaign was a singular achievement for the Housewives and an indication of the depth of their support in a country of less than thirteen million residents. The delegation confronted legislators with an unambiguous expression of the country's preoccupation with high prices and the popular demand for government controls. The number and diversity of delegates further testified to the broad consensus across the country that the escalating crisis justified state intervention in the economy on a scale similar to its role in managing prices during the war. Such an event, if allowed to go unchallenged, would constitute a major political embarrassment for the Liberals.

Government management of the economy in peacetime was, of course, a socialist policy of long standing, given powerful momentum by the Keynesian challenge to economic orthodoxy that had reshaped economic thought in the 1930s and was continuing to influence policy-makers everywhere. As everyone knew, an experiment with state economic planning was underway in Britain, where the Labour Party had won a landslide victory in 1945 on a platform of state planning, full employment, an enlarged welfare state, nationalized industries, and enhanced equality.[29] Although it was opposed by the conservative British Housewives' League,[30] Canada's Housewives, along with both the CCF and the LPP, advocated a similar program. Absent the stigma that the Cold War would soon attach to such ideas, thousands of people who were not socialists supported it. That support was evident in the composition of the Housewives' delegation, which united middle- and working-class Canadians from virtually every region. The delegates came from towns and cities from Nova Scotia to British Columbia, and included civic officials, members of community and professional

Citizen Consumers or Kitchen Communists? 173

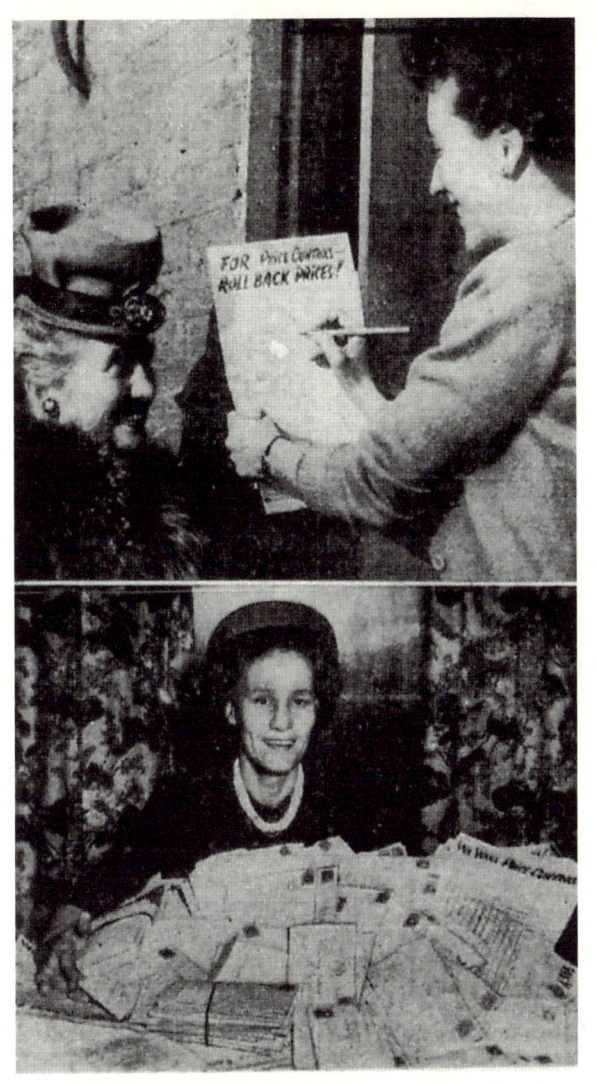

TOP, Mrs. Rae Luckock, president Toronto Housewives Consumer Assoc., gets neighbor's signature to petition. LOWER, some of the many letters she received following broadcast.

—Photos by Helene Wasser

5.3 "Nation Is Aroused," *Canadian Tribune*, 14 February 1948, 1

organizations, labour unions and municipal labour councils, faith organizations, parents' associations, and women's auxiliaries, as well as members of more than forty Housewives and Consumers groups that now spanned the nation.

Confident they had every reason to anticipate continued growth, the delegates had come to Ottawa not only to deliver their petitions and lobby politicians, but also to establish a national association to coordinate the work of affiliated consumer groups and other organizations. As early as 1938, the Housewives had attempted to forge a national federation, but even then some consumer groups that considered themselves part of the same movement had declined to affiliate. During the war years, when the absence of media articles and RCMP surveillance reports suggests that many Housewives Associations, Consumers Leagues, and Homemakers Clubs lapsed, the nascent Housewives federation dissolved. For eleven years, the Toronto Housewives Consumers Association had, to varying degrees, coordinated the network of Housewives' Leagues and consumers groups across the country, held together by women's networks across the labour, ethnic, and party left.[31] But as Toronto HCA President and delegation chair Rae Luckock told the hundreds of delegates to the new organization's founding convention, the Housewives and Consumers Federation of Canada (HCFC) aimed to do more than force down prices. The Housewives were "on the march for freedom," and to be strong, a Housewives-led "peoples' movement" for "more justice and freedom" and greater "opportunity for the people" required "a national association." Such was the plan for the HCFC. In addition to its emphasis on lobbying government and engaging in direct action to bring down the cost of living, the newly formed HCFC would, they agreed, continue to prepare and present briefs to government, investigate prices and standards of consumer goods, and provide reliable information on prices and profits to consumers.[32]

The HCFC may well have been influenced to expand its already broad mandate to include consumer advocacy in matters of product quality and reliability by the emergence of a rival organization, the Canadian Association of Consumers (CAC). Established in April 1947, the CAC was initiated by the conservative National Council of Women of Canada (NCWC) with the financial support of the King government. At least two prominent Housewives, Winnipeg Housewives President Anne Ross and Toronto Housewives President Lily Phelps, were invited to participate in the new organization.[33] But the CAC was created expressly as a non-radical, non-activist alternative to the Housewives. As Joy Parr notes in her comparison of the two groups, "The more Housewives brandishing rolling pins on Parliament Hill became identified with women's concern to roll back prices, the more eager the government grew to encourage and finance the CAC." Indeed, she notes, "The Canadian Association of Consumers owed its government grant partly to its willingness to adopt many government priorities as its own, and partly to the Housewives' political work." While the Housewives led consumers in "class-based struggles to defend workers' living standards," she continues, the CAC "emphasized consensus building based on mutual understanding" between consumers and manufacturers. The CAC thus opposed buyers' strikes and protests. Instead, their mandate was to negotiate on behalf of consumers to influence product standards and bring those shared interests to the attention of regulatory bodies.[34]

Despite their nod to product standardization and accurate labelling, matters of concern to any consumer, the Housewives remained focused on the politics of prices and the impact of government economic policies on working people's standard of living. Indeed, their mandate, broadly similar to those of the CCF and the LPP, encompassed more than consumer rights; it envisioned a more egalitarian society.[35] Delegates pledged to "propose necessary changes" in federal legislation to advance the "health and well-being of the nation," support better social conditions, and ensure more adequate social security. They also endorsed unionization, union wages, and "equal pay for equal work" for women workers.[36] Conference resolutions covered an extensive array of social issues, including long-standing Housewives' demands regarding prices, freight rates, rent controls, and excise, income, and sales taxes, in addition to their more recent call for changes to the cost-of-living index. Some of their other resolutions, such as those calling for publicly funded health insurance, income security for seniors and veterans, civil and women's rights, fair employment practices, and the diversion of atomic energy from military to peaceful uses, were indicative of both their enlarged ambitions as a force to usher in a better world and their close relationship to, and the overlapping memberships of some in, the communist labour, party, and ethnic left.

In recognition of the broader composition of their new federation, the delegates voted, after some debate, that the HCFC would not be solely a women's organization, and elected a number of male union delegates to official positions.[37] In so doing, the Housewives defied the gender implications of their organization's focus on "housewives" and "consumers" by the expedient of announcing that men could be responsible for homes, too. Indeed, as early as 1938 the BC Housewives League had invited men to join, contending that, although, as everyone knew, only (married) women could be housewives, in a province with many single men, "Lots of men are housekeepers just as much as women."[38] Drawing on a version of socialist feminism that called for working-class solidarity, and consistent with the general refusal of the left to prioritize gender differences over those of class, the Housewives asserted that "if we women can work together for higher wages, better working conditions, and a higher standard of living for all," then "surely the men, both leadership and members, can bury their differences that we may in one united effort achieve these aims."[39] These statements and actions of the Housewives bring to mind the socialist feminism described by Johanna Brenner.[40] Indeed, with this small gesture, they suggested an alternative way of "reasoning about the consumer interest" that, as Parr has argued, "was always about the rights and responsibilities of people who were women rather than men."[41] Perhaps informed by the working-class feminism implicit in their radical political vision, they signalled their willingness to reconceive normal gender ascriptions by becoming the only consumer organization of their era that was not solely identified with women. Unfortunately, there is no evidence that their male comrades shared this vision.

Confident that they spoke for a majority of Canadians, the Housewives warned the government that the crisis was far from over. The four-page brief they submitted to the Cabinet detailed an unprecedented rise in the official cost-of-living index to 150.8, an increase, they noted, of 48.6 per cent since the base period of 1935–9 and a startling 17 per cent increase over the past year. Much of the increase, they pointed out, was due to an exceptional rise in the food index, which had risen even higher than the overall average. The Toronto Welfare Council confirmed that a bare subsistence diet – food alone – would cost a family of five $885.96 annually, an increase of 135 per cent since 1939, whereas average total family income was only $1,896. Despite repeated official assurances that the economy was rebounding quickly and Canadians were "enjoying their most prosperous time in memory," living costs, the press agreed, had never been higher.[42] Scoffing at government economists' predictions that prices would find their "natural level," the Housewives pointed to evidence of widespread profiteering and price-fixing, which the government was doing little to control.

Since the elimination of controls, they noted, prices had risen faster than at any time in the past, an increase that the Housewives and their allies in the union movement argued was not, as the business press argued, the result of high wages but the consequence of an "enormous growth in profits," which, they pointed out, had increased an astonishing 302 per cent between 1938 and 1946.[43] Contending that "the present policy of the government is a disastrous one," an "evasion of responsibility" and evidence of its "subservience to the monied interests of this country," they proposed that the state reduce prices immediately "to the January 1946 level" and restore price controls and subsidies on essential items, policies that they proposed be paid for by the re-imposition of the excess profits tax.[44] While the Cabinet was preoccupied with the dampening impact of the Marshall Plan and the dollar crisis on Canada's export trade and the escalating Cold War in Europe, they accused, the real crisis was "here in our Canadian homes." Finance Minister Douglas Abbott "has dared to say that our children and our families should do with less food, less clothing, less medical care, less education, less of the necessities of life," they inveighed. "We are of a different opinion."[45]

Barred from Parliament

Yet despite the obvious validity of their arguments and the widespread support for their demands, and unlike their four previous delegations, all of which had met with members of the Cabinet, this delegation was denied an audience with the finance minister. The prime minister likewise did his best to avoid accepting their petitions. As would soon become clear, their 1948 delegation was a turning point for the Housewives, who had so far managed to evade anticommunist attacks with minimal damage. By 1948, as Whitaker and Marcuse argue, with the support of organizations such as the Canadian Legion and the Chamber of Commerce, and MPs and MPPs from both the mainstream parties, Cold War anticommunism had taken hold across the country.[46] The government that had met with all their previous delegations, pressured by their maternalist credentials and the breadth of their support, now refused to do so. Emboldened by the hyperbolic media campaign that attempted to redefine them publicly as radical political agitators who were not genuinely interested in prices or the well-being of ordinary people, and indeed, were neither loyal Canadians nor genuine housewives, but agents of a hostile foreign power, the Cabinet could safely refuse to see them.

The day before their confrontation with the Cabinet, as the delegates met in conference before dispersing to the Houses of Parliament to lobby MPs, delegation leader and newly elected president of the HCFC Rae Luckock received a letter from the Cabinet secretary stating that the ministers had a "strong impression" that the delegation was "being used for Communist propaganda." Finance Minister Abbott had therefore cancelled their appointment. The next day, using similar anticommunist rhetoric, he explained his decision in the House of Commons. To the approval of all but the CCF members, he justified his rebuke to the delegation on the grounds that the government would no longer receive Housewives' delegations because their "primary purpose" was to "foster communist propaganda."[47] Immediately after receiving the cancellation, Luckock had tracked Abbott to the parliamentary restaurant, where he agreed to "a short interview," but insisted that he was "receiving her only as a private citizen" and not as a "representative of the Housewives Convention." While there, Luckock attempted to give him their brief, but he refused it, suggesting she send it by post to the Clerk of the Privy Council "who would lay it on the Cabinet table." But, he insisted, "he would not read it or touch it." Nor would he accept the petitions, which three Housewives later delivered to the prime minister's residence, where, to underscore the insult, they were directed to the trade entrance.[48]

The Housewives' rally on Parliament Hill was the apex of their ambitious attempt to gather a million signatures on their "roll back prices" petition. Flush with the success of their previous campaigns, they were confident that their large bundle of petitions would provide such compelling evidence of the popular demand for price control that it would shame the government into taking remedial action to halt inflation and freeze prices. But the Liberals were committed to different priorities. Although the government would certainly have framed the issues differently, the Housewives' accusation that it had no interest in containing the "mad hungry profiteers" who had "made millions out of the war" was substantially accurate.[49] The Liberals' postwar economic program, developed by the redoubtable Minister of Supply and Reconstruction C.D. Howe, was predicated on promoting Canadian business as the route to general economic prosperity. Canadians would eventually get the greater economic equality and enhanced social welfare they had been promised, but not immediately and only indirectly as a result of Canada's reconstruction program.[50] Wartime promises of full employment, general prosperity, and a more vibrant democracy would never be fulfilled, although progress towards these objectives would be made in due course. Such reforms were, however, secondary to the corporatist agenda of the pro-business faction of Howe, Abbott, and Ilsley that dominated the Cabinet.[51] Indeed, under Howe's direction, Canada's reconstruction program of low corporate taxes and non-interference by government earned it the approval of *Fortune* magazine, which subsequently dubbed it a "businessman's country."[52] To address their immediate priorities of reducing the federal deficit, improving the balance of trade with the U.S., and attracting more foreign investment, the Liberals reduced the tax on profits, imposed excise duties on exports, revaluated the dollar, and increased federally controlled freight rates, all of which increased prices and led to shortages.[53] Reconstruction was thus pursued in a manner intended to improve the business climate for capital with the understanding that, in the short term, at least, households would suffer.

Demonizing the Housewives enabled the Liberals to pursue these policies, which were naturally unpopular with wage-earners and consumers, unhampered by the broad-based popular movement they led. Redefined as communists and therefore no longer citizens, the massive parade of delegates, stretching for blocks and complete with a pony cart piled high with petitions, was denied entrance to Parliament, the buildings that Anne Ross reminded the other Housewives "belong to Canada's people."[54] To compound their frustration, the Prince of Belgium, a minor dignitary, was "whisked inside" while the Housewives stood outside in the rain, their way blocked by Mounties "arrayed in their scarlet coats."[55] The delegates stood their ground, and after an hour and a half in the "cold and rain," were admitted to the public gallery.[56] But even their well-honed skills in constructing media-friendly public spectacles, which had provided such favourable imagery of motherly housewives in the past, failed to provide the necessary maternalist cover. Papers hostile to the Housewives mocked the "irate" and "bedraggled" delegates – "Communist and non-Communist alike" – and smirked that it was a "bad day for the Housewives."[57] The Communist *Tribune*, by contrast, ran a large photo of Rae Luckock with an armload of petitions, flanked by two bulky Mounties in full dress uniform blocking her access to the House of Commons, under the caption, "How the King Government Received a Delegation of Electors."[58]

Anne Ross later assured her group that although the delegation was discouraged they refused to be silenced, remaining "united as one in

Millions of Canadians want price controls restored, but when they make democratic representations to Mr. King, he meets them at the door with RCMP — as in case of Housewives' delegation.

5.4 "Somebody Is Lying," *Canadian Tribune*, 19 June 1948, 9

our determination to go on fighting against high prices." Delegates underlined the Liberals' inertia on the economic crisis by attending a session of the parliamentary committee to study prices, a toothless body created by the Liberals to silence discussion in the House about prices by the simple expedient of forbidding discussion of the committee's investigation until it was done.[59] At the time the committee was struck in February, Toronto HCA President Rae Luckock insisted that the urgency of the problem called for "action, not talk." She predicted that the inquiry would achieve nothing, but was merely an attempt by the government to "avoid responsibility" rather than taking "immediate action on prices – the number one headache of every Canadian today."[60] Five months of hearings generated front-page news about the "record profits" earned by retailers and the salaries of corporate executives and raised popular expectations, but even in the face of this evidence and the public outrage it generated, the committee recommended increased production as the only solution to rising prices.[61] Housewives, supported by the LPP, ridiculed their conclusion, pointing out that gross national product had increased by over $10 billion in less than nine years without curbing inflation.[62]

Fostering Communism

A number of the delegates were, of course, communists, and by invoking their presence as a valid reason to refuse an audience with the Housewives, Abbott was able to avoid the problems created by the previous delegations, which had asked awkward questions and focused unflattering attention on the disastrous effects on households of the Liberals' reconversion program. His stratagem was an unqualified success.[63] Overnight, the price issue was sidelined by the suddenly more urgent and vexing questions of the Cold War. In the House, CCF leader M.J. Coldwell challenged the government's right to refuse the delegation, but not by pointing out that their political views or party affiliations were irrelevant and insisting that the Housewives be treated like any other Canadian citizens. Instead, no doubt anxious to avoid giving ammunition to those who would, in any case, label him a "fellow traveler," he cautiously observed that not all of "the ladies" were Communists, but were "members of all parties," including, of course, his own CCF. Abbott responded as a liberal Cold Warrior, acknowledging that many of the delegates were not communists, but because the delegation's "primary purpose" was to "foster communist propaganda," he argued, the government was only doing its duty by refusing to "facilitate movements of this kind."[64] The Housewives countered with vocal outrage, insisted that their organization had never "been used for Communistic propaganda," and accused Abbott of using the charge of Communism "as an excuse" to avoid them. Mrs Florence Theodore, president of the Regina Housewives and leader of the Saskatchewan LPP, confirmed that she was an LPP member. But, she explained, "The party has nothing to do with the league," pointing out what would have been obvious in the case of any other party, that not everything communists did was directed by the Communist party. HCFC President Luckcock reminded the government that "as elected representatives," they were responsible for "learning the wishes and desires of all Canadians," and instructed the press that although she was not a Communist, it should not matter if she was. "I'm a democrat," she snapped. "Are you?"[65]

Bolstered by the Finance Minister's refusal to receive them, media that had previously emphasized the matronly femininity of the previous delegation with descriptions of their "chic print dresses" and "picture hats" erupted in polemical debate about Communist subterfuge, the defence of democracy, and the limits of freedom. Right-leaning papers such as the *Ottawa Journal*, the *Halifax Chronicle*, and the *Montreal Gazette* hastily condemned the Housewives, counting it "high time" people "became more wary" of organizations, such as the Housewives, with "high-sounding names." Editors endeavoured to educate their readers about "Communist techniques" designed to "trap the unwary" into "advancing the Communist cause," apparently unconcerned about the general vagueness regarding the nature of the threat they posed but nonetheless confidently identifying the Housewives as "dangerous" and their supporters as otherwise "honest and reliable people" who are "drawn into the Communist net as collaborators."[66] Further tarnishing the Housewives' reputation as respectable mothers and homemakers and employing the standard anticommunist method of assigning guilt by association was the news that "press releases" and "other documents" related to the Housewives were found in a police raid on the office of the Montreal Communist paper *Le Combat*.[67]

Most HCA members were, of course, aware that the organization included communists and, when questioned, defended anti-discriminatory policies as an expression of their organization's commitment to social justice, civil liberties, and democracy. In response to the deluge of attack articles, Toronto HCA President Rae Luckock scolded reporters, who she said "don't tell the truth" about the Housewives. In a reference to the wooden "dummy" doll of the well-known ventriloquist Edgar Bergen, a household name in the 1940s, she accused them of "taking orders from the Charley McCarthys [sic] who are our elected representatives."[68]

Such characterizations, historian Ian McKay argues, have always been used to attack and delegitimize the left. Leftists, those who believe a better world is possible and who organize collectively in an effort to bring that change about, he reminds us, have consistently been dismissed by those who benefit from the prevailing power arrangements as delusional idealists who promote dangerous ideas.[69] They are also, as were the Housewives, vilified as subversives. The Cold Warriors who attacked the Housewives were quite explicit in this regard, seizing upon their efforts to "usher in a new and better world" as self-evidently "the work of Moscow" and evidence that the organization was a Communist front. Housewives' protests against rising prices and calls for democracy, they insisted, cloaked a more "sinister purpose" as evinced by the "serious embarrassment" such activities caused the government. Indeed, in this view, embarrassing the government by pointing out its failings could not be legitimate criticism, but was inevitably intended to undermine the state and was therefore evidence of communism. As delusional idealists, moreover, the *Ottawa Journal*'s editor huffed, they failed to recognize that not only was their collection of over 700,000 signatures "one of the easiest jobs in the world," but it was a "lesson in futility." Economic policy was a matter of "far-reaching difficulties and complications" that was best left to "those who are possessed of all the facts," who are "competent to study them" and who "understand their ramifications," a category that, by implication, did not include women and most certainly excluded the Housewives.[70]

In the face of the anticommunist onslaught against the Housewives, liberal-populist papers such as the *Toronto Star* and the *Ottawa Citizen* defended the Housewives but did so cautiously, questioning whether their demands actually constituted "Communist propaganda" and suggesting, in mild tones, that the government's refusal to see them or recognize their petition might be undemocratic. Editorially, the *Star* poked fun at red-baiters' overly enthusiastic identification of suspicious targets, observing that there were "Plenty of Decoys" to confuse anticommunists. Pointing out that the Housewives were overwhelmingly the "wives of wage-earners and lower-paid 'white-collar' workers," and that their demands reflected the "worries gripping most working-class people about the rising cost of living," its editor, social reformer Joseph E. "Holy Joe" Atkinson, urged the Cabinet to alter its decision, stating that "a million signatures from citizens worried about high prices are not to be ignored!"[71] The *Citizen*'s editor suggested that, even if the Housewives Association was "Communist-led" and its real goal was to "embarrass the government," their call for the re-imposition of price controls and subsidies was nonetheless popular "throughout the country." Invoking the liberal argument that the evisceration of civil liberties in the pursuit of communists would actually foster more radicalism and was thus hindering the anticommunist cause, he argued that the finance minister's action aided the Communists by confirming their claim that the government rode roughshod over the "elementary right of the citizen."[72]

Not only was there no consensus on the exact nature of the threat posed by the Housewives' brand of domestic Communism, but anyone who attempted a more reasoned approach found themselves similarly vilified. An editorial in the liberal *Saturday Night* magazine denounced the Housewives' "protest-against-prices business" as "undoubtedly a Communist racket," but worried that "liberal and progressive thinkers will be frightened out of all such activities by the fact that there are two or three Communists engaged in them," leaving the "nation's affairs to be entirely run by illiberal and unprogressive thinkers." Quite a lot of non-communists, the magazine's editor, B.K. Sandwell, noted, supported the Housewives, including "the research director of the United Welfare Chest" (precursor of the United Way), a United Church deaconess, and the Health League of Canada. But, he concluded, "the most infuriating thing" about the communists was "the excellence" of their causes, and the risk that some would be "delighted" to "mask their illiberalism by calling it anti-Communism."[73]

It was precisely this kind of liberal thinking that red-baiters used to attack liberals and progressives, attacks that fuelled the anticommunism that was sweeping the nation. Indeed, *Saturday Night*'s cautious warning about the risks of anticommunism probably contributed to Sandwell's vilification. Like many other progressive liberals, Sandwell refused to work with communists in the human rights community in which he was active, but that did not save him from being red-baited because of his liberal views.[74] Many others who expressed liberal views were also targeted, not just the entire CCF, but also a number of publishers, lawyers, writers, and politicians, including some conservatives.[75] In this way, red-baiting and fear of being thought "soft" on communism effectively silenced legitimate dissent.⁷⁶ Some, such as Dr J.R. Mutchmore, articulated the liberal argument that unaccountable governments that ignored the popular will contributed to the spread of communism. It was "no use our talking about communism," he informed a gathering of the Canadian Council of Churches, while "high prices" posed the real threat to "world peace." The Council agreed, sending a resolution to Prime Minister King requesting a Parliamentary committee to study the cost of living.⁷⁷ But quiet appeals to reason were hard to hear over the vitriolic rhetoric of red-baiters like Ontario Premier George Drew, who, in an unmistakeable reference to the Housewives, warned all Canadians "to examine all political organizations they are asked to join – all petitions they are asked to sign" for evidence of subversion.⁷⁸

The Housewives had survived anticommunist attacks since 1938, but it was clear that escalating Cold War anticommunism, encouraged by a number of highly regarded public figures, including members of Parliament, had shifted the terrain. Days before the Housewives' delegation arrived on Parliament Hill, the House debated a private members' bill introduced by a back-bench MP, Wilfred LaCroix, modelled on the U.S. anticommunist Smith Act. Like the U.S. legislation, it proposed draconian penalties for even the most casual association with a Communist organization, or even an organization the police had reason to suspect might be communist. Parliamentarians who had rejected the same bill as a "crank" proposal in 1947 were willing to debate it in 1948, even proposing an amendment requiring Communists to register as agents of a foreign power. Both measures failed, and despite the efforts of powerful public figures, including Justice Minister J.L. Ilsley, to have the Labor-Progressive Party (LPP), created in 1943 to replace the banned Communist Party of Canada (CPC), declared an illegal organization, it remained a legal political party. It was evident, however, that tolerance for communists in the House, and indeed the nation, was becoming increasingly risky. Indeed, two years later, Conservative MP George Drew introduced a similar motion in the House, which failed, Whitaker and Marcuse contend, only because of its overly broad scope and because the top ranks of the RCMP opposed banning communists, preferring to "keep them out in the open" where they could watch them.⁷⁹

The Housewives' community credentials, acquired over a decade of local organizing, their maternalism and domesticity, their reputation as respectable, highly competent, civic-minded women, and their obvious distinction from all other organizations of the left, which had insulated them from attack through the late 1930s and early 1940s, became less effective as the Cold War progressed. Labour, human rights, and immigration historians have amply demonstrated how virtually all social movements, including those that were explicitly anticommunist, struggled through the Cold War years to retain their credibility against anticommunist attacks.[80] As Cold War sensibilities crept into mainstream discourse, organizations in which communists were active, and many whose goals were merely endorsed by communists, were demonized as "Communist front" organizations that were accused of being under the "direct control" of the Communist Party. Left-led unions were attacked by anticommunists, including the leaders of the CCF-dominated Congress of Canadian Labour, who expelled the unions that defied their orders to purge communists.[81]

The Housewives' alliances with labour organizations, many of which were left-led, their memberships in left-wing ethnic organizations and the LPP, and the support of those and other organizations on the left made them obvious targets. As a grassroots movement, the Housewives had cultivated alliances with labour organizations across the political spectrum, participated in Labour Day parades, spoken to labour councils and at union conventions, and supported strikes as flying pickets. But their closest ties in the labour movement were with the left-led United Electrical, Radio and Machine Workers (UE) and International Woodworkers (IWA) and their auxiliaries, in which a number of leading Housewives, including open Communists, were active. They had also worked closely with pro-communist, left-led, and communist-tolerant labour councils in Cape Breton, Montreal, Toronto, Port Arthur, and Vancouver, areas where the left was strong. Vancouver Housewives Vice-President Mona Morgan recalled that the women's auxiliary of the IWA, of which she was president, had been "protesting the milk subsidy removal" for "over a year" in spring 1947, when the Saskatchewan Housewives invited them to join the Western delegation. Two hundred women at the IWA's International Women's Day meeting elected Morgan and Marge Croy, both IWA auxiliary officers (and LPP members), as delegates. BC unions and their auxiliaries, most of which were pro-communist, "were all supportive of us," she recalled. "So when it came time to having any kind of a campaign then we would call on the different organizations. They were part of what formed the Housewives." Union women were energetic activists, she remembered. "We'd send a notice to everybody and they'd come …

They packed the halls in meetings." Such women were also skilled fund-raisers, a critical quality in this self-funded organization. Morgan recalled that there were about twenty-five such ethnic organizations in BC, including the Association of United Ukrainian Canadians (AUUC) and the Scandinavian groups, which collectively raised enough money to finance the delegations to Ottawa, including a stop-over for a meeting in Winnipeg.[82]

The ethnic organizations of the left, particularly the AUUC and the United Jewish People's Order (UJPO), were critical to the Housewives' success. Left ethnic newspapers regularly reported on Housewives events and urged their members to support their campaigns, and ethnic organizations offered their halls for Housewives' events. AUUC activist Sinefta Kizema toured AUUC halls through Alberta in May and June 1947 reporting to the members on the Housewives' delegation to Ottawa, closely observed by the RCMP and its informers.[83] But anticommunism exacerbated the existing nativism of Canadian society, which was encouraged by the large number of communists who were members of the so-called language federations that constituted the ethnic organizations of the Communist left. As Franca Iacovetta, Carmela Patrias, and others have noted, the Cold War added legitimacy to discrimination against Eastern European immigrants, Canadian-born people with "foreign" last names, as well as Jews and African Canadians with long tenure in Canada, by reinforcing assumptions that such people were untrustworthy "foreigners" and very likely also dangerous subversives.[84] This was certainly the case with the Mounties, who watched the Housewives, collected articles from the left-wing press, and recorded who attended Housewives meetings and participated in their events. Steve Hewitt argues that the RCMP's culture of racism and xenophobia encouraged agents to regard Eastern European birth, language, or ancestry with suspicion.[85] Larry Hannant argues differently, contending that "during the war," the RCMP adopted a "judicious attitude toward people of foreign extraction," taking pains to "contradict the notion" that had guided earlier police work, that "a foreigner equalled an enemy agent." As of 1941, he writes, for the Mounties, "it was not the alien but the communist who was the country's greatest adversary."[86] Reg Whitaker and Gregory Kealey, in their chapter on wartime internment in the edited collection *Enemies Within*, suggest that the role of the RCMP in targeting "unpopular minorities" has been exaggerated, noting that the interment of German-, Italian- and Japanese-Canadians was "widely applauded at the time by the majority" of

Canadians. Still, they affirm that, "When ethnicity was mixed with left-wing ideology, it was a different story." In the case of "pro-communist Ukrainians, Red Finns, and other ethnic associations of red bent," they state, the Mounties were "implacable."[87] Xenophobic assumptions are clearly evident in their surveillance reports on the Housewives, which treat the presence of so many Eastern European and Jewish women as prima facie evidence of subversion. Agents placed great emphasis on identifying individuals' membership in, or sympathy with, the ethnic left, often by tracking membership in or attendance at such organizations' meetings. One record, for instance, noted that "most of the women who are active workers in the AUUC are interested in, and support, the Housewives Consumers Association," and that twenty-one of the 1948 delegates were members of the AUUC or the association's Workers' Benevolent Association. Another considered it important to note that Mrs A.J. Beveridge, a member of the Communist-affiliated University of Toronto club, was of "Finnish extraction."[88]

Housewives or Communists?

Red-baiting articles cited anonymous Housewives who claimed that Communists "inculcated" others with "Communistic ideals" at their meetings, and that "somehow" the women who were elected "were mainly Communists."[89] But many others, all of whom, in contrast to their critics, were willing to be named, defended their organization's political tolerance. These women acknowledged that, while "members were aware" that some Housewives were communists, they described them as a small if "very vocal element" that "had not always had their way" and "conducted themselves to the satisfaction of us all." Communist and non-communist members alike applauded their organization's principled non-partisan membership policy, insisting that the Housewives included "women from all walks of life," including "some very high Liberals," and that "the political affiliations of the members are their private concern."[90] Others observed presciently that Cold War anticommunism of the sort directed at their organization threatened to silence legitimate dissent. Non-communist Mrs A.C. Latham of Moose Jaw, for instance, complained that "you can't raise your voice in protest about anything anymore without having a charge of Communist levelled at you." Similarly, another non-communist, Toronto Housewife Ann Arland, observed that "anyone who is out to demand something for the working people is branded a Communist," noting with irony that, if the Housewives Association was really dominated by Communists, "then there are a lot of Communists in Canada."[91] Helen Wheaton and Dorothy Walls, representing the Saskatoon Housewives, issued a press release in which they advised the press that it "might better serve the interests of the people by publicizing our fight against depression" rather than "trying to disrupt" Housewives' work with "red herrings."[92] Despite these rebuttals, public denunciation of the Housewives as Communists inflicted considerable damage by undermining their identities as respectable mothers and homemakers, casting doubt on their legitimacy as reluctant political actors, and destabilizing the "maternalist cover" that had made them such a powerful force. This erosion of their protective maternalism was evident in their treatment by the police, who began disrupting their parades, intimidating the participants, and "manhandling" Housewives engaged in support pickets.[93] In their translation from genuine housewives into subversives, they were stripped of not only their maternalism, but also their protective femininity. Like so many other female activists, the Housewives were publicly redefined as protestors, subversives, and Communists and thus not entitled to be treated with respect and deference as women.

Were the Housewives, as their detractors alleged at the time, and as a number of contemporary scholars have accepted, really a "Communist front" organization that took its orders from the party's national leaders, who got theirs, in turn, from Moscow? Was its real objective, as its accusers contended, not state control of prices or more responsive and humane government, but to foment discord and inspire discontent, or as more recent references to them suggest, recruit women to the party? Did communist Housewives covertly direct the organization in accordance with instructions from the party's central committee and the current party line from Moscow? Remote as we are from the hysteria of the Cold War, even the questions now seem absurd, yet surprisingly, the description of the Housewives as Communist-led or a Communist front continues to be accepted uncritically by some scholars of the left.[94]

Like other women's organizations of this era, its commitment to take seriously principles of non-discrimination and welcome women regardless of their political views facilitated anticommunist attacks. The Women's International League for Peace and Freedom (WILPF), Canada's most prominent peace organization before the Second World War, founded with the objective of uniting "women of different political views and philosophical and religious backgrounds," was, as Tarah Brookfield shows, isolated and marginalized during the Cold war by official anticommunism, and its successor, the Voice of Women (VOW), established in 1960, also encountered red-baiting.[95] With few openly communist members, however, such charges appear to have been based more on the VOW's criticisms of Canada's pro-nuclear policy and its own direct action tactics than on political identity. VOW's American counterpart, Women Strike for Peace, similarly refused to ban communists, a principled stand that pitted them against the House Committee on Un-American Activities (HUAC), which, outraged by their defiant stance, called them to testify.[96]

As an organization led by members of the left, the Housewives, like other activists in the social justice movements of the 1930s and 1940s, wanted what Ian McKay, historian of the Canadian left, describes as a "top-to-bottom transformation of Canadian society." But, as McKay argues, such activists were not the "monolithic army of 'steeled militants'" demanded by the Comintern and imagined by anticommunists. Drawing on new evidence from the recently released Comintern papers, as well as his own critical reading of the scholarship, he challenges the characterization of the entire communist left as "subservient to an authoritarian style of politics" and obedient to Moscow. Although most hoped for a social revolution that would overturn the existing order and usher in a people's democracy, he argues, their immediate goals were more reformist than revolutionary. Moreover, the party leadership, based in Toronto, had "neither the will nor the capacity" to control this relatively small, mostly grassroots movement, "spread out across a vast land-mass" and "encompassing discrete language federations," only a "minority of whom were in a given year officially party members." Rather than a tightly disciplined "monolith," he suggests, the communist left was a "diversity of communisms, a movement of movements," a "variegated and diffuse *cohort*," that "headquarters struggled, with very uneven success, to homogenize and discipline."[97] There is some debate about the adherence of the party's leadership to Moscow's dictates, however. John Manley, an important scholar of this movement, argues that the Canadian party was consistently subservient to Moscow's rules, not only during the Party's insular United Front period (1928–35), but also during its more open Popular Front period (1935–39). Others, he acknowledges, disagree.[98] Yet the accumulated evidence suggests that, regardless of compliance by party leaders, this was not the case for the broad communist left.

At the heart of the Canadian state's embrace of the Cold War was the RCMP's Special Branch, whose sole function was to monitor domestic

Communists. The promotion of John Leopold to Superintendent in 1948 signalled the heightened priority the state assigned to locating, exposing, and containing Communists. Leopold, the RCMP's chief expert on Communists and an ardent anticommunist, was an expert at infiltrating and providing extensive intelligence from the very core of the Communist party. It is instructive, Hewitt notes, that those skills had become sufficiently valuable to the Mounties that they overcame his Eastern European and Jewish ethnicity and short physical stature, qualities that would normally have disqualified him from holding any regular position on the force.[99] Leopold, along with Superintendents Mortimer, McClellan, and Zaneth, uniformly convinced that the Communist party controlled the Housewives, charged their agents repeatedly to find corroborating evidence. Yet despite their extensive surveillance of the Housewives, the Mounties found no proof that it was "merely a front organization" of the Party.[100]

The Housewives themselves regarded charges of "Communist domination" as a red herring. Toronto Housewife and life-long Communist Mary Prokop, an active member of the AUUC, recalled that, "in comparison with the rest of the [non-Communist] women, we were just a few." Communists, she believed, "had the know-how to carry on such activities. That was why the other women who were with us were not afraid of us even though in the media they tried to intimidate them." Both communist and non-communist Housewives struggled towards the same goals: "They could see that we were fighting for milk for the children, for cheaper bread, for lower rents. And later on, for pensions for women at fifty-five. All these things, they affected them, those were their demands. That's what we were fighting for."[101] Non-communist Housewives concurred, asserting that they elected known LPP members "at open meetings," as "housewives, not as Labor-progressives."[102] RCMP surveillance files confirmed that "allegations" of communist domination of the Housewives "published in the news have made little difference in the recent elections to HCA office, and if anything, more radicals were elected."[103]

Housewives and the Labor-Progressive Party

The Housewives' critics correctly identified the Labor-Progressive Party as one of their closest allies, but the relationship between the HCA and the LPP cannot be reduced to simple Communist Party domination. Both the CCF and the LPP lobbied for postwar price control, but unlike its social democratic counterpart, the LPP encouraged its members to join, support, and lead the Housewives. Indeed, Communist party women's protests over high prices predated those of the Housewives and reports of their delegations to Toronto city council may well have inspired Bertha Lamb to organize consumers in a more widely acceptable, non-politically affiliated movement. The party's Women's Progressive Associations had called for state control of prices during the 1930s, years before both the CCF's and the Housewives' campaigns. Through the last years of the Depression, the Communist *Daily Clarion* maintained a steady flow of articles celebrating the Housewives' campaigns and detailing the shady practices, high profits, and exorbitant executive salaries of the firms that were charging such high food prices. Officially banned in 1940 and with most of its leaders underground, the party was quiescent during the war years. But it was reinvigorated as the Labor-Progressive Party (LPP) in the immediate postwar period and became especially active in local politics, including the price campaign. LPP city councillors Stuart Smith and Dewar Ferguson in Toronto and Peggy Chunn in Winnipeg were elected, at least in part, on milk price platforms and, while in office, fought for public inquiries into milk price, public control of milk delivery, free milk for school children, and consumer representation on milk boards. Communist Housewives also ran for political office in campaigns that gave them a public platform to promote the price movement, even if they rarely won seats. Perhaps the most tenacious was Vancouver Housewives League founder Effie Jones, whose campaigns spanned some two decades, but others, such as Elizabeth Wilson and Jean Mason in BC, Saskatchewan LPP head and Housewives' President Florence Theodore, and Montrealer Gertrude P. Partridge, also campaigned on milk price platforms. Housewife Peggy Chunn was elected to the Winnipeg school board in 1947 and at least four Housewives ran as candidates in the 1946 Toronto civic elections, including Elizabeth Morton, who also ran in a federal by-election in Toronto's Parkdale riding on a platform denouncing illegally and unjustly high milk prices and promising "a free glass of milk for every school child every day" and an expanded, state-funded day care program.[104]

The LPP's enthusiastic support and the presence of well-known communists among the Housewives' leadership, together with the party leaders' unfortunate and misguided attempts to control popular front alliances, led inevitably to charges that the Housewives Association was no more than a "front" organization of the LPP. Many historians of the left accept this view, but a more careful consideration, together with new evidence, reveals a more complex relationship between the Housewives and the Communist party.[105] To be sure, Communists were active in the price campaign and, as in virtually all their social justice work, were more influential than their numbers alone would suggest. Even so, Party leaders often complained that the comrades in these "mass organizations" failed to lead those struggles or use them to build the party. Leaders considered work in the trade union movement and the Housewives as the most successful of the party's efforts to engage women in party work, and were encouraged by its apparent success in the Housewives.[106] The party's Director of Women's Work – an elected position occupied at different times during this period by Alice Cooke, Elizabeth Morton, and Louise Watson – was always active in the Housewives, reported on the HCA's activities at party conferences, instructed party women to join the organization, urged the party to lead the campaign, and probably conferred with the national executive about the LPP's role in the HCA on a regular basis.[107] Some provincial branches also reported to the comrades on the Housewives, as did Florence Theodore at the 1948 Saskatchewan convention, where she commended the "splendid work of the housewives' associations," in which "our party women played a leading part," and applauded the "keener appreciation" they had developed of the "leadership they must give to these movements." Yet her comments seem more aspirational than descriptive, since the same panel advised that "a greater number of our members" must participate in, and do more recruiting from, the Housewives.[108] Assertions about the importance within the party of the price campaign were also contradicted by its inclusion in "work among women," which the comrades regarded as less important than other party activities and where the emphasis was on waged workers, who were perceived to be more accessible to class consciousness.[109]

Party men rarely took an interest in any aspect of women's work, and prices, and therefore the price campaign, were regarded as primarily women's concern. As Manitoba Housewife Ann Ross complained, "many claim to be too busy" to participate in the prices campaign and it was even "hard to interest party women to get more active."[110] The party's efforts to recruit women were chronically disappointing, and men always far outnumbered women in the party. Although leaders repeatedly instructed the comrades that "special attention must be given to recruiting women," they acknowledged that "very little leadership is given to the women's work." When the party initiated such efforts, it frequently "let them drop." The male comrades don't "look upon work among women as a Party task," while women members fail to regard it as "their main task."[111] Minutes of Communist party conventions, although incomplete in the archives, reveal a constant struggle by the leadership to encourage "work among women," which included urging their members to join the Housewives. Two of the longest-serving women members of the party's national executive, Annie Buller and Becky Buhay, claimed to have worked on the price campaign, but their participation appears to have been nominal, and they are not linked to the Housewives by the press or in police surveillance reports. Member of Parliament Dorise Nielsen, a Communist elected as a United Progressive in 1940, provided more concrete support to the Housewives. As her biographer, Faith Johnston, recounts, Nielsen was active in efforts to engage women in left causes. She spoke at a number of Housewives groups when she toured the Western provinces in 1947, and urged women to join the prices campaign and sign the Housewives' petitions.[112] Buhay's twenty-two page pamphlet, *Woman and the Fight for Peace and Socialism*, devoted only one page to the "Position of Housewife: The Fight against Profiteering and for Peace," and referred only in passing to the struggle against "inflationary prices."[113] As late as 1948, provincial LPP resolutions on "work among women" enjoined party faithful to "conduct a fight on the question of prices," through "special assignment of tasks to your women party comrades."[114] Into the 1950s, national leader Tim Buck acknowledged that the party's "worst weakness" was "that we do not give our party women a role in the party."[115]

Party leaders often lamented how difficult it was to interest party women in the Housewives. Annual reports of party work in the HCA indicate that the leaders exhorted the women members to join the Housewives, support their campaigns, and "take leadership in any way possible."[116] But little came of it. Anne Ross, wife of Manitoba Party leader Bill Ross but, she insisted, not a party member herself, complained that it was "hard to interest party women to get more active" in the Housewives. The party's failure to attract more comrades to the Housewives may have helped rather than hurt them. Housewives organizations in which LPP women dominated appear to have been least successful. This was the case of the Halifax Housewives League, which, according to RCMP surveillance reports, was almost entirely made up of party women. Surveillance revealed that a group of eight LPP women organized the league at a meeting on 19 May 1947, at which sixty-nine women were present. A meeting of the LPP "Annie Buller Club" in June records Mrs Ethel Meade, education director of the Halifax Housewives League, lamenting that "there were not enough outside people working in" the League. But she advised the party women that they "would just have to go ahead and do as good a job as [they] each could do."[117]

As scholars of the left point out, party leaders fought a losing battle trying to persuade the comrades to recruit from within the various social justice organizations in which they were active.[118] The party members in the Housewives were no exception, being, like members of other such community organizations, more interested in their immediate campaigns for reform than in building the revolutionary capacity of the party. Most Communist women, moreover, regarded their activity in the Housewives as quite distinct from their party work, as something "of concern to women," and thus not genuinely political. This failure may have been due, in part, to the party's conflicting admonitions to its members, urging them, on the one hand, to support the Housewives, while on the other hand attempting to lead them by advocating "stronger action to bring the trade union movement into the prices campaign" and "more independent activity by our Party on the prices issue."[119]

The Housewives, who refused to affiliate with any organization, accepted the Party's support but, far from taking direction, rarely even accepted its advice. Articles in the Communist press by members of the party's Women's Committee and others regularly urged Canadians to "get up on their hind legs and demand higher wages and lower prices," and suggested that "a little unrefined language may help."[120] Similarly, Party leaders regularly urged "all women Party members" to "join the HCA and assist by giving leadership," suggesting that they present briefs to the various councils, ask MPs and MPPs to sign the petitions, and embarrass any who refused to sign by issuing press releases.[121] But the Housewives, perhaps in part because they were conscious that their popularity depended on their maternalism, their good reputation as civic-minded women, and their diverse appeal, preferred to present themselves as well-behaved women and stringently avoided the aggressive tactics and hortatory language advocated by the Party.

Far more important to the HCA than the support of the male left was the work of women in the ethnic and labour left. Housewives associations tended to organize and flourish in cities that had a significant

Communist presence, and communist Housewives, with their well-honed organizing skills, nationwide networks of like-minded women, and activist orientation, influenced the association's strategy and tactics disproportionately to their numbers. The ethnic organizations themselves had complicated relationships with the Party, and certainly not all members of these organizations or members of left-led unions or auxiliaries were Party members. Those who were tended to be quite open about their political affiliations. Housewives such as Florence Theodore, Louise Watson, Alice Buck, Josephine Gehl, Peggy Chunn, Elizabeth Morton, Helen Weir, and Mary Kardash, who served on provincial LPP executives or ran for local office as LPP candidates, certainly made no attempt to hide their party membership. Mary Prokop, a Toronto-based Housewife, AUUC activist, and life-long Communist, thought calling the Housewives a "Communist front organization" was "just stupid." In any social justice organization, she scoffed, "if they happen to see a few Communists here and there, they immediately label the whole organization as Communist." In any case, she recalled, there were "were just a few" Communists in the organization.[122]

Demonized as Reds

Housewives continued to campaign against high prices through the end of the decade and into the 1950s. Following their disappointing encounter with Finance Minister Abbott, six housewives applied for an investigation of the six big bread companies for alleged price-fixing. BC Housewives who, they reminded consumers, had "gone around with petitions, written letters to our MPs, and argued with our storekeepers" for months, called a two-day, province-wide meat boycott with the support of the Vancouver Labor Council.[123] In the ensuing months, Toronto Housewives organized the unemployed, protested the high price of meat, and lobbied governments to reinstitute the milk subsidy. They denounced peacetime profiteering, called for free milk for school children, and organized delegations to Toronto city council to demand affordable meat, milk, butter, and margarine; they protested high telephone rates and demanded that wartime day nurseries be retained in peacetime. With the support of their ally, MP Dorise Nielsen, the first Communist elected to federal Parliament, Housewives linked calls for lower prices to demands for peace, joining with other left women in the emerging peace movement.[124]

But the damage was irreparable. The stigma of communism frightened Housewives' allies in women's, community, and faith organizations, most of whom dropped their support. The RCMP reported that a Sunday school teacher who had been part of the April 1948 delegation told the press that she was "profoundly shocked at being classed with Reds," and "admitted she did not know how she could go back to face her class."[125] The Canadian Association of Consumers seized the opportunity to distance itself from the Housewives with a statement to the press emphasizing their own nationalist credentials, stressing that it had "no connection with any other group which did not carry the designation 'Canadian' in its name." Its invitation to appear before the Liberals' Price Committee, it stated, confirmed that it alone was "competent to speak for consumers generally," ignoring the possibility that its invitation may have been prompted by its Liberal origins. Lest there be any remaining confusion, it denied any connection to "groups which term themselves roll back the prices groups," and which "advocate the reimposition of subsidies and price controls."[126] The annual convention of the Catholic Women's League resolved to petition the federal government to retain price control and restore the work of the Consumers Branch, proposals advanced by the Housewives. But based on hearing reports that "some leaders of the Housewives Consumers League were communists," they warned members explicitly against supporting the HCA.[127] In March 1949, Toronto Housewives held a public meeting on the housing crisis, supported by the Toronto District Labour Council, the Building Trades Council, and the left-led United Electrical, Radio and Machine Workers union. They called for a government housing program and formed a tenants' association to "deal with tenants' problems." But in contrast to their earlier events, the mayor and several city councillors who had been expected did not attend. Days later, the Toronto Labour Council, a Housewives' ally since 1938, voted to end its affiliation on the grounds that the Housewives were a "Communist organization."[128] In April 1949, yet another article by Ronald Williams vilifying the Housewives, posing the provocative question, "Are you a Stooge for a Communist?" appeared in *Chatelaine*, Canada's premier women's magazine.[129] In late 1950, the Housewives signalled their resignation to the new reality of the Cold War by helping to found a new organization, the Congress of Canadian Women, a women's group that included a number of CCF women, such as Rae Luckock, who were long-term Housewives, but was, unlike the HCA, little more than the women's wing of the LPP.[130]

6
"Reds," Housewives, and the Cold War

In 1954, former Housewife and Labor-Progressive Party member Frances Sim contacted the Halifax RCMP. A sole-support mother recently divorced from her husband – a life-long communist who had grown up in the party – Sim planned to change her name and make a new life for herself and her two children in Vancouver, far away from her ex-husband and the left community of which she had been a part. According to the RCMP's report on the incident, by taking such extreme measures, she hoped to escape the "stigma attached to her name." Awarded sole custody of the children, but with support of only $50 a month, she had sought paid work, but discovered that she was disqualified for a government job or one in a private-sector aviation firm by her inability to obtain the required security clearance. Throwing herself on the mercy of the RCMP, she begged them to lift the restrictions that excluded her from jobs. She assured the two agents who interviewed her in her sister's home that she had become active in the church, renounced her former associates, and had no intention of renewing her contact with anyone associated with the left. The Mounties confirmed the details of her divorce, and noted that she had "attended only a few meetings" of the LPP-led Halifax Housewives and Consumers Association. She had also had no contact with "any left-wing group or organization" for almost five years. They record with apparent approval that Sim was "very bitter towards" the left, which she blamed for her current difficulties and those of her brother and brother-in-law, both of whom had been denied promotions because of her and her husband's past. Yet there is no indication that they granted her request. Rather, they advised her that "the only way to prove" her good intentions was "in the manner in which she conducted her future life" and, in particular, the "organizations to which she might become connected with [sic]." Nothing in the report suggests that Sim might be considered a genuine threat to national security, and indeed, it concludes with the agents' assessment that she "will live up to her remarks in her new surroundings." Nonetheless, they arranged to forward her file to the RCMP's Vancouver division, thus ensuring that the past she had taken such pains to renounce would follow her into her new life.[1]

As Sim's case illuminates, the RCMP, the principal organization of the Canadian state's security apparatus, used their power to define subversion and conduct surveillance of those identified as threats to domestic security, not only to protect Canadians, but to suppress dissent. For criticizing and embarrassing the government, the Housewives, like other organizations of the left, were defined as subversives and subjected to invasive police surveillance, state policy that encouraged and supported the anticommunists who red-baited and demonized them in the media and the community. Some shrugged this off, but others suffered the damaging and sometimes life-altering consequences of anticommunist persecution, punishment that was meted out not only to genuine and suspected communists, but also to those thought to be too friendly with communists. Individual Housewives were named and described derogatively as "reds" in the press, and the organization was accused publicly, by prominent politicians, business people, and others in positions of authority, of insincerity, deceit, and of being a "Communist front" rather than a genuine consumers' organization. As the Cold War escalated, so too did the red-baiting. By the end of 1948, the demonization of Housewives, and their supporters' fears of being similarly stigmatized, had driven most non-communists out of the movement. Housewife and life-long communist Mary Prokop, who saw this at work, expressed no rancour towards the many members and supporters who abandoned the Housewives Association and the movement they led during this difficult time. "Don't forget," she explained, "there was intimidation at work. If you support the Communists, you don't get the job."[2] Reduced to a small cadre of mostly party members and left-wing CCFers, along with a small number of others who likewise refused to be intimidated, and widely discredited as a "Communist front," the Housewives lost its legitimacy and ceased to be the kind of broad-based grassroots movement that was capable of influencing politicians and forcing them to revise policies in the interests of ordinary Canadians.

Cold War anticommunism continues to be debated, at least among scholars, some of whom contend that the Western democracies' wholesale suppression of civil liberties was justified by the genuine threat posed by the U.S.S.R.[3] Others argue that the "red scare" was deliberately exaggerated by business and political elites who used the threat of a communist takeover to "scare the hell" out of people, particularly those who were vocal critics of state policies.[4] Whitaker and Marcuse, for instance, argue that powerful social conservatives used this extremist position to subdue popular resistance to the right's consolidation of power by tarring dissenters "with the brush of illegitimacy" by convicting them in the court of public opinion (although never in any real court) of "disloyalty, subversion, [and] connections to an external enemy."[5] Ellen Schrecker, writing about the U.S., observes that, while the Communist Party of the USA (CPUSA)'s ability to mobilize workers and others in support of progressive social change infuriated the right and thus made it a target, the comrades did, in fact, regard themselves as members of a revolutionary party whose stated objective was to challenge and eventually overthrow the capitalist state. Although there is no evidence that Communists ever represented a serious security threat, she argues, Communists' principled commitment to a Soviet-led conspiracy, and their own rigid adherence to the Moscow "line," provided ammunition to their enemies.[6] Much the same argument could be made about the Communist party in Canada, which similarly aspired to proletarian revolution, although the effect of the Cold War in the U.S. was ultimately more devastating to leftists and liberals.[7] It was the Cold War culture of fear, inflamed by hyperbolic anticommunism, that enabled the governments of the Western powers to renege on their wartime promises of a peace dividend of security, prosperity, and a more pervasive democracy.[8] It also enabled the Housewives' enemies to destroy the nationwide movement that had taken them years to organize and that, by the beginning of 1948, had seemed ready to become a permanent, national consumers' organization.

Police Surveillance

Information provided by the Mounties was critical to the process of demonizing, and thus silencing, the Housewives. RCMP Commissioner S.T. Wood kept the Minister of Justice and other Cabinet ministers up to date about the Housewives' activities, affiliations, and identities, including the information that their 1947 delegation was led by

Mrs Florence Theodore, "a well-known Communist," and that Communists were among the April 1948 delegation, details that Finance Minister Abbott used to justify turning them away.[9] But the Mounties also appear to have shared information about suspected "subversives" with other elected members, determined Cold Warriors who claimed to have had close contact with the security service and access to classified information. MPs shared this information publicly, and by this subterfuge, information gathered covertly by the Mounties and designated as "top secret" was released to the press.

H.A. Bruce and John Diefenbaker were two of the MPs who revealed secret information that helped demonize the Housewives. Dr Herbert (H.A.) Bruce was a Conservative MP who represented Toronto's Parkdale riding from 1940 to 1946, a former Army Medical Corps surgeon, Lieutenant Governor of Ontario (1932–7), and a dedicated Cold Warrior.[10] In June 1940, Bruce wrote to Commissioner Wood, the RCMP's top-ranking officer, with a list of "subversive organizations" that included the Housewives Association, a group, he advised, that "should be carefully watched." In addition to advising the police, Bruce, like several other MPs, seemed to have had privileged access to secret police information. Citing "police authorities" and "information received" – a term typically used to identify information from informers – he announced in the House of Commons that the Housewives Association was one of nineteen subversive organizations that were under police surveillance and was "definitely controlled by the Communist Party of Canada." Based on this information, he advised federal Justice Minister Ernest Lapointe that Canada's ability to "take action" to "safeguard the country against subversion" was woefully inadequate.[11] Not only did Bruce have a reciprocal relationship with the RCMP, but his access to information seems to have been better than Justice Minister Lapointe's. The Deputy Minister's letter to the RCMP, copied in the archives, suggests that Lapointe responded to these accusations by contacting the RCMP immediately to request more detail.[12]

Eight years later, another Conservative MP and future Prime Minister, John Diefenbaker, drew an implicit link between ethnically identified "foreigners" and dangerous communists when he announced to the House that "mounted policeman after mounted policeman" had told him that Communists were using threats against relatives in their "home countries" to extort contributions from members of their own ethnic groups. "The mounted police did not fail us during the war," Diefenbaker told the MPs. "They had complete lists of those who would have undermined the state and they are not failing us today, operating, as they have in the past, as a silent force." Diefenbaker advised the police be given added powers that would allow them to "tell the country" about the imminent dangers they all faced. But he also extolled the Mounties' covert methods, operating as a "silent force" compiling "complete lists" of those involved in activities that exposed the failings of the state.[13] Diefenbaker may well have been referring to the RCMP program code-named "operation PROFUNC."[14] This was a vast system of surveillance and the creation of security files on an estimated 800,000 individuals and organizations that would be used to intern hundreds of thousands of Canadians in the event of an actual national emergency. Such methods were also used to persecute the Housewives. Such "extraordinary peacetime political policing," which, as Reg Whitaker and Greg Kealey observe, included the surveillance of a large number of Canadians, none of whom had committed any crime, was justified by the exaggerated threat of Communism.[15]

The Mounties were not just the instruments of the state's security program; RCMP top brass were key participants in its development and of course in identifying individuals and groups, such as the Housewives, as threats to security. Assisted by informers, the RCMP maintained close surveillance of the Housewives, and their detailed reports fill tens of thousands of files, records that informed the actions of the federal Cabinet, which was eager to eliminate the irritant that the Housewives had become. RCMP agents and informers watched the Housewives, attended their meetings, collected their literature, and gathered articles about them from the mainstream, Communist, and left ethnic press. But despite persistent effort, including cross-checking names and events across the wide spectrum of left organizations designated within the security service as subversive, the Mounties were unable to find proof that the Housewives were controlled by the Communist party. One revealing memo from the noted RCMP red-hunter Inspector K. Shakespeare, for instance, confirmed that police efforts to determine "whether the LPP is providing copying services for *The Housewives News*" had produced no such proof. Yet the Mounties remained convinced that the Communist party was "publishing literature" for the organizations, like the Housewives, that they believed were "under Party dominance."[16] In fact, Housewives' claims to be self-supporting are bolstered by their many fund-raising activities, although they did acknowledged that they got help with their research from left-led unions.

File notes and memos show that the police continued to search for evidence to support their conviction that, "in the majority of cases," the "Communist movement" was "in control" of Housewives organizations. Such evidence, had they found it, would have supported their belief that neither the LPP nor the Housewives were genuinely interested in prices, but that the "wide-spread resentment to the present high prices" that "exists among the public" had merely been "seized upon by the Labour Progressive Party" and was "a very welcome instrument of agitation for them."[17] This conviction, unshaken by the absence of evidence, was reflected in internal communications, such as the memo identifying the "quite favorable" public reaction to a series of red-baiting articles on the topic of "Communism in B.C" that appeared in February 1948 in the Vancouver *Daily Province*. It also noted with approval that many readers "have come to the realization that there is actually a serious Communist threat in their midst."[18] Agents preferred to target only bona fide Communists, and endeavoured to distinguish party members from non-communists. But they often erred, in part because they treated such things as marriage to a communist, membership in a left-wing ethnic organization, a left-led union or its auxiliary, or an agent's assessment that a person was inclined to "radicalism" as evidence of probable communism. Such an expansive definition of subversion enabled them to include staunch CCFers such as Lily Phelps. The Mounties were well aware that Phelps was "not a member of the Labor Progressive Party," but, because she was active in the Housewives, they considered her to be "susceptible to Labor Progressive Party guile." Likewise, they decided that Rae Luckock, a life-long CCFer, was "led by the LPP" because the party endorsed the Housewives and, they believed, was secretly behind the prices campaign.[19]

Mounting evidence challenges the popular notion that Canada pursued communists and others on the left less aggressively than the U.S., where, from the mid-1940s to the mid-1950s, the House Committee on Un-American Activities (HUAC) famously persecuted U.S. communists, as well as unaffiliated leftists, social democrats, left-leaning liberals, and many others who were merely suspected of sympathizing with the ideas of the left.[20] Canadians suspected of being too far to the left were also persecuted. Moreover, as a number of Cold War scholars have pointed out, they had, if anything, less recourse to justice than those in the U.S.[21] Unlike HUAC, whose inquisition was largely public, the Canadian state acted covertly, and was thus even less accountable to its citizens than its U.S. counterpart. Sim and countless others discovered that their involvement in legitimate protest resulted in persistent and intrusive surveillance that often included police visits to their employers or neighbours, denial of security clearances needed to get jobs or promotions, and many other police intrusions into their private lives that amounted to punishment for their left-wing politics.

Police in a number of cities denied Housewives' parade permits and red squads broke up their protests, confiscated their placards, and, on at least two occasions, raided Housewives' homes. Although it is possible that, as they claimed, they were targeting the homes because the occupants were reported to be Communists (despite party membership being quite legal), both their own surveillance reports and the newspapers made a point of identifying the women as Housewives. A police raid on the home of a British Columbia Housewives League member in January 1941 spawned a lively series of newspaper articles when the Housewives complained to Justice Minister Ernest Lapointe, described the raid, which interrupted one of their meetings, as "an act of intimidation," and demanded an apology. Lapointe rejected their claim on the grounds that the raid was not meant to coincide with their meeting. His admission appears to be at odds with the responses of both the RCMP and the provincial police, who denied any knowledge of the incident.[22] In November, police raided the home of Toronto Housewife Mrs M. Jeffries. Although, on this occasion, there appear to have been no reports in the press, the Mounties who conducted the raid noted that the premises contained donation cards for the "Committee for the Release of Labour Internees" (probably the National Committee for Democratic Rights, a communist-led organization to which several Housewives belonged), and membership cards for the Housewives Consumers Association.[23]

All of the seven former Housewives who were interviewed for this project agreed that the Housewives were subjected to intrusive police surveillance and political persecution. Vancouver Housewives President Mona Morgan blamed the police when her gas tank was sugared and her windows broken.[24] Housewife Mary Prokop, an activist in the Ukrainian Labour Farmer Temple Association (ULFTA) who joined the Communist party in Winnipeg, but moved to Toronto during the war years as secretary of the National Committee for Democratic Rights when her husband, Peter, was interned, was familiar with police surveillance. She recalled that, in Winnipeg, the police would follow those, like herself, whom "they suspected of doing what they called subversion." She described being followed by police "in these big black cars. They'd be out there day and night." She was also certain that "they used to come undercover" to some Housewives' meetings. RCMP surveillance reports confirm that suspicion, although the names of their informants have been redacted from the records. As a life-long activist in the communist movement, she expected and shrugged off the intrusive surveillance. "So what?" she recalled. "You want to follow me, go ahead."[25] Mona Morgan similarly regarded red-baiting and police surveillance as a manageable problem. Harassment, she explained, was just "one of the things we were up against." But the Housewives' "issues were good" and she thought the organization lost fewer members as a result of such harassment than "people would think." The press, in her recollection, was generally supportive, and many mainstream columnists "gave us credit for the things we were doing."[26] Others were less sanguine. Dee Dee Rizzo, Winnipeg Housewives President Anne Ross's daughter, recalled that, despite her many political activities, Ross was "passionate about her kids" and "by and large" organized her life around her responsibilities as a mother. She was therefore distraught when Dee Dee and her brother Arthur were persecuted at school in response to a newspaper story that identified her as a communist. The RCMP, as well, identified Ross in their surveillance reports as a "well-known Communist," and she was often referred to as such by the press. To be sure, Ross was well-known as a community activist, and her husband, Bill Ross, was not merely an open party member but head of the Manitoba Communist party. But Rizzo was adamant that, regardless of her father's political affiliations, her mother was not a Communist. Ross, she said, was frustrated that the press and the Mounties routinely assumed that Communists' wives were "ipso facto" also Communists.[27]

Non-communist Housewives, such as Toronto Housewife Margaret McBride, were also persecuted. Alice Maigis, who had joined the Communist party after emigrating to Canada as a war bride and was active in the prices committee as a member of the Congress of Canadian Women in the 1950s, recalled that the RCMP harassed McBride by trying to "make trouble" for her anticommunist husband who was already "angry with her for doing any political work." Margaret "wasn't a communist," she explained. But "because she was close to [Communist] party people," the RCMP "tried to destroy" her husband. "They found out where he worked," she recalled, and "talked to his boss." When confronted, he refuted the charges against himself and his wife. Fortunately, "he was a good worker," and because of that, his boss told him they were "prepared to overlook a lot of sins" – which, in his case, meant false accusations of Communism. Had he been less valuable as a worker, she thought, "they might have fired him."[28]

Vectors of Suspicion

Some Housewives attracted suspicion because their husbands were Communists, which the police assumed was evidence of their wives' political views. A memo from the Toronto division, for example, reported that the HCA was "pretty much in the hands of the women members of the LPP or wives of prominent members."[29] Housewife-activists, both communists and non-communists, expressed outrage at the assumption that married women's political views would simply echo those of their spouses. As BC Housewives President Mona Morgan pointed out, she was not simply the wife of provincial LPP leader Nigel Morgan. She was also a prominent member of the left (and proudly a Communist) in her own right. In addition to being president of the Vancouver Housewives, she was president of the left-led International Woodworkers (IWA) women's auxiliary, a member of the BC LPP club and the LPP city and provincial committees, and active in the peace movement and the opposition to the Spanish Civil War. Yet when the red-baiting began, she noted, the press stopped identifying her as Mona Morgan and referred to her by her husband's name. "Almost immediately," she recalled, "I was Mrs Nigel Morgan."[30] References to Housewives' communist husbands seem intended to cast doubt on Housewives' insistence that their organization was not under communist control. In the wake of a series of red-baiting articles that first appeared in the *Windsor Star* and were picked up and reprinted in papers across the country, the *Edmonton Journal* ran an article asking rhetorically, "Do Reds Guide League? 'No,' Says Leaders' Wife." Underscoring the matrimonial link to the Communist party, it identified Edmonton Housewives President "Mrs. Ben Swankey" as the wife of the well-known "Alberta Communist leader."[31] Similarly, the Regina *Leader-Post* announced "Housewives Deny Control by Reds," in which it identified Regina HCA President "Mrs. Norman Brudy" with reference to her son, also named Norman Brudy, a well-known LPP member who had run as a Labor candidate in the recent civic election.[32]

Not only were some Housewives related to known communists, but as their accusers noted, some were also members of the ethnic left. In Cold War-era Canada, a xenophobic society in which citizens of British ancestry were regarded as more authentically Canadian, and by extension more trustworthy, than others, certain ethnicities were regarded as grounds for suspicion.[33] By contrast, the communist left, philosophically committed to fighting discrimination and intolerance, even if it did so imperfectly, was so ethnically diverse that any working-class person with an Eastern European background, Jews of any national origin, and people with "foreign-sounding" names were often suspected of being communists. So uncritically did many accept the assumed link between these ethnicities and "subversion" that one anticommunist MP confidently advised the police that a suspicious person's "nationality should be traced," citing his father's "undoubtedly" ethnic "appearance" and his own "very pronounced anti-British" attitude.[34] RCMP surveillance records indicate that at least some agents found information about ethnicity noteworthy. A report on a 1947 meeting of the Halifax Housewives association, for instance, notes that Mrs Katie Tzakarakas is the "Polish wife of Greek Steve Tzakarakas," and another identifies Toronto Housewife Mrs A.J. Beveridge as being "of Finnish extraction."[35]

By the late 1940s, the Housewives' support for human rights and social justice had also become cause for suspicion. Like other organizations of the left, including the Communist party and the left-led unions, the Housewives not only endorsed acceptance of religious, political, ethnic, and racial differences but put those values into daily practice, welcoming as members women of any ethnicity or race, all political views, and any social class. They also advocated many of the same social justice causes as other organizations of both the communist and non-communist left. In the 1930s, Housewives protested Quebec's anticommunist Padlock Law, created ostensibly to "protect" Quebecers from "Communistic propaganda."[36] They also organized alongside activist clergy and the CCF, as well as the Communist-led Toronto Youth Council and the organization of unemployed, to demand work and wages for unemployed single men, protest work requirements for relief recipients, and demand more adequate relief benefits. During the war, along with left-liberal community activist May Birchard, the Toronto Labour Council, the CCF-affiliated League for Social Reconstruction, the Quakers, and the Women's International League for Peace and Freedom, they protested the militarization of youth by opposing compulsory cadet training in the public schools.[37] In tandem with others on the left, they called for rent control and protested wartime legislation forbidding workers from changing jobs. They also advanced their own campaign against the imposition of a 50-cent-per-month service charge by the gas utility as an unaffordable assault on the poor. At war's end, along with the increasingly popular CCF, the LPP, and the labour movement, they called for state-funded maternity and child care, affordable education, higher old-age pensions at 65 with no means test, state-funded medical care, and human rights legislation.[38]

But like other organizations that were red-baited because they included communists, the Housewives were abandoned by the human rights community, which either accepted their attackers' claims that they were a Communist "front," or were anxious to avoid being discredited as being "soft on communism." By the late 1940s, Cold War anticommunism had taken hold among non-communist leftists and liberals, who not only failed to defend Canadians' right to hold unpopular political views or join the LPP – a legal political party – but did their best to purge communists from the human rights community. Although some, as human rights historian Dominique Clément notes, were "appalled by the persecution of communists," others were themselves adamantly anticommunist.[39] One of the latter was human rights advocate and publisher B.K. Sandwell, whose popular *Saturday Night* magazine denounced the Housewives, while tacitly acknowledging their commitment to social justice and the "excellence of the causes they advocate."[40]

We will never know how many Housewives were thus punished for their activism, but one of the most prominent was Rae Luckock, who had joined the Housewives in 1937 and remained active, serving several terms as president, into the 1950s. Both a practicing Baptist and a farmer, Luckock explained that it was "Christ's sermon on the mount" that made her a socialist. One of the founding members of the Ontario CCF, she had entered politics following the death of her 12-year-old daughter due in part to the hardship suffered by the family during the Depression. Her search for solutions to the social inequality that created such terrible hardships led her to the CCF. The same commitment to social justice that underpinned her commitment to social democracy prompted her to join the Housewives.[41] By the late 1930s, already a seasoned politician, she was aware that an organization that challenged powerful business and government leaders would engender opposition, but urged her sister-Housewives not to "fear criticism, nor fear to be different," assuring them that if their "grandmothers had been different," they would already be "enjoying a better life." The only way out of their "present predicaments," she advised, was "through organization." She urged them to never "miss a chance to ask our political representatives in government to help us better our lives."[42]

It is instructive that, although Luckock was one of the first two women elected to the Ontario legislature in 1933, she has been all but forgotten. Agnes Macphail, who was elected at the same time, is remembered as the "first woman" elected to the Ontario legislature, a position she actually shared with Luckock.[43] But because of her work in the Housewives, Luckock was effectively air-brushed out of CCF history. In spring 1948, amidst the maelstrom of attacks against the Housewives, the CCF executive, who had for years supported the Housewives' campaigns, reversed their position and joined the chorus of red-baiters who labelled the Housewives Consumers Association a Communist "front." Their shift was probably instigated by CCF Women's Committee chair Marjorie Mann, who insisted that Luckock "was a communist, no question." But, as Luckock's biographer points out, the entire process was a sham. The charges against the Housewives and Luckock were not investigated, Mann's "evidence" amounted to seeing Luckock's name in the Communist newspapers, and Luckock was not permitted to respond to the accusations. Instead, three prominent CCF officers, David Lewis, F.R. Scott, and M.J. Coldwell, arrived at her home and demanded she quit the Housewives or be "excommunicated." They were confident that she would choose the CCF. Instead, Luckock quit the party she had helped to found on the spot. The party never forgave her.[44]

Margaret Laurence, one of Canada's best-known and most beloved writers, was active in the Winnipeg Housewives. In his account of Laurence's early years, Donez Xiques notes that, for six months in the winter of 1947–8, the twenty-two year old Peggy (Wemyss) Laurence worked as a journalist and wrote about labour issues and social problems for two left-wing papers, the cooperatively owned, pro-union *Winnipeg Citizen* and the Communist party paper, *The Westerner*. At the latter, she worked under the direction of editor Mitch Sago and manager Bill Tuomi, both of whom were well-known Winnipeg Communists and civic activists. She left the *Winnipeg Citizen* in protest "over allegations that she was a Communist," although one-time party member Roland Penner affirmed that she never joined the party.[45] Laurence's ties to the communist left were more than incidental, however, and revolved around the Housewives. John Marshall, the education director of the People's Cooperative Dairy, a business operated by the Communist-affiliated Association of United Ukrainian Canadians (AUUC) that collaborated with the Manitoba Housewives Consumers Association in protesting the termination of the milk subsidy, was best man at her wedding. She wrote an article celebrating the work of prominent Housewife, LPP member, and fellow *Westerner* reporter Peggy Chunn, and was editor at least until May 1948 of the *Manitoba Housewives' News*. Her living arrangements, on the upper floor of a house above Manitoba Housewives founding president Anne Ross and her husband and Manitoba LPP leader Bill Ross, suggest that Laurence was immersed, at least for a time, in the social as well as the political life of the Winnipeg left during the time the Housewives was its most active organization.[46] We may never know precisely the extent of Laurence's involvement in the Housewives, but it is clear that her work in the Housewives was motivated by the same passion for social justice and activism that has been so much celebrated in her writing.

Other women who later became prominent conveniently "forgot" about their early involvement in the left. Labour activist and CCF member Eileen Tallman Sufrin, who is best known for her attempt to organize Eaton's workers, worked briefly for the Toronto Housewives. Such political amnesia is a product of the Cold War, and those who buried their connections to the communist left can be forgiven for wishing to avoid notoriety and possible persecution. One of the most notable of these is the famous Second Wave feminist icon, Betty Friedan, whose pivotal 1963 book, *The Feminine Mystique*, helped frame the popular critique of gender relations. Friedan, as Daniel Horowitz's biography reveals, refused to acknowledge her early involvement in Marxist circles or her brief career as a journalist writing for the left-wing *Federated Press* and the *UE News*, the paper of the Communist-led United Electrical, Radio and Machine Workers union.[47] Friedan was an American and not, of course, a consumer activist. But she exemplifies those who, for understandable reasons, denied their radical pasts.

Housewives and Anticommunism in the CCF

The CCF, too, turned its back on the Housewives, and the loss of its support was a serious blow to their legitimacy. As they had often reminded the Housewives, Canada's social democrats had advocated social planning, public ownership, and state economic management in peacetime well before the end of the war, a position that party stalwarts David Lewis and F.R. Scott articulated in their widely read 1943 book, *Make this Your Canada*. With a broad base of popular support and, between

1945 and 1949, twenty-eight MPs in the federal Parliament, the CCF played a crucial role in the campaign for peacetime price control. CCF MPs used their access to Parliament to bring HCA campaigns, petitions, delegations, and letters to members of Parliament to the attention of the House. At the grassroots, CCF women were active in Housewives' campaigns and participated in delegations to Ottawa; other party members supported their effort by providing billets.[48] Housewives collaborated with CCF aldermen, city councillors, and members of provincial legislatures in shared campaigns for social justice and fairer prices. They counted on the endorsements of prominent CCFers such as Gladys Strum, Angus McInnis, Morton Lazarus, M.J. Coldwell, and Tommy Douglas to minimize the effect of red-baiting, sometimes by issuing press releases designed to confirm CCF support.[49] But in 1948, anxious to distance themselves from raging anticommunism, and urged on by Cold Warriors such as David Lewis within the party, the CCF recast itself as less a part of Canada's diverse left than a "bulwark to oppose reds" on the front lines of anticommunism.[50] As Housewife Mary Prokop recalled, some members of the CCF "were good people," but "when it came to take a real stand they buckled under. They were intimidated."[51]

The CCF Ontario executive were under particular pressure to abandon their support of the Housewives from the party's own Ontario CCF Women's Committee, which initially resisted requests from the executive to support the Housewives and then persuaded them to withdraw the party's support. Shortly after its founding in May 1947,[52] the Women's Committee was invited to join the HCA, but the executive, believing they detected "a Commie odour about the whole thing," declined.[53] Committee members were not only convinced that the Housewives was a Communist organization, but regarded it as a competitor that threatened to draw women away from the CCF. Determined to "find ways and means of bringing more women into the CCF so that with their added strength the CCF may come into office as the government of Ontario," the committee was particularly interested in "the occupational group known as 'housewives,'" women who, they believed, "needed some special attention before they would come into the CCF."[54] The committee was therefore alarmed to see that many CCF women were joining the HCA, attracted by the "very capable manner in which [the Housewives] handled their advance."[55] Committee chairman Marjorie Mann advised members that they should not support the Housewives because it was "LPP controlled."[56] Yet despite resolute investigation, the committee found no more conclusive evidence of such control than had the Mounties. Undeterred, they based their conclusions on their personal knowledge that some Housewives were Communists, their collective disbelief in some Housewives' denials that they were LPP members, and their conviction that others were "fellow travelers." The rest, they concluded, were "politically naïve people and non-political, public spirited citizens who carry no responsibility in the organization."[57] On this evidence, the Committee informed the October 1948 Ontario CCF convention that, rather than supporting the Housewives, "the only effective method of achieving lower prices and a better standard of living for all is by the election of a CCF government." However, if women "wish to take part in work of this type," the Committee suggested, they could join the Liberal Party-funded Canadian Association of Consumers.[58] They dropped their endorsement of the CAC a month later, following an investigation by CCF activist Peg Stewart. In her scathing report to the Women's Joint Committee, Stewart described the CAC as a "reactionary" organization of elite women that received ongoing, although unacknowledged, financial support from the Liberals and was designed to "keep the girls quiet." After floating several ideas for organizing consumers into the CCF, they admitted failure in their efforts to "galvanize" their "own women."[59] CCF historian Dan Azoulay, although sympathetic to the Women's Committee, acknowledges the ruthlessness with which they fought the Housewives.[60] Discrediting the Housewives was a major preoccupation, which, Mann noted in her report to 1948 annual meeting of the CCF Women's Committee, "took more of our time last year than any other single subject and is one which we feel is terribly important."[61] She was especially proud of their part in the attack on former Ontario CCF MLA Rae Lucock, observing, in a letter to sister CCFer Roxie Tait, that, "as a result of our pointing out to provincial council and convincing them of the nature" of the Housewives, the party refused to "endorse her as a provincial candidate in the recent election."[62]

Housewives and Anticommunism in the Labour Movement

By 1949, organized labour's immediate postwar priorities of raising wages, lowering prices, and increasing working people's purchasing power had been almost eclipsed by its determination to drive Communists out of the unions. Only a year earlier, not yet ready to abandon their demand for price control, which they acknowledged had worked "superlatively well" to control inflation, but anxious to demonstrate their intolerance of Communism, the leaders of labour's most powerful organization, the CCF-led Canadian Congress of Labour, had portrayed these struggles as linked. As the Congress explained to the 1948 Royal Commission on Prices, "one of the main battlefronts" of the Cold War was "the fight against inflation," and the only way to "preserve our free society" was to restore price control.[63] But after 1948, these Cold Warriors were obliged to conduct their battles against prices without the Housewives' help. Anticommunist purges drove the left-led unions out of the CCL, eroding union support even in Housewives' strongholds, such as Montreal, where the Housewives and Consumers Federation had organized a number of broadly based community meetings and from which it had sent two diverse delegations to Ottawa.[64] Former supporters such as R.J. Lamoureux, international director of the United Steelworkers union (USW), proclaimed, in a clear reference to the Housewives, that "labour can stand on its own feet and does not need any support from Communists or any of their fronts in fighting the present battle against increased prices." CCL regional organizing director Paul Emile Marquette sneered that no CCL union "would fall for the latest Communist approach of the Housewives Consumers League."[65] Even in Cape Breton, where the LPP was particularly strong in the unions and was leading the fight for price control, the RCMP reported that red-baiting in the press had "considerably retarded" the collection of signatures on the Housewives' petitions.[66]

The Congress' resolutions to "organize public opinion behind its demands" for peacetime price controls produced no action on its part, although from 1946 to 1948 a demand for price control was an item in its annual memorandum to the government.[67] In its 1949 meeting with the Cabinet, the CCL executive did point out that the elimination of price controls had "cost Canadian consumers hundreds of millions of dollars," but Prime Minister King disputed their figures and cautioned "responsible labour organizations" to address their concerns to the employers, where they could be resolved "through collective bargaining."[68] The same year, the Congress underscored its opposition to the Housewives by publicly endorsing the rival Canadian Association of Consumers (CAC). A two-page article in the November 1949 issue of *The Canadian Unionist* described the work of the CAC, in which the Congress had "a special interest," and in which it was represented by "Mrs. Patrick Conroy," wife of the CCL's president (although by 1951, belatedly following the lead of other CCF women, Esther Conroy had quit the CAC).[69] Affiliation with the Liberal-funded and elite-run CAC was consistent with the CCL's self-described role as an organization of "labour statesmen" and its anticipation of a bipartisan labour relations system in which it would be a respected collaborator with employers and the state. Among the fifty delegates to the CAC's annual meeting, the *Unionist* reported with evident pride, were such respected, mainstream, and in some cases reactionary organizations as the Imperial Order Daughters of the Empire, the National Council of Women, the Federal Women's Institutes of Canada, les Cercles des Fermières, the National Council of Hadassah, and the Women's Christian Temperance Union, several of which were, like itself, on the front lines of anticommunism.[70]

Silencing Dissent

Housewives who had pinned such high hopes on their movement were dismayed by these attacks, which they felt were unjust and politically motivated. President Luckock assured her members that Finance Minister Abbott's refusal to re-instate price controls was "an infringement of the democratic rights of the citizens, who were promised in the Atlantic Charter freedom from want and fear would be guaranteed to them. Both of these promises have been broken." "Our task," she exhorted them, is to "pick up the torch of justice and raise it high. Our children and their children will call us blessed as we go forward to the day when true freedom will prevail throughout the land."[71] "Only by action," she reminded the organization's supporters, "can we do something to really protect the health of our nation."[72] Some ordinary members were equally eloquent. Elderly Manitoba Housewife Elizabeth Green, in an undated commentary found among Anne Ross's records of the Manitoba Housewives Association, expressed in emotionally charged terms her profound commitment to what she regarded as the lofty goals of the organization. She wrote that, "having not only reached but passed the allotted span of years," she regarded "with great alarm and dismay the attempt of certain forces to destroy this great organization, which already has become National, by labeling it Communist, and in that way obscuring the main issue, viz: the desire on the part of the housewives to bring prices down to a reasonable level so that we may feed, clothe and house our families adequately." She affirmed her undiminished hope of achieving the aims for which she joined the Housewives, "which may be summed up thus: To unite all women irrespective of religious beliefs, color of skin, or political affiliations to protect the basic needs of the Canadian family."[73]

The widespread outrage about high food costs, unchecked inflation, and a government that refused to account for its failure to resolve these problems for ordinary people remained, but without the HCA at the helm of a popular mobilization, these matters faded from the popular discourse. The CAC, which replaced the HCA as Canada's only consumer organization, adopted a very different approach, advising, rather than arguing with, the government, and putting its energies into consumer education and unsuccessful attempts to develop collaborative relationships between consumers and manufacturers rather than mobilization.[74] Like the HCA, the CAC presented briefs to government, but in contrast to the Housewives, who confronted politicians and demanded radical change, it prided itself on having "gained the confidence of government [and] industry." Far from being a grassroots organization, the CAC attributed its success to the elite women who led it. A 1951 internal review concluded that the willingness of these women to assume leadership of the CAC was "most fortunate." The "CAC was organized from the top down," it explained, and led by "well-educated" women of the "highest caliber." If the organization had been left to the "rank-and-file," it "would never have got off the ground." Nor did the organization offer much to working-class women; indeed, it dismissed their concerns outright. "Labour women," it noted, were "enthusiastic at the start," but "parted company with the CAC" soon after its founding, when the organization endorsed wage ceilings. Remarkably, it blamed the women themselves for this. Those who left the organization, the report concluded, were "unthinking women" who "found it easier to pressure their husbands to get higher wages" than to learn how to "use their existing pay cheques more wisely."[75]

The state's suppression of the Housewives, primarily through the intrusive surveillance work of the RCMP and its own official encouragement of anticommunists in the labour movement, the media, and the wider community, was a key factor in the movement's loss of legitimacy and subsequent decline. The Housewives' maternalism, which had protected them from such attacks for far longer than the male-dominated organizations of the left, in the end contributed to their demise. In the hyperbolic atmosphere of the Cold War, the Housewives' maternalism was successfully transformed by their opponents from proof of their sincerity to evidence of their perfidiousness and treachery. Stripped of the protective cloak of motherhood, the HCA was abandoned by the many allies and supporters who had made their movement a broad-based expression of the popular will, too numerous for even reluctant politicians to safely ignore. Virtually unopposed, the Liberals continued to pursue the policies that had so outraged Canadians for most of the next decade under their new leader, Louis St. Laurent, who replaced King in November 1948. Demonized by powerful anticommunists, the radical consumer movement had been successfully silenced.

Notes

Introduction

1 For most of its existence, the HCA was a loosely linked network of consumers' associations rather than a centrally organized association, but it was widely regarded by the media, public officials, and the police as a single entity. Its constituent organizations also took direction from the de facto headquarters in Toronto. I have endeavoured to clarify this throughout the book, but the tendency of some, including the Housewives themselves, to refer to their organization as if it were one entity can be confusing.

2 See, for instance, Sarah Elvins, *Sales & Celebrations: Retailing and Regional Identity in Western New York State, 1920–1940* (Athens: Ohio University Press, 2004); Dana Frank, *Purchasing Power: Consumer Organizing, Gender, and the Seattle Labor Movement, 1919–1929* (Cambridge: Cambridge University Press, 1994); Lawrence B. Glickman, *Buying Power: A History of Consumer Activism in America* (Chicago: University of Chicago Press, 2009); Lawrence B. Glickman, *Consumer Society in American History: A Reader* (Ithaca, NY: Cornell University Press, 1999); Lawrence B. Glickman, *A Living Wage: American Workers and the Making of Consumer Society* (Ithaca, NY: Cornell University Press, 1997); Meg Jacobs, *Pocketbook Politics: Economic Citizenship in Twentieth-Century America* (Princeton, NJ: Princeton University Press, 2005); Patricia L. MacLachlan, *Consumer Politics in Postwar Japan: The Institutional Boundaries of Citizen Activism* (New York: Columbia University Press, 2002); Kathy M. Newman, *Radio Active Advertising and Consumer Activism, 1935–1947* (Berkeley: University of California Press, 2004); Heidi Tinsman, *Buying into the Regime: Grapes and Consumption in Cold War Chile and the United States* (Durham, NC: Duke University Press, 2014).

3 Examples of this include Robert Bothwell, Ian M Drummond, and John English, *Canada since 1945: Power, Politics and Provincialism* (Toronto: University of Toronto Press, 1989) and, more recently, Richard Harris, *Creeping Conformity: How Canada Became Suburban, 1900–1960* (Toronto: University of Toronto Press, 2004). The traditional view of the postwar has been challenged by some historians, and particularly by historians of women. See, for instance, Tarah Brookfield, *Cold War Comforts: Canadian Women, Child Safety, and Global Insecurity, 1945–1975* (Waterloo, ON: Wilfrid Laurier University Press, 2012). For the U.S., see, for instance, Joanne Meyerowitz, ed., *Not June Cleaver: Women and Gender in Postwar America* (Philadelphia: Temple University Press, 1994).
4 Peter S. McInnis, "Planning Prosperity: Canadians Debate Postwar Reconstruction," in *Uncertain Horizons: Canadians and Their World in 1945*, ed. Greg Donaghy (Ottawa: Canadian Committee for the History of the Second World War, 1997), 231–60.
5 James Naylor, *The Fate of Labour Socialism: The Co-operative Commonwealth Federation and the Dream of a Working-Class Future* (Toronto: University of Toronto Press, 2016). See also, Michael S. Beaulieu, *Labour at the Lakehead: Ethnicity, Socialism, and Politics, 1900–35* (Vancouver: UBC Press, 2011), 207.
6 Ivan Avakumoic, *Socialism in Canada: A Study of the CCF-NDP in Federal and Provincial Politics* (Toronto: McClelland and Stewart, 1978), 143.
7 Robert Bothwell, Ian M. Drummond, and John English, *Canada, 1900–1945* (Toronto: University of Toronto Press, 1987), 329.
8 In this discussion and throughout the book, I distinguish between the Communist party and the individuals and organizations that formed the broad communist left by capitalizing "Communist" only in the case of the party and those known to be party members. This usage is consistent throughout; for instance, I make the same distinction between the Liberal party and unaffiliated liberals.
9 Norman Penner, *Canadian Communism: The Stalin Years and Beyond* (Toronto: Methuen, 1988), 28, 166, 193; Labor-Progressive Party collection, Finding Aid, The William Ready Division of Archives and Research Collection, McMaster University, http://archives.mcmaster.ca/index.php/labor-progressive-party-collection. The ethnic composition of the Communist party has been extensively documented. For example, see Benjamin Isitt, *Militant Minority: British Columbia Workers and the Rise of a New Left, 1948–1972* (Toronto: University of Toronto Press, 2011), 44–83; Ian McKay, *Rebels, Reds, Radicals: Rethinking Canada's Left History* (Toronto: Between the Lines, 2005), 167. Relevant histories of these lefts include Rhonda L. Hinther and Jim Mochoruk, *Re-imagining Ukrainian Canadians:*

History, Politics, and Identity (Toronto: University of Toronto Press, 2011); Rhonda L. Hinther, "Raised in the Spirit of the Class Struggle: Children, Youth, and the Interwar Ukrainian Left in Canada," *Labour/Le Travail* 60 (2007): 43–76; Varpu Lindström, *From Heroes to Enemies: Finns in Canada, 1937–1947* (Beaverton, ON: Aspasia Books, 2000); Ester Reiter, *A Future without Hate or Need: The Promise of the Jewish Left in Canada* (Toronto: Between the Lines, 2016); Frances Swyripa, *Wedded to the Cause: Ukrainian-Canadian Women and Ethnic Identity, 1891–1991* (Toronto: University of Toronto Press, 1993).

10 Graham Broad, *A Small Price to Pay: Consumer Culture on the Canadian Home Front, 1939–45* (Vancouver: UBC Press, 2013), 203.

11 Craig Heron, *The Canadian Labour Movement: A Short History* (Toronto: James Lorimer, 1989); Isitt, *Militant Minority*; Peter S. McInnis, *Harnessing Labour Confrontation: Shaping the Postwar Settlement in Canada* (Toronto: University of Toronto Press, 2002); Bryan D. Palmer, *Working-Class Experience: Rethinking the History of Canadian Labour, 1800–1991* (Toronto: McClelland and Stewart, 1992).

12 Lara Campbell, *Respectable Citizens: Gender, Family, and Unemployment in Ontario's Great Depression* (Toronto: University of Toronto Press, 2009). See also, Carmela Patrias, *Relief Strike: Immigrant Workers and the Great Depression in Crowland, Ontario, 1930–1935* (Toronto: New Hogtown Press, 1990); Patricia V. Schulz, *The East York Workers' Association: A Response to the Great Depression* (Toronto: New Hogtown Press, 1975).

13 Broad, *A Small Price to Pay,* 16–49, 207–8; Ian Mosby, *Food Will Win the War: The Politics, Culture, and Science of Food on Canada's Home Front* (Vancouver: UBC Press, 2014), 90, 94.

14 Mosby, *Food Will Win the War.*

15 Roy Barnes, "The Rise of Corporatist Regulation in the English and Canadian Dairy Industries," *Social Science History* 25 (2001): 381–406; Andrew Ebejer, "'Milking' the Consumer? Consumer Dissatisfaction and Regulatory Intervention in the Ontario Milk Industry during the Great Depression," *Ontario History* 102 (2010): 20–39; Ian MacPherson, "An Authoritative Voice: The Reorientation of the Canadian Farmers' Movement, 1935 to 1945," *Historical Papers* (1979): 164–81.

16 Joy Parr, *Domestic Goods: The Material, the Moral, and the Economic in the Postwar Years* (Toronto: University of Toronto Press, 1999), 64–83.

17 Mosby, *Food Will Win the War,* 42–63.

18 On CPC women, see Joan Sangster, *Dreams of Equality: Women on the Canadian Left, 1920–60* (Don Mills, ON: McClelland & Stewart, 1989; reprinted 2015 by University of Toronto Press).

19 The reference to "Communists in women's clothes" is from Parr, *Domestic Goods*, 93. See also her account of the HCA: *Domestic Goods*, 40–63. For other accounts of the Housewives, see Joy Parr and Gunilla Ekberg, "Mrs. Consumer and Mr. Keynes in Postwar Canada and Sweden," *Gender and History* 8 (1996): 212–30; Sangster, *Dreams of Equality*, 139, 173, 178, 185–8, 220. Two who erroneously identify the Housewives as a Communist front are Dan Azoulay, "'Ruthless in a Ladylike Way': CCF Women Confront the Postwar Communist Menace," *Ontario History* 89 (1997): 23–52 and, perhaps influenced by Azoulay, Donica Belisle, "Toward a Canadian Consumer History," *Labour/Le Travail* 52 (2003): 181–206.

20 John Manley, "Moscow Rules? 'Red' Unionism and 'Class against Class' in Britain, Canada, and the United States, 1928–1935," *Labour/Le Travail* 56 (2005): 9–49; Ian McKay, "Rethinking the History of Depression-Era Communism in Canada," a paper delivered to the Oyfn Veg [On the Road], in honor of Gerald Tulchinsky, November 2013. Recent work on the CPUSA draws a similar distinction. See, for instance, Ellen Schrecker, *Many Are the Crimes: McCarthyism in America* (Boston: Little, Brown and Company, 1998).

21 See, for example, Linda Kealey, *Enlisting Women for the Cause: Women, Labour, and the Left in Canada, 1890–1920* (Toronto: University of Toronto Press, 1998); John Manley, "Women and the Left in the 1930s: The Case of the Toronto CCF Women's Joint Committee," *Atlantis: Critical Studies in Gender, Culture & Social Justice/Études critiques sur le genre, la culture, et la justice* 5 (1980): 100–19; Joan Sangster, "Radical Ruptures: Feminism, Labor, and the Left in the Long Sixties in Canada," *American Review of Canadian Studies* 40 (2010): 1–21; Sangster, *Dreams of Equality*; Brian T. Thorn, "'Healthy Activity and Worthwhile Ideas': Left- and Right-Wing Women Confront Juvenile Delinquency in Post-World-War-II Canada," *Social History / Histoire sociale* 42 (2009): 327–59; Candida Rifkind, *Comrades and Critics: Women, Literature and the Left in 1930s Canada* (Toronto: University of Toronto Press, 2009).

22 Marlene Epp, Franca Iacovetta, and Frances Swyripa, eds., *Sisters or Strangers: Immigrant, Ethnic, and Racialized Women in Canadian History* (Toronto: University of Toronto Press, 2004); Rhonda L. Hinther, *Perogies and Politics: Canada's Ukrainian Left, 1891–1991* (Toronto: University of Toronto Press, 2017); Rhonda L. Hinther, "'They Said the Course Would Be Wasted on Me Because I Was a Girl': Mothers, Daughters, and Shifting Forms of Female Activism in the Ukrainian Left in Twentieth-Century Canada," *Atlantis: Critical Studies in Gender, Culture & Social Justice/Études critiques sur le genre, la culture, et la justice* 32 (2007): 100–10; Donna R.

Gabaccia and Franca Iacovetta, eds., *Women, Gender, and Transnational Lives: Italian Workers of the World* (Toronto: University of Toronto Press, 2002); Lindström, *From Heroes to Enemies*; Irene Howard, "The Mothers' Council of Vancouver: Holding the Fort for the Unemployed, 1935–1938," *BC Studies* (Spring/Summer 1986): 249–87; Reiter, *A Future without Hate or Need*; Joan Sangster, "Robitnytsia, Ukrainian Communists, and the 'Porcupinism' Debate: Reassessing Ethnicity, Gender, and Class in Early Canadian Communism, 1922–1930," *Labour/Le Travail* 56 (2005): 51–89; Swyripa, *Wedded to the Cause*.

23 Dana Frank, "Housewives, Socialists, and the Politics of Food: The 1917 New York Cost-of-Living Protests," *Feminist Studies* 11, no. 2 (1985): 255–86; Lawrence B. Glickman, "The Strike in the Temple of Consumption: Consumer Activism and Twentieth-Century American Political Culture," *The Journal of American History* 88 (2001): 99–128; Glickman, *Buying Power*; Jacobs, *Pocketbook Politics*; Annelise Orleck, "We Are That Mythical Thing Called the Public: Militant Housewives during the Great Depression," *Feminist Studies* 19, no. 1 (1993): 147–73.

24 Landon R.Y. Storrs, *The Second Red Scare and the Unmaking of the New Deal Left* (Princeton, NJ: Princeton University Press, 2013).

25 Joseph Tohill, "'The Consumer Goes to War': Consumer Politics in the United States and Canada during the Second World War," in *Shopping for Change: Consumer Activism and the Possibilities of Purchasing Power*, ed. Louis Hyman and Joseph Tohill (Toronto and Ithaca: Between the Lines Press and Cornell University Press, 2017): 137–50, 144. See also, Joseph Tohill, "'A Consumers' War': Price Control and Political Consumerism in the United States and Canada during World War II" (PhD dissertation, York University, 2012).

26 Barry Glen Ferguson, *Remaking Liberalism: The Intellectual Legacy of Adam Shortt, O.D. Skelton, W.C. Clark and W.A. Mackintosh, 1890–1925* (Montreal: McGill-Queen's University Press, 1993).

27 Robert B. Bryce, "Prices, Wages and the Ceiling," in David Slater with Robert B. Bryce, *War, Finance and Reconstruction: The Role of Canada's Department of Finance 1939–1946* (Ottawa: Department of Finance, 1995), 127.

28 On the surveillance activities of the RCMP, see Larry Hannant, *The Infernal Machine: Investigating the Loyalty of Canada's Citizens* (Toronto: University of Toronto Press, 1995); Gregory S. Kealey and Reginald Whitaker, eds., *R.C.M.P. Security Bulletins: The War Series* (St. John's, Nfld.: Committee on Canadian Labour History, 1989); Gregory S. Kealey and Reginald Whitaker, eds., *R.C.M.P. Security Bulletins: The Depression Years* (St. John's, Nfld.: Committee on Canadian Labour History, 1993).

29 The documentary evidence for this book includes items from two national newspapers, the *Globe and Mail* and the *Financial Post*; from local papers including the *Toronto Tribune, The Toronto Daily Star*, the *Montreal Standard*, the *Hamilton Spectator*, the *Port Arthur News Chronicle*, the *Winnipeg News* (1944–8), and others, as well as clippings in the RCMP files from local papers such as the Vancouver *Daily Province*, the *Albertan*, the *Calgary Herald*, the Saskatoon *Star-Phoenix*, the Regina *Leader-Post*, the *Winnipeg Free Press*, the *Ottawa Citizen*, the *Ottawa Journal*, the *Windsor Star*, the *Montreal Standard*, the *Montreal Gazette*, and the *Halifax Herald*.

30 The Communist Party of Canada's newspapers from which evidence about the Housewives was drawn include the *Clarion* (1939–40), the *Canadian Tribune* (1940–52), the *Pacific Tribune* (1939–44), and *National Affairs Monthly* (1944–52), as well as clippings from *The Westerner* and the *Pacific Tribune* found in RCMP files.

31 Brookfield, *Cold War Comforts*, 78. Irene Howard has also commented on the tendency of women to undervalue their records and destroy them. See Irene Howard, "The Mothers' Council of Vancouver: Holding the Fort for the Unemployed, 1935–1938," *BC Studies* (Spring/Summer 1986): 249–87.

32 Some useful anthologies that address this point include, Vicki L. Ruiz and Ellen Carol DuBois, eds., *Unequal Sisters: A Multicultural Reader in U.S. Women's History*, 3rd ed. (New York: Routledge, 2000); Sheila Rowbotham and Stephanie Linkogle, eds., *Women Resist Globalization: Mobilizing for Livelihood and Rights* (London: Zed Books, 2001); Alexis Jetter, Annelise Orleck, and Diana Taylor, eds., *The Politics of Motherhood: Activist Voices from Left to Right* (Hanover, NH: 1997); Judith Fingard and Janet Guildford, eds., *Mothers of the Municipality: Women, Work and Social Policy in Post-1945 Halifax* (Toronto: University of Toronto Press, 2005).

33 Some examples include, Eileen Boris, *Home to Work: Motherhood and the Politics of Industrial Homework in the United States* (Cambridge: Cambridge University Press, 1994); Georgina Denton, "'Neither Guns nor Bombs – Neither the State nor God – Will Stop Us from Fighting for Our Children': Motherhood and Protest in 1960s and 1970s America," *The Sixties* 5 (2012): 205–28; Cynthia Edmonds-Cady, "Mobilizing Motherhood: Race, Class, and the Uses of Maternalism in the Welfare Rights Movement," *Women's Studies Quarterly* 37 (2009): 206–22; Marilyn Fischer, "Addams's Internationalist Pacifism and the Rhetoric of Maternalism," *NWSA Journal* 18 (2006): 1–19; Glen Jeansonne, *Women of the Far Right: The Mothers' Movement and World War II* (Chicago: University of Chicago Press, 1996); Molly Ladd-Taylor, *Mother-work: Women, Child Welfare, and the*

State, 1890–1930 (Urbana: University of Illinois Press, 1995); Ellen Reese, "Maternalism and Political Mobilization: How California's Postwar Child Care Campaign Was Won," *Gender and Society* 10 (1996): 566–89.

34 Temma Kaplan, *Taking Back the Streets: Women, Youth, and Direct Democracy* (Berkeley: University of California Press, 2004), 46. See also, Sheila Rowbotham, "Facets of Emancipation: Women in Movement from the Eighteenth Century to the Present," in Rowbotham and Linkogle, *Women Resist Globalization*, 13–27.

35 Ann Taylor Allen, "Maternalism in German Feminist Movements"; Eileen Boris, "What about the Working of the Working Mother?"; Molly Ladd-Taylor, "Toward Defining Maternalism in US History"; Lynn Y. Weiner, "Maternalism as a Paradigm: Defining the Issues," all in *Journal of Women's History* 5, no. 2 (1993): 96–131. See also the articles by Adele Lindemeyr and Kathleen S. Uno in the same issue.

36 Denise Baillargeon, *Babies for the Nation: The Medicalization of Motherhood in Quebec, 1910–1970* (Waterloo, ON: Wilfrid Laurier University Press, 2009).

37 Annelise Orleck, "Tradition Unbound: Radical Mothers in International Perspective," in Jetter, Orleck, and Taylor, *The Politics of Motherhood*, 3–20.

38 On the social historical construction of motherhood, see Katherine Arnup, *Education for Motherhood: Advice for Mothers in Twentieth-Century Canada* (Toronto: University of Toronto Press, 1994), and the chapters in Rima D. Apple and Janet Golden, eds., *Mothers and Motherhood: Readings in American History* (Columbus: Ohio State University Press, 1997). On the social historical construction of adolescence, see Cynthia R. Comacchio, *The Dominion of Youth: Adolescence and the Making of a Modern Canada* (Waterloo: Wilfrid Laurier Press, 2006).

39 Faith Johnston, *A Great Restlessness: The Life and Politics of Dorise Nielsen* (Winnipeg: University of Manitoba Press, 2006).

40 For instance, in her biography of Annie Buller, Louise Watson devotes only three pages to Buller's family life, and makes only passing reference to the long absences from her son occasioned by the demands of Party work. Louise Watson, *She Never Was Afraid: The Biography of Annie Buller* (Toronto: Progress Press, 1976), 15–17, 66–7, 103.

41 Brookfield, *Cold War Comforts*, 23–50.

42 Brian T. Thorn, *From Left to Right: Maternalism and Women's Activism in Postwar Canada* (Vancouver: UBC Press, 2016).

43 Gisela Bock and Pat Thane, eds., *Maternity and Gender Policies: Women and the Rise of the European Welfare States, 1880s–1950s* (New York: Routledge, 1991); Seth Koven and Sonya Michel, eds., *Mothers of a New World:*

Maternalist Policies and the Origins of Welfare States (New York: Routledge, 1993).

44 Tarah Brookfield makes this argument in relation to women organizing on both the left and the right in Cold War Canada in *Cold War Comforts*. Landon Storrs makes a similar argument with regard to the lack of attention paid to the U.S. consumer movement of the 1930s and 1940s because its activists were women. Landon R.Y. Storrs, "Left-Feminism, the Consumer Movement, and Red Scare Politics in the United States, 1935–1960," *Journal of Women's History* 18 (2006): 40–67; Storrs, *The Second Red Scare*. The neglect of women activists by historians has been noted by a number of feminist scholars. See, for instance, Elizabeth Faue, *Community of Suffering and Struggle: Women, Men, and the Labor Movement in Minneapolis, 1915–1945* (Chapel Hill: University of North Carolina Press, 1991).

45 Brookfield, *Cold War Comforts*, 5.

46 There is an extensive literature on working-class feminism. See, for example, Dorothy Sue Cobble, *The Other Women's Movement: Workplace Justice and Social Rights in Modern America* (Princeton, NJ: Princeton University Press, 2004); Dennis A. Deslippe, *"Rights, Not Roses": Unions and the Rise of Working-Class Feminism, 1945–80* (Urbana: University of Illinois Press, 2000); Carol Kates, "Working Class Feminism and Feminist Unions: Title VII, the UAW and NOW," *Labor Studies Journal* 14 (1989): 28–45; Meg Luxton, "Feminism as a Class Act: Working-Class Feminism and the Women's Movement in Canada," *Labour/Le Travail* 48 (2001): 63–88; Joan Sangster, "Feminism and the Making of Canadian Working-Class History: Exploring the Past, Present and Future," *Labour/Le Travail* 46 (2000): 127–65. Landon Storrs argues, in *The Second Red Scare* and other places, that U.S. consumer activists of the same period were left feminists. Eric McDuffy makes a related argument for Black left feminism in Eric S. McDuffy, *Sojourning for Freedom: Black Women, American Communism, and the Making of Black Left Feminism* (Durham, NC: Duke University Press, 2011). On a related topic, see Kate Weigand, *Red Feminism: American Communism and the Making of Women's Liberation* (Baltimore: Johns Hopkins University Press, 2001).

47 See, for instance, Julia Smith, "An 'Entirely Different' Kind of Union: The Service, Office, and Retail Workers' Union of Canada (SORWUC), 1972–1986," *Labour/Le Travail* 73 (2014): 23–65; Pamela Sugiman, *Labour's Dilemma: The Gender Politics of Auto Workers in Canada, 1937–1979* (Toronto: University of Toronto Press, 1994); Sangster, "Radical Ruptures."

48 James C. Scott, *Weapons of the Weak: Everyday Forms of Peasant Resistance* (New Haven, CT: Yale University Press, 1985).

1. Price War

1 Aleck Samuel Ostry, *Nutrition Policy in Canada, 1870–1939* (Vancouver: UBC Press, 2006), 7.
2 "Housewives Plan Boycott of Milk," *Daily Clarion*, 4 November 1937, 1.
3 "Housewives Plan 'High Prices' Boycott," *Toronto Daily Star*, 4 November 1937, 1; "Women Uniting against Prices Mrs. Lamb Says," *Daily Clarion*, 8 November 1937, 1.
4 "Women Call Mass Meeting on Milk Boycott," *Toronto Evening Telegram*, 5 November 1937, 18; "Housewives in Toronto Launch Boycott on Milk to Force Three-Cent Cut," *Toronto Daily Star*, 5 November 1937; "Farmers, Consumers to Fight Trust," *Daily Clarion*, 6 November 1937, 1; "Women Uniting against Prices, Mrs. Lamb Says," *Daily Clarion*, 8 November 1937, 1; "Housewives Limit Milk Boycott Meeting to Women," *Toronto Evening Telegram*, 8 November 1937, 26.
5 "Farmers, Consumers to Fight Trust: Housewives to Meet Monday, Discuss Action," *Daily Clarion*, 6 November 1937, 1; "Housewives Plan Union to Conduct Milk Strike," *Globe and Mail*, 6 November 1937, 4; "Threatened for Her Fight against High Prices," *Daily Clarion*, 9 November 1937, 1.
6 "Housewives Plan 'High Prices' Boycott: Plan City-Wide Union To Fight Food Costs Control Board Told," *Toronto Daily Star*, 3 November 1937, 1; "Women Uniting against Prices Mrs. Lamb Says," *Daily Clarion*, 8 November 1937, 1; "Housewives Association Starts War on Prices," *Toronto Evening Telegram*, 9 November 1937, 21; "Meeting Hectic as Women Vote to Force Milk Cut," *Toronto Daily Star*, 9 November 1937, 9; "Reeve Offers Housewives Support in Milk-Price War," *Toronto Daily Star*, 9 November 1937, 6; "Housewives' Union Starts to Organize," *Globe and Mail*, 10 November 1937, 5.
7 "Milk Boycott Leader Spurns Police Guard Despite Threat," *Globe and Mail*, 9 November 1937, 1; "Disgruntled Milk Driver Blamed for Threat Note," *Toronto Daily Star*, 9 November 1937, 5.
8 "Women Demand Milk Probe, Public Distribution Plan," *Toronto Daily Star*, 10 November 1937, 2; "Women Urge Publicly Owned Milk Delivery," *Daily Clarion*, 11 November 1937, 1.
9 "Women Milk Boycotters Now Claim 5,000 Members," *Toronto Daily Star*, 16 November 1937, 7; "Orderly Boycott Is Intent in Toronto Milk Battle," *Toronto Evening Telegram*, 18 November 1937, 30.
10 "Ald. Saunders to Ask Probe Staple Prices," *Toronto Evening Telegram*, 6 December 1937, 12; "Toronto Urges Investigation of Milk Prices," *Daily Clarion*, 20 December 1937, 1.

11 "Housewives in Toronto Launch Boycott on Milk to Force Three-Cent Cut," *Toronto Daily Star*, 5 November 1937.
12 "Women Call Mass Meeting on Milk Boycott," *Toronto Evening Telegram*, 5 November 1937, 18; "Holds 10-Cent Milk Is Out of the Question," *Toronto Daily Star*, 9 November 1937, 9; "Dairies Feel No Effect of Boycott Threat," *Globe and Mail*, 10 November 1937, 5; "Housewives' Union Starts to Organize," *Globe and Mail*, 10 November 1937, 5; "Price Boycott Cuts Milk Consumption," *Daily Clarion*, 12 November 1937, 1.
13 "5000 Housewives Cut Milk Some Drinking Only Water," *Toronto Daily Star*, 18 November 1937, 25.
14 "Wives Mark One Day for Buying No Milk," *Toronto Daily Star*, 20 November 1937, 9.
15 Ebejer, "'Milking' the Consumer"; "Milk-Price Boost of One Cent per Quart as Aid to Producers," *Globe and Mail*, 16 January 1941, 4; "Women Consumers Decide to Ask for Lower Milk Prices," *Globe and Mail*, 14 February 1941, 4; "Milk Prices Go Up Sunday," *Globe and Mail*, 22 February 1941, 8.
16 "Repeat Stand against Rise in Milk Price," *Toronto Evening Telegram*, 24 October 1937, 7; "Cent Increase in Milk Price Forecast," *Toronto Evening Telegram*, 29 October 1937, 1; "Wants Full Public Inquiry of Milk Price Situation as Result of Cent Jump," *Toronto Evening Telegram*, 2 November 1937, 21; "Increase in Milk Price Opposed by Councillors," *Toronto Evening Telegram*, 2 November 1937, 4; "Dairies Feel No Effect of Boycott Threat," *Globe and Mail*, 10 November 1937, 5.
17 "Milk Consumers' Voice is Termed 'Obnoxious,'" *Toronto Evening Telegram*, 29 November 1937, 4.
18 "Dairyman Defies Board's Milk Price Boost," *Toronto Evening Telegram*, 5 November 1937, 13; "Milk at Ten Cents Is Possible Claim," *Toronto Daily Star*, 8 December 1937, 6.
19 "Trying to Weld Milk Producers in One Big Unit," *Toronto Daily Star*, 17 February 1938, 1.
20 Powdered milk was not mentioned.
21 "Suburban Dairies Form Association to Sell 12-Cent Milk," *Toronto Evening Telegram*, 18 November 1937, 25; "Milk Producers Informed Boycott 'Flash in Pan,'" *Toronto Daily Star*, 29 November 1937, 6; "Toronto Milk Distribution Abominable, Says Hepburn," *Toronto Daily Star*, 23 December 1937, 7.
22 "Lakeshore Women Unite to Fight Milk Increase," *Toronto Daily Star*, 13 November 1937, 6.
23 "Women Milk Boycotters Now Claim 5,000 Members," *Toronto Daily Star*, 16 November 1937, 7.

24 "Striking Milk Drivers Seek Union Recognition," *Globe and Mail*, 23 September 1937, 4; "General Milk Strike Looms," *Globe and Mail*, 21 October 1937, 1; "Will Toronto Have a General Milk Strike, or Not?" *Toronto Daily Star*, 22 October 1937, 11; "Would Urge Minimum Wage for Milk Producers Here," *Toronto Daily Star*, 27 October 1937, 2; "Suburbs May Join in Protest," *Globe and Mail*, 4 November 1937, 1–2; "Dairies Make $8,000,000 in Year," *Daily Clarion*, 4 November 1937, 1; "Six Unionists Are Fined in Dairy Strike Assault," *Globe and Mail*, 25 November 1937, 4.

25 "Oppose Boost in Milk Price," *Daily Clarion*, 28 January 1937, 1; "Women Call Mass Meeting on Milk Boycott," *Toronto Evening Telegram*, 5 November 1937, 18; "Wives Mark One Day for Buying No Milk," *Toronto Daily Star*, 26 November 1937, 9; Ebejer, "'Milking' the Consumer," 34; Jim Mochoruk, *The People's Co-op: The Life and Times of a North End Institution* (Halifax: Fernwood Publishing, 2000): 59–64.

26 "Woman Insists Milk Too High at 12 Cents," *Toronto Daily Star*, 18 November 1937, 11.

27 Roy C. Barnes, "Rise of Corporatist Regulation"; "Milk Price Cut by Cent for Toronto," *Toronto Telegram*, 14 May 1938, cited in, Ebejer, "'Milking' the Consumer," 34.

28 "Dairies Make $8,000,000 in Year," *Daily Clarion*, 4 November 1937, 1.

29 "Farmer's Daughter Is Heartsick," letter to the editor, *Globe and Mail*, 5 March 1938, 6.

30 "Thinks City Should Sell Milk as Public Utility," *Toronto Daily Star*, 9 November 1937, 1.

31 "Dairies Decide on Lower Price as Women Band," *Daily Clarion*, 17 November 1937, 1.

32 "Lakeshore Women Unite to Fight Milk Increase," *Toronto Daily Star*, 13 November 1937, 6.

33 "Declares Municipalization Overdue in Milk, Coal, Bread," *Toronto Daily Star*, 30 November 1937, 6.

34 "School Club Joins in Milk Protest," *Toronto Evening Telegram*, 1 November 1937, 4; "Increase in Milk Price Is Opposed by Councillors," *Toronto Evening Telegram*, 2 November 1937, 4; "Wants Full Public Inquiry of Milk Price Situation as a Result of Cent Jump," *Toronto Evening Telegram*, 2 November 1937, 21; "Church Seeks Ottawa's Aid in Milk Price," *Toronto Evening Telegram*, 4 November 1937, 25; "Will Ask Curb on Milk Board," *Toronto Evening Telegram*, 10 November 1937, 21; "Farmers May Unite against Milk Trust," *Daily Clarion*, 11 November 1937, 1; "Urge Study of Milk Price," *Toronto Evening Telegram*, 17 November 1937, 9; "York Council

Calls Meeting to Protest Milk Increase," *Toronto Evening Telegram*, 6 November 1937, 13; "Urge Study of Milk Price," *Toronto Evening Telegram*, 17 November 1937, 9; "Abolition of Milk Board Urged at County Council," *Toronto Daily Star*, 23 November 1937, 1; "Inquiry by Government into Milk Cost Structure Asked by County Council," *Toronto Evening Telegram*, 23 November 1937, 1; "Declares Municipalization Overdue in Milk, Coal, Bread," *Toronto Daily Star*, 30 November 1937, 6.
35 "Millions Flow from Ontario's Milk Cans," *Toronto Evening Telegram*, 13 November 1937, 31.
36 "Nation-Wide Inquiry on Milk Price-Spread Opened by Committee," *Globe and Mail*, 1 March 1933, 1.
37 Ebejer, "'Milking' the Consumer," 20–39.
38 Ebejer, "'Milking' the Consumer," 36; "Housewives Seek Law Allowing 'Co-op' Dairies," *Toronto Evening Telegram*, 17 March 1938, 20.
39 "Housewives Seek Law Allowing 'Co-op' Dairies," *Toronto Evening Telegram*, 17 March 1938, 20.
40 "Housewives Sign Contract with Farmers," *Toronto Evening Telegram*, 23 June 1938, 30; "Farmers Join Housewives' Cooperative," *Globe and Mail*, 23 June 1938, 5; "First Vegetables Friday for Housewives' Union," *Toronto Daily Star*, 7 July 1938, 6; "Housewives' Plan Held Success," *Globe and Mail*, 9 July 1938, 4.
41 "Housewives' Association," in "With Our Women," *Daily Clarion*, 7 May 1938, 7.
42 "Housewives' Paper a Credit," *Daily Clarion*, 18 January 1938; "Toronto Housewives to Publish Paper," *Daily Clarion*, 6 April 1938.
43 For a longer discussion about the social significance of milk, see Julie Guard, "A Mighty Power against the Cost of Living: Canadian Housewives Organize in the 1930s," *International Labor and Working-Class History* 77 (2010): 27–47, http://dx.doi.org/10.1017/S0147547909990238
44 "Wives Ask for Representation on Ontario Milk Board," *Toronto Evening Telegram*, 10 December 1937, 30.
45 "Housewives Widen Scope of Cheapness Campaign," *Toronto Evening Telegram*, 19 November 1937, 4; "Lakeshore Women Unite to Fight Milk Increase," *Toronto Daily Star*, 19 November 1937, 6.
46 "Women Plan Mass Protest to Milk Board," *Toronto Evening Telegram*, 23 November 1937, 4.
47 "Up to Housewives," letter to the editor, *Toronto Daily Star*, 3 November 1937, 4.
48 "To Speak in Arena," *Daily Clarion*, 18 February 1938, 1; "Expect 8,000 Wives to Boycott Butter," *Toronto Daily Star*, 22 February 1938, 8; "Toronto

Women Picket High Food Cost," "Women Boycott Costly Butter, Groups Grow," *Daily Clarion*, 26 February 1938; Phyllis Poland, "International Women's Day: The Cost of Living and March the Eighth," *Daily Clarion*, 28 February 1938.

49 "Radio Privilege May Be Denied to Housewives," *Toronto Evening Telegram*, 18 March 1938, 29; "Housewives Plan Fight to Bring Down Butter Prices," "Ontario MPPs Asked to Support Changes to Milk Control Act," *Daily Clarion*, 18 March 1938, 1; "Butter Boycott Broadcast Permitted by Station," *Globe and Mail*, 19 March 1938, 5.

50 Thomas Kriger, "Syndicalism and Spilled Milk: The Origins of Dairy Farmer Activism in New York State, 1936–1941," *Labor History* 38, no. 2–3 (1997): 266–86.

51 "Women Insist on Food Probe," *Daily Clarion*, 25 March 1938.

52 "Housewives Seek Law Allowing 'Co-op' Dairies," *Toronto Evening Telegram*, 17 March 1938, 20; "Use Telephone to Popularize Boycott Week: Women throughout City Favor Plan for Campaign," *Daily Clarion*, 18 March 1938; "Urge Officials Query Spread in Food Price," *Toronto Evening Telegram*, 22 March 1938, 34; "Butter Boycott Is Still Busy," *Globe and Mail*, 23 March 1938, 5; "Ask Control Board Aid on Prices," "Housewives Present Resolution Demanding Probe into High Costs," *Daily Clarion*, 24 March 1938, 1; "Deluge of Protests Mailed to Hepburn, Housewives Parade to Post Office to Write Their Cards," *Toronto Daily Star*, 25 March 1938; "Women Insist on Food Probe," *Daily Clarion*, 25 March 1938, 1; "Housewives Consider Entering Candidates," *Globe and Mail*, 28 March 1938, 5.

53 Christine Chappel, Executive Secretary, Housewives Association, to Eric W. Cross, Member of Ontario Parliament, 31 January 1940, 9.

54 "Gas Bills Are Too High," *Daily Clarion*, 25 June 1938, 1.

55 Gerald Tulchinsky has produced an excellent account of Salsberg's contribution to Canada. Gerald J.J. Tulchinsky, *Joe Salsberg: A Life of Commitment* (Toronto: University of Toronto Press, 2013); "Take Over Gas Firm Housewives Suggest," *Toronto Daily Star*, 28 September 1938, 6; "Effort to Cut Dividends of Gas Company Defeated," *Toronto Daily Star*, 4 October 1938, 5; "City to Ask Gas Company to Abolish Meter Charge," *Toronto Daily Star*, 15 November 1938, 8.

56 "Consumers Gas Got $2,500,000 in Year's Profits," *Daily Clarion*, 17 November 1938, 1; "Aid Housewives Gas Campaign," *Daily Clarion*, 18 February 1939.

57 Mosby, *Food Will Win the War*, 165ff; "Housewives Plan Boycott to Fight Gas Meter Fee," *Toronto Daily Star*, 1 December 1938, 22; "Chart Great Crusade to Lower Prices," *Daily Clarion*, 2 December 1938, 2.

58 "200 Women Invade Office to Protest Gas Meter Fee," *Toronto Daily Star*, 8 February 1939, 3; "Toronto Women Seek Abolition of Gas Meter Fee," *Toronto Daily Star*, 8 February 1939, 3; "Women Halted on Steps to Gas Company Office," *Toronto Daily Star*, 10 February 1939, 7.
59 "Refuse to Permit Toronto to End Gas Meter Rental," *Toronto Daily Star*, 15 February 1938, 15; Bertha Lamb, President, Housewives Association, to The Hon. E. W. Cross, Minister of Public Welfare, 4 February 1938.
60 "Parley Called on Gas Meters," *Daily Clarion*, 1 May 1939; "Housewives Rally on Gas-Meter Issue," *Daily Clarion*, 2 May 1939, 3; "Gas Meter Conference Tonight," *Daily Clarion*, 4 May 1939; "Gas Conference Brief Strikes at Monopoly," *Daily Clarion*, 6 May 1939, 5.
61 Library and Archives Canada (LAC), RG 146, vol. 3353, Housewives and Consumers Federation of Canada, supp. 1, vol. 2, clipping, "Profiteer Prices Kernel of Emergency – Smith," *Canadian Tribune*, [December 1947] ATIP request 96-A-00007.
62 "Toronto Women Picket High Food Cost," "Women Boycott Costly Butter, Groups Grow," *Daily Clarion*, 26 February 1938, 1; "Housewives Declare Resistance to High Butter Price," *Daily Clarion*, 28 February 1938, 1, 5; Phyllis Poland, "International Women's Day: The Cost of Living and March the Eighth," *Daily Clarion*, 28 February 1938, 4.
63 "Housewives' Union Battles Milk Trust," *Daily Clarion*, 6 January 1938, 1.
64 "Housewives' Association," in "With Our Women," *Daily Clarion*, 7 May 1938, 4.
65 "Mrs. Lamb Blames Reds as Housewives Disband," *Toronto Telegram*, 22 September 1938, 30.
66 "Montreal Housewives Will Fight Attempts to Raise Rent Rates," *Daily Clarion*, 19 February 1938.
67 Catharine Vance, *Not by Gods but by People: The Story of Bella Hall Gauld* (Toronto: Progress Books, 1968).
68 LAC, RG146, Housewives League, Montreal, Quebec, ATIP request A-2007–00010, vol. 1, RCMP "C" Division file, "Canadian Housewives League," 27 January 1936.
69 "Buck Detained at Montreal," *Globe and Mail*, 4 February 1939, 2; "Montreal Housewives Will Fight Attempts to Raise Rent Rates," *Daily Clarion*, 19 February 1938; "Mont'l Women Propose Anti-Profiteering Action," *The Clarion*, 28 October 1939; LAC, RG146, Housewives League, Montreal, Quebec, RCMP report re: Federated Youth Clubs of Montreal (Young Communist League), 27 November 1939; "Fighting Higher Rents, Montreal Housewives Placard Homes," *Globe and Mail*, 19 February 1940, 2.

70 Effie Jones, interview by Sara Diamond, 21 November 1979, Women's Labour History Project, BC Archives, call number T3588:0001.
71 Wm. Purvis, "B.C. Organizes to Cut Prices," *Daily Clarion*, 16 March 1938; "B.C. Housewives Ask Men to Join," *Globe and Mail*, 11 November 1938, 10.
72 "Housewives Call Strike vs. Meat Cost," *Daily Clarion*, 10 May 1939.
73 "Councils, Unions, Women Protest against Profiteering: Wide Conferences to Discuss Action by Citizens Being Called in London, Vancouver, Toronto," *Daily Clarion*, 21 October 1939; "B.C. Housewives Ask Men to Join," *Globe and Mail*, 11 November 1938, 10; LAC, RG146, Housewives League, BC, ATIP request A-2007–00010, clippings, "Food Prices Still Soaring, Housewives Call Protest Rally," *The Pacific Advocate*, 22 September 1939; RCMP report on Housewives' League of BC, 2 October 1939; clipping, "Anti-Profiteering Council Is Named," 1 November 1939; RCMP report, 20 April 1940. Along with others on the left, Mrs Jamieson was a patron of the progressive Vancouver Folk Festival. Gary Cristall, "The Vancouver Folk Song and Dance Festival with Arts and Crafts Exhibition: The First Ongoing Multicultural Festival in Canada," *Canadian Folk Music Bulletin* 46 (2012): 19–27, www.folkmusichistory.com/528-2078-1-PB.pdf
74 On Consumers' Research, see Glickman, *Buying Power*, 189ff.
75 Jones, interview.
76 Jones, interview. On the history of the RCWU, see John Manley, "'Starve, Be Damned!' Communists and Canada's Urban Unemployed, 1929–39," *Canadian Historical Review* 79 (1998): 466–91.
77 "Winnipeg Women Forget All Dignity When They Talk about Milk Prices," *Globe and Mail*, 11 January 1938, 13; "Winnipeg Hits Profiteering," *Daily Clarion*, 28 October 1939.
78 "'Peg Wives Campaign against High Prices: Will Hold Mass Meeting, Radio Broadcast, Get Mayor's Support," *Daily Clarion*, 11 May 1938, 1; "Winnipeg Housewives Association Calls Milk Boycott," *Port Arthur News Chronicle*, 12 September 1938; "Winnipeg Hits Profiteering," *Toronto Clarion*, 28 October 1939.
79 "Call Conference on Living Standards/City Councils, Unions, Women Join Protest against Profiteering: Wide Conferences to Discuss Action by Citizens Being Called in London, Vancouver, Toronto," *Toronto Clarion*, 21 October 1939.
80 "Women Uniting against Prices Mrs. Lamb Says," *Daily Clarion*, 8 November 1937, 1.

81 "Meeting Hectic as Women Vote to Force Milk Cut," *Toronto Daily Star*, 9 November 1937, 9.
82 "Toronto and Suburbs Protest Milk Boost Delay Is Demanded," *Toronto Daily Star*, 2 November 1937, 1.
83 Ewart Gladstone Humphreys married Ethel May Watts in York, Ontario, on 1 August 1923. http://www.ancestry.ca/
84 Laurel Sefton MacDowell, *Renegade Lawyer: The Life of J.L. Cohen* (Toronto: University of Toronto Press, 2014), 56; RCMP, "Weekly Summary: Report on Revolutionary Organizations and Agitation in Canada," 15 July 1936, in Gregory S. Kealey and Reginald Whitaker, eds. *R.C.M.P. Security Bulletins: The Depression Years* (St. John's, Nfld.: Canadian Committee on Canadian Labour History, 1993): 291 https://journals.lib.unb.ca/index.php/RCMP/article/viewFile/9497/9552; Manley, "'Starve, be Damned!'"
85 Schulz, *East York Workers' Association*; Mary Flanigan, "A Tribute to the Women of East York," *Daily Clarion*, 13 June 1936, 1; "East York Jobless Move Toward C.I.O.," *Toronto Daily Star*, 1 May 1937; "'No More Babies' Strike Suggested in East York," *Toronto Daily Star*, 13 October 1937.
86 "Meeting Hectic as Women Vote to Force Milk Cut," *Toronto Daily Star*, 9 November 1937, 9; Michael Dawber, *After You, Agnes: Mrs. Rae Luckock, MPP* (Tweed, ON: Quinte Web Press, 1994): 21–2.
87 Benjamin Isitt, "Tug-of-War: The Working Class and Political Change in British Columbia, 1948–1972," (PhD dissertation, University of New Brunswick, Department of History, 2008): 205–6.
88 Maurice Rush, *We Have a Glowing Dream: Recollections of Working-Class and People's Struggles in B.C. from 1935 to 1996* (Vancouver: Centre for Socialist Education, 1996), 163–5, 184n22.
89 Howard, "The Mothers' Council of Vancouver," 252–3.
90 Jennifer Anderson, *Propaganda and Persuasion in the Cold War: The Canadian Soviet Friendship Society* (Winnipeg: University of Manitoba Press, 2017); Francisca de Haan, "The Women's International Democratic Federation (WIDF): History, Main Agenda, and Contributions, 1945–1991," (Alexandria, VA: Alexander Street, 2012), https://search.alexanderstreet.com/view/work/bibliographic_entity%7Cbibliographic_details%7C2476925
91 The episode is also mentioned in Louise Watson's biography of the Communist Party's most prominent woman member, Annie Buller, which suggests that Rodd was also a party member: Watson, *She Never Was Afraid*, 126; "Windsor Women Organize League," *Toronto Telegram*, 31 March 1938, 16; Arthur Blakely, "Ottawa Day by Day," *Montreal Gazette*, 26 May 1951, 2.

92 "Professor, Air Office Held Incommunicado," *Globe and Mail*, 23 March 1946, 1; "Soviet Files Link Lunan, Mazerall, Halperin and Smith with 'Network,'" *Ottawa Journal*, 23 March 1946, 1; Reg Whitaker and Gary Marcuse, *Cold War Canada: The Making of a National Insecurity State, 1945–1957* (Toronto: University of Toronto Press, 1994), 70, 432n36.

93 Michiel Horn, *The League for Social Reconstruction: Intellectual Origins of the Democratic Left in Canada 1930–1942* (Toronto: University of Toronto Press, 1980), 23–4, 28, 38, 187ff; Michiel Horn, "Professors in the Public Eye: Canadian Universities, Academic Freedom, and the League for Social Reconstruction," *History of Education Quarterly* 20 (1980): 433.

94 Ebejer, "'Milking' the Consumer," 36; "Relief System in Toronto Said Costly to Taxpayers," *Toronto Evening Telegram*, 10 March 1938, 28; "Milk Price Goes Up Infant Deaths Follow," *Daily Clarion*, 7 September 1938, 1; "Dairies Make $8,000,000 in Year: Toronto Citizens Pay Higher Rates," *Daily Clarion*, 4 November 1937, 1.

95 Dave Richards, *Milk for Millions* (New York: New York State Committee, Communist Party, [1938]).

96 "Oppose Boost in Milk Price," *Daily Clarion*, 28 January 1937; "Rise in Food Cost Fought by Women," *Daily Clarion*, 11 February 1937; "Would Probe Spread before Price Raised," *Toronto Daily Star*, 3 November 1937, 6; "York Council Calls Meeting to Protest Milk Price Increase," *Toronto Evening Telegram*, 6 November 1937, 13.

97 "City Wide Meet of Women's Clubs," *Daily Clarion*, 23 May 1936, 1; "Council of Women Is Organized," *Daily Clarion*, 9 May 1936, 2; "Tag Day for Kiddies," *Daily Clarion*, 30 May 1936.

98 Peter Campbell, *Rose Henderson: A Woman for the People* (Montreal: McGill-Queen's University Press, 2010): 7, 10ff.

99 John Manley, "'Audacity, Audacity, Still More Audacity': Tim Buck, the Party, and the People, 1932–1939," *Labour/Le Travail* 49 (April 2002): 9–41; Manley, "'Starve, Be Damned!'"

100 "Meeting Hectic as Women Vote to Force Milk Cut," *Toronto Daily Star*, 9 November 1937, 9.

101 Len de Caux, *Labor Radical: From the Wobblies to the CIO, a Personal History* (Boston: Beacon Press, 1970), cited in Frances Fox Piven and Richard A. Cloward, *Poor People's Movements: Why They Succeed, How They Fail* (New York: Vintage Books, 1979), 52, 69.

102 "Mrs. Lamb Blames Reds as Housewives Disbanded," *Toronto Evening Telegram*, 22 September 1938, 30; "Housewives' Army Disbands, 'Red Charge' Is Good Joke," *Toronto Daily Star*, 22 September 1938; "Housewives Condemn Mrs. Lamb's Antics," *Daily Clarion*, 24 September 1938.

103 "Housewives Association Is Disbanded; Communism Blamed," *Port Arthur News Chronicle*, 23 September 1938, 12; "Housewives' Head Denies Communism," *Daily Province* (Vancouver), 30 July 1940.
104 Bertha Lamb, "The Housewives Want No Padlocks," in "Women's World," *Daily Clarion*, 14 May 1938, 1.
105 "Mrs. Lamb Blames Reds as Housewives Disband," *Toronto Evening Telegram*, 22 September 1938, 30; "Full Inquiry into Activities of Reds Likely," *Hamilton Spectator*, 22 September 1938, 1; "Housewives' Army Disbands, 'Red Charge' Is Good Joke," *Toronto Daily Star*, 22 September 1938; "Housewives' Officers at Loggerheads over Dissolution Claim," *Globe and Mail*, 23 September 1938; "The Methods of the Reds," editorial, *Globe and Mail*, 23 September 1938, 6; LAC, RG146, Vol. 3440, Housewives Consumers Association, Toronto, ON, part 1, clippings, "Housewives Condemn Mrs. Lamb's Antics," *Daily Clarion*, 24 September 1938, "Ready to Investigate Any Communistic Angle," *Ottawa Journal*, 23 September 1938; "Legal Advisor of Housewives Denies Charge," *Globe and Mail*, 24 September 1938, 4. On Gordon Conant, see Reg Whitaker, "Official Repression of Communism during World War II," *Labour/Le Travail* 17 (1986): 135–66.
106 "Housewives Unit Dissolved; Reds Blamed," *Globe and Mail*, 22 September 1938, 13; "Housewives' Army Disbands, 'Red Charge' Is Good Joke," *Toronto Daily Star*, 22 September 1938; "Housewives' Officers at Loggerheads over Dissolution Claim," *Globe and Mail*, 23 September 1938; "Housewives Condemn Mrs. Lamb's Antics," *Daily Clarion*, 24 September 1938.
107 LAC, RG146, Housewives Consumers Association, Toronto, ON, part 1, memo to the commissioner, RCMP, from Superintendent W. Munday, Commander, O Division.
108 Lara Campbell, *Respectable Citizens*, 178.
109 "Housewives Reorganize," *Globe and Mail*, 24 November 1938, 1; "Housewives Reorganized," *Toronto Telegram*, 25 November 1938, 1, 2.
110 "Housewives Seek to Work with Farmers," *Daily Clarion*, 23 November 1938; "Housewives Plan Parleys to Terminate 'Monopolies,'" *Toronto Evening Telegram*, 30 November 1938, 1; Beatrice Ferneyhough, "Housewives' Resolutions Present Plan of Action: Clear-Cut Program, Inner Democracy Characterize Women's Movement," *Daily Clarion*, 2 December 1938.
111 "Meetings to Hear Woodsworth, Gould, Alderman Davy," *Daily Clarion*, 10 May 1939; "Unemployed Ask Women for Food," *Daily Clarion*, 10 May 1939; Rose L. Metcalfe and Mrs. Jennie Cook, Ward Five

Housewives, "The Unemployed Transients," letter to the editor, *Toronto Daily Star*, 19 October 1939, 7; "Winnipeg Hits Profiteering," *Toronto Clarion*, 28 October 1939, 1; *Toronto Daily Star*, 2 January 1940; LAC, RG146, Housewives Consumers Association, Toronto, ON, part 1, RCMP file, "Re; C.P. Activity among Single Unemployed, 53 Duke St., Toronto, Ont." 21 June 1940.

112 "Housewives' Association Must Pay Rent for Hall," *Globe and Mail*, 29 Nov 1938, 28; "Boycott Paraders Outwit Montreal Police Squads," *Daily Clarion*, 20 December 1938, 3.

113 On Drummond Wren, see Ian Radforth and Joan Sangster, "'A Link between Labour and Learning': The Workers Educational Association in Ontario, 1917–1951," *Labour/Le Travail* 8/9 (1981): 41–78.

114 "Excess Taxes and Profits Hit by Housewives' Meeting; Annual Election Is Protested," *Globe and Mail*, 30 November 1939, 22.

115 "Purge of Red Schools in Toronto to Be Demanded by Housewives: National Association Is Also Going to Ask That Circulation of Godless Literature Be Stopped Lanphier Is Speaker," *Globe and Mail*, 21 January 1939, 4.

116 Patrias, *Relief Strike*; Schulz, *The East York Workers' Association*.

117 Campbell, *Respectable Citizens*.

118 Paula Maurutto, "Private Policing and Surveillance of Catholics: Anti-Communism in the Roman Catholic Archdiocese of Toronto, 1920–60," in *Whose National Security?: Canadian State Surveillance and the Creation of Enemies*, ed. Gary Kinsman, Dieter K Buse, and Mercedes Steedman (Toronto: Between the Lines, 2000): 37–54.

119 "Purge of Red Schools in Toronto to Be Demanded by Housewives: National Association Is Also Going to Ask That Circulation of Godless Literature Be Stopped Lanphier Is Speaker," *Globe and Mail*, 21 January 1939, 4; "Probe to Seek Red in Schools," *Globe and Mail*, 7 February 1939, 13; "Provincial Ban on Red Schools May Be Sought," *Globe and Mail*, 14 Mar 1939, 2; "Committee Favors Inquiry into 'Red' Schools," *Globe and Mail*, 15 Mar 1939, 15; "Housewives Union Approves League," *Globe and Mail*, 18 March 1939, 7.

120 "Red Schools in Toronto," editorial, *Globe and Mail*, 16 March 1939, 6.

121 H. Ivers Kelly, "Millions of Dollars Back Red Teaching," *Globe and Mail*, 23 March 1939, 21.

122 "Organizations Confused, East York Group Complains," *Globe and Mail*, 21 February 1939, 8; "Deny They Authored Communist Charges," *Toronto Daily Star*, 21 February 1939, 6.

123 Bertha Lamb bears the same last name as Majorie Lamb, a well-known anticommunist crusader, but there is no evidence of any relationship.
124 Phyllis Poland, "The Cost of Living and International Women's Day, March the Eighth," *Daily Clarion*, 28 February 1938.
125 "Tory Leader Backs Hepburn about Relief," *Globe and Mail*, 2 March 1938, 1.
126 Franca Iacovetta, *Gatekeepers: Reshaping Immigrant Lives in Cold War Canada* (Toronto: Between the Lines, 2006); Whitaker and Marcuse, *Cold War Canada*.

2. Housewife-Patriots and Wartime Price Controls

1 On National Farm Radio Forum, see Eleanor Beattie, "Public Education in the Mass Media: National Farm Radio Forum on CBC Radio" (PhD dissertation, Concordia University, 1999); Leonard Kuffert, "'Stabbing Our Spirits Broad Awake': Reconstructing Canadian Culture, 1940–1948," in *Cultures of Citizenship in Post-war Canada, 1940–1955*, ed. Nancy Christie and Michael Gauvreau (Montreal: McGill-Queen's University Press, 2004), 27–62.
2 By mid-1942, both agricultural production and exports had increased significantly, doubling in some cases, in response to wartime demand. G.E. Britnell and V.C. Fowke, *Canadian Agriculture in War and Peace 1935–50* (Stanford, CA: Stanford University Press, 1962), 104.
3 "Is Rationing Rational?" *National Farm Radio Forum*, broadcast on 1 March 1943, http://www.cbc.ca/archives/entry/farm-forum-is-rationing-rational
4 Graham Broad supplies this excellent image. See Broad, *A Small Price to Pay*, 91.
5 J.L. Granatstein, *Canada's War: The Politics of the Mackenzie King Government, 1939–1945* (Toronto: University of Toronto Press, 1990), 180.
6 Broad, *A Small Price to Pay*, 16–49; Mosby, *Food Will Win the War*, 74–83, 95.
7 "Local Consumers, Dealers, Pleased with National Butter Rationing," *Globe and Mail*, 21 December 1942, 13.
8 Granatstein, *Canada's War*, 252.
9 Mosby, *Food Will Win the War*, 5–8.
10 Mosby, *Food Will Win the War*, 64–6; David W. Slater with Robert B. Bryce, *War, Finance and Reconstruction: The Role of Canada's Department of Finance 1939–1946* (Ottawa: Department of Finance, 1995), 129–32.
11 Jeffrey A. Keshen, *Saints, Sinners, and Soldiers: Canada's Second World War* (Vancouver: UBC Press, 2004), 55, 57; Slater, *War, Finance and Reconstruction*, 129–32.

12 "No Profiteering Scandal This War, M'Larty Says," *Toronto Daily Star*, 20 February 1940, 31; "Search of Private Homes Likely in Hoarding Drive," *Toronto Daily Star*, 20 September 1939, 1, 10.
13 "Nation-Wide Public Meetings Protest High Living Costs; Windsor Meet Sets Up League against War Profiteering," *Toronto Clarion*, 30 September 1939.
14 Jules Backman, *War Time Price Control* (New York: New York University School of Law, 1940), 3–4, 20–1, 45–6.
15 Broad, *A Small Price to Pay*, 23, 27, 30, 35, 40, 43, 48, 207ff.
16 "Toronto Housewives to Publish Paper," *Daily Clarion*, 6 April 1938; Alice Cooke, "Housewives' Association," in "With Our Women," *Daily Clarion*, 7 May 1938; LAC, RG146, Housewives League, British Columbia, AITP request A-2007–00010, report from RCMP "E" Division, "The Housewives' League, Vancouver, B.C.," 25 April 1941; LAC, RG146, Housewives League, British Columbia, AITP request A-2007–00010, report from RCMP E Division, "The Housewives' League," 16 September 1941.
17 On the WEA, see Radforth and Sangster, "A Link between Labour and Learning."
18 Mary Prokop, interview by author, Toronto, ON, 15 December 1998.
19 "Housewives Plan Conference on Profiteering," *Toronto Clarion*, 7 October 1939, 1.
20 "Winnipeg Hits Profiteering," *Toronto Clarion*, 28 October 1939.
21 "Nation-Wide Meets Urge Ottawa Take Effective Measures: Want Consumers Represented on Prices Control Board; Vets, Unions, Youth in Movement," *Toronto Clarion*, 7 October 1939; "300 Housewives Sponsor Move to Curb Profiteering, Regulate Prices," *Toronto Clarion*, 7 October 1939; "Montreal Women Propose Anti-Profiteering Action: Would Tax Profits, Fix Prices, Ration Scarce Commodities: Housewives' League Meeting Sends Resolution to All Montreal M.P.s," *Toronto Clarion*, 28 October 1939; LAC, RG146, Housewives League, British Columbia, AITP request A-2007–00010, clippings, "Anti-Profiteering Council Is Named," 1 November 1939, "Survey of Housewives," BC Housewives League [probably April/May 1941].
22 On Regina's city council, see William J. Brennan, "'The Common People Have Spoken with a Mighty Voice': Regina's Labour City Councils, 1936–1939," *Labour/Le Travail* 71 (2013): 49–86. On Lyle Telford, see Jean Barman, "Neighbourhood and Community in Interwar Vancouver: Residential Differentiation and Civic Voting Behaviour," *B.C. Studies* 69/70 (1986), reprinted in Robert A.J. McDonald and Jean Barman, eds., *Vancouver Past: Essays in Social History* (Vancouver: UBC Press, 1986), 97–141; "Nation-

Wide Public Meetings Protest High Living Costs: Windsor Meet Sets Up League against War Profiteering," *Toronto Clarion*, 30 September 1939.
23 "Hoarders Disgorge 330,000 lbs. Butter," *Toronto Daily Star*, 21 February 1940, 33; "Search of Private Homes Likely in Hoarding Drive," *Toronto Daily Star*, 20 September 1939, 1, 10.
24 See, Broad, *A Small Price to Pay*, for a discussion of advertising in wartime.
25 Keshen, *Saints, Sinners, and Soldiers*, 107–11. On meat consumption and rationing, see also, Broad, *A Small Price to Pay*, 16–38.
26 Canada's wartime and postwar housing shortage has been well-documented. See, for example, Kevin Brushett, "'Where Will the People Go': Toronto's Emergency Housing Program and the Limits of Canadian Social Housing Policy, 1944–1957," *Journal of Urban History* 33, no. 3 (2007): 375–99; Veronica Strong-Boag, "Home Dreams: Women and the Suburban Experiment in Canada, 1945–60," *Canadian Historical Review* 72, no. 4 (1991): 471–504; Jill Wade, "'A Palace for the Public': Housing Reform and the 1946 Occupation of the Old Hotel Vancouver," *BC Studies* 69/70 (1986): 288–310.
27 Broad, *A Small Price to Pay*, 35–9; Mosby, *Food Will Win the War*, 66; Slater, *War, Finance and Reconstruction*, 160.
28 Slater, *War, Finance and Reconstruction*, 131.
29 Broad, *A Small Price to Pay*, 40; see also, Mosby, *Food Will Win the War*, 65.
30 W. H. Heick, *A Propensity to Protect: Butter, Margarine and the Rise of Urban Culture in Canada* (Waterloo, ON: Wilfrid Laurier University Press, 1991), 56.
31 LAC, RG146, Housewives League, British Columbia, AITP request A-2007-00010, clippings, "Housewives' League Threatens Butter Strike If Prices Increased," *Daily Province* (Vancouver), 29 November 1940, "Housewives on Warpath: League Meeting Denounces Canada's Wartime Measures," *Daily Province* (Vancouver), 30 November 1940.
32 "Call Sent for Police as Crowds of Women Raise Clamour for Butter," *Toronto Telegram*, 28 November 1942, 1, cited in Broad, *A Small Price to Pay*, 36.
33 "Butter Action Demand Sent to Government," *Globe and Mail*, 3 December 1942, 4.
34 "Local Consumers, Dealers Pleased with National Butter Rationing," *Globe and Mail*, 21 December 1942, 13; "Butter Action Demand Sent to Government," *Globe and Mail*, 3 December 1942, 4; "Butter Rationing Suggestion 'Conboy's Opinion': Taggart," *Globe and Mail*, 10 December 1942, 4.

35 For example, "Hoarders Create Butter Shortage," *Globe and Mail*, 3 November 1942, 2.
36 Mosby, *Food Will Win the War*, 145.
37 "Cost of Living Index Lower for December," *Globe and Mail*, 4 February 1943, 9.
38 "Consider Boost in Milk Price," *Globe and Mail*, 15 January 1941, 3; "Plan Milk-Price Boost of One Cent per Quart as Aid to Producers," *Globe and Mail*, 16 January 1941, 4.
39 Granatstein, *Canada's War*, 160–74; "Offers Cheese Subsidy If Butter Peg Removed," *Globe and Mail*, 18 January 1941, 1–2; "A Subsidy with Strings," *Globe and Mail*, 20 January 1941, 6; "Increase in Milk Price Is Regarded as Certain," *Globe and Mail*, 22 January 1941, 4; "Farmers Given Benefit as Milk Up to 13 Cents," *Globe and Mail*, 23 January 1941, 4.
40 "Council Demands Probe under the Combine Act of Milk Control Board," *Globe and Mail*, 6 May 1941, 4.
41 "Powers Override Regulations Made in Any Province," *Globe and Mail*, 30 August 1941, 1; "Plan Meeting on Milk Price," *Globe and Mail*, 4 September 1941, 4; "Civic Body Asks Ottawa to Peg Price of Milk," *Globe and Mail*, 9 September 1941, 5.
42 "6 Centres Join Toronto Seek Milk Act Change," *Globe and Mail*, 24 September 1941, 4; "Saunders Acts on Milk Price," *Globe and Mail*, 24 September 1941, 13.
43 "Milk Shortage Is Seen Unless Price Goes Up," *Globe and Mail*, 5 December 1941, 8.
44 "Payment of Milk Subsidies Ordered to Aid Producers," *Globe and Mail*, 20 December 1941, 1–2.
45 Backman, *War Time Price Control*, 45–7; "Citizens Make $1,520,000 Saving in Milk Outlay," *Globe and Mail*, 11 December 1942, 4.
46 "Housewives Plan Protest on Coal," *Globe and Mail*, 14 April 1943, 10.
47 Mrs Mary Aveline, "Housewives Played Part," letter to the editor, *Globe and Mail*, 14 December 1942, 6
48 "Higher Prices Seen for Milk at War's End," *Globe and Mail*, 18 November 1943, 4.
49 Mosby, *Food Will Win the War*, 80.
50 "Housewives Claim Living Cost Inflated," *Globe and Mail*, 22 April 1942, 4.
51 "Housewives Plan Boycott to Fight Gas Meter Fee," *Toronto Daily Star*, December 1938, 22; "Women to Aid Jobless Men," *Globe and Mail*, 23 January 1939, 4; "Trustees Fail to Take Stand on Cadet Work," *Globe and Mail*, 17 March 1939, 4; "Housewives' Meetings Oppose Cadet Revival," *Toronto Daily Star*, 1 August 1939, 10; "Seek Parley of All Parties in Milk

Dispute," *Globe and Mail*, 15 November 1941, 4; "Housewives Claim Living Cost Inflated," *Globe and Mail*, 22 April 1942, 4; "Lack of Coordination in Day Nurseries Plan Claimed by Delegation," *Globe and Mail*, 12 December 1942, 14; "B.C. Consumer Group Has Wide Program," *Globe and Mail*, 25 February 1943, 10; "Housewives Plan Protest on Coal," *Globe and Mail*, 14 April 1943, 10; "Toronto Householders Want Ottawa to Name City Fuel Controller," *Globe and Mail*, 22 April 1943, 4; LAC, RG146, Housewives League, Vancouver, BC, AITP request A-2007–00010, clipping, "Unions Back Franchise Move," *Daily Province* (Vancouver), 13 August 1943; "Housewives Elect Mrs. E. Bartlett," *Globe and Mail*, 18 April 1944, 9. On Toronto's Day Nursery struggle, see Susan Prentice, "Workers, Mothers, Reds: Toronto's Postwar Daycare Fight," *Studies in Political Economy* 30 (1989): 115–41.

52 "Taxation Problem Vital for East York, by Elizabeth Morton, Candidate for East York Council," *Daily Clarion*, 3 January 1939; LAC, RG146, Housewives League, Montreal, Quebec, AITP request A-2007–00010, report from RCMP "C" Division re: Labour Progressive Party, Montreal, P.Q., 10 October 1946; LAC, RG146, Housewives League, Montreal, Quebec, AITP request A-2007–00010, RCMP memorandum re: "Pacific Advocate," 16 October 1945.

53 Donald Gordon, *Report of the Wartime Prices and Trade Board January 1, 1944 to December 31, 1944* (Ottawa: Wartime Prices and Trade Board, 12 March 1945), 43.

54 "Mobilize Housewives Diet to Aid Win War," *Toronto Daily Star*, 13 January 1940, 2.

55 Backman, *War Time Price Control*, 60–1.

56 Lillian D. Millar, "Price Control Depends Largely on the Women," *Saturday Night*, 10 October 1942, 20; Lillian D. Millar, "Has This Structure of a Million Women Post-War Potentialities?" *Saturday Night*, 8 July 1944, 22–3.

57 Phyllis Poland, publicity director of the Housewives' Association of Canada, "International Women's Day: The Cost of Living and March the Eighth," *Daily Clarion*, 28 February 1938.

58 Mosby, *Food Will Win the War*, 99.

59 Meg Jacobs, *Pocketbook Politics*, 204–12 passim; Martin Hart-Landsberg, "Popular Mobilization and Progressive Policy Making: Lessons from World War II Price Control Struggles in the United States," *Science and Society* 67, no. 4 (2003–4): 399–428. For Canada, see Broad, *A Small Price to Pay*, 16–49; Mosby, *Food Will Win the War*, 61–132. See also, Matthew Hilton, *Consumerism in 20th-Century Britain: The Search for a Historical Movement* (Cambridge: Cambridge University Press, 2003); Martin

Daunton and Matthew Hilton, eds., *The Politics of Consumption: Material Culture and Citizenship in Europe and America* (Oxford: Berg, 2001).

60 "Women from Many Walks Urge Action on Hospitals," *Globe and Mail*, 15 August 1944, 10; "Citizenship in Action," *Globe and Mail*, 16 August 1944, 6; "Make Plea to Mr. King for Wartime Hospitals," *Globe and Mail*, 23 August 1944, 4. On the life of Margaret Hyndman, see Shirley Tillotson, "Human Rights Law as Prism: Women's Organizations, Unions, and Ontario's Female Employees Fair Remuneration Act, 1951," *Canadian Historical Review* 72, no. 4 (1991): 532–57.

61 A contemporary example is Ontario's declaration of Agnes Macphail Day, Hansard Transcripts, Legislative Assembly of Ontario, 25 June 1992, http://www.ontla.on.ca/web/house-proceedings/house_detail.do?locale=en&Date=1992-06-25. Terry Crowley is one of the few to acknowledge Luckock: *Agnes Macphail and the Politics of Equality* (Toronto: James Lorimer, 1990), 185, 189. Doris Pennington includes one mention but misspells her name as "Lulock": *Agnes Macphail, Reformer: Canada's First Female M.P.* (Toronto: Simon & Pierre, 1989), 230. Rachel Wyatt, *Agnes Macphail: Champion of the Underdog* (Toronto: Dundurn, 2000), includes no mention of Luckock at all.

62 Dawber, *After You, Agnes*.

63 Parr, *Domestic Goods*, 92. Terry Crowley also makes this observation in *Agnes Macphail and the Politics of Equality*, 190.

64 LAC, MG32, Marjorie Mann fonds, G12, Vol. 1, "CCF Women's Committee Conference, September 25 and 26, 1948," Ontario CCF Women's Committee, Chairman's Business File, correspondence, minutes, etc., 1948.

65 Agnes Macphail, "Milk Price May Force Diversion," *Globe and Mail*, 13 December 1941, 15.

66 Peter Campbell's biography of Rose Henderson does not mention Luckock, but Michael Dawber's biography of Luckock confirms that she worked to elect Henderson in 1934. Campbell, *Rose Henderson*.

67 "Liberal Slate Wiped Off at Toronto-York Polls; Many New Members," *Globe and Mail*, 5 August 1943, 4; "Candidate Raps Listlessness," *Globe and Mail*, 30 December 1942, 4.

68 "Votes $3000 to Maintain Scholarships," *Globe and Mail*, 5 February 1943, 4; "Noisy Council Brings Police; Housing Voted," *Globe and Mail*, 6 September 1944, 4.

69 Henry Srebrnik, *Jerusalem on the Amur: Birobidzhan and the Canadian Jewish Communist Movement, 1924–1951* (Montreal: McGill-Queen's University Press, 2007), 158–9.

70 Reg Whitaker, helpfully, identifies this organization. See Whitaker, "Repression of Communism," 156.
71 Watson, *She Never Was Afraid*; "Dewson School Club," *Globe and Mail*, 3 December 1941, 11; "Power Is Necessary with League Responsibility, President Frank J. Day Claims," *Globe & Mail*, 4 April 1939, 11; "Russia Study Group Has Christmas Party," *Globe and Mail*, 19 December 1942, 5; J.V. McAbee, "Women Offer Proof of Their Brightness," op-ed, *Globe and Mail*, 1 March 1944, 6; F.S. Northedge, *The League of Nations: Its Life and Times, 1920–1946* (New York: Holmes & Meier, 1986); "Ask Clothing for Russians," *Globe and Mail*, 22 December 1942, 4; "Clothing Depot Hive of Industry," *Globe and Mail*, 30 December 1942, 11; "17,000 Clothing Units Start on Trip to Russia," *Globe and Mail*, 13 January 1943, 4; "Gifts Appreciated, Says Russ Envoy; Need Is Great for Children's Things," *Globe and Mail*, 19 January 1943, 5; "99,000 Pounds Clothing Sent to Russ People," *Globe and Mail*, 3 February 1943, 4; "12,000 Articles Sorted Every Day for Russia," *Globe and Mail*, 17 February 1943, 9. On the identification of Ukrainian organizations, see Bogdan S. Kordan, *Canada and the Ukrainian Question, 1939–1945: A Study in Statecraft* (Montreal: McGill-Queen's University Press, 2001).
72 "Women's School for Citizenship," *Globe and Mail*, 25 January 1944, 8; J.V. McAbee, "Women Offer Proof of Their Brightness," op-ed, *Globe and Mail*, 1 March 1944, 6.
73 LAC, RG146, Vol. 3440, Housewives Consumers Association of Toronto, part 1, HCA telegram to Ernest Lapointe, Minister of Justice, 13 June 1940; "Over 140 Women's Groups Are Aiding Health League," *Toronto Daily Star*, 17 January 1940, 23; "Prisoners of War Get Yule Boxes," *Globe and Mail*, 4 March 1943, 12.
74 Ruth Roach Pierson, *They're Still Women After All: The Second World War and Canadian Womanhood* (Toronto: McClelland and Stewart, 1986), 33, 44.
75 Slater, *War, Finance, and Reconstruction*; Douglas McCalla, "The Economic Impact of the Great War," in *Canada and the First World War: Essays in Honour of Robert Craig Brown*, ed. David Clark MacKenzie (Toronto: University of Toronto Press, 2005), 138–53.
76 K.W. Taylor, "Canadian War-Time Price Controls, 1941–6," *The Canadian Journal of Economics and Political Science* 13, no. 1 (1947): 87.
77 "Cost-of-Living Cuts Made Effective Today," *Globe and Mail*, 7 December 1942, 1–2; "Winning the War," *Proceedings of the Academy of Political Science* 20, no. 1 (1942). For a detailed account of the wartime Finance department, see Slater, *War, Finance and Reconstruction*.

78 Jules Backman, *The Price Control and Subsidy Program in Canada* (Washington, D.C.: The Brookings Institute, 1943); A. F. W. Plumptre, "Price and Wage Control in Canada," Proceedings of the Academy of Political Science, vol. 20, no. 1, *Winning the War* (May, 1942): 23–34, http://www.jstor.org/stable/1173088; Taylor, "Canadian War-Time Price Controls," 87.

79 Bryce, "Prices, Wages and the Ceiling," in Slater, *War, Finance and Reconstruction*, 127, 131.

80 Backman, *War Time Price Control*; Backman, *Price Control and Subsidy Program*; Taylor, "Canadian War-Time Price Controls."

81 Dominion Bureau of Statistics, *Canada Year Book 1946* (Ottawa: King's Printer, 1946), 862; Backman, *Price Control and Subsidy Program*, 21; John English, "Wartime Prices and Trade Board," *Canadian Encyclopedia*, http://www.thecanadianencyclopedia.ca/en/article/wartime-prices-and-trade-board/, modified 17 February 2015; Keshen, *Saints, Sinners, and Soldiers*, 55, 57; Slater, *War, Finance and Reconstruction*, 128–34, 153, 159. In December 1940, the Cabinet approved Privy Council order PC 7440, which fixed wage rates, permitting increases only in the form of cost-of-living bonuses. Salaries of white-collar workers were controlled a year later, at the same time as prices.

82 John Riddell and Ian Angus, *The Left in Canada in World War II*, Socialist History Project, 9 October 2004, http://www.socialisthistory.ca/Docs/History/Left-in-WW2.htm

83 Chris Frazer, "From Pariahs to Patriots: Canadian Communists and the Second World War," *Past Imperfect* 5 (1996), reprinted by Socialist History Project: http://www.socialisthistory.ca/Docs/History/Pariahs_to_Patriots.htm#_ftnref18

84 For example, Peter Krawchuk, *Interned without Cause: The Internment of Canadian Anti-fascists during World War Two* (Toronto: Kobzar, 1985); Ian Radforth, "Political Prisoners: The Communist Internees," in *Enemies Within: Italian and Other Internees in Canada and Abroad*, ed. Franca Iacovetta, Roberto Perin, and Angelo Principe (Toronto: University of Toronto Press, 2000), 194–224; Whitaker, "Repression of Communism."

85 "Canada Outlaws 16 Groups as Subversive," *Globe and Mail*, 6 June 1940, 1; "Bruce Indicts Nineteen Units as Subversive," *Globe and Mail*, 13 June 1940, 9.

86 Whitaker, "Repression of Communism," 135–66.

87 Whitaker, "Repression of Communism," 137.

88 Frazer, "From Pariahs to Patriots"; Whitaker, "Repression of Communism," 146; Penner, *Canadian Communism*, 169–70.

89 LAC, RG146, vol. 3440, Housewives Consumers Association of Toronto, part 1, telegram, Central Executive Council Housewives Consumers Association, 13 June 1940; LAC, RG146, vol. 3440, part 1, letter from Elizabeth Brown, President, and Christine Chappel, Secretary, to Honorable Ernest Lapointe, 19 June 1940.
90 Krawchuk, *Interned without Cause*; Radforth, "Political Prisoners"; John Stanton, *My Past Is Now: Further Memoirs of a Labour Lawyer* (St. John's, Nfld.: Canadian Committee on Labour History, 1994), 53–60.
91 Radforth, "Political Prisoners," 214.
92 Mary Prokop, in William Repka and Kathleen Repka, *Dangerous Patriots: Canada's Unknown Prisoners of War* (Vancouver: New Star Books, 1982): 96–117.
93 See, for instance, Ross Lambertson, "The Rosedale Red," *Beaver* 83, no. 3 (2003), 22–7.
94 Norman Penner, "They Fought for Labor, Now Interned," pamphlet (Winnipeg: Committee for the Release of Labor Prisoners, April 1941), reprinted by Socialist History Project: http://www.socialisthistory.ca/Docs/CPC/WW2/FoughtFor.htm
95 Mary Prokop, interview by author, Toronto, ON, 15 December 1998.
96 J. Petryshyn, "Class Conflict and Civil Liberties: The Origins and Activities of the Canadian Labour Defense League, 1925–1940," *Labour/Le Travail* 10 (1982): 39–63.
97 Radforth, "Political Prisoners"; Prokop, *Dangerous Patriots*, 96–117.
98 Mary Prokop, interview by author, Toronto, ON, 15 December 1998.
99 LAC, RG146, Housewives League, Vancouver, BC, AITP request A-2007-00010, RCMP "E" Division, copies of telegrams to Committee to Review Defence of Canada Regulations, 9 June 1942.
100 LAC, RG146, Housewives League, Vancouver, BC, AITP request A-2007-00010, clippings, "Editor Repeats Charges," *Daily Province* (Vancouver), 16 December 1939, "Housewives' Interest Comes First," *Daily Province* (Vancouver), 16 December 1939, "Mrs. Norton Explains Action," *Sun* (Vancouver), 13 July 1940, "Rift Looms in Consumers' Organization," *Daily Province* (Vancouver), 16 July 1940, "Red Influence in Housewives' Body Charged," *Daily Province* (Vancouver), 26 July 1940, "Housewives' League Issues Statement," *Daily Province* (Vancouver), 26 July 1940, "Housewives' Head Denies Communism," *Daily Province* (Vancouver), 30 July 1940, report, "E" Division, "The Housewives' League, Vancouver, B.C."
101 LAC, RG146, Housewives League, Vancouver, BC, AITP request A-2007–00010, RCMP "E" Division report re: The Housewives' League, Vancouver, BC, 31 August 1940.

102 Granatstein, *Canada's War*, 249–52.
103 Leonard Marsh, *Report on Social Security for Canada* (Toronto: University of Toronto Press, 1975), xvi.
104 Storrs, *The Second Red Scare*, 26, 213. See also, Alan Brinkely, "The New Deal and the Idea of the State," in *The Rise and Fall of the New Deal Order, 1930–1980*, ed. Steve Fraser and Gary Gerstle (Princeton, NJ: Princeton University Press, 1990), 85–121.
105 Jeff Keshen and Raymond Benjamin Blake, eds., *Social Fabric or Patchwork Quilt: The Development of Social Policy in Canada* (Peterborough, ON: Broadview Press, 2006), 207.
106 H.S. Gordon, "Why Today's Students Look to Socialism," *Saturday Night*, 8 July 1944, 6–7; Edward Murray, "Let's Have Long Range Food Planning Now," *Saturday Night*, 15 July 1944, 10–11.
107 Marsh, *Report on Social Security*, xiii–xviii; McInnis, "Planning Prosperity"; Slater, *War, Finance and Reconstruction*, 41.
108 LAC, RG 146, vol. 3353, Housewives and Consumers Federation of Canada, part sup. 1, Vol. 1, clipping, *Ottawa Citizen*, 24 June 1947.

3. Fighting for the Working Class

1 Canadian Institute of Public Opinion, *Gallup Poll* 25 July 1942. A Gallup poll of 12 July 1947 found that 55 per cent of Canadians blame "big profits" for high prices and 54 per cent think price controls came off too fast; LAC, RG 146 Vol. 3353, Housewives and Consumers Federation of Canada (HCFC), part 1, clipping, *Daily Tribune*, 17 July 1947; Communist Party of Manitoba files, *The Manitoba Housewife*, vol. 1, number 1, February 1948. Most public opinion polls were conducted by federal wartime agencies such as the Wartime Prices and Trade Board. For a summary of polls on price controls, see Broad, *A Small Price to Pay*, 16–49, 207–8. On popular calls for permanent economic management, see, for instance, Edward Murray, "Let's Have Long Range Food Planning Now," *Saturday Night*, 15 July 1944, 10–11.
2 Broad, *A Small Price to Pay*, 208.
3 "Ottawa Soon to Relax Price Control," *Globe and Mail*, 17 January 1946, 1–2.
4 LAC, RG19, Department of Finance, Central Registry (items related to Price Control), Series E2C, vol. 389, file 101–102–38–0-147, unattributed clipping, "Other Raises Predicted," 3 April 1946; "Up Go Shirt Prices and Costs of Living But Controls to Stay," *Globe and Mail*, 3 April 1946: 1–2.

5 Archives of Manitoba (AM), Ann Ross fonds, P5941/10, Donald Gordon, "Your Bread and Butter," *The Facts about Price Control: Second Broadcast*, 4 November 1946.
6 "Panic-Buying of Meat Starts; Back Market Terms Out of Control," *Globe and Mail*, 19 April 1946, 1–2; "Irate Milk Producers Talk 'Drastic Action,'" *Globe and Mail*, 1 May 1946, 1–2; "Butchers Won't Pledge Black Market Boycott," *Globe and Mail*, 1 May 1946, 1–2; "Packers on Sit Down, Union Leaders Charge," *Globe and Mail*, 2 May 1946, 1–2.
7 Slater, *War, Finance and Reconstruction*, 153.
8 LAC, RG19, Finance Central Files, file number 101–102–38–0-28, letter from Lillian Colgate, Executive Secretary, Housewives' Association, to Hon. J.L. Ilsley, 19 March 1946.
9 LAC, RG19, Finance Central Files, file number 101–102–38–0-28, letter from Lillian Colgate, Executive Secretary, Housewives' Association, to J.L. Ilsley, 15 April 1946.
10 LAC, RG19, Finance Central Files, file number 101–102–38–0-28, letter from Lillian Colgate, Executive Secretary, Housewives' Association, to Prime Minister King and Finance Minister Ilsley, 25 April 1946; "Panic-Buying of Meat Starts; Black Market Terms Out of Control," *Globe and Mail*, 19 April 1946, 1; "See Little Meat in City Stores in Coming Week," *Toronto Daily Star*, 20 April 1946; "Beef Strike Seen in Four Provinces," *Toronto Daily Star*, 23 April 1946.
11 LAC, RG19, Finance Central Files, vol. 389, memo from the Private Secretary [PMO] to C.H. Blair, Assistant Secretary, Wartime Prices and Trade Board, 24 April 1946; letter from Byrne Hope Sanders to Mrs Lillian Colgate, 27 April 1946; LAC, RG 19, Series E2C, vol. 389, memo from Paul Rochon to A.L. Wickwire, 1 May 1946; letter from W.P.T.B. to Mrs Lillian Colgate, 6 May 1946.
12 "Women Fear Milk Price Boost to 15 Cents, Appeal to City Hall," *Toronto Daily Star*, 8 April 1946; "Maintain Controls, Housewives Advise," *Globe and Mail*, 14 April 1945.
13 "Milk Price Will Rise Two Cents per Quart," *Globe and Mail*, 17 May 1946, 1; "Explains Government Will Cease Paying Part of Consumers' Milk Bill," *Globe and Mail*, 17 May 1946, 12.
14 "Suggests Liquor Revenue Be Used as Milk Subsidy," *Toronto Daily Star*, 18 May 1946.
15 "See Little Meat in City Stores in Coming Week," *Toronto Daily Star*, 20 April 1946; "Meat Crisis Said Wedge in Price Control Fight," *Toronto Daily Star*, 22 April 1946, 1; "Shortage, Not Price to Blame, Gordon Says," *Toronto*

Daily Star, 23 April 1946, 2; "Meat in Canada to Fill Ration, Gordon States," *Toronto Daily Star*, 16 May 1946.
16 "'Stick to End' Women Told in Anti-Inflation Fight," *Globe and Mail*, 8 May 1946, 12.
17 "Ottawa Tells Just Where Those Price Ceilings Apply," *Toronto Daily Star*, 6 July 1946, 3; "Housewives to Check Prices of Groceries," *Toronto Daily Star*, 30 July 1946, 11.
18 LAC, RG19, Finance Central Files, series E2C, vol. 389, "W.P.T.B. & Decontrol Procedures Now and Post-War," [1945], Confidential report.
19 Parr, *Domestic Goods*, 69–73.
20 "Panic-Buying of Meat Starts; Black Market Termed Out of Control," *Globe and Mail*, 19 April 1946, 1–2; "Butchers Won't Pledge Black Market Boycott," *Globe and Mail*, 1 May 1946, 1; "Packers on Sit-Down, Union Leaders Charge," *Globe and Mail*, 7 May 1946, 1–2.
21 "Loaf 20 Ounces Instead of 24 Bakers Predict," *Toronto Daily Star*, 22 April 1946, 1; "Milk Ration Is Possible If Subsidy Ends – Producers," *Toronto Daily Star*, 1 May 1946, 3; "Milk-Bottle Barrage Trained on Mr. King," *Globe and Mail*, 23 May 1946, 17.
22 "Milk Price Will Rise Two Cents per Quart," *Globe and Mail*, 17 May 1946, 1–2; "Mass Protest Sweeps Dominion Following End of Milk Subsidy," *Globe and Mail*, 18 May 1946, 5.
23 LAC, RG19, Finance Central Files, series E2C, vol. 389, 1946–47, letter from Mrs Lillian Colegate, Secretary, Housewives Association, to Prime Minister King, 25 April 1946.
24 "Price Control Saved $18 for Each Family Monthly," *Toronto Daily Star*, 31 January 1946.
25 "Hour-Wage Rates across Dominion Found Declining," *Globe and Mail*, 13 February 1946, 8; Emil Bjarnason and Bert Marcuse, *The Case of the Dwindling Dollar* (Trade Union Research Bureau [1948]).
26 Alvin Finkel, *Our Lives: Canada after 1945* (Toronto: James Lorimer, 1997), 9–10.
27 LAC, RG19, Finance Central Registry Files, series E2C, vol. 389, letter from Ann Emard, Vancouver, BC, to Mr Ilsley, 8 April 1946.
28 LAC, RG19, Finance Central Registry Files, series E2C, vol. 389, letter from Mrs Cecilia Hill, 3 April 1946; letter from Mrs E. A. Lightfoot, Regina Saskatchewan, 31 May 1946; letter from A. F. Smith, Toronto, Ontario, to The Hon. J.L. Ilsley, 1 December 1946.
29 LAC, RG19, Finance Central Registry Files, letter from Mrs Ethel Clare to Walter Tucker, M.P., 9 April 1946; letter from W. Garfield Chase, M.P., to

Ilsley, 12 April 1946; petition from Rev. Anthony Friedbert, Hartney, MB, 8 April 1946.
30 "Mass Protest Sweeps Dominion Following End of Milk Subsidy," *Globe and Mail*, 18 May 1946, 5.
31 AM, Ross papers, P5941/1, clipping, "Housewives Protest Govt. Lifting of Price Controls," *Winnipeg News*, 10 May 1946.
32 "Call Milk Meeting in 'Park' This Saturday," *Toronto Daily Star*, 23 May 1946.
33 "Suggests Liquor Revenue Be Used as Milk Subsidy," *Toronto Daily Star*, 18 May 1946.
34 LAC, RG19, Finance Central Files, series E2C, vol. 389, 1946–7, part 1, "Union News," Mine Mill and Smelter Workers Local 241, 10 April 1946.
35 LAC, RG19, Finance Central Files, series E2C, vol. 389, Fort William Trades and Labor Council, "Resolution on Re-establishment and Retention of Price Controls," attached to letter from the Labour Council to Finance Minister J.L. Ilsley, 13 May 1946.
36 AM, Ross Papers, P5941/11, clipping, "Urges United Church Back Higher Wages, Labor Code," *Toronto Daily Star*, 28 May 1946.
37 "Milk Price Will Rise Two Cents per Quart," *Globe and Mail*, 17 May 1946, 1–2; "Mass Protest Sweeps Dominion Following End of Milk Subsidy," *Globe and Mail*, 18 May 1946, 5; "Mayor Leaves for Ottawa Milk Parley," *Globe and Mail*, 21 May 1946, 5; "Cabinet Refuses to Change Decision on Milk Subsidies," *Toronto Daily Star*, 21 May 1946; "Ottawa Firm on Milk Subsidy Ilsley Tells Toronto Delegates," *Globe and Mail*, 22 May 1946, 5; "Call Milk Meeting in 'Park' Saturday," *Toronto Daily Star*, 23 May 1946; "Milk-Bottle Barrage Trained on Mr. King," *Toronto Daily Star*, 23 May 1946, 17.
38 AM, Ross Papers, P5941/1, clipping, "Housewives Protest Govt. Lifting of Price Controls," *Winnipeg News*, 10 May 1946; AM, Ross papers, P5941/3, clipping, "Housewives March on Legislative Building; Seek Return of Subsidy," *Winnipeg News*, 24 May 1946.
39 LAC, RG 19, Finance Central Files, series E2C, vol. 389, letter from Mrs Betty Lowe, secretary, Saskatoon Housewives' Consumers Association, to Prime Minister Mackenzie King, 26 July 1946.
40 AM, Ross papers, P5941/1, letter from Anne Ross to James Gardiner, Minister of Agriculture, 23 December 1946.
41 LAC, RG19, Finance Central Files, series E2C, vol. 389, "Statement by the Minister of Finance, House of Commons, Evening of July 5, 1946."

42 AM, Ross papers, P5941/10, Donald Gordon, "The Facts about Price Control," radio scripts for broadcast, 1 November 1946 and 4 November 1946.
43 On the termination of the OPA, see Meg Jacobs, *Pocketbook Politics*, 221–31.
44 LAC, RG19, Finance Central Files, series E2C, vol. 389, "Notes on Trip to Washington of Mr. Donald Gordon, Accompanied by Mr. J.D. Gibson," [1946]; "Canada to Hold Ceiling Despite O.P.A. – Ottawa," *Toronto Daily Star*, 2 July 1946, 1.
45 Meg Jacobs, "'How about Some Meat?': The Office of Price Administration, Consumption Politics, and State Building from the Bottom Up, 1941–1946," *The Journal of American History* 84, no. 3 (1997), 910–41.
46 "Toronto Women Strike against Beef Price Rise," *Toronto Daily Star*, 19 July 1946, 1.
47 "Wives' Beef Strike Hits Some Butchers," *Toronto Daily Star*, 29 July 1946, 11; "Guess Who's Getting Hooked?" *The Globe and Mail*, 25 April 1946, 6.
48 AM, Ross papers, P5941/1, clipping, "Consumers' Association Formed by Sudbury Women," *Sudbury Daily Star*, 31 August 1946; Charlie Angus and Louie Palu, *Mirrors of Stone: Fragments from the Porcupine Frontier* (Toronto: Between the Lines, 2001); Mercedes Steedman, Peter Suschnigg, and Dieter K. Buse, eds. *Hard Lessons: The Mine Mill Union in the Canadian Labour Movement* (Toronto: Dundurn Press, 1995).
49 LAC, RG19, Finance Central Files, letter from Mrs Betty Lowe, Secretary, Saskatoon Housewives' Consumers Association, to Mackenzie King, 26 July 1946.
50 LAC, RG146, Housewives Consumer League, Windsor, ON, vol. 1, AITP request A-2007–00089, RCMP file, "Re: Labour Progressive Party Windsor. Ont.," 24 October 1946; RCMP file, "Canadian Federation of Democratic Hungarians, Canada, General," 27 December 1946.
51 LAC, RG146, Housewives League, Montreal, Quebec, AITP request A-2007–00010, RCMP "C" Division file, "Labour Progressive Party Montreal, PQ"; "Crowsnest Pass Historical Driving Tour: Coleman," Alberta Culture and Multiculturalism, https://www.culturetourism.alberta.ca/heritage-and-museums/resources/historical-walking-and-driving-tours/docs/Tour-Coleman.pdf; Tom Langford and Chris Frazer, "The Cold War and Working-Class Politics in the Coal Mining Communities of the Crowsnest Pass, 1945–1958," *Labour/Le Travail* 49 (2002): 43–81.
52 Prokop, interview.

53 Iacovetta, *Gatekeepers*.
54 J.M. Bumsted, "Ross, Anne Glaz," *Dictionary of Manitoba Biography* (Winnipeg: University of Manitoba Press 2014), 214; "Anne Glaz Ross (1911–1998)," Memorable Manitobans, http://www.mhs.mb.ca/docs/people/ross_ag.shtml; "Ross, Anne," RULA Archives and Special Collections, http://archives.library.ryerson.ca/index.php/ross-anne
55 "Wants Subsidy Kept as Less Milk Drunk," *Toronto Daily Star*, 17 August 1946, 7; AM, Ross papers, P5941/5, flyer from John Marshall, Provisional Chairman, Citizens Committee on Milk, to all committee members, 31 December 1946.
56 AM, Ross papers, P5941/11, "Mrs. Housewife the Price of Milk Must Not Go Up!" flyer advertising public protest meeting, 12 September 1946, [n.d.]; AM, Ross papers, P5941/6, "Saskatchewan Housewives Consumers Association rally at the Technical school, 8 pm"; AM, Ross papers, P5941/10, "Milk: Facts behind the Rise in Price," *Labour News*, vol. 6, no. 13, 16 September 1946; "Saskatchewan May Start Its Own Subsidy for Milk," *Toronto Daily Star*, 27 September 1946, 1; LAC, RG146, Housewives Consumers Association, Regina, Saskatchewan, AITP request A-2007–00051, RCMP file, transcript, "Regina and Moose Jaw Women Ask Province Subsidize Milk," *Canadian Tribune*, 21 October 1946; AM, Ross papers, P5941/5, letter from D.L. Campbell, Minister of Agriculture and Immigration (MB) to Anne Ross, 8 November 1946.
57 AM, Ross papers, P5941/1, letter from Douglas Abbott, Acting Finance Minister, to Gladys Steiman, Secretary, Manitoba Housewives Consumers Association, 26 July 1946.
58 AM, Ross papers, P5941/1, letter from Anne Ross to James Gardiner, Minister of Agriculture, 23 December 1946.
59 Dominion Bureau of Statistics, *Canada Year Book 1946* (Ottawa: King's Printer, 1946), 853–6; "Milk Prices Up Two Cents," *Toronto Daily Star*, 17 May 1946, 6; "Price Protection," *The Globe and Mail* 4 July 1946, 15; "Three-Cent Rise Expected Milk Going to 15 Cents," *Toronto Star*, 14 August 1946, 1.
60 AM, Ross papers, P5941/5, letter from Mrs E. Molinski, President of the Mothers' Club of All People's Church to the Housewives' Association, 28 September 1946.
61 "Milk 16 Cents a Quart, Toronto Cost $300,000," *Globe and Mail*, 27 September 1946, 1.
62 "Milk Subsidy Extension after Sept. 30 Deadline Forecast as Certainty," *Globe and Mail*, 24 September 1946, 3.

63 Jacobs, *Pocketbook Politics*, 220–4.
64 Glickman, *Buying Power*.
65 Landon R.Y. Storrs, *Civilizing Capitalism: The National Consumers' League, Women's Activism, and Labor Standards in the New Deal Era* (Chapel Hill: University of North Carolina Press, 2000).
66 Jacobs, *Pocketbook Politics*, 179–245.
67 AM, Ross papers, P5941/6, Gladys Steiman, "News Round-Up on the Fight against High Prices," *The Manitoba Housewife*, July 1946, 3–4. On other consumer movements, see Glickman, "The Strike in the Temple"; Hilton, *Consumerism in Twentieth-Century Britain*; Karen Hunt, "Negotiating the Boundaries of the Domestic: British Socialist Women and the Politics of Consumption," *Women's History Review* 9, no. 2 (2000): 389–410; Rebecca Pulju, "Consumers for the Nation: Women, Politics, and Consumer Organization in France, 1944–1965," *Journal of Women's History* 18, no. 3 (2006): 68–90; Judith Smart, "The Politics of Consumption: The Housewives' Associations in South-Eastern Australia before 1950," *Journal of Women's History* 18, no. 3 (2006): 13–39; Iselin Theien, "Campaigning for Milk: Housewives as Consumer Activists in Post-War Norway," in *Twentieth-Century Housewives: Meanings and Implications of Unpaid Work*, ed. Gro Hagemann and Hege Roll-Hansen (Norway: Unipub forlag–Oslo Academic Press, 2005): 105–76.
68 "Post-War Price Control Problem in Canada and in the United States," *Toronto Daily Star*, 1 February 1946.
69 Commentators provided varied figures on the total public expenditure on subsidies. See, for instance, Jim Mochoruk, *The People's Co-op: The Life and Times of a North End Institution* (Winnipeg: The Wind-up Committee of the People's Co-operative Ltd., 2000), 100; "Milk Price Will Rise Two Cents per Quart," *Globe and Mail*, 17 May 1946, 1–2; "Keep Controls or Prices May Rise 50 P.C. – Gordon," *Toronto Daily Star*, 5 November 1946, 7; "Ottawa Soon to Relax Price Control," *Globe and Mail*, 17 January 1946, 1–2.
70 "Curb Corporation Profits, Housewives' Brief Demands," *Toronto Daily Star*, 31 May 1947, 15.
71 AM, Ross papers, P5941/5, Edmonton Housewives League, October 1946.
72 On the CCN and its nutritional studies, see Mosby, *Food Will Win the War*, 25–6, 32–3, 171–2.
73 "Two-Cent Subsidy on Milk Will Be One of the Last to Go," *Toronto Daily Star*, 11 January 1946; "East York Survey of Health Shows Nutrition Lack," *Globe and Mail*, 4 October 1946, 8.

74 "Suggests Liquor Revenue Be Used as Milk Subsidy," *Toronto Daily Star*, 18 May 1946; "Mayor Leaves for Ottawa Milk Parley," *Globe and Mail*, 21 May 1946, 5; H.H. Armstrong, "Cabinet Refuses to Change Decision on Milk Subsidies," *Toronto Daily Star*, 21 May 1946; AM, Ross papers, P5941/5, Edmonton Housewives League, October 1946.

75 "Price Control Saved $18 for Each Family Monthly," *Toronto Daily Star*, 31 January 1946.

76 AM, Ross papers, P5941/5, Radio Broadcast script, no title, [2 October 1946]; AM, Ross papers, P5941/5, "Memorandum on Milk Subsidies," presented by Manitoba Housewives Consumers Association to Prime Minister W.L. Mackenzie King, by courtesy of Premier Stuart S. Garson, 11 October 1946; MA, Ross papers, P5941/5, Berry Richards [CCF-Manitoba], "Submission to the Citizens' Conference on Milk," 28 October 1946.

77 LAC, RG 19, Finance Department, Central Registry, Series E2C, vol. 389, 1946–7, part 1, letter from James Tester, Secretary, Workers' Cooperative of New Ontario Limited to Finance Minister Abbott, 14 April 1947; "Curb Corporation Profits, Housewives' Brief Demands," *Toronto Daily Star*, 31 May 1947, 15.

78 On the improvement in people's diets during the war, see Broad, *A Small Price to Pay*, 16–49, 196–209. The democratizing benefits of wartime rationing were experienced in other war-affected countries. See, for example, Amy Bently, *Eating for Victory: Food Rationing and the Politics of Domesticity* (Urbana: University of Illinois Press, 1998); James Vernon, *Hunger: A Modern History* (Cambridge, MA: The Belknap Press of Harvard University Press, 2007), 133–211.

79 "Imply Milk Subsidies Continue after Oct 1," *Globe and Mail*, 15 August 1946, 1.

80 Jeffrey Keshen reports that overall meat consumption rose during the war, but since much of the increase was bought on the black market, and legally available rationed meat was often scarce, it's unclear how much meat those on low incomes could buy. Keshen, *Saints, Sinners, and Soldiers*, 107–11.

81 "Cabinet Refuses to Change Decision on Milk Subsidies," *Toronto Daily Star*, 21 May 1946.

82 AM, Ross papers, P5941/5, "Edmonton Housewives League"; "Prices Must Come Down," *The Canadian Unionist*, May 1947, 99.

83 Noah M. Meltz, "Section E: Wages and Working Conditions," Statistics Canada, *Historical Statistics of Canada*, 1983, http://www.statcan.gc.ca/pub/11-516-x/sectione/4147438-eng.htm

84 Palmer, *Working-Class Experience*, 268–339.
85 Wendy Cuthbertson, *Labour Goes to War: The CIO and the Construction of a New Social Order, 1939–45* (Vancouver: UBC Press, 2012), 8.
86 LAC, RG 146, vol. 3353, Housewives and Consumers Federation of Canada, part 1a, clipping, "Buyers Strike Wins Canada-Wide Support," *Daily Tribune*, 21 June 1947; AM, Ross papers, P5941/8, "Presentation of the Petition of [blank] signatures favoring controls and subsidies where necessary to roll back prices to January 1946 levels," submitted to The Rt. Hon. W.L. Mackenzie King Prime Minister, and members of the Government of Canada, Roll Back Prices Conference, Ottawa Ontario April 15–16–17, 1948.
87 Eugene Forsey, "Price-Control and the Worker's Dollar," *The Canadian Unionist*, September 1946, 209.
88 Parr, *Domestic Goods*, 89–93; "The Congress Memorandum," *The Canadian Unionist*, April 1946; "The Congress Memorandum," *The Canadian Unionist*, April 1947, 78–81, 84; "Prices Must Come Down," *The Canadian Unionist*, May 1947; "The Congress Memorandum," *The Canadian Unionist*, 5 March 1948, 55–6; "The Congress Meets the Government," *The Canadian Unionist*, April 1949, 75–8; "Consumers' Association Holds Annual Meeting," *The Canadian Unionist*, November 1949, 267–9, 272; LAC, Trades and Labor Congress of Canada fonds, MG28, vol. 103, file: Price Control, "Submission on Price Control to the Government of Canada," Trades and Labor Congress of Canada, Canadian Congress of Labor, Canadian and Catholic Confederation of Labour, Dominion Joint Legislative Committee of the Railway Transportation Brotherhoods, Ottawa, 20 February 1951.
89 Eugene Forsey, "Congress Memorandum on Prices and Price-Control," *The Canadian Unionist*, January 1949, 6–8, 16, 18; "Freeze Prices, Freeze Wages," *Globe and Mail* editorial, 10 January 1948, 6; "Guns, Not Butter – King," *Canadian Tribune*, 24 January 1948.
90 The best full-length study is, Peter S. McInnis, *Harnessing Labour Confrontation: Shaping the Postwar Settlement in Canada, 1943–1950* (Toronto: University of Toronto Press, 2001). See also, Michael Lynk, "Labour Law and Labour Rights: The Wagner Act in Canada," in *Unions Matter: Advancing Democracy, Economic Equality, and Social Justice*, ed. Matthew Berens (Toronto: Between the Lines, 2014): 79–90; Carmela Patrias, "Employers' Anti-Unionism in Niagara, 1942–1965: Questioning the Postwar Compromise," *Labour/Le Travail*, 76 (2015): 37–77; Don Wells, "The Impact of the Postwar Compromise on Canadian Unionism: The Formation of an Auto Worker Local in the 1950s," *Labour/Le Travail*, 36 (1995): 147–73.

91 "Prices Must Come Down," *The Canadian Unionist*, May 1947, 104; "Important Resolutions at Congress Convention," *The Canadian Unionist*, December 1948, 289. On the CCL's strategic shift, see McInnis, *Harnessing Postwar Confrontation*.
92 LAC, RG19, Finance Central Files, Series E2C, vol. 389, part 1, 1946–7, "Ilsley Says Living Costs Will Rise, Workers Will Pay," *Union News*, Mine Mill Local 241, 10 April 1946; "Mayor Leaves for Ottawa Milk Parley," *Globe and Mail*, 21 May 1946, 5; "Milk-Bottle Barrage Trained on Mr. King," *Globe and Mail*, 23 May 1946, 17; York University Archives and Special Collections (YUA), United Electrical, Radio and Machine Workers of America fonds, fonds F0438, UE-HCA Prices Campaign, 1984, 018–001, circular letter from Stewart Smith to "Dear Fellow Citizen," sent to UE Director of Organization Ross Russell, 10 September 1946; YUA, UE-HCA Prices Campaign, UE National office, "S" Miscellaneous Correspondence, circular letter from Ross Russell, 30 September 1946; YUA, UE-HCA Prices Campaign, "Here Are Some Talking Points about the UE 'Lower Prices' Campaign," [n.d.].
93 LAC, RG146, vol. 3305, Housewives Consumers League of BC, 1940–1965, letter from [Minerva Miller] to Stanley Ryerson, 25 March 1948. On Stanley Ryerson, see Gregory S. Kealey, "Stanley Brehaut Ryerson: Canadian Revolutionary Intellectual," *Studies in Political Economy* 9 (1982), 105; on Minerva Miller, see Johnston, *A Great Restlessness*, 310. Information about Miller's position is from *The Daily Ubyssey* 30, no. 70, 25 February 1948, http://www.library.ubc.ca/archives/pdfs/ubyssey/UBYSSEY_1948_02_25.pdf.
94 LAC, RG146, vol. 3305, Housewives and Consumers League of BC, letter from Miller to Ryerson; "The Force of Public Opinion," *Daily Tribune*, 30 June 1947.
95 "'Come Out and Fight' Is Reaction of Labor as Prices Skyrocket," *Toronto Daily Star*, 19 September 1947, 21. Lawrence Glickman's history of union struggles that linked wages to prices in the U.S. offers a valuable context to this discussion. See Glickman, *A Living Wage*.
96 On the history of women's militancy in Mine-Mill, see Mercedes Steedman, "The Red Petticoat Brigade: Mine-Mill Women's Auxiliary and the 'Threat from Within,' 1940–1970," in Kinsman, Buse, and Steedman, *Whose National Security?*, 55–71.
97 Mona Morgan, Peggy Chunn, and Audrey Modzir (Staples), interview by author, Vancouver, BC, 24 July 1998.
98 LAC, RG19, Finance Central Files, series E2C, vol. 389, part 1, "Resolution #6, Price Control," attached to letter from Marge Croy, Secretary-Treasurer,

International Woodworkers of America, CIO, Ladies' Auxiliary, to the Honourable J.L. Ilsley, 28 February 1946; Letter from Women's Auxiliary, Port Arthur Trades and Labour Council, to J.L. Ilsley, MP, 1 June 1946; and letter from Ladies' Auxiliary, Local 117, IUMM&SW, to Leo Gauthier, MP, 20 February 1947.

99 LAC, RG19, Finance Central Files, series E2C, vol. 389, parts 1 and 2.
100 AM, Ross papers, P5941/5, International Woodworkers of America, BC District Council, IWA Education Department, pamphlet, "High Profits = High Prices," [probably early 1947]; AM, Ross papers, P5941/4, Saskatchewan Federation of Labour, "Removal of Price Control and Subsidies Leading Canada to Economic Recession," [1947]; AM, Ross papers, P5941/9, Emile Bjarnason and Bert Marcuse, "The Case of the Dwindling Dollar," Trade Union Research Bureau [1948].
101 Manitoba Communist Party collection, flyer, "Mrs. Housewife" [1946].
102 "City Is Urged to Take Over Sale of Milk," *Globe and Mail*, 4 July 1941, 4.
103 "Urges Vote on Milk Sale on Public Utility Plan," *Globe and Mail*, 14 February 1941, 4; "Direct Representation of Farmers and Labor on War Boards Is Asked," *Globe and Mail*, 14 April 1941, 4; "Ask Replacement If Milk Subsidy," *Globe and Mail*, 11 June 1946, 12; "City Is Urged to Take Over Sale of Milk," *Globe and Mail*, 4 July 1941, 4; "Milk Shortage Stories Are Termed Propaganda," *Globe and Mail*, 11 July 1941, 4; "Milk Subsidy Lift Said 'Sabotage,'" *Globe and Mail*, 27 May 1946, 4; "Milk Cost Soars, Says M.P. Backs Plea to Keep Subsidy," *Toronto Daily Star*, 27 August 1946, 2.
104 "Ottawa Prepares People for Bread Milk Price Boost," *Toronto Daily Star*, 15 August 1946.
105 "Vote Forces Cabinet Review Milk Subsidy," *Globe and Mail*, 28 August 1946, 1–2.
106 "Jurisdiction Returned to Provinces," *Globe and Mail*, 26 September 1946, 1–2.
107 Thomas Fisher Rare Book Library (Fisher Library), Robert S. Kenny papers, MSS 179, box 49, flyer, "Mr. and Mrs. Consumer: 16 Cent Milk Is Illegal" [n. d.]; "5 to Fight By-Election in Parkdale Riding," *Globe and Mail*, 16 October 1946, 4; "No Injunction as Milk Board Made No Order," *Toronto Daily Star*, 17 October 1946, 1; "11th Hour Word Battle in Parkdale," *Globe and Mail*, 19 October 1946, 3; "Voice of Consumers in Milk-Price Talks Sought by Injunction," *Globe and Mail*, 21 October 1946, 11; "Court Rejects Move to Restrain Milk Price Rise," *Globe and Mail*, 21 November 1946, 5; Fisher Library, Kenny papers, MSS 179, box 57, "Conference on the Rising Cost of Living and the Increased Price of Milk, Toronto," 8 October 1946; Fisher Library, Kenny papers, MSS

179, box 57, "Milk: What You Must Make Drew Do!" October 1946, LPP pamphlet, October 1946; "16 Cent Milk Is Illegal," LPP pamphlet, [n.d.]; LAC, RG146, Housewives Consumer League, Windsor, ON, vol. 1, AITP request A-2007–00089, RCMP file, "Re: Labour Progressive Party Windsor. Ont.," 24 October 1946; "Injunction Is Sought to Stay Milk Price," *Globe and Mail*, 8 October 1946, 1–2; "Voice of Consumers in Milk-Price Talks Sought by Injunctions," *Globe and Mail*, 21 October 1946, 11; "Board Rules Out Municipal Dairy Referendum Plea," *Globe and Mail*, 31 October 1946, 5.

108 Fisher Library, Kenny papers, MSS 179, boxes 1 and 57: copy of letter from Consumers' Federated Council to the Government of Ontario, 13 November 1946; Copy of Submission to the Board of Control [Toronto] by a deputation representing the Consumers' Federated Council, [13 November 1946]; Submission of the Consumers' Federated Council of the City of Toronto to Mr Justice Dalton C. Wells, of the Royal Commission enquiring into the Milk Situation, 26 November 1946; "16 Cent Milk Is Illegal," circular letter, Executive Committee, Consumers' Federated Council, [n.d.]; "Consumer Meeting Demands Municipal Milk Control," *Toronto Daily Star*, 9 October 1946, 22.

109 On George Drew, see Whitaker and Marcuse, *Cold War Canada*, 133, 191–2. On royal commissions, see Thomas J. Lockwood, "A History of Royal Commissions," *Osgood Hall Law Journal* 5, no. 2 (1967): 172–209, http://digitalcommons.osgoode.yorku.ca/ohlj/vol5/iss2/3

110 "Blackwell Asks Report on Milk Rise," *Globe and Mail*, 28 September 1946, 1.

111 "Province to Probe Milk Price," *Globe and Mail*, 1 October 1946, 1–2; "Probe Milk, Price-Spread, Financing," *Globe and Mail*, 5 October 1946, 1; "Milk Commission Plans Sittings at Key Points," *Globe and Mail*, 26 October 1946, 5.

112 "Province to Probe Milk Price," *Globe and Mail*, 1 October 1946, 1–2.

113 Ontario Royal Commission on Milk, *Report of the Ontario Royal Commission on Milk, 1947* (Toronto: B. Johnson, 1947). These arguments were advanced in many of the briefs submitted to the Commission, all of which are found in Archives of Ontario, RG18–126, Royal Commission on Milk 1947, container 1, boxes 1 and 2.

114 Kuffert, "Stabbing Our Spirits Broad Awake."

115 One of the few scholars who has documented this debate is Peter S. McInnis, "Planning Prosperity."

116 Harry M. Cassidy, *Social Security and Reconstruction in Canada* (Toronto: The Ryerson Press, 1943); McInnis, "Planning Prosperity."

117 LAC, RG19, Finance Central Files, series E2C, vol. 390; Norman S. Buchanan, *Price Control in the Postwar Period* (New York: The Committee on International Economic Policy, 1944); Erick T.H. Kjellstrom, Gustav Henry Gluck, Per Jacobsson, and Ivan Wright, *Price Control: The War against Inflation* (New Brunswick, NJ: Rutgers University Press, 1942); "Collegiate Pupils Strike over High Price of Milk," *Globe and Mail*, 6 November 1946, 4.

4. Mothers, Breadwinners, and Citizens

1 "Three of Four Voters Want Price Controls Back, Survey Reveals," *Toronto Daily Star*, 20 December 1947, 21.
2 Hande D'Arcy, "Parity Prices and the Farmers' Strike," *Saskatchewan History* 38, no. 3 (1985): 81–96. See also, Johnston, *A Great Restlessness*, 98; Bruce E. Field, *Harvest of Dissent: The National Farmers' Union and the Early Cold War* (Lawrence: University of Kansas, 1998).
3 LAC, RG146, vol. 3353, Housewives and Consumers Federation of Canada (HCFC), supp. 1, vol. 1, clipping, "Western Women Determined to See Finance Minister," *Ottawa Evening Citizen*, 31 March 1947.
4 LAC, HCFC, supp. 1, vol. 1, clippings, "Western Women Find Trip to Ottawa Futile," *Montreal Standard*, 5 April 1947; "Among Those Women from the West," *Ottawa Journal*, 7 April 1947.
5 The most complete account of the state's imposition of Cold War thinking in Canada remains Whitaker and Marcuse, *Cold War Canada*, although it overlooks the state's treatment of immigrants and ethnically marked Canadians. Iacovetta, *Gatekeepers* addresses this gap with a comprehensive account of the Canadian state's systematic program of eradicating socialist views among recent immigrants, who were a particularly vulnerable segment of the population.
6 The Housewives got extensive press coverage for these events. Two examples are: LAC, RG146, vol. 3440, Housewives Consumers Association, Toronto, ON, part 1, clipping, "Ottawa Trip Parley Plan of Housewives," *Daily Tribune*, 9 May 1947; and "Twins Feature Baby Parade to Protest Rise in Butter," *Toronto Daily Star*, 6 May 1947, 19.
7 LAC, HCFC, supp. 1, vol. 2, clipping, "Profiteer Prices Kernel of Emergency – Smith," *Canadian Tribune*, [December 1947].
8 "Early Shopper Favorite in City's Meat Derby," *Globe and Mail*, 10 January 1947, 5; "Butter, Bread Up Soon – Ottawa," *Toronto Daily Star*, 20 January 1947, 1.
9 LAC, HCFC, supp. 1, vol. 1, text of radio broadcast, 25 March 1947, station CFQC (Saskatoon).

10 YUA, United Electrical, Radio and Machine Workers of America fonds, fonds F0438, UE-HCA Prices Campaign, 1984, 018–001, "Special Supplement to Consumers' News," April 1947; LAC, RG19, Finance Central Files, vol. 390, "Notes for Speech on Price Control," 22 September 1947.
11 Kenneth Norrie, Douglas Owram, and J.C. Herbert Emery, *A History of the Canadian Economy*, 4th ed. (Toronto: Nelson, 2008), 371–3.
12 McInnis, "Planning Prosperity."
13 LAC, HCFC, supp. 1, vol. 1, clippings, "Rolling Pin Brigade Opens Local Campaign," Ottawa *Citizen*, 24 June 1947, "Controls Stay Off Abbott Declares," *Ottawa Evening Citizen*, 25 June 1947.
14 LAC, HCFC, supp. 1, vol. 1, clipping, "Believe They Got 'Brush-Off' Housewives Angry, Return Home," *Ottawa Citizen*, 26 June 1947.
15 Dominion Bureau of Statistics, *Canada Year Book 1947–1948* (Ottawa: King's Printer, 1946); calculations by John Loxley. See also, "Living Costs on the Up-and-Up," *Toronto Daily Star*, 29 April 1947, 6; "Abbott Eases Load on Pocketbook," *Toronto Daily Star*, 30 April 1947, 1; "More Purchase Power Workers' Need Labor," *Toronto Daily Star*, 28 May 1947, 19; "Five Need $40.11 Now Was $28.35, She Says," *Toronto Daily Star*, 26 May 1947; AM, Ross papers, P5941/10, speakers' notes, Roll Back Prices Campaign, 6 February 1948.
16 Social scientists argue that particular social conditions encourage mass protest. See, for instance, Piven and Cloward, *Poor People's Movements*, 6–13.
17 AM, Ross papers, P5941/1, letter from Anne Ross to James Gardiner, Minister of Agriculture, 23 December 1946.
18 LAC, HCFC, supp. 1, vol. 1, clipping, "Western Women Determined to See Finance Minister," *Ottawa Evening Citizen*, 31 March 1947; LAC, HCFC, part 1, clipping, *Ukrainian Life*, vol. 7, no. 20 (302), 15 May 1947, 10.
19 LAC, HCFC, supp. 1, vol. 1, clippings, "Controls Sought," *Leader-Post* (Regina) 29 March 1947, "Western Women Determined to See Finance Minister," *Evening Citizen*, 31 March 1947, "Women Fail to Have Controls Restored," *Winnipeg Free Press*, 3 April 1947, "Western Women Find Trip to Ottawa Futile," *Montreal Standard*, 5 April 1947; "Restore Price Controls, Demand from Women," *Globe and Mail*, 1 April 1947, 11; AM, Ross papers, P5941/6, Annual Report, MHCA, 26 May 1948.
20 LAC, HCFC, clipping, "Western Women Find Trip to Ottawa Futile," *Montreal Standard*, 5 April 1947; LAC, HCFC, supp. 1, vol. 1, RCMP surveillance report, 15 April 1947.
21 LAC, HCFC, supp. 1, vol. 1, clippings, "Winnipeg Women Fail to Have Controls Restored," *Winnipeg Free Press*, 3 April 1947, "Western Women Find Trip to Ottawa Futile," *Montreal Standard*, 5 April 1947.

22 LAC, HCFC, supp. 1, vol. 1, memorandum for file Re: Housewives' Consumers League, Ottawa, 23 June 1947.
23 LAC, HCFC, part 1, clippings, "Communist Officials Head Up Housewives Consumers' Group," *Winnipeg Free Press*, 22 April 1947, Don Cameron, "Winnipeg Central Headquarters for Communist-Led Housewives," *Winnipeg Free Press*, 23 April 1947, "Communist Strategy Is Exposed," *Winnipeg Free Press*, 23 April 1947, "Wives Duped by Reds," *Calgary Herald*, 23 April 1947, "Housewives Protest 'Communist' Label," *Toronto Daily Star*, 24 April 1947, "Communists Are Angry at the Truth," *Winnipeg Free Press* [n.d.].
24 LAC, HCFC, part 1, clippings, "Unions Will Fight Communists' 'Help,'" *Montreal Gazette*, 24 April 1947, "Regina Housewives League Plans Picketing Programme," *Winnipeg Free Press*, 7 May 1947, "Hoping to Spread Strike of Buyers," *Ottawa Citizen*, 10 May 1947, "Housewives To Protest Here on High Prices," *Ottawa Citizen*, 14 May 1947; "Butter Price Cut Encourages Women to New Boycotts," *Ottawa Citizen*, 16 May 1947; "One-Day Protest Strike Planned at Vancouver," *Toronto Daily Star*, 24 April 1947, 21; "Boycott Butter for Week Toronto Housewives Urge," *Toronto Daily Star*, 1 May 1947, 1; "Twins Feature Baby Parade to Protest Rise in Butter," *Toronto Daily Star*, 6 May 1947, 19; "Labor Backs Women in Picketing Stores," *Toronto Daily Star*, 14 May 1947, 17.
25 "The High Prices," letter to the editor, *Toronto Daily Star*, 28 April 1947, 6.
26 Canadian Broadcasting Corporation Archives, CBC radio broadcast, "News Round-up," 1 May 1947; Phillip Daniels and S. Wyeth Clarkson, "The Five-Cent War," documentary film, Telefilm Canada (Toronto: Travesty Productions, 2003).
27 LAC, HCFC, part 1, RCMP report, "Housewives Consumers Association Saskatoon, Saskatchewan," 25 April 1947; LAC, HCFC, part 1, clippings, "Buyers' Strike Started in BC by Housewives," *Montreal Standard*, 10 May 1947, "Report Progress on Buyers' Strike," *Montreal Gazette*, 26 May 1947; "Youth 'Chain Picket' Backs 8-Cent Candy Bar Boycott," *Toronto Daily Star*, 28 April 1947, 1; "Pupils Storm B.C. Chamber Price Protests Bring Cuts," *Toronto Daily Star*, 30 April 1947, 2; "Parading Pupils Launch 8-cent Candy Boycott," *Globe and Mail*, 1 May 1947, 5; "Trustee Offers to Mediate Student Candy Bar Boycott," *Toronto Daily Star*, 1 May 1947, 3; "'We'll Eat Worms First' Students Spurn 8-Cent Bar," *Toronto Daily Star*, 3 May 1947, 2; "Reds Seen Duping Youth in 8-Cent Bar Campaign," *Toronto Telegram*, 3 May 1947.
28 Frances Early, "Canadian Women and the International Arena in the Sixties: The Voice of Women/La voix des femmes and the Opposition to

the Vietnam War," in *The Sixties: Passion, Politics, and Style*, ed. Dimitry Anastakis (Montreal: McGill-Queen's University Press, 2008), 25–41; Frances Early, "Re-imaging War: The Voice of Women, the Canadian Aid for Vietnam Civilians, and the Knitting Project for Vietnamese Children, 1966–1976," *Peace & Change* 34, no. 2 (2009): 148–163.

29 LAC, HCFC, part 1, clipping, "Communist 'Boycotts' Attacked," *Daily Province* (Vancouver), 9 May 1947; LAC, RG146, vol. 3305; Housewives Consumers League of BC 1940–1965 (HCLBC), AITP request A-2007–00010, clippings, "Housewives Planning Buyer Strike," *Leader-Post* (Regina), 24 April 1947, "Housewives' Vancouver Strike Communist, Says B of T Head," 10 May 1947, "Buyers' Strike Started in BC by Housewives," 10 May 1947, "Labor Backs Women in Picketing Stores," *Toronto Star*, 14 May 1947, "Vancouver Unions Back Buyers' Strike," 16 May 1947, Beland Honderich, "Is Buyers' Strike Any Good as Price-Reducing Weapon?" 3 June 1947, untitled clipping, *Winnipeg Free Press*, 4 June 1947.

30 "Montreal Housewives Ponder Buyers' Strike to Cut Prices," *Globe and Mail*, 2 May 1947, 15; LAC, RG146, Housewives League, Montreal, Quebec, AITP request A-2007–00010, RCMP "C" Division report, 21 June 1947, RCMP memorandum to Inspector Leopold, re: Housewives' Consumers League, Montreal, Quebec, 28 June 1947, clippings, "Parade Right Not Refused, No Such Request Made by Consumers' Body," *Montreal Star*, 16 June 1947, "Housewives to Seek Renewal of Controls," *Montreal Gazette*, 18 June 1947, "Protest," caption, and "Protest Hike an 'Outrage,'" *Montreal Herald*, 20 June 1947, "Police Break Parade," *Montreal Star*, 20 June 1947, "Anti-Red Squad Breaks Up Parade of Women's Consumers Federation," *Montreal Gazette*, 21 June 1947, "Militant Mothers Protest High Prices," *Montreal Star*, 21 June 1947, letter from Mrs Ethel Leigh, Chairman, and Mrs Rose Petch, Secretary, The Montreal Consumers' Federation, to Mayor Camillien Houde, 11 September 1947.

31 "Twins Feature Baby Parade to Protest Rise in Butter," *Toronto Daily Star*, 6 May 1947, 19; "Ban Protest March by 20 Sets of Twins," *Toronto Daily Star*, 17 May 1947; LAC, RG146, vol. 3466, Housewives Consumers League of Regina, Saskatchewan, 1946–1952 (HCAR), AITP request A-2007–00051, clippings, "Youngsters Tie Up Regina Traffic in Parade against 8c Chocolate Bars," *Daily Tribune*, 6 May 1947, "Baby Parade Is Cancelled," *Leader-Post* (Regina), 16 May 1947, "Refusal Is Rapped," *Leader-Post* (Regina), 17 May 1947, "Chief Is under Fire," *Leader-Post* (Regina), 21 May 1947, "Halts Women, Babies, Call Chief Fascist," *Leader-Post* (Regina), 22 May 1947, "Council Disclaims Authority," *Leader-Post* (Regina), 23 May 1947, "Chief Explains Parade Refusal," *Leader-Post* (Regina), 26

May 1947; LAC, HCAR, RCMP memorandum from "F" Division to the Commissioner, Ottawa, re: Labor Progressive Party, Regina Saskatchewan, 14 June 1947; "Premier Douglas at Regina Rally," *Canadian Tribune*, 14 February 1948; RCMP "F" Division report re: "Newspaper Clipping Taken from the Canadian Tribune," 21 February 1948.

32 Beland Honderich, "Is Buyers' Strike Any Good as Price-Reducing Weapon?" *Toronto Daily Star*, 3 June 1947, 10.

33 LAC, HCFC, part 1, clippings, "Twins Feature Baby Parade to Protest Rise in Butter," *Toronto Daily Star*, 6 May 1947, 19, "Buyers' Strike Started in BC by Housewives," *Montreal Standard*, 10 May 1947, "Strikes of Buyers Gather Strength," *Montreal Gazette*, 12 May 1947, "Western Stores Minimize Effort of Buying Strike," *Ottawa Journal*, 13 May 1947, "Regina Wives Win 11-Cent Price Cut," *Toronto Daily Star*, 14 May 1947, 17, "Butter Price Cut Encourages Women to New Boycotts," *Ottawa Citizen*, 16 May 1947, "Report Progress on Buyers' Strike," *Montreal Gazette*, 26 May 1947; LAC, HCFC, part 1a, clippings, Ronald Williams, "Will Fellow-Travellers Control Housewives' Cavalcade to Ottawa?" *Financial Post*, 7 June 1947, "Those Rolling-Pin Women and Their Demands," *Ottawa Journal*, 25 June 1947.

34 LAC, HCFC, part 2, clipping, Ronald Williams, "Reds and Housewives," *Financial Post* [June 1948]. On Ronald Williams' career as an anticommunist writer, see Iacovetta, *Gatekeepers*, 106, 124.

35 LAC, HCFC, supp. 1, vol. 1, clipping, "Women Fail to Have Controls Restored," *Winnipeg Free Press*, 3 April 1947; LAC, RG 146, vol. 3440, Housewives Consumers Association of Toronto, part 1, clipping, "Get Dizzy Spells, Tired Feeling? Here's Tonic from Mrs. Luckock," *Daily Tribune*, 3 April 1947.

36 LAC, HCFC, part 1a, press release, Housewives Consumer Association, 20 February 1948. The estimate of 100,000 members is from an anticommunist article by Don Cameron, and may be exaggerated. "Communist Officials Head Up Housewives Consumer' Group," *Winnipeg Free Press*, 22 April 1947, 1, 8.

37 Sociologists Frances Fox Piven and Richard A. Cloward describe "strategic disruption" in their classic study of social movements, in which they argue that disruptive strategies are more effective than lobbying and similar, peaceful tactics. Piven and Cloward, *Poor People's Movements*.

38 "Curb Corporation Profits, Housewives' Brief Demands," *Toronto Daily Star*, 31 May 1947, 15.

39 "Curb Corporation Profits, Housewives' Brief Demands," *Toronto Daily Star*, 31 May 1947, 15.

40 LAC, HCFC, part 1a, clipping, "18,000 Citizens Sign Price Protest Cards," *Daily Tribune*, 2 June 1947; "18,000 Sign Protests against Rising Prices," *Toronto Daily Star*, 2 June 1947, 5; "18,000 Housewives Call Buyers' Strike June 21," *Toronto Daily Star*, 12 June 1947, 25.

41 LAC, A200700010_2007–10–16–13–53–33.PDF, stack 3, Housewives League, Montreal, Quebec, clipping, "Parade Right Not Refused," *Montreal Star*, 16 June 1947.

42 "Get Dizzy Spells, Tired Feeling? Here's Tonic from Mrs. Luckock," *Daily Tribune*, 3 April 1947.

43 LAC, HCFC, part 1a, clippings, "Issuing Call for Buyers' Strike as Decontrol Protest," *Ottawa Citizen*, 12 June 1947, "Housewives Plan Resistance Week," *Winnipeg Free Press*, 19 June 1947, "35,000 Add Names to Cards Demanding Gov't Reduce Prices," *Daily Tribune*, 23 June 1947; "400 Housewives to Protest High Prices of Commodities," *Globe and Mail*, 20 June 1947, 15; "Buyers' Protest," *Toronto Daily Star*, 21 June 1947, 17.

44 James M. Jasper, *The Art of Moral Protest: Culture, Biography, and Creativity in Social Movements* (Chicago: University of Chicago Press, 1997), 253–66.

45 "18,000 Sign Protests against Rising Prices," *Toronto Daily Star*, 2 June 1947, 5. On the Montgomery bus boycott, see Pamela E. Brooks, *Boycotts, Buses, and Passes: Black Women's Resistance in the U.S. South and South Africa* (Amherst: University of Massachusetts Press, 2008). On the United Farm Workers' struggles, see Marshall Ganz, *Why David Sometimes Wins: Leadership, Organization, and Strategy in the California Farm Worker Movement* (Oxford: Oxford University Press, 2010); Miriam Pawel, *The Union of Their Dreams: Power, Hope, and Struggle in Cesar Chavez's Farm Worker Movement* (New York: Bloomsbury Press, 2009).

46 LAC, HCFC, supp. 1, vol. 1, clippings, "Rolling Pin Brigade Opens Local Campaign," *Ottawa Citizen*, 24 June 1947, "Housewives Bent on Rolling Back Prices," *Ottawa Journal*, 24 June 1947.

47 Henderson's biographer, Peter Campbell, argues that the conviction that maternalism is inherently apolitical persists, and contributes to her near erasure from our historical memory. Campbell, *Rose Henderson*, 6–7.

48 LAC, HCFC, supp. 1, vol. 1, clippings, "Rolling Pin Protest Badges as Women Move on Ottawa," *Toronto Evening Telegram*, 23 June 1947, "Women Attack Prices – With Rolling Pins," *Winnipeg Free Press*, 24 June 1947, "Rolling Pin Brigade Opens Local Campaign," *Ottawa Citizen*, 24 June 1947, "Would Wield Pins on MP's," *Ottawa Citizen*, 24 June 1947, "Housewives in Capital Demand 10% Price Cut, Sales Tax Repeal," *Daily Tribune*, 24 June 1947; LAC, HCFC, part 1a, clipping, "Women with Rolling

Pins Seek Control of Prices," *Calgary Herald*, 25 June 1947; "Women Wield Rolling-Pins to Help Roll Back Prices," *Globe and Mail*, 25 June 1947, 12.

49 LAC, HCFC, supp. 1, vol. 1, clippings, "Housewives Chase Abbott for Roll-Back in Prices," *Ottawa Journal*, 25 June 1947, "Only His Speed on Foot Saves Him as Irate Housewives Storm Abbott," *Montreal Gazette*, 26 June 1947.

50 Thorn, *From Left to Right*; Brian T. Thorn, "Peace Is the Concern of Every Mother: Communist and Social Democratic Women's Anti-War Activism in British Columbia, 1948–1960," *Peace and Change* 35, no. 4 (2010): 626–57.

51 José Moya, "Italians in Buenos Aires's Anarchist Movement: Gender Ideology and Women's Participation, 1890–1910," in Gabaccia and Iacovetta, *Women, Gender, and Transnational Lives* (Toronto: University of Toronto Press, 2002), 189–216.

52 Caroline Waldron Merithew, "Anarchist Motherhood: Toward the Making of a Revolutionary Proletariat in Illinois Coal Towns," in Gabaccia and Iacovetta, *Women, Gender, and Transnational Lives*, 217–46.

53 Jennifer Guglielmo, "Italian Women's Proletarian Feminism in the New York City Garment Trades, 1890s–1940s," in Gabaccia and Iacovetta, *Women, Gender, and Transnational Lives*, 247–98; Jennifer Guglielmo, *Living the Revolution: Italian Women's Resistance and Radicalism in New York City, 1880–1945* (Chapel Hill: University of North Carolina Press, 2010).

54 Kaplan, *Taking Back the Streets*, 43–4, 51–2, 80, 194.

55 Moya, "Italians in Buenos Aires's Anarchist Movement." See also, Jose C. Moya, *Cousins and Strangers: Spanish Immigrants in Buenos Aires, 1860–1930* (Berkeley: University of California Press, 1998).

56 Kathleen Kennedy, *Disloyal Mothers and Scurrilous Citizens: Women and Subversion during World War I* (Bloomington: Indiana University Press, 1999), 21–2.

57 There is an extensive literature on radical women and claims by themselves or others to their maternalism. Of note are Brooks, *Boycotts, Buses and Passes*; Ardis Cameron, *Radicals of the Worst Sort: Laboring Women in Lawrence, Massachusetts, 1860–1912* (Urbana: University of Illinois Press, 1995); Victoria González-Rivera and Karen Kampwirth, eds., *Radical Women in Latin America: Left and Right* (University Park: Pennsylvania State University Press, 2010).

58 Brookfield, *Cold War Comforts*, 71–97 passim.

59 LAC, HCFC, supp. 1, vol. 1, note on file distribution slip, to RCMP Inspector Leopold, 27 June 1947.

60 On the hostility of the CCF Women's Committee to the HCA, see Azoulay, "Ruthless in a Ladylike Way."

61 LAC, HCFC, supp. 1, vol. 1, clippings, "Would Wield Pins on MP's," *Ottawa Citizen*, 24 June 1947, [No headline], *Ottawa Citizen*, 24 June 1947; "Ahead of CCF on Prices but Wives Late for Talk," *Toronto Daily Star*, 26 June 1947.

62 LAC, HCFC, supp. 1, vol. 1, clippings, "Rolling Pin Brigade Opens Local Campaign," *Ottawa Citizen*, 24 June 1947, "Controls Stay Off Abbott Declares," *Ottawa Citizen*, 25 June 1947, "Believe They Got 'Brush-Off' Housewives Angry, Return Home," *Ottawa Citizen*, 26 June 1947; "What Goes Up Had Better Come Down!" editorial cartoon, *Toronto Daily Star*, 24 June 1947, 6.

63 LAC, HCFC, supp. 1, part 1, clipping, "Rolling-Pin Economics," *Ottawa Citizen*, 25 June 1947.

64 "Housewives Deny Ottawa Gave Delegates Brush-Off," *Globe and Mail*, 17 July 1947.

65 LAC, HCFC, part 1a, clippings, "Housewives Group Voices Displeasure," *Winnipeg Free Press*, 24 June 1947, "Montreal Wives Not Dismayed by Ottawa Reception," *Ottawa Journal*, 27 June 1947, "'Won Victory Won't Take Abbott's No for Answer'- Housewives," *Daily Tribune*, 27 June 1947, "Canadian Housewives to Form National Organization Following 'Brush-off' by Government," *Daily Tribune*, 27 June 1947.

66 "When Prices Run Wild," *Toronto Daily Star*, 5 September 1947, 6; "Ward Two's Opportunity," *Toronto Daily Star*, 31 December 1947, 6; "Up 38 P.C. since Decontrol U.S. Food Still Going Up," *Toronto Daily Star*, 25 September 1947, 22. On the U.S. price control protests, see Jacobs, *Pocketbook Politics*. The 1947 period is addressed in chapter 6.

67 "Clothing Prices Lead Rise in Living Costs, Index 136.6," *Toronto Daily Star*, 5 September 1947, 2; "Food Going Up, Up, How Long Will We Stand It?" *Toronto Daily Star*, 6 September 1947, 1.

68 "To Keep Prices Down by Exposing Profiteers Said Ottawa Program," *Toronto Daily Star*, 19 September 1947, 1.

69 "Restored Price Control No Help to Consumers, Say Bracken, Coldwell," *Globe and Mail*, 17 January 1948, 1–2; "Price Control Debate Billed for First Week of 6 Months' Session," *Globe and Mail*, 24 January 1948, 3.

70 "Shortages, High Prices in Wake of Restrictions Predicted by Abbott," *Globe and Mail*, 19 November 1947, 3; "Prices Push Incomes Below Family Health 'Danger Line,'" *Globe and Mail*, 8 January 1948, 1–2; LAC, HCFC, supp. 1, vol. 2, clipping, "Wages: Dollar Shrinks," *The Westerner*, 17 April 1948; LAC, HCFC, part 2, letter from the Housewives Consumers Delegation to the Right Honourable Mackenzie King, 21 April 1948.

71 "Coldwell Deplores 'Lack of Planning' to Meet Crisis," *Globe and Mail*, 22 May 1947, 7; "Coldwell Charges Canada in Throes of Economic Crisis," *Globe and Mail*, 7 January 1948, 3.
72 LAC, HCFC, part 1a, clipping, "The Gallup Poll Proves the Trib Is Right," *Daily Tribune*, 17 July 1947; "Three of Four Voters Want Price Controls Back, Survey Reveals," *Toronto Daily Star*, 20 December 1947, 21.
73 "How Will Ottawa Handle Price Control Demands?" *Toronto Daily Star*, 22 December 1947, 16.
74 "Tax Excess Profits 100 p.c., Keep Controls Union Urges Ottawa," *Toronto Daily Star*, 18 December 1947, 25.
75 "Church Urges Ottawa Name M.P. Committee to Probe Living Costs," *Toronto Daily Star*, 23 October 1947, 1.
76 "Fought Price Control Now Tories Protesting High Prices, CCF Jibe," *Toronto Daily Star*, 12 December 1947, 26; Beland Honderich, "How Will Ottawa Handle Price Control Demands?" *Toronto Daily Star*, 22 December 1947, 16.
77 "Government Aids Profiteer Say White Collar Workers," *Toronto Daily Star*, 16 September 1947, 31.
78 Tim Rooth, "Britain's Other Dollar Problem: Economic Relations with Canada, 1945–1950," *Journal of Imperial and Commonwealth History* 27, no. 1 (1999): 81–108.
79 "U.S. Imports May Solve Dollar Crisis," *Globe and Mail*, 17 November 1947, 1–2; "Excise Taxes of 25 P.C. Announced," *Globe and Mail*, 18 November 1947, 1–2; "Abbott Tells Program to Cut Spending in U.S.," *Globe and Mail*, 18 November 1947, 2; Robert Bothwell and William Kilbourn, *C.D. Howe: A Biography* (Toronto: McClelland and Stewart, 1979), 216–17.
80 LAC, HCFC, part 1a, RCMP file, "Housewives Consumers Association, Ottawa, Ontario," 12 December 1947; Warren Baldwin, "Canada Cuts Spending in U.S: Bans Cars, Curbs Travel, Big List of U.S. Goods Is under Import Ban, Excise Taxes of 25 P.C. Announced," *Globe and Mail*, 18 November 1947, 1; Warren Baldwin, "Lowered Tariff Walls May Assist Dominion," *Globe and Mail*, 18 November 1947, 1–2; "The Right Way Is Still Open," *Globe and Mail*, 27 November 1947, 6; "End Not in Sight Meat to Double Is Prices View," *Toronto Daily Star*, 8 December 1947, 1; "Price Control Possible, Up to House: Abbott," *Globe and Mail*, 10 January 1948, 1.
81 "Cabbage Supply Gone, Meat Sales Cut 40 p.c.," *The Globe and Mail*, 13 January 1948, 1–2.
82 "$16.36 Feeds Family of Five for a Week," *The Globe and Mail*, 16 January 1948, 1.

83 AM, Ross papers, P5941/10, speakers' notes, Roll Back Prices Campaign, 6 February 1948; LAC, HCAR, Housewives Consumers Association, brief to the City of Regina Council, "Reduce the Cost of Living," 13 April 1948; Table E60–68, Average annual, weekly and hourly earnings, male and female wage earners, manufacturing industries, Canada, 1934 to 1969, in Noah M. Meltz, "Section E: Wages and Working Conditions," *Historical Statistics of Canada*, Statistics Canada, 1983, http://www.statcan.gc.ca/pub/11-516-x/sectione/4147438-eng.htm#2. Ian Mosby has documented the federal government's failure to measure nutritional requirements: Ian Mosby, "Making and Breaking Canada's Food Rules; Science, the State, and the Government of Nutrition, 1942–1949," in *Edible Histories, Cultural Politics: Towards a Canadian Food History*, ed. Franca Iacovetta, Valerie J. Korinek, and Marlene Epp (Toronto: University of Toronto Press, 2012), 409–32. See also, Mosby, *Food Will Win the War*.

84 LAC, HCFC, supp. 1, vol. 2, clippings, "Consumers Said Disappointed by Visit to Abbott," *Ottawa Citizen*, 13 December 1947, "Claim Abbott Gave Visitors 'Frozen Front,'" *Ottawa Citizen*, 13 December 1947; "Housewives Petition Mr. Drew on Milk," *Globe and Mail*, 18 November 1947, 31; "Group Protests Milk Price Boost," *Globe and Mail*, 27 November 1947, 8; "Only Set Ceiling, Milk Board Tells Consumer Body," *Globe and Mail*, 29 November 1947, 4.

85 "Baffled, Muttering Delegates Seek Austerity Plan Data," *Globe and Mail*, 18 December 1947, 1.

86 LAC, HCFC, part 1a, "Canada Heading for Inflation," undated document [probably December 1947].

87 LAC, HCFC, part 1a, clipping, "Consumer Federation Will Trek to Ottawa," *Montreal Gazette*, 12 December 1947, RCMP memo, "Organizations Attending Conference to Roll Back Prices in Montreal," November-December 1947, Ottawa Consumers' Association, "Canada Heading for Inflation: Consumers Demanding a Return to Price Control and Rationing to Steady Living Costs and Prevent Hardship on the Lower Income Groups," December 1947.

88 Fisher Library, Robert S. Kenny papers, MSS 179, box 20, "Act Now! Tell Ottawa Prices Must Be Held!" CCF leaflet, [1948].

89 Ian McKay, *Rebels, Reds, Radicals*, 169–83 passim.

90 LAC, HCFC, part 1a, clipping, "'Million Names' Drive Backed by Coldwell, Issue Convention Called," *Canadian Tribune*, 28 February 1948.

91 Historian Peter McInnis argues persuasively that the federal government encouraged ordinary Canadians to participate in postwar planning. McInnis, "Planning Prosperity,"47–85.

92 McInnis, *Harnessing Labour Confrontation.*
93 The labour militancy of this period has been well-documented by generations of labour historians, of which McInnis, *Harnessing Labour Confrontation,* is the most relevant. For a more general treatment, see Heron, *The Canadian Labour Movement.* The limitations of labour's struggle for social justice in the matter of discrimination on the basis of race and ethnicity are well-documented in chapter six, "Labour and the Left," of Carmela Patrias, *Jobs and Justice: Fighting Discrimination in Wartime Canada, 1939–1945* (Toronto: University of Toronto Press, 2012), 132–50. On the history of labour's struggle for a living wage in the U.S., see Glickman, *A Living Wage.*
94 Table E175–177 in Noah M. Meltz, "Section E: Wages and Working Conditions," *Historical Statistics of Canada,* Statistics Canada, 1983, http://www.statcan.gc.ca/pub/11-516-x/sectione/E175_177-eng.csv
95 "If Minimum for Family $40 How Can One Live on $36?" *Toronto Daily Star,* 20 May 1947, 9.
96 "'Come Out and Fight' Is Reaction of Labor as Prices Skyrocket," *Toronto Daily Star,* 19 September 1947, 21.
97 "37,000 Workers to Demand New Raise If Ceiling Goes," *Toronto Daily Star,* 13 January 1947, 2; "Fear New Wave of Strikes If Living Costs Soar Higher," *Toronto Daily Star,* 14 January 1947, 17; "Curb Price Spiral or Wage Demands Coming – Labor," *Toronto Daily Star,* 21 February 1947, 1.
98 "Must Ask Pay Boosts If Bread Is 14 Cents Steel Union Head Says," *Toronto Daily Star,* 15 September 1947, 1.
99 "'Come Out and Fight' Is Reaction of Labor as Prices Skyrocket," *Toronto Daily Star,* 19 September 1947, 21.
100 Jacobs, *Pocketbook Politics,* 224.
101 The Congress's memoranda to the government were published in its monthly magazine, *The Canadian Unionist.* See *The Canadian Unionist,* 1940 to 1949.
102 Iacovetta, *Gatekeepers,* 62–3, 121–34 passim.
103 The classic sources are Ruth Frager, *Sweatshop Strife: Class, Ethnicity and Gender in the Jewish Labour Movement of Toronto, 1900–1939* (Toronto: University of Toronto Press, 1992); Franca Iacovetta, *Such Hardworking People: Italian Immigrants in Postwar Toronto* (Montreal: McGill-Queen's University Press, 1992); Varpu Lindström, *Defiant Sisters: A Social History of Finnish Immigrant Women in Canada* (Toronto: Multicultural History Society of Ontario, 1992); Swyripa, *Wedded to the Cause.* More recent sources include Epp, Iacovetta, and Swyripa, *Sisters or Strangers?;* Ruth

Frager and Carmela Patrias, *Discounted Labour: Women Workers in Canada, 1870–1939* (Toronto: University of Toronto Press, 2005); Varpu Lindström, *"I Won't Be a Slave!" Selected Articles on Finnish Canadian Women's History* (Beaverton, ON: Aspasia Books, 2010).

104 Lil Ilomak and Alice Maigis, interview by author, Toronto, ON, 12 December 1996.
105 Pat Chytyk, interview by author, Sudbury, ON, 27 February 1997.
106 Mona Morgan, interview by author, Vancouver, BC, 24 July 1998.
107 Peggy Chunn, interview with Mona Morgan, Peggy Chunn, and Audrey Modzir (Staples), by author, Vancouver, BC, 24 July 1998; Prokop, interview.
108 LAC, HCFC, part 1, RCMP Saskatoon Division, Report, "Housewives Consumers Association, Saskatoon, Saskatchewan," 25 April 1947.
109 AM, Ross papers, P5941/6, Manitoba Housewives Consumers Association (MHCA) Annual Report, 26 May 1948.
110 Becky Lapedes, interview by Karen Levine, Toronto, ON, 7 June 1978; Anne Ross, interview by Kathryn McPherson, Winnipeg, MB, 4 August 1988, Archives of Manitoba, Winnipeg General Hospital Alumni, C934–935; Mona Morgan, Peggy Chunn, and Audrey Modzir, interview by author, Vancouver, BC, 24 July 1998; Prokop, interview.
111 "Consumer Group Anxious for Opinions on U.S. Bans," *Globe and Mail*, 6 August 1948, 13.
112 Valerie Korinek, *Roughing It in the Suburbs: Reading Chatelaine Magazine in the Fifties and Sixties* (Toronto: University of Toronto Press, 2000).
113 Mrs R.J. Marshall was president of the National Council of Women of Canada from 1946–51: National Council of Women of Canada, http://www.ncwcanada.com/our-team/past-presidents/; Mrs W.P.M. (Pauline) Kennedy was prominent in a number of charities and the Anglican church, and president of the Toronto Women's Canadian Club: Martin Friedland, "Introduction," in W.P.M. Kennedy, *The Constitution of Canada: An Introduction to Its Development and Law* (Oxford: Oxford University Press, 1938), 16.
114 "Consumers to Battle for Ottawa Price-Cut," *Globe and Mail*, 1 Oct. 1947, 7.
115 "Women on Warpath against Soaring Prices," *Globe and Mail*, 8 January 1948, 10.
116 John Lewis Gaddis, *The United States and the Origins of the Cold War, 1941–1947* (New York: Columbia University Press, 1972); Whitaker and Marcuse, *Cold War Canada*.

5. Citizen Consumers or Kitchen Communists?

1 Whitaker and Marcuse, *Cold War Canada*, 188–90.
2 Dominique Clément, *Canada's Rights Revolution: Social Movements and Social Change, 1937–82* (Vancouver: UBC Press, 2008); Dominique Clément, "Alberta's Rights Revolution," *British Journal of Canadian Studies* 26, no. 1 (2013): 59–77. See also, Ross Lambertson, *Repression and Resistance: Canadian Human Rights Activists, 1930–1960* (Toronto: University of Toronto Press, 2005); Patrias, *Jobs and Justice*.
3 Harvey Hickey, "Housewives' Group Said Propagandists for Reds," *Globe and Mail*, 15 April 1948.
4 On the role of the IWA and its president, Bruce Magnuson, in the community, see Michel Beaulieu, *Labour at the Lakehead: Ethnicity, Socialism, and Politics, 1900–35* (Vancouver: UBC Press, 2011) and Ian Radforth, *Bush Workers and Bosses: Logging in Northern Ontario 1900–1980* (Toronto: University of Toronto Press, 1987), 135–40.
5 "Housewives Unit Dissolved; Reds Blamed," *Globe and Mail*, 22 September 1938, 13.
6 "Housewives Condemn Mrs. Lamb's Antics," *Daily Clarion*, 24 September 1938.
7 LAC, RG146, vol. 3305, Housewives League of BC 1940–1965 (henceforth HLBC), AITP request A-2007–00010, clippings, "Mrs. Norton Explains Action," *Vancouver Sun*, 13 July 1940, "Housewives' Head Denies Communism" *Daily Province* (Vancouver), 30 July 1940.
8 Schrecker, *Many Are the Crimes*, 90.
9 LAC, RG146, Vol. 3440, HCA Toronto, ON (henceforth HCAT), vol. 2, clipping, "Some Enlightenment," *Hamilton Spectator*, 24 January 1948.
10 LAC, HLBC, clipping, "Reds Proficient in Exploitation," *Daily Province* (Vancouver), 5 February 1948; Howard, "The Mother's Council of Vancouver"; Bert Whyte, *Champagne and Meatballs: Adventures of a Canadian Communist* (Athabasca, AB: Athabasca University Press, 2011), 244–7; Rush, *We Have a Glowing Dream*, 164–5.
11 "Mr. Abbott Makes a Discovery," editorial, *Ottawa Journal*, 16 April 1948.
12 Storrs, *The Second Red Scare*.
13 Whitaker and Marcuse, *Cold War Canada*, 161–87; on security screening of suspected homosexuals, see Gary Kinsman, "'Character Weaknesses' and 'Fruit Machines': Towards an Analysis of the Anti-Homosexual Security Campaign in the Canadian Civil Service," *Labour/Le Travail* 35 (1995): 133–61.
14 "Ilsley Accuses CCF Left Wing of Being Close to Communism," *Globe and Mail*, 26 March 1948, 17; "Threat to Free Nations from within Grave,

Need Action: Mr. King," *Globe and Mail*, 3 April 1948, 7; Penner, *Canadian Communism*, 224–5.
15 Steve Hewitt, "Royal Canadian Mounted Spy: The Secret Life of John Leopold/Jack Esselwein," *Intelligence and National Security* 15, no. 1 (2000): 144–68.
16 The essays in Richard Cavell, ed., *Love, Hate, and Fear in Canada's Cold War* (Toronto: University of Toronto Press, 2004), provide an excellent overview of the repressiveness of the Cold War for individuals. See also, Elaine Tyler May, *Homeward Bound: American Families in the Cold War* (New York: Basic Books, 1988).
17 Ivan Avakumovic, *The Communist Party in Canada: A History* (Toronto: McClelland and Stewart, 1975); McKay, *Rebels, Reds, Radicals*, 158–62.
18 Clément, *Canada's Rights Revolution*; Patrias, *Jobs and Justice*.
19 The Cominform (Communist Information Bureau) replaced the Comintern (Communist Third International) in 1947.
20 Penner, *Canadian Communism*, 216–27.
21 "Police Nab 56 at Reds' Party When Liquor Sold," *Globe and Mail*, 5 April 1948, 17; LAC, HCAT, part 2, clipping, "Raid in Montreal on 'Party' Sponsored by LPP," *Ottawa Citizen*, 5 April 1948; LAC, HCAT, part 2a, clipping, "Quebec Liquor Police Smash Rally of Communists in Montreal House," *Montreal Gazette*, 5 April 1948.
22 LAC, HCFC, part 2, clipping, Don Cameron, "Loyal Canadian Duped to Aid Red 5th Column," *Windsor Star*, 10 March 1948.
23 Ronald Williams, "Are Reds behind Housewives?" *Financial Post*, 24 April 1948, 1, 3; LAC, HCFC, part 2, clipping, Ronald Williams, "Reds and Housewives," *Financial Post*, 1948.
24 Ronald Williams, "Are Reds behind Housewives?" *Financial Post*, 24 April 1948, 1.
25 May, *Homeward Bound*.
26 The HCA claimed 500; the *Globe and Mail* reported 300. "Housewives and Royalty Arrive Simultaneously in Rain on Capitol Hill," *Globe and Mail*, 17 April, 1–2.
27 AM, Ross papers, P5941/8, MHCA Releases, Reports, Activities, [1946–1948], "Presentation of the Petition of [blank] signatures favoring controls and subsidies where necessary to roll back prices to January 1946 levels accompanied by the following brief, submitted to The Rt. Hon. W.L. Mackenzie King Prime Minister, and Members of the Government of Canada, Roll Back Prices Conference, Ottawa Ontario April 15-16-17, 1948."
28 LAC, HCAT, part 2a, clipping, "But Housewives Take Huge Price Petitions to King's Front Door," *Canadian Tribune*, 24 April 1948.

29 Ina Zweiniger-Bargielowska, *Austerity in Britain: Rationing, Controls, and Consumption, 1939–1955* (Oxford: Oxford University Press, 2002).
30 Hilton, *Consumerism in Twentieth-Century Britain*; James Hinton, "Militant Housewives: The British Housewives' League and the Attlee Government," *History Workshop* 38 (1994): 128–56.
31 These complexities evidently eluded the RCMP, whose various memoranda and surveillance reports reveal agents' largely unsuccessful efforts to understand the episodic nature of Housewives organizing.
32 AM, Ross papers, P5941/9, "Minutes of First Annual Convention of the Housewives and Consumers Federation of Canada," 17 April 1948.
33 "City Housewives Launch Buyer's Strike," *Globe and Mail*, 14 May 1947, 15; AM, Ross papers, P5941/1, letter from Mrs R.J. Marshall to Mrs Anne Ross, 20 September 1947.
34 Parr, *Domestic Goods*, 87–93 passim.
35 Norman Penner, *Canadian Communism*, 216–27.
36 LAC, HCFC, part 2, "Draft Constitution: The Housewives' and Consumers' Federation of Canada," 21 April 1948.
37 LAC, HCFC, part 3, clipping, "Opposes Food Subsidy Skey Tells Housewives," *Canadian Tribune*, 4 April 1949.
38 "B.C. Housewives Ask Men to Join," *Globe and Mail*, 11 November 1938, 10.
39 "Opposes Food Subsidy Skey Tells Housewives," *Canadian Tribune*, 4 April 1949.
40 Johanna Brenner, "Twenty-First Century Socialist Feminism," *Socialist Studies* 10, no. 1 (Summer 2014): 31–49, http://dx.doi.org/10.18740/S4RP43
41 Joy Parr argues that "the reasoning about the consumer interest in the first fifteen years after the war was always about the rights and responsibilities of people who were women rather than men." Parr, *Domestic Goods*, 86.
42 "Abbott Budget Eases Load on Canadian Pocketbooks," caption, *Toronto Daily Star*, 30 April 1947, 1; "Basic Needs Jump 139 pc Since 1939," *Globe and Mail*, 8 January 1948, 1–2; "50.4 Per Cent Increase over 1939 Living Cost," *Globe and Mail*, 5 May 1948, 1; LAC, HCFC, part 3, clipping, "Somebody Is Lying," *Canadian Tribune*, 19 June 1948.
43 Tim Buck, "The Wage Movement, Prices and Profits," *National Affairs Monthly* 3, no. 6 (June 1946): 165–71 identifies the publications that argued that inflation is caused by high wages as the *Calgary Herald*, *The Globe and Mail*, the *Financial Post*, and *Saturday Night*.
44 AM, Ross papers, P5941/8, "Presentation of the Petition of [blank] signatures favoring controls and subsidies where necessary to roll back prices to January 1946 levels accompanied by the following brief,

submitted to The Rt. Hon. W.L. Mackenzie King Prime Minister, and Members of the Government of Canada, Roll Back Prices Conference, Ottawa Ontario April 15-16-17, 1948."

45 LAC, HCFC, part 2, letter from Rae Luckock to Prime Minister Mackenzie King, 21 April 1948. On the dollar crisis, see H.S. Ellis, "The Dollar Shortage in Theory and Fact," *The Canadian Journal of Economics and Political Science* 14, no. 3 (1948): 358–72; Parr, *Domestic Goods*, 74; J.A. Stevenson, "The Political Situation in Canada," *The Political Quarterly* 19, no. 3 (1948): 234–43; Kenneth R. Wilson, "Dollar Famine," *Behind the Headlines* 7, no. 7 (Canadian Association for Adult Education, 1948).

46 Whitaker and Marcuse, *Cold War Canada*, 191.

47 "Housewives' Group Said Propagandists for Reds; Denied Cabinet Hearing," *Globe and Mail*, 15 April, 1948; LAC, HCFC, supp. 1, vol. 2, clippings, "Abbott Charges Housewives Inspired by Communists," *Ottawa Journal*; "Abbott Tells Why Cabinet Wouldn't See Housewives," *Toronto Daily Star*, 15 April 1948; "Cabinet Refuses to See Women, March Planned," *Toronto Daily Star*; "Housewives Consumers Association," House of Commons Debates, 14 April 1948: 2952.

48 AM, Ross papers, PAM P5941/8, Anne Ross, speaking notes, no title, no date; AM, Ross papers, P5941/9, "Minutes of First Annual Convention of the Housewives and Consumers Federation of Canada," 17 April 1948; LAC, HCFC, part 2, RCMP report re: Housewives and Consumers Federation of Canada, 21 April 1948.

49 AM, Ross papers, P5941/10, "Speakers' Notes, Roll Back Prices Campaign," 6 February 1948.

50 Bothwell, Drummond, and English, *Canada Since 1945*; Greg Donaghy, *Uncertain Horizons*.

51 Bothwell and Kilbourn, *C.D. Howe*; Bothwell, Drummond, and English, *Canada Since 1945*; Don Nerbas, *Dominion of Capital: The Politics of Big Business and the Crisis of the Canadian Bourgeoisie, 1914–1947* (Toronto: University of Toronto Press, 2013), 201–41.

52 Robert Bothwell, "Clarence Decatur Howe," *Dictionary of Canadian Biography*, vol. 18 (Toronto: University of Toronto Press, 2003), http://www.biographi.ca/en/bio/howe_clarence_decatur_18E.html

53 "Mantle of Martyrdom a Misfit," editorial, *Globe and Mail*, 10 June 1948, 6.

54 AM, Ross papers, P5941/8, Anne Ross, untitled document, "Report of 'March of a Million Names' Conference," no date.

55 AM, Ross papers, P5941/8, Louise Watson, MHCA Executive Secretary, "Report of 'March of a Million Names' Conference, Little Elgin Theatre, Ottawa, Ont., April 15–16, 1948."

56 LAC, HCFC, part 2, clipping, "709,573 Citizens Spurned by Gov't," *The Westerner*, 1 May 1948.
57 "Housewives and Royalty Arrive Simultaneously in Rain on Capitol Hill," *Globe and Mail*, 17 April 1948, 1; LAC, HCFC, supp. 1, vol. 2, clipping, "Abbott, MPs. Weather Turn against 'Wives,'" *Montreal Gazette*, 17 April 1948.
58 LAC, HCFC, supp. 1, vol. 2, clipping, "Abbott Gives Curt 'No' to Prices Delegation," *Canadian Tribune*, no date.
59 "3-Hour Debate on Cost of Living Billed for House," *Globe and Mail*, 25 June 1948, 1–2.
60 LAC, HCFC, part 1a, clipping, "Petition Campaign," *Canadian Tribune*, 7 February 1948; LAC, HCFC, part 1, clipping, "Toronto Supports Coldwell Stand," *The Westerner*, 21 February 1948.
61 "Tells Officials' Salary Bakery Firm Ordered over Tory Opposition," *Toronto Daily Star*, 1 March 1946, 1; "Toronto Firms Admit Making Record Profits," *Globe and Mail*, 21 May 1948, 1–2.
62 LAC, HCFC, part 3, clipping, "Housewives Get Big Support in Downtown Prices Protest," *Pacific Tribune*, 24 July 1948.
63 The Liberals may well have taken instruction from their U.S. counterparts on use of anticommunism to neutralize the problem represented by the Housewives. On the attacks on consumer activists in the U.S., see Storrs, "Left-Feminism."
64 "Housewives Consumers Association," *House of Commons Debates*, 14 April 1948; LAC, RG146, vol. 3268, Housewives Consumers League of Saskatchewan, 1946–49 (HCLS), AITP request A-2007–00166, clipping, "Consumers' Group Denies 'Red' Sway," *Prince Albert Herald*, 24 April 1947.
65 LAC, HCFC, part 1, clippings, "Women's Groups Plan March to 'The Hill' Unshaken by House Charges," *Ottawa Evening Citizen*, 15 April 1948, 1, "Abbott Charges Housewives Inspired by Communists," *Ottawa Journal*, 15 April 1948, "Biggest Petition in History Demands King Act on Prices" *Canadian Tribune*, 17 April 1948, "Housewives Deny Control by Reds," *Leader-Post* (Regina), 23 April 1947.
66 LAC, HCAT, Vol. 2, clipping, Don Cameron, "Loyal Canadian Duped to Aid Red 5th Column," *Windsor Star*, 10 March 1948; reprinted in *Halifax Herald*, 13 March 1948.
67 LAC, HCAT, part 2, clipping, "Rain in Montreal on 'Party' Sponsored by LPP," *Ottawa Citizen*, 5 April 1948.
68 "Only Set Ceiling, Milk Board Tells Consumer Body," *Globe and Mail*, 29 November 1947, 4; "Women's Groups Plan March to 'The Hill' Unshaken by House Charges," *Ottawa Evening Citizen* 15 April 1948, 1.

69 McKay, *Rebels, Reds, and Radicals*, 1–21 passim.
70 LAC, HCFC, part 2, clippings, "Mr. Abbott Makes a Discovery," *Ottawa Journal*, 16 April 1948, 6, "The Effort to Embarrass," *Halifax Chronicle*, 16 April 1948; LAC, HCFC, supp. 1, vol. 2, clipping, "Good Women with a Bad Case," *Ottawa Journal*, editorial, 19 April 1948.
71 On Joseph E. Atkinson, see Trista Vincent, "Manufacturing Concern," *Ryerson Review of Journalism*, 1 March 1999, http://rrj.ca/manufacturing-concern/
72 LAC, HCFC, supp. 1, vol. 2, clippings, "The Government and the Housewives," *Toronto Daily Star*, 15 April 1948, 6, "The Housewives' Petition," *Ottawa Citizen*, 19 April 1948; "Plenty of Decoys Anyhow, Mister!," *Toronto Daily Star*, 24 October 1947, 6.
73 LAC, HCFC, part 1a, clipping, "Call It Anti-Communism," *Saturday Night*, 28 June 1947.
74 Clément, *Canada's Rights Revolution*, 40, and Dominique Clément, "Spies, Lies and a Commission: A Case Study in the Mobilization of the Canadian Civil Liberties Movement," *Left History* 7, no. 2 (2000): 53–79.
75 "MP Charges Canadians Duped into Aiding Reds," *Globe and Mail*, 13 April 1948, 3.
76 Clément, *Canada's Rights Revolution*; Lambertson, *Repression and Resistance*.
77 "Church Urges Ottawa Name M.P. Committee to Probe Living Costs," *Toronto Daily Star*, 23 October 1947, 1.
78 LAC, HCFC, part 1, clipping, "Drew Asks Women to Check Moves of Political Groups," *Ottawa Citizen*, May 1947.
79 "Measure Asking Canada to Outlaw Communists Up for Debate Tuesday," *Globe and Mail*, 9 April 1948, 3; Whitaker and Marcuse, *Cold War Canada*, 188–92.
80 Some recent examples include: Clément, *Canada's Rights Revolution*; Iacovetta, *Gatekeepers*; Lambertson, *Repression and Resistance*.
81 Irving Martin Abella, *Nationalism, Communism, and Canadian Labour: The CIO, the Communist Party, and the Canadian Congress of Labour 1935–1956* (Toronto: University of Toronto Press, 1973); Whitaker and Marcuse, *Cold War Canada*, 342–63.
82 Peggy Chunn, Mona Morgan, and Audrey Modzir (Staples), interview by author, Vancouver, BC, 24 July 1998.
83 LAC, HCFC, part 1, RCMP "O" Division report re: "Ukrainian Life," vol. 7, no. 20, 15 May 1947.
84 Iacovetta, *Gatekeepers*; Patrias, *Jobs and Justice*. See also the essays in, Epp, Iacovetta, and Swyripa, *Sisters or Strangers*. Although it does

not address the Cold War years, Donald Avery, *Dangerous Foreigners: European Immigrant Workers and Labour Radicalism in Canada, 1896–1932* (Toronto: McClelland and Stewart, 1979), continues to inform the scholarship.

85 Steve Hewitt observes that the Mounties routinely used racial slurs in their reports and treated non-Anglo-Saxon ethnicity or race as evidence of probable subversion. Hewitt, "Royal Canadian Mounted Spy."
86 Hannant, *The Infernal Machine*, 89.
87 Reg Whitaker and Gregory S. Kealey, "A War on Ethnicity? The RCMP and Internment," in Iacovetta, Perin, and Principe, *Enemies Within*, 130.
88 LAC, HCFC, part 2, RCMP file re: "Ukrainian Life," 6 May 1948; 5 June 1948: LAC, HCAT, part 2a, RCMP file extract re: Association of United Ukrainian Canadians.
89 LAC, HCFC, part 1, clipping, "Communist Officials Head Up Housewives Consumers' Group," *Winnipeg Free Press*, 22 April 1947.
90 LAC, HCFC, part 1, clippings, "Wives Duped by Reds," *Calgary Herald*, 23 April 1947, "Housewives Deny Press Allegations of Red Domination of Organization," *Star-Phoenix* (Saskatoon), 24 April 1947, "Housewives Protest 'Communist' Label," *Toronto Daily Star*, 24 April 1947; "Housewives Refute Charge Reds Dominate Society," *Globe and Mail*, 24 April 1947, 7.
91 "Housewives Refute Charge Reds Dominate Society," *Globe and Mail*, 24 April 1947, 7; LAC, HCFC, part 1, clipping, "Housewives Protest 'Communist' Label," *Toronto Daily Star*, 24 April 1947.
92 LAC, HCFC, part 1, clipping, "Housewives Deny Press Allegations of Red Domination of Organization," *Star-Phoenix* (Saskatoon), 24 April 1947; LAC, HCFC, part 1, RCMP file "Re: Housewives Consumers Association Saskatoon Saskatchewan," 25 April 1947.
93 LAC, HCFC, supp. 1, vol. 1, clipping, "Believe They Got 'Brush-Off' Housewives Angry, Return Home," *Ottawa Citizen*, 26 June 1947; LAC, HCFC, supp. 1, vol. 2, RCMP report, 13 March 1948; LAC, HCFC, part 3, clipping, "All B.C. Backs Beef Prices Opposition," *Pacific Tribune*, 20 August 1948.
94 This assumption is quite common among writers who mention the Housewives, and may be due in part to the absence, until now, of a full-length history of the organization. Of particular interest in this regard among those who write about the Housewives is Azoulay, "Ruthless in a Ladylike Way." For a more nuanced account, see Sangster, *Dreams of Equality*, 185–8.
95 Brookfield, *Cold War Comforts*, 71–92.

96 Amy Swerdlow, *Women Strike for Peace: Traditional Motherhood and Radical Politics in the 1960s* (Chicago: University of Chicago Press, 1993); Amy Swerdlow, "Ladies' Day at the Capitol: Women Strike for Peace versus HUAC," *Feminist Studies* 8, no. 3 (1982): 493–520, http://www.jstor.org/stable/3177709

97 Ian McKay, "Rethinking the History of Depression-Era Communism"; see also, McKay, *Rebels, Reds, Radicals*, 145–217 passim.

98 Manley, "Moscow Rules?"; John Manley, "'Communists Love Canada!': The Communist Party of Canada, the 'People' and the Popular Front, 1933–1939," *Journal of Canadian Studies* 36, no. 4 (2001): 59–86.

99 Hewitt, "Royal Canadian Mounted Spy." For insight into the activities and culture of the RCMP, see also, Gregory S. Kealey and Reg Whitaker, eds., *R.C.M.P. Security Bulletins: The Early Years, 1919–1929* (St. John's, Nfld.: Canadian Committee on Labour History, 1994); Kealey and Whitaker, *R.C.M.P. Security Bulletins: The Depression Years*; and Kealey and Whitaker, *R.C.M.P. Security Bulletins: The War Series.*

100 LAC, HCAR, RCMP memo from W. Mortimer, Superintendent CIB, "Subversive Activity in Housewives Consumers League, Regina Sask.," 1 May 1947; LAC, HCFC, part 1a, RCMP memo from Sgt. R.D. Robertson to Superintendent McClellan, 9 February 1948; LAC, HCAT, part 2, RCMP memorandum from Sgt. R.D. Robertson to Superintendent McClellan, 10 February 1948; LAC, HCAR, RCMP memorandum from Superintendent F.W. Zaneth re: Subversive Activity in Housewives Consumers League, Regina, Saskatchewan, 8 September 1948.

101 Mary Prokop, interview by author, Toronto, ON, 15 December 1998.

102 LAC, HCLS, clipping, "Consumers' Group Denies 'Red' Sway," *Prince Albert Herald*, 24 April 1947.

103 LAC, HCFC, part 1, RCMP file, "Housewives Consumers Association, Saskatoon, Saskatchewan," 25 April 1947.

104 AM, Ross papers, P5941/5, Milk bottle shaped campaign flyer; Election results, *Globe and Mail*, 2 January 1947, 1–2; "Four Trustee Seats Won by Communists," *Globe and Mail*, 2 January 1947, 5.

105 Joan Sangster and Dan Azoulay erroneously identify the Housewives as an organization of the Communist Party. Sangster, *Dreams of Equality*, 139, 173, 178, 185–8, 220; Azoulay, "Ruthless in a Ladylike Way."

106 Fisher Library, Robert S. Kenny papers, MSS 179, Box 57, "Discussion on Panel of Work among Women," by LPP National Executive Committee, [c. 1950].

107 LAC, MG28 IV4, Communist Party of Canada fonds, vol. 29, file 66, "Proceedings," Second Ontario Convention, 8–10 October 1938; LAC,

Communist Party fonds, vol. 30, file 3, "Report on Panel on Women's Work," LPP Third Annual Convention, 1946.
108 LAC, Communist Party fonds, vol. 35, file 37, "Report of Panel on Women's Work," LPP Saskatchewan Convention 1948.
109 This particular orthodoxy has been widely noted. See, for instance, Joan Sangster, "The Communist Party and the Woman Question, 1922–1929," *Labour/Le Travail*, 15 (1985): 25–56. It is also apparent in the party's educational materials. One example is LAC, Communist Party fonds, vol. 9, file 23, "Key Questions and Reading Material" in "Women and the Fight for Peace and Justice," 1948.
110 AM, Ross papers, P5941/3, handwritten notes [1946].
111 LAC, Communist Party fonds, vol. 24, file 49, "Winning the Women for the Broad People's Front," BC District Provincial Convention, 20–24 March 1937; Fisher Library, Kenny papers, box 57, circular letter from Leslie Morris to all Regional Committees and all Members of the Ontario Committee LPP, 2 July 1946.
112 Johnston, *A Great Restlessness*, 75, 94–5, 204.
113 LAC, Communist Party fonds, vol. 9, file 23, Becky Buhay, *Woman and the Fight for Peace and Socialism*, National Woman's Commission, Labor-Progressive Party, February 1948.
114 LAC, Communist Party fonds, vol. 9, file 23, "Resolution on Work among Women," Saskatchewan LPP Convention 1948.
115 Fisher Library, Kenny papers, box 57, "Discussion on Panel on Work among Women," [1950].
116 LAC, HCAT, part 2, RCMP file, "CPof C Activities in the LPP, York Township," 13 February 1948.
117 LAC, RG146, vol. 3389, Housewives Consumers Association of Halifax, 1947–64 (HCAH), "RCMP 'H' Division report re: Labour Progressive Party, Nova Scotia," 5 June 1947.
118 Avakumovic, *The Communist Party in Canada*.
119 LAC, HCFC, part 1a, Tim Buck, letter to all provincial committee, editors of labour press and national executive committee, 10 February 1948.
120 LAC, HCFC, supp. 1, vol. 1, clipping, "Demand March on Ottawa to Protest Prices," *Ottawa Journal* 7 February 1947; "Boycott Butter for Week Toronto Housewives Urge," *Toronto Daily Star*, 1 May 1947, 1; RG 146, HCFC, part 1, clipping, "Regina Housewives League Plans Picketing Programme," *Winnipeg Free Press*, 7 May 1947.
121 LAC, HCAT, part 2, RCMP file, "CP of C Activities in the LPP, York Township," 13 February 1948.
122 Prokop, interview.

123 LAC, HCFC, part 2, clippings, "The Daily Round," *Pacific Tribune*, 7 May 1948, "Beef about Beef: Join Housewives' Boycott This Week," *Pacific Tribune*, 14 May 1948, "Probe Leading Bakeries on Housewives' Demand," *The Westerner*, May 1948.
124 "Fighting High Prices Is Fighting for Peace!" *Canadian Tribune*, 2 October 1950; "HCA Asks Gov't Action against Profiteering," *Canadian Tribune*, 30 October 1950.
125 "Housewives and Royalty Arrive Simultaneously in Rain on Capitol Hill," *Globe and Mail*, 17 April 1948, 1–2.
126 "Housewives' Groups Said Propagandists for Reds, Denied Cabinet Hearing," *Globe and Mail*, 15 April 1948.
127 "Prayer Crusade Planned by CWL for Soviet Benefit," *Globe and Mail*, 26 June 1947, 12.
128 "Housewives to Organize Tenants for Housing Fight, Eviction End," *Canadian Tribune*, 28 March 1948; "Labor Backs Atlantic Pact Blasts Red-Tinged Union," *Toronto Telegram*, 30 March 1949.
129 Ronald Williams, "Are You a Stooge for a Communist?" *Chatelaine*, April 1949, 90–4.
130 "HCA Asks Gov't Action against Profiteering," *Canadian Tribune*, 30 October 1950.

6. "Reds," Housewives, and the Cold War

1 LAC, HCOH, RCMP report re: Frances M. (Mrs James C.) Sim, 16 July 1954.
2 Prokop, interview.
3 There is a voluminous literature on this topic. See, for instance, John Lewis Gaddis, *The Cold War: A New History* (New York: Penguin Press, 2005); John Earl Haynes and Harvey Klehr, *In Denial: Historians, Communism and Espionage* (San Francisco: Encounter Books, 2003); and many essays in the *Journal of Cold War Studies*. For a response to this perspective, see Ellen Schrecker, ed., *Cold War Triumphalism: The Misuse of History after the Fall of Communism* (New York: The New Press, 2004).
4 The reference is to President Truman's speech of 12 March 1946, intended to "scare the hell out of the country," and may well be the most referenced quote of the Cold War. For one such reference, see Otto H. Olsen and Ephraim Schulman, "John Lewis Gaddis and the Perpetuation of the Cold War," *Nature, Society, and Thought* 11, no. 2 (1998): 187–218.
5 Whitaker and Marcuse, *Cold War Canada*, 24.
6 Schrecker, *Many Are the Crimes*.

7 Storrs, *The Second Red Scare*.
8 Alvin Finkel, "Paradise Postponed: A Re-Examination of the Green Book Proposals of 1945," *Journal of the Canadian Historical Association* 4 (1993):120–142; McInnis, *Harnessing Labour Confrontation*.
9 LAC, HCFC, letter from RCMP Commissioner S. T. Wood to J.L. Ilsley, Min. of Justice, 12 April 1948.
10 Herbert A. Bruce, *Varied Operations: An Autobiography* (Toronto: Longmans, Green, 1958).
11 "Bruce Indicts Nineteen Units as Subversive," *Globe and Mail*, 13 June 1940, 9; LAC, RG 146, vol. 3440, Housewives Consumers Association, Toronto, Ontario, part 1, letter from H.A. Bruce to RCMP Commissioner S.T. Wood, Ottawa, Ontario, 18 June 1940; LAC, RG 146, vol. 3440, Housewives Consumers Association, Toronto, Ontario, part 1, Memorandum from RCMP Sgt. J.H. Pepper, 18 June 1940.
12 LAC, HCAT, part 1, letter from the Deputy Minister of Justice to the Commissioner, RCMP, Ottawa, Ontario, 14 June 1940.
13 "Compulsory Registration of Reds as Foreign Power Agents Proposed," *Globe and Mail*, 27 April 1948, 15.
14 On Operation PROFUNC, see Frances V. Reilly, "Controlling Contagion: Policing and Prescribing Sexual and Political Normalcy in Cold War Canada," (PhD dissertation, University of Saskatchewan, 2016), https://ecommons.usask.ca/bitstream/handle/10388/7396/REILLY-DISSERTATION-2016.pdf?sequence=1&isAllowed=y
15 Whitaker and Kealey, "A War on Ethnicity?" 141–2.
16 LAC, HCAT, part 2, RCMP memo, 6 March 1948. New scholarship is in progress on the RCMP's continued use of secret lists of suspected subversives. See Frances Reilly, "Confining the Enemy in the Cold War: Operation Profunc and the Planned Internment of Canadian Communists," paper presented at Civilian Internment in Canada conference, 17–19 June 2015, Winnipeg, Manitoba.
17 LAC, HCFC, part 1a, RCMP memo, 20 February 1948.
18 LAC, HCLBC, RCMP report, "Housewives' League of B.C.," 6 February 1948.
19 LAC, HCFC, part 1, RCMP file, letter from S.T. Wood to Ilsley, 10 June 1947; LAC, HCFC, part 2, RCMP report, D/A/Cpl. W.D. Fast to the Commissioner, 7 May 1948.
20 Whitaker and Marcuse, *Cold War Canada*; Iacovetta, *Gatekeepers*. New work documenting the Canadian state's extra-legal persecution of innocents was presented at a recent conference on Civilian Internment in Canada, 17–19 June 2015, Winnipeg, Manitoba.

21 See, for example, the essays in Gary Kinsman, Dieter K. Buse, and Mercedes Steedman, eds., *Whose National Security? Canadian State Surveillance and the Creation of Enemies* (Toronto: Between the Lines, 2000); Iacovetta, Perin, and Principe, *Enemies Within*; Repka and Repka, *Dangerous Patriots*.

22 LAC, HCLBC, letters from G. [Grace] Greenwood, corresponding secretary, Central Executive Council, Housewives' League of BC to Colonel Edgett, Vancouver Police Department, and to Hon. E. LaPointe, Minister of Justice, Ottawa, 17 January 1941, BC Housewives League; "Women Say Meeting 'Raided,'" *Daily Province* (Vancouver), 18 January 1941, clipping, "B.C. Housewives' League Protests Raid on Meeting by 3 Police Forces," 20 January [1941]; Letter to BC Housewives from LaPointe, 24 January 1941.

23 LAC, HCAT, part 1, RCMP file "Re: Mrs. M. Jeffries, 31 Rose Ave., MI 8176 Toronto, Ont.," 17 November 1941.

24 Mona Morgan, Interview with Mona Morgan, Peggy Chunn, and Audrey Modzir (Staples) by author, Vancouver, BC, 24 July 1998.

25 Prokop, interview.

26 Mona Morgan, interview by author, Vancouver, BC, 24 July 1998.

27 Dee Dee Rizzo, interview by author, Winnipeg, Manitoba, 6 December 2001; Anne Ross, interview by K. McPherson, 4 August 1988, Manitoba Archives, Winnipeg General Hospital Alumni, C934–935.

28 Lil Ilomaki and Alice Maigis, interview by author, Toronto, Ontario, 12 December 1996.

29 LAC, HCAT, part 2, RCMP memorandum, 30 July 1947.

30 Morgan, interview.

31 LAC, HCFC, part 1, "Do Reds Guide League? 'No' Says Leader's Wife," *Edmonton Journal*, 23 April 1947.

32 LAC, HCLS, clipping, "Housewives Deny Control by Reds," *Regina Leader Post*, 23 April 1947.

33 See, for example, Clément, *Canada's Rights Revolution*; Lambertson, *Repression and Resistance*.

34 LAC, HCAT, part 1, letter from H.A. Bruce to RCMP Commissioner S.T. Wood, Ottawa, Ontario, 18 June 1940.

35 LAC, HCOH, RCMP report, "Labor Progressive Party, Nova Scotia," 7 June 1947; RCMP, file note, 23 June 1947.

36 On the scope of such resistance to the Padlock Law, see Lambertson, *Repression and Resistance*, 16–67.

37 "Trustees Fail to Take Stand on Cadet Work," *Globe & Mail*, 17 March 1939, 4.

38 AM, Ross papers, P5941/9, "Proposed Program to Be Presented to the Housewives' and Consumers' Federation of Canada Convention, April 15 to 18, 1948 at Ottawa."
39 Clément, *Canada's Rights Revolution*, 40.
40 LAC, HCFC, part 1a, "Call It Anti-communism," *Toronto Saturday Night*, 28 June 1947.
41 Dawber, *After You, Agnes*, 19–20.
42 "London Women Elect Officers," *Daily Clarion*, 25 February 1939.
43 One of the many articles and books that overlook Luckock is Terry Crowley, "Agnes Macphail and Canadian Working Women," *Labour/Le Travail*, 28 (1991): 129–48.
44 Dawber, *After You, Agnes*, 9–10.
45 Donez Xiques, *Margaret Laurence: The Making of a Writer* (Toronto: Dundurn Press, 2005): 135–50; Donez Xiques, "Early Influences," in *Challenging Territory: The Writing of Margaret Laurence*, ed. Christian Riegel (Edmonton: University of Alberta Press, 1997), 187–210.
46 AM, Ross papers, P5941/6, "Annual report, MHCA, 26 May 1948."
47 Daniel Horowitz, *Betty Friedan and the Making of The Feminine Mystique* (Amherst: University of Massachusetts Press, 1998); Daniel Horowitz, "Rethinking Betty Friedan and The Feminine Mystique: Labor Union Radicalism and Feminism in Cold War America," *American Quarterly* 48, no. 1 (1996): 1–42.
48 LAC, Marjorie Mann Papers, MG32, G12, vol. 1, letter from Marjorie Mann to Morden Lazarus, Executive Secretary, CCF, Ontario Section, 23 June 1947.
49 "Milk Cost Soars, Says M.P. Backs Plea to Keep Subsidy," *Toronto Star*, 27 August 1946, 2; LAC, HCFC, part 2, clippings, "Public Protests Price Decontrol on Food Products," *Daily Tribune*, 10 June 1947; "Gladys Strum, CCF MP, Endorses HCA Delegation," *Daily Tribune*, 21 June 1947; LAC, HCFC, part 2, press release, Housewives Consumer Association, 20 February 1948.
50 "Lewis Says CCF Is Only Bulwark to Oppose Reds," *Globe and Mail*, 29 March 1948, 4.
51 Mary Prokop, interview by author, Toronto, ON, 15 December 1998.
52 Dan Azoulay, "Winning Women for Socialism: The Ontario CCF and Women, 1947–1961," *Labour/Le Travail* 36 (1995): 59–90.
53 LAC, Mann papers, vol. 2, Peg Stewart to Marjorie Mann, 6 July 1947.
54 LAC, Mann papers, vol. 1, circular letter to "Toronto Member of the Steering Committee," 11 May 1947, and "Report of Discussion Groups, Ontario Women's Conference, Woodsworth House, Ottawa, 30–31 May 1947."

55 LAC, Mann papers, vol. 2, letter from Irene Knechtel to Marjorie Mann, 10 July 1947.
56 LAC, Mann papers, vol. 1, circular letter, Ontario Provincial Women's Committee to corresponding members, 17 October 1947.
57 LAC, Mann papers, vol. 1, letter from Marjorie Mann to Mrs Peck, 30 September 1948.
58 LAC, Mann Papers, vol. 1, "CCF Women's Committee Conference, September 25 and 26, 1948," Ontario CCF Women's Committee, Chairman's Business File, correspondence, minutes, etc., 1948.
59 LAC, Mann papers, vol. 1, letter from Peg Stewart to Marjorie Mann, 21 November 1948; letter from Marion Brydon to Marjorie Mann, 24 April 1951; letter from Marjorie Mann to Marion Brydon, 3 May 1951.
60 Azoulay, "Ruthless in a Ladylike Way."
61 LAC, Mann papers, vol. 1, "CCF Women's Committee Conference, September 25 and 26, 1948," Ontario CCF Women's Committee, Chairman's Business File, correspondence, minutes, etc., 1948.
62 LAC, Mann papers, vol. 1, letter from Marjorie Mann to Mrs [Roxie] Tait, 19 October 1948.
63 "Congress Memorandum on Prices and Price-Control," *The Canadian Unionist*, January 1949, 6.
64 LAC, RG 146, ATIP request A-2007–00010, Housewives League, Montreal, Que., vol. 1, 5 April 1940–9 June 1948. On the Montreal Consumers League, see Magdalena Fahrni, *Household Politics: Montreal Families and Postwar Reconstruction* (Toronto: University of Toronto Press, 2005).
65 LAC, HCFC, part 1, clipping, "Union Will Fight Communists' 'Help,'" *Montreal Gazette*, 24 April 1947.
66 LAC, HCOH, RCMP memo re: Housewives and Consumers Organization, 5 April 1948.
67 "The Congress Meets the Government," *The Canadian Unionist*, April 1946, 77; "The Congress Memorandum," *The Canadian Unionist*, April 1947, 79; "Important Resolutions at Congress Convention," *The Canadian Unionist*, December 1948, 289.
68 "The Congress Meets the Government," *The Canadian Unionist*, April 1949, 75.
69 LAC, Mann papers, vol. 1, letter from Marjorie Mann to Marion Bryden, 3 May 1951.
70 "Consumers' Association Holds Annual Meeting," *The Canadian Unionist*, November 1949, 267–9.
71 AM, Ross papers, P5941/9, *The Housewives' News*, December 1947.
72 Rae Luckock, letter to the editor, *Toronto Daily Star*, 2 February 1948, 6.

73 AM, Ross papers, P5941/6, Untitled statement by Elizabeth Green, Member of the Executive, Manitoba Housewives Consumers Association, n.d.
74 "Housewives Doubtful Cost-of-Living Figures Prove Accurate Mirror," *Globe and Mail*, 13 March 1948, 3.
75 University of Manitoba Archives, Canadian Association of Consumers, MSS 23, Box 1, Folder 1100–30, Untitled report, [1951].

Index

Bold page numbers indicate photos or illustrations.

Abbott, Douglas: and Austerity Plan, 146–7; AUUC writes to, 96; Housewives' view of meeting with, 143; meets Housewives, 122, 138, 177; plan for foreign trade crisis, 145–6; on price control, 121; refuses to see Housewives in 1948, 164, 178, 181–2
Albon, Ena, 29, 42, 45
anarchist women, 138–9
Anderson, Helen, 165
anticommunism: attacks in media of Housewives, 132; attacks in media of teenagers in boycott, 128; attacks in media of western delegation of Housewives, 122–4; bills on voted down in Parliament, 185; of B. Lamb, 35, 41, 42–3, 44, 45, 192; Canadian government's move toward, 41, 73–5, 163–4, 166–7, 177–8, 201; of CCF, 118, 166, 209, 211–12; comparison of US *vs* Canadian, 203–4; effect on Housewives, 164–5, 188–9, 196–7; failure of pre-Second World War, 49; Housewives' resilience towards, 118, 119; legacy of its effect during Cold War, 200; media debate over, 182–4; of MPs, 200–2; of National Housewives, 45–7; of organized labour, 130, 149–50, 213–4; red-baiting by Board of Trade, 129–30; red-baiting Housewives, 78, 116, 117, 165–6, 168–9; in US during war, 79
Arland, Ann, 83, 84, 188–9
Association for Jewish Colonization in the Soviet Union (ICOR), 28
Association of United Ukrainian Canadians (AUUC), 151–2, 187, 188
Atkinson, Joseph E., 184
Aveline, Mary, 64–5

baby parades, 118, 125, 128, 131
Backman, Jules, 72
bakeries, 85, 86
Balfour, David, 45, 46
B.C. Consumer (newspaper), 55, 77–8
BC Housewives Consumers Association, 128–9, 196

BC Housewives League: and butter prices, 60–1; campaign against profiteering, 35; early work of, 33–4; establishes Consumers' Research Council, 56, 59; fight against DOCR, 77; open to male members, 176; during Second World War, 55; variety of causes worked for, 66
beef strike, 82, 92, **93**
Bell, Marjorie, 56
Beveridge, Edith (Mrs A.J.), 121, 133, 140, 188, 207
Bilecki, Andrew, 34
Binley, Mrs A. (Toronto Housewives), **170**
Birchard, May, 83, 107, 110, 141, 143, 207
black market, 59, 60, 82, 84, 85
Blumberg, Jack, 34
Board of Control (Toronto), 17, 19, 30, 61, 88
Bogart, Ernest, 63
Bolton, Mrs K. (Winnipeg Housewives), 90
Braidwood, Thomas, 129–30
Britain, 172
Bronstein, Rose, 28
Brown, Elizabeth: as Housewives president, 30; and milk price war, 63, 64–5; and Ontario Legislature protest, 28; on profiteering, 56; speaks on war shortages, 50; view of butter rationing, 52; view of communist infiltration, 43
Bruce, Herbert, 73, 75, 109, 201
Brudy, Mrs Norman, 123, 206
Brudy, Norman, 206
Bryce, Robert B., 71
Bryce, William, 108

Buck, Alice, 36, 66
Buck, Tim, 33, 41, 194
Buckley, Dorothy, 22
Buckley, John W., 22
Buhay, Becky, 32, 194
Buller, Annie, 32, 194
business profits, 120, 133, 145, 155, 177, 178–9
butter boycott, 124, 129
butter price, 88
butter rationing, 52, 62
butter shortage, 60–2
buyers' strikes, 124–31, 133, 135–6

CAC. *See* Canadian Association of Consumers
Cadwell, J.R., 43
Cameron, Don, 168
Canada, Government of: actions taken against communism during war, 73–4; appeals to for price control, 35, 87–8; backs private investment over consumers, 84–5, 178–9; comparison of its anticommunism with that of US, 203–4; dealing carefully with Housewives post-Second World War, 9, 82–3; and Defence of Canada Regulations, 73–4; end of wartime price controls and subsidies, 6, 81–3, 99, 120, 121; Housewives' brief on economy to, 176–7; and Housewives second delegation, 141, 143; ignores Housewives delegations, 122–3; manipulation of cost of living index, 65; move towards policy of anticommunism, 41, 73–5, 163–4, 166–7, 177–8, 201; and N. Rodd, 38; opposition to postwar

reconversion plan of, 91, 96–7, 143–5; and parliamentary committee to study prices, 181; policies of 1950s, 216; and politicization of food during war, 6–7; refusal to see Housewives 1948 delegation, 177–8, 179–**80**; response to foreign trade crisis, 145–6; takes control of economy in Second World War, 5–6, 50–1, 53–4; xenophobia of, 154. *See also* Abbott, Douglas; King, McKenzie; Wartime Prices and Trade Board (WPTB)

Canadian Aid to Russia campaign, 69–70

Canadian Association of Consumers (CAC): approach of, 215; and CCF, 212; CCL support for, 102–3, 213–14; distances itself from Housewives, 197; as non-foreign alternative to Housewives, 154–5, 174–5

Canadian Congress of Labour (CCL), 102–3, 118, 137, 144, 149, 213–14

Canadian Council of Churches, 145, 185

Canadian Council on Nutrition, 99

Canadian Labor Defence League (CLDL), 77

Canadian Youth Congress, 45

Catholic Women's League, 197

CCF. *See* Co-operative Commonwealth Federation (CCF)

Chappel, Christine, 65

chocolate bar boycott, 125, 128, **129**, 130, 131

Chunn, Peggy: as colleague of M. Prokop, 77; Housewives support for, 153; labelled as communist by media, 123; M. Laurence article on, 210; and price control campaign, 105, 107; runs for office, 192; view of ethnic left, 152

Chytyk, Pat, 151, 154

citizen-consumers, 6–7, 67–8, 114–15, 119

Citizens Committee on Milk, 96, 107–8

Clare, Ethel, 88

Clark, H.J., 65

Clarke, Nelson, 131

Cold War: adds legitimacy to discrimination, 187–8; and demonization of organizations on left, 166, 186; legacy of anticommunist movement, 200; and media debate over Housewives, 182–4; overwhelms other issues, 181; seen as necessary to demonize communists, 48–9; transition to from postwar period, 155, 163–4, 165. *See also* anticommunism

Coldwell, M.J., 122, 141, 144, 145, 181, 209

Colgate, Lillian, 82

communism: cause of 1938 rift within Housewives, 41–4; and supposed infiltration of schools, 46–7. *See also* anticommunism; Communist Party of Canada (CPC); Labor-Progressive Party (LPP)

communist left: growing popularity of, 46; organizing ability of its adherents, 41; as part of Housewives second delegation, 140–1; and protest of high prices, 39–40; and red-baiting, 45; role in organized labour, 34, 149–50

Communist Party of Canada (CPC): banning of its press, 34–5; campaigns against high prices, 28, 39; ethnic left's tie to, 150–4; history, 5; marginalization of ethnic groups, 152; as part of background of many Housewives, 7, 32; pledges full support for war, 76; repressive state response to, 41; and research on nationalization of food, 39; ruled illegal, 73; support for Housewives during war, 55; tie to many early Housewives, 35–6, 38–9; tie to Montreal Housewives, 32, 33. *See also* Labor-Progressive Party (LPP)
Conant, Gordon, 43, 46
Conboy, Frederick, 61, 62
Congress of Canadian Women, 197
Conroy, Esther, 213–14
consumer movements of late 1930s, 17–22
Consumers' Federated Council, 110
Consumers' Gas Company, 29–31
Consumers' Research Council, 33
Cooke, Alice, 31, 36, 193
Co-operative Commonwealth Federation (CCF): abandons Housewives, 211–12; as allies of Housewives, 9, 107–8, 122, 141, 147–8, 181, 210–11; anticommunism of, 118, 166, 209, 211–12; differing attitude towards first women elected to Ontario legislature, 68–9; early history of, 4–5; and milk subsidy vote in Parliament, 109; opposition to government reconversion program, 144; and price controls, 39, 40, 108, 147; role of in press red-baiting, 169; and R. Luckock, 209, 212
cost of living index, 62, 64, 65, 146, 176
Cotterell, Murray, 149–50
Craig, Kenneth, 97
Croll, David, 83
Cross, Eric, 31
Croy, Marge, 105, 186

dairy cooperatives, 25
dairy farmers: and cooperatives, 25; effect of Milk Control Act on, 25; and milk price war, 63, 64, 65, 96; reaction to milk boycott, 22–3; threaten milk shortages over price control, 85
dairy industry: blamed for milk price increase, 63; call for government regulation, 25; claims of profiteering against, 61; instability in, 24–5; left's desire for nationalization of, 39; and municipalization, 39; offer of free butter to protesters, 19, 21; penalizes drivers, 22; response to milk boycott, 21–2; and Royal Commission on milk, 113; squeezing out of small dairies, 25
Defence of Canada Regulations (DOCR), 73–4, 77–8
Dennison, William, 39, 63, 107–8
Diefenbaker, John, 201–2
Douglas, T.C. "Tommy," 131
Drew, George, 110, 113, 185

East York Housewives Association, 18, 36, 47
Eaton, Flora McCrea, 68
Edmonton Housewives League, 99, 101, 125, 169, 206

Elliott, Lorna, 88
Emard, Ann, 87
Emergency Committee of Canadian Women, 68
Endicott, Shirley, 136
ethnic left: and Canadian welfare state, 8; importance of to Housewives, 150–4, 195–6; and price control fight, 105; RCMP interest in, 187–8; support for Housewives, 55–6, 92, 94, 96; tie to communism, 5, 206–7
evictions, fighting, 34

farmers, 44
Farrow, Evelyn (Mrs C.A.), 131
fascism, 73, 74
feminism, 14–15, 40, 70
Ferguson, Dewar, 107, 110, 132
Ferguson, Margery, 132, **170**
Flowerdale, Florence, 138
food boycotts, 124, 133, 135–6
food security movement, 11
food shortages: postwar, 82, 84, 85; during war, 50, 51–2, 54, 60–2, 252n80; WPTB's answer for, 56, 59–60
Forsey, Eugene, 102
Franklin, Ursula, 140
Friebert, Anthony, 88
Friedan, Betty, 210

Gardiner, James, 83, 97, 108–9, 121
Garrison, Mrs M. (Toronto Housewives), 26
gas meter campaign, 29–31
Gauld, Bella Hall, 32
Geddes, Mrs J. (Edmonton Housewives), 169
Gehl, Josephine, 123

Gordon, Donald: and concern with Housewives, 9; on importance of public belief in economic controls, 67; on postwar shortages, 60, 84; response to calls for reinstatement of controls, 81, 89; takes over as WPTB head, 64; view of price controls, 71–2, 91, 99
Gould, Margaret, 30
Great Britain, 172
Great Depression, 5, 6, 24, 46
Green, Elizabeth, 214–15
Guest, Edmund T., 28

Hahn, Edna, 132, **170**
Halifax Housewives League, 194–5
Hannam, Herbert H., 25, 56
Hanway, Mable, 131
Harrison, Edith, 26
Hart, Mrs S. (Toronto Housewives), **170**
Havelock, Ellen (Mrs E.A.), 19, 38–9
Havelock, Eric, 38
Henderson, Rose, 40, 68, 137
Hepburn, Mitchell, 28, 63
Hill, Cecilia L., 87–8
Hill, Mrs Claude, 42
hoarding, 56, 59–60, 61
Honderich, Beland, 131, 146
Houde, Camillien, 74
Hougham, George H., 56
Housewives and Consumers Federation of Canada (HCFC), 143, 174–6
Housewives Associations, 24
Housewives Consumers Association (HCA): abandoned by CCF, 211–12; abandoned by human rights community, 208; abandoned by organized labour,

212–14; accusations of communist domination of, 119, 153, 191–6; accusations that they were controlled by Moscow, 189–90, 191; achievements of, 3, 7, 15–16, 131; as activist consumers, 6–7, 67–8, 114, argument for milk subsidy, 99–100; array of historical sources for, 10, 11–12; belief in state management of economy, 5; call for food boycotts, 133, 135–6; campaigns against rising prices, 84, 88–97, 196; campaigns for continuation of price controls, 59, 81, 86, 133, 150, 176–7, 197; CCF support for, 9, 107–8, 122, 141, 147–8, 181, 210–11; cements reputation as voice of consumers, 52, 65, 68, 98; character of women in, 117–18; as colleagues of Second World War interned, 75–7; as communist front, 168–9; 119; communist links of its leaders, 35–6, 38–9; compromised by association with Labor-Progressive Party, 167–8; decline of, 185–6, 189, 214–16; defined as subversive, 73–4, 199; delegations to Ottawa in 1947–8, 115, 116, 117–18, 121–4, 136–8, 140–3, 164, 177–8, 179–80; effect of anticommunism on, 164–5, 188–9, 196–7; establishes HCFC, 174–6; evolution into mainstream organization, 78–80; as feminists, 14–15; fight against DOCR, 77–8; formation and mandate of, 31–2; growth of post-Second World War, 92–3, 115, 117, 120, 131, 132–3; importance of ethnic left to, 55–6, 92, 94, 96, 150–4; lack of faith in government postwar plans, 71, 98, 120–1, 144, 146–7; legacy of, 8; local allies of, 107–8; and March of a Million Names, 155, 168, 169–74, 177–8, 179–**80**; maternalism of, 15, 35, 118, 136–8, 189, 195, 215–16; membership in, 31, 32, 54; members judged as communist through husband, 37, 123, 132, 169, 206; members whom history has forgotten, 68–9, 208–10; members who ran for political office, 66; overlooked history of, 7, 37; performance activism of, 119, 128, 129; police obstruction of, 130–1, 135; political program of, 116–17, 119, 133; political tolerance of, 188; as a Popular Front organization, 7–8; popularity of, 119, 132–3, 144; press coverage of, 10–11, 42, 182–4; press coverage of delegations to Ottawa, 117, 121, 122, 137–8, 141, **142**; press red-baiting of, 78, 116, 117, 122–4, 132, 165–6, 182–4, 197, 203; RCMP surveillance of, 10, 45, 75, 197, 202–6; redefining notions of gender by, 67; and R. Luckock's election to Ontario legislature, 68–9; and Royal Commission on milk, 110–13; status of on brink of Second World War, 48, 54–5; support for chocolate bar boycott, 128; support for human rights and social justice, 196, 207–8; support from organized labour, 100–7, 148–9, 186–7; use of labour research, **106**, 107; as volunteer price checkers during war, 66–7; women who "forgot" connection

to, 210; women's auxiliaries as allies of, 105, 107; work during Second World War, 53, 54, 66–7, 70–1. *See also* BC Housewives League; Toronto Housewives Association
Housewives' National Association, 44
Housewives' News (newspaper), 54
Housewives' Report, 31
Houston, Mrs (*Globe* letter writer), 97
Howe, C.D., 109, 178–9
Humphreys, Ethel (Mrs Ewart), 22, 36
Humphreys, Ewart, 36
Hunt, Donna, 153
Hyndman, Margaret, 68

Ilomaki, Lil, 151
Ilsley, J.L., 81, 82, 87, 166, 185
Independent Milk Distributors Association, 23
inflation: organized labour's campaign on, 149–50, 213; and parliamentary committee solution to, 181; as part of Housewives message to government, 176–7; postwar, 82, 84, 88, 99, 117, 120, 121, 122, 143–5, 163; as real target of price control policy, 71–2, 73; as response to government's austerity plan, 145–6; during Second World War, 53–4, 60
Innes, John, 63
International Woodworkers of America (IWA), 103, 105, 186
internment during Second World War, 74, 75–7
Irwin, R.J., 24

Jackman, Harry, 83
Jacobs, Meg, 68

Jamieson, Mrs. Stuart, 33
Jeffries, Mrs M. (Toronto Housewives), 204
Jennison, Mary, 165
Johnson, Isobel, 30
Jones, Effie, 33–4, 36–7, 66, 165, 192

Kardash, Mary, 107, 124, 154
Kelly, H. Ivers, 47
Kellythorne, J. (Toronto Labour Council), 22
Kemppfer, Mrs B. (Toronto Housewives), 42
Kennedy, Mrs W.P.M. (WPTB Advisor), 61
Kenny, Robert, 12
King, McKenzie: change in attitude toward anticommunism, 164, 166; Communist Party registers complaint against, 28; and foreign trade crisis, 145; and milk subsidy, 109; and removal of price controls, 91; resignation, 216; response to labour on price controls, 213; and wage control, 103. *See also* Canada, Government of
Kizema, Sinefta (Cynest, Cynefta), 141, 153, 187
Knowles, Stanley, 108, 141

Labor-Progressive Party (LPP): achievements of, 5; and beginning of Winnipeg Housewives, 89; extent of tie to Housewives, 123–4, 191–6; gender split in, 193–4; government efforts to make illegal, 185; members who ran for political office, 192–3; RCMP inability to prove it controlled Housewives, 202–3;

and Royal Commission, 110–13; tie to Moscow, 167–8. *See also* Communist Party of Canada (CPC)
LaCroix, Wilfred, 185
Lakeshore Housewives Association, 26
Lamb, Bertha: announces dissolving of Housewives, 42, 43; announces new organization, 44; anticommunism of, 35, 41, 42–3, 44, 45, 192; defection of from Housewives, 164; last public notice of, 48; and milk politics, 17, 18, **20**, 22, 26; receives threat, 18–19, 22
Lamoureux, R.J., 213
Lanphier, Charles, 45, 46
Lapedes, Becky, 110, 151, 154
Lapedes, Sam, 110
Lapointe, Ernest, 34, 73, 74, 76, 201, 204
Latham, Ann, 122–3, 188
Latva, Mary, 141
Laurence, Margaret, 209–10
League for Social Reconstruction (LSR), 38
League of Women Shoppers, 98
Ledoux, Sylvia, 33
Leigh, Ethel, 147
Leopold, John, 191
Levis, Beatrice, 123
Lewis, David, 209, 210, 211
Liberal Party (federal), 147, 148. *See also* Canada, Government of
Lightfoot, E.A., 87
Low, Solon, 108
Luckock, Rae: announces founding of HCFC, 174; background, 208–9; celebrity of, 68; and Congress of Canadian Women, 197; on delegations to Ottawa, 135, 136, 178, 179; election to provincial legislature, 68–9; on extent of communist influence in Housewives, 43; forgotten by history, 68–9, 209; forsaken by CCF, 209, 212; as founding member of Housewives, 36, 40; pictures, **170**, **173**; and price controls, 145, 181, 214; RCMP surveillance of, 203; red-baiting of, 165, 182–3

Macaulay, Leopold, 48
MacDougall, Duncan, 131
MacKinnon, James, 61
Macphail, Agnes, 68–9
Magnuson, Bruce, 75, 164
Magnuson, Kate, 75–6, 100, 164
Maigis, Alice, 151, 205–6
Malloy, Mrs Malcolm, 42
Mann, Marjorie, 11–12, 69, 209, 211, 212
Maple Spring student protests, 139
March of a Million Names: demonstration at Parliament, 169–74, 177–8, 179–**80**; media coverage, **161**; posters for, **156**, **160**; preparation for, 155, 168
Marquette, Paul Emile, 213
Marshall, John, 96, 124, 209–10
Marshall, Mrs R.J., 155
Martin, Mrs A.E., 153
Mason, Jean, 66, 192
maternalism: of E. Brown, 51; of ethnic left, 150–1; Housewives' use of, 15, 35, 118, 136–8, 189, 195; how women's protest has been judged by, 138–40; as source of Housewives danger to

anticommunists, 168, 169; survey of its use as political strategy, 12–14; of Toronto Housewives Association, 18, 19; used by enemies of Housewives against, 215–16; and volunteer war work, 70–1; and VOW, 128
McBride, Margaret, 205–6
McCallum, Hiram, 63
McCullagh, Mrs H.E., 45
McKean, Fergus, 75, 77
McKean, Nellie, 75, 77
McKinnon, Hector, 63–4
Meade, Ethel, 195
meat boycotts, 98, 125, **126–7**, 196
meat shortage, 59, 85, 252n80
meat strike, 33
media. *See* press
milk boycott, 18–19, 21–3, 34, 44, 48
Milk Control Act, 25, 31
Milk Control Board: control of milk pricing, 17, 21, 23, 25; creation of, 23; fight over price of during war, 62–5; press view of, 24; protest movement demands on, 19; and Royal Commission, 110, 113
milk delivery drivers, 22
Milk Distributors Association, 22
Milk for Millions (booklet), 39
milk price: effect on consumption, 99, 101; and E. Morton's file for injunction on, 109–10; and end of subsidy, 85–6; fight over during Second World War, 62–5; as prominent campaign policy, 192; protest against rise in, 19, 21, 22, 24, 25, 63, 64–5, 83, 89, **95**, 96, 104, **159**; and real value of wages, 101; and Royal Commission, 110–13
Milk Producers Association, 21, 96

Miller, Minerva, 104
Mitchell, Humphrey, 143
Molinski, Mrs E. (Mothers' Club), 97
Montreal Housewives, 32, 33, 59, 130, 135
Montreal Labor College, 32
Morgan, Mona: on ethnic left, 151; and Housewives' ties to labour, 186; invites women to join consumers league, 125; as IWA auxiliary president, 100, 105; judged through her husband, 123, 206; response to RCMP surveillance, 204, 205
Morgan, Nigel, 206
Morrison, Neil, 51
Morton, Elizabeth: files for an injunction against milk producers, 109–10; at Housewives founding meeting, 36; as LPP Director of Women's Work, 193; as political candidate, 66, 192; and rise in price of milk, 83; and Royal Commission, 110
Mount Carmel Clinic, 94, 96
Munday, W. (RCMP superintendent), 43–4
municipalization, 24
Murray, Hilda, 43, 165
Murray, Philip, 89
Mutchmore, J.F., 89, 143, 185

National Council of Women, 37, 102
National Council on Democratic Rights (NCDR), 76, 77
National Farm Radio Forum, 50
National Federation of Labor Youth (NFLY), 125
National Housewives Association, 45, 46–7

National Unity Party, 73
network of consumer groups, 124
Newey, Mrs (Montreal Housewives), 32, 33
Nielsen, Dorise, 13, 194, 196
Noble, Helen, 125
Noble, John, 22
Norton, Mable, 77–8, 165
Nursey, William, 47

O'Hare, Kate Richards, 139–40
Ontario, Government of, 25, 28, 40, 43, 110–13
Ontario CCF Women's Committee, 211–12
Ontario Legislature, 25, 26–8, 31
Ontario Milk Control Act, 25
Ontario Milk Producers Association, 65
operation PROFUNC, 202
organized labour: abandons Housewives, 212–14; anticommunism of, 130, 149–50, 213–14; and cost of living index, 65; fight against inflation, 149–50, 213; and fight for price controls, 88–9, 100–7, 149–50, 212–13; growth of, 101–2; opposition to government reconversion program, 144–5; research of, **106**, 107; role in milk price war, 22, 64; and support for consumer movement in US, 98; support for Housewives, 100–7, 148–9, 186–7. *See also* Canadian Congress of Labour (CCL)
Ottawa Consumers Association, 146–7

Padlock law, 165, 207
Parliament of Canada: anticommunist bills voted down in, 185; anticommunist petitions in, 201–2; CCF defends Housewives in, 181; Housewives refused entrance to, 177–8, 179–**80**, 181–2; petitioned by Housewives, 33; and price controls, 108–9
Partridge, Gertrude, 66, 192
Paska, Mrs., 141
paternalism, 19, 30
Pawley, Russell, 28
peace movement, 196
Pearson, Lester, 38
Penner, Jacob, 124
Penner, Norman, 125
Penner, Roland, 209
People's Cooperative Dairy, 89–90, 96
performance activism, 10–11, 26–7, 128
Pett, L.B., 146
Phelps, Lily: announces food boycotts, 124; causes supported by, 69–70; celebrity of, 68; defends use of boycotts, 136; and government postwar plans, 121; invited to join CAC, 174; as leader of second delegation, 136, 137, 143; RCMP surveillance of, 203
Plumptre, Adelaide, 45
Poland, Fred, 38
Poland, Phyllis, **27**, 28, 31, 38, 48
press: and anticommunist attacks on Housewives, 78, 116, 117, 122–4, 132, 165–6, 182–4, 197, 203; and anticommunist attacks on teenagers in boycott, 128; banning of communist, 34–5; and chocolate bar boycott, 125; coverage of anticommunist rift within Housewives, 42; coverage of beef strike, 92; coverage of gas meter campaign, 29, 30, 31;

coverage of Housewives delegations in Ottawa, 117, 121, 122, 137–8, 141, **142**; coverage of Housewives during wartime, 54, 79–80; coverage of milk politics, 18, 24, 97; coverage of Toronto Housewives meetings, 45; paternalism of, 30; positive coverage of Housewives by, 10–11, 67, 131; reaction to communist school scare, 47; red-baits Housewives as communist front, 168–9; and Second World War butter shortage, 62; support for Aid to Russia, 70

price controls: CCF fight for, 39, 40, 108, 147; compared to wage controls, 67; ethnic left's support for restoration of, 92, 94, 151; government termination of after war, 6, 81–3, 99, 120, 121; Housewives campaign for, 59, 81, 86, 133, 150, 176–7, 197; LPP support for, 192; and March of a Million Names, 169–72; M. King's view of, 91, 213; organized labour's campaign for, 88–9, 100–7, 149–50, 212–13; popularity of, 72–3, 86–8, 116; pro-business push to end, 155; removal of in US, 88–9, 91–2; R. Luckock and, 145, 181, 214; societal debate on, 114–15; support for in Parliament, 108–9; unions see as women's fight, 104; wartime policy sold to public under false pretenses, 71–2; and women's auxiliaries, 105, 107; WPTB announces end of, 81; WPTB view of, 71–2, 91, 99. *See also* subsidies

price-fixing, 176, 196
private investment, 84–5, 120
profiteering: and butter shortage, 60–2; Housewives denounce, 196; postwar evidence of, 176; report on, 32; during Second World War, 35, 52, 54, 56, 59
Prokop, Mary: background, 77; describes work of price control campaigns, 151–2; on importance of ethnic left to Housewives, 55–6; and internment of husband, 75, 76–7; reaction to members leaving Housewives, 199; responds to Housewives being branded communist, 191, 196; response to RCMP surveillance, 204–5
Prokop, Peter, 75–7, 153

Queen, John, 34, 39
Quinn, John, 63

racism, 152–4, 187–8, 207
RCMP. *See* Royal Canadian Mounted Police
Red Squads, 46–7, 130, 146
Regina city council, 59
Regina Housewives League, 124–5, 130–1
Reid, Minerva, 68
Relief Project Workers Union, 34
Reynolds, J.B., 21
Rivett-Carnac, Mr (RCMP Inspector), 74
Rizzo, Dee Dee, 205
Rodd, Nora, 37–8
Ross, Anne: background, 94; connection to M. Laurence, 210; on difficulty recruiting LPP women to Housewives, 193, 194;

and end of milk subsidy, 90–1, 97; Housewives support for, 153; on Housewives victories, 131; invited to join CAC, 174; labelled as communist by media, 123; and March of Million Names, 179, 181; and Mount Carmel Clinic, 94, 96; name change, 153; personal papers of, 11; and RCMP surveillance, 205; reaction to government postwar programs, 121
Ross, Bill C., 94, 153, 210
Ross, Mrs H. (BC Housewives president), 165
Royal Canadian Mounted Police (RCMP): and BC Housewives, 129; blocks Housewives from Parliament, 179, **180**; communist persecution of during Cold War, 167, 187–8, 190–1; and F. Sim, 198–9; and Housewives delegations, 123; and Montreal Housewives, 130; operation PROFUNC, 202; passing secret information to MPs, 200–2; report on profiteering symposium, 32; reports on Housewives during war, 55, 78; role in anticommunist bill before Parliament, 185; role in Defence of Canada Regulations, 74; surveillance of ethnic left, 187; surveillance of Housewives, 10, 45, 75, 197, 202–6; suspicions of ethnic protesters, 152; view of rift within Housewives, 43–4
Royal Commission on Milk (1947), 110–13
Royal Commission on Prices (1948), 213
Rush, Maurice, 37

Russell, Ross, 104
Ryerson, Stanley, 104

Sago, Mitch, 124, 209
Salsberg, Joe, 29, 46
Sanders, Byrne Hope, 84
Sandwell, B.K., 184, 208
Saskatchewan, Government of, 96
Saskatchewan Housewives, 125
Saskatoon Housewives Consumers Association, 91, 120, 189
Saunders, R.H.: as ally of Housewives, 107; and end of milk subsidy, 85, 89; on milk committee, 63; praises Housewives, 19; on rise of price of milk, 62, 83
Scott, F.R., 209
Second World War: Canada's declaration of war in, 34; fear over social breakdown during, 71; fight over price of milk, 62–5; and food shortages, 50, 51–2, 54, 60–2, 252n80; and hoarding, 59–60; Housewives activity during, 44, 56, 59–60; and management of economy, 5–6; and politicization of food, 6–7, 53; and poverty, 52; and protest, 53; and support for Russia during, 69–70; and system of price control and subsidies, 50–1, 71–3; volunteer work for, 70–1
Shakespeare, K. (RCMP Inspector), 202
Sim, David, 59
Sim, Frances, 198–9
Simpson, James "Jimmy," 39
Single Unemployed Men's Association, 45
Smith, A.F., 88
Smith, Stuart: on communist school scare, 47; elected, 46;

joins Housewives protest, 35; and milk politics, 83, 85; red-baited in press, 165; and Royal Commission, 110

Smith Act (US), 185

Social Credit Party, 108

social welfare, 78–80

Spaulding, Margaret, 45

Staples (Modzir), Audrey, 123, 154

Stewart, Peg, 212

St. Laurent, Louis, 216

subsidies: Canadian government use to protect industry, 147; CCF support for, 108; government terminates after war, 6, 81–3, 99, 109, 120, 121; Housewives argue for, 99–100; imposed on milk during war, 64–5; and issue of postwar stabilization, 97–8; Parliament vote on, 109; protests against ending milk, 85–6, 89, 90–1, 97; and Saskatchewan government, 96. *See also* price controls

Swanky, Ann, 123, 206

Taggart, J.G., 61–2

Tait, Roxie, 212

Tallman, Eileen (Sufrin), 141, 210

Taylor, K.W., 71

Telford, Lyle, 33, 39, 59

Theodore, Forence, 96, 123, 182, 192, 193, 201

Tisdale, F.F., 67

Toronto, City of, 46–7, 85–6

Toronto city council, 28, 40, 45, 62–3, 83, 107

Toronto District Labour Council, 24, 29, 104, 150, 197

Toronto Housewives Association: bread price war, 44; butter boycott, 26–8, 31; campaigns against high price of meat, 196; collecting signatures showing support for delegation, 135; committee to study food prices, 26; communist rift within 1938, 41–4; founding meeting of, 18; gas meter campaign, 29–31, 44; growing legitimacy of, 31, 45, 174; membership, 45; and milk politics, 19, 21, 22, 24, 25, 63, 64–5, 83, 89; petitions Consumers' Gas Company, 29–31; proposes changes to cost of living index, 65; reacts to end of price controls, 82; red-baiting of, 45, 75; in Second World War, 44, 50, 52, 56; social causes of, 45, 197; and support for Aid to Russia, 69–70; variety of causes worked for, 65–6

Toronto Welfare Council, 146

Treadway, George, 45, 47

Tuomi, Bill, 209

Tzakarakas, Katie, 207

Ukrainian Labour Farmer Temple Association (ULFTA), 34, 76, 77

unions. *See* organized labour

United Church, 89, 143

United Electrical, Radio and Machine Workers of America (UE), 103–4, 144–5, 186

United Farmers Party, 144

United Jewish People's Order (UJPO), 34, 152, 187

United States: anticommunism in during war, 79; and Cold War anticommunism, 185, 200; comparison of its anticommunism with Canada's, 203–4; comparison of its consumer movement with Canada's, 8–9; consumer activism in, 26, 28, 97–8; and HUAC, 165, 190, 203; inflation in post-Second World War, 88, 143; and Office of Price Administration, 68, 72; removal of price controls in, 88–9, 91–2; role in Canada's foreign trade crisis, 145

United Ukrainian Canadians. *See* Association of United Ukrainian Canadians (AUUC)

Usprich, Anne, **27**

Usprich, Cecile, **27**

Vickery, Dorothy, 47

Voice of Women (VOW), 128, 140, 190

wage controls: compared to price controls, 67; drop in post-Second World War, 86–7; unions fight against, 101, 103, 149; unions see as man's fight, 104

Walls, Dorothy, 189

Wartime Prices and Trade Board (WPTB): announces end of price controls, 81; denial of butter shortage by, 61–2; early failure to control prices, 53–4; encouraged to appoint a woman to, 35, 56; focus of Housewives protest, 35; mandate of, 51; price control policy of, 71–3; role in price of milk, 63–4; starts coupon rationing, 60; view of wartime shortages, 56, 59–60; volunteer price-checker system of, 66–7. *See also* Gordon, Donald

Watson, George, 28

Watson, Louise, 110, 132, 140, **170**, 193

WEA Labour News, 55, **57–8**

Weir, Helen, 75, 132, 153

Weir, John, 75, 132, 153–4

Wells, Dalton C., 113

Wheaton, Helen, 189

White, Christine, 61

Williams, Ronald, 169, 197

Wilson, Elizabeth, 66, 192

Wingham, Mrs Anderson, 45

Winnipeg Homemakers' Club, 34, 35, 56

Winnipeg Housewives Consumers Association, 89, 90, 96, 125

women's auxiliaries, 105, 107

Women's International Democratic Federation (WIDF), 37

Women's International League for Peace and Freedom (WILPF), 78, 189–90

Women's Progressive Associations, 40, 44

Women Strike for Peace, 190

Wood, S.T., 74, 200, 201

Woodsworth, Lucy, 108

Workers' Cooperative (Timmins), 59

Workers' Cooperative of New Ontario, 100

WPTB. *See* Wartime Prices and Trade Board

Wren, Drummond, 45

Wright, Reg, 132

xenophobia, 152–4, 187–8, 207

York Township Housewives Association, 26

Zailing, Abe, 124

Zuken, Joseph, 107, 124

STUDIES IN GENDER AND HISTORY

General Editors: Franca Iacovetta and Karen Dubinsky

1 Suzanne Morton, *Ideal Surroundings: Domestic Life in a Working-Class Suburb in the 1920s*
2 Joan Sangster, *Earning Respect: The Lives of Working Women in Small-Town Ontario, 1920–1960*
3 Carolyn Strange, *Toronto's Girl Problem: The Perils and Pleasures of the City, 1880–1930*
4 Sara Z. Burke, *Seeking the Highest Good: Social Service and Gender at the University of Toronto, 1888–1937*
5 Lynne Marks, *Revivals and Roller Rinks: Religion, Leisure, and Identity in Late-Nineteenth-Century Small-Town Ontario*
6 Cecilia Morgan, *Public Men and Virtuous Women: The Gendered Languages of Religion and Politics in Upper Canada, 1791–1850*
7 Mary Louise Adams, *The Trouble with Normal: Postwar Youth and the Making of Heterosexuality*
8 Linda Kealey, *Enlisting Women for the Cause: Women, Labour, and the Left in Canada, 1890–1920*
9 Christina Burr, *Spreading the Light: Work and Labour Reform in Late-Nineteenth-Century Toronto*
10 Mona Gleason, *Normalizing the Ideal: Psychology, Schooling, and the Family in Postwar Canada*
11 Deborah Gorham, *Vera Brittain: A Feminist Life*
12 Marlene Epp, *Women without Men: Mennonite Refugees of the Second World War*
13 Shirley Tillotson, *The Public at Play: Gender and the Politics of Recreation in Postwar Ontario*
14 Veronica Strong-Boag and Carole Gerson, *Paddling Her Own Canoe: The Times and Texts of E. Pauline Johnson (Tekahionwake)*
15 Stephen Heathorn, *For Home, Country, and Race: Constructing Gender, Class, and Englishness in the Elementary School, 1880–1914*
16 Valerie J. Korinek, *Roughing It in the Suburbs: Reading* Chatelaine *Magazine in the Fifties and Sixties*
17 Adele Perry, *On the Edge of Empire: Gender, Race, and the Making of British Columbia, 1849–1871*
18 Robert A. Campbell, *Sit Down and Drink Your Beer: Regulating Vancouver's Beer Parlours, 1925–1954*
19 Wendy Mitchinson, *Giving Birth in Canada, 1900–1950*

20 Roberta Hamilton, *Setting the Agenda: Jean Royce and the Shaping of Queen's University*
21 Donna Gabaccia and Franca Iacovetta, eds, *Women, Gender, and Transnational Lives: Italian Workers of the World*
22 Linda Reeder, *Widows in White: Migration and the Transformation of Rural Women, Sicily, 1880–1928*
23 Terry Crowley, *Marriage of Minds: Isabel and Oscar Skelton Reinventing Canada*
24 Marlene Epp, Franca Iacovetta, and Frances Swyripa, eds, *Sisters or Strangers? Immigrant, Ethnic, and Racialized Women in Canadian History*
25 John G. Reid, *Viola Florence Barnes, 1885–1979: A Historian's Biography*
26 Catherine Carstairs, *Jailed for Possession: Illegal Drug Use, Regulation, and Power in Canada, 1920–1961*
27 Magda Fahrni, *Household Politics: Montreal Families and Postwar Reconstruction*
28 Tamara Myers, *Caught: Montreal's Modern Girls and the Law, 1869–1945*
29 Jennifer A. Stephen, *Pick One Intelligent Girl: Employability, Domesticity, and the Gendering of Canada's Welfare State, 1939–1947*
30 Lisa Chilton, *Agents of Empire: British Female Migration to Canada and Australia, 1860–1930*
31 Esyllt W. Jones, *Influenza 1918: Disease, Death, and Struggle in Winnipeg*
32 Elise Chenier, *Strangers in Our Midst: Sexual Deviancy in Postwar Ontario*
33 Lara Campbell, *Respectable Citizens: Gender, Family, and Unemployment in Ontario's Great Depression*
34 Katrina Srigley, *Breadwinning Daughters: Young Working Women in a Depression-Era City, 1929–1939*
35 Maureen Moynagh with Nancy Forestell, eds, *Documenting First Wave Feminisms, Volume 1: Transnational Collaborations and Crosscurrents*
36 Mona Oikawa, *Cartographies of Violence: Japanese Canadian Women, Memory, and the Subjects of the Internment*
37 Karen Flynn, *Moving beyond Borders: A History of Black Canadian and Caribbean Women in the Diaspora*
38 Karen A. Balcom, *The Traffic in Babies: Cross-Border Adoption and Baby-Selling between the United States and Canada, 1930–1972*

39 Nancy M. Forestell with Maureen Moynagh, eds, *Documenting First Wave Feminisms, Volume II: Canada – National and Transnational Contexts*
40 Patrizia Gentile and Jane Nicholas, eds, *Contesting Bodies and Nation in Canadian History*
41 Suzanne Morton, *Wisdom, Justice, and Charity: Canadian Social Welfare through the Life of Jane B. Wisdom, 1884–1975*
42 Jane Nicholas, *The Modern Girl: Feminine Modernities, the Body, and Commodities in the 1920s*
43 Pauline A. Phipps, *Constance Maynard's Passions: Religion, Sexuality, and an English Educational Pioneer, 1849–1935*
44 Marlene Epp and Franca Iacovetta, eds, *Sisters or Strangers? Immigrant, Ethnic, and Racialized Women in Canadian History*, Second Edition
45 Rhonda L. Hinther, *Perogies and Politics: Canada's Ukrainian Left, 1891–1991*
46 Valerie J. Korinek, *Prairie Fairies: A History of Queer Communities and People in Western Canada, 1930–1985*
47 Julie Guard, *Radical Housewives: Price Wars and Food Politics in Mid-Twentieth-Century Canada*